MW01070441

Biopsychosocial
Practice

Biopsychosocial Practice

A SCIENCE-BASED FRAMEWORK FOR BEHAVIORAL HEALTH CARE

TIMOTHY P. MELCHERT

AMERICAN PSYCHOLOGICAL ASSOCIATION • WASHINGTON, DC

Copyright © 2015 by the American Psychological Association. All rights reserved. Except as permitted under the United States Copyright Act of 1976, no part of this publication may be reproduced or distributed in any form or by any means, including, but not limited to, the process of scanning and digitization, or stored in a database or retrieval system, without the prior written permission of the publisher.

Published by
American Psychological Association
750 First Street, NE
Washington, DC 20002
www.apa.org

To order
APA Order Department
P.O. Box 92984
Washington, DC 20090-2984
Tel: (800) 374-2721; Direct: (202) 336-5510
Fax: (202) 336-5502; TDD/TTY: (202) 336-6123
Online: www.apa.org/pubs/books
E-mail: order@apa.org

In the U.K., Europe, Africa, and the Middle East, copies may be ordered from
American Psychological Association
3 Henrietta Street
Covent Garden, London
WC2E 8LU England

Typeset in Goudy by Circle Graphics, Inc., Columbia, MD

Printer: Maple Press, York, PA
Cover Designer: Mercury Publishing Services, Inc., Rockville, MD

The opinions and statements published are the responsibility of the authors, and such opinions and statements do not necessarily represent the policies of the American Psychological Association.

Library of Congress Cataloging-in-Publication Data

Melchert, Timothy P. (Timothy Peter)
  Biopsychosocial practice : a science-based framework for behavioral health care /
by Timothy P. Melchert. — First edition.
    pages cm
  Includes bibliographical references and index.
  ISBN-13: 978-1-4338-1761-8
  ISBN-10: 1-4338-1761-6
  1. Clinical health psychology. 2. Science and psychology. 3. Psychobiology. I. Title.
  R726.7.M45 2015
  616.89—dc23
                          2014006056

British Library Cataloguing-in-Publication Data
A CIP record is available from the British Library.

Printed in the United States of America
First Edition

http://dx.doi.org/10.1037/14441-000

To Maya, Jack, Drew, and Susan.

CONTENTS

Biopsychosocial Practice

INTRODUCTION

Behavioral health care and the behavioral sciences are currently at one of the most significant points in their historical development. There has been remarkable progress in both the basic and applied sides of the discipline, and behavioral health care is arguably now emerging as a true clinical science. This volume is based on the view that the behavioral health care field has reached a tipping point where clinical practice can now be based on a unified, scientifically grounded understanding of human development, functioning, and behavior change. Historically, clinical education and practice in the field have relied heavily on a diverse array of irreconcilable theoretical orientations for conceptualizing personality, psychopathology, and psychotherapy. The conceptual confusion and conflict associated with that approach are well known. This volume is based on a very different approach where a unified, paradigmatic, scientific perspective replaces the array of orientations that have been used to understand psychological functioning and the treatment

DOI: 10.1037/14441-001
Biopsychosocial Practice: A Science-Based Framework for Behavioral Health Care, by T. P. Melchert
Copyright © 2015 by the American Psychological Association. All rights reserved.

process. This volume documents the scientific progress that supports that approach and then goes on to describe how clinical practice is informed by a current biopsychosocial understanding of human psychology along with professional ethics, which also play a foundational role in informing health care practice and research.

Both the conceptual foundations of a unified science-based biopsychosocial approach to behavioral health care and the practical implementation of this approach in contemporary clinical practice are presented herein. I cover the whole treatment process from intake through termination and include numerous clinical illustrations that demonstrate how the biopsychosocial approach is applied in common behavioral health care settings. Going beyond standard therapy practice, I discuss important emerging issues related to prevention and integrated primary care (where medical and behavioral health issues are treated in single primary care settings).

I first discuss in detail the scientific and ethical foundations for practicing behavioral health care from a unified, evidence-based perspective, prior to addressing their application in clinical practice. These conceptual foundations are critically important because a science-based approach to understanding human psychology and behavioral health care is very different from traditional approaches that relied heavily on the various theoretical orientations, either singly or in some integrative or eclectic fashion. Indeed, when taking a science-based biopsychosocial approach, one generally no longer even uses the term *theoretical orientation* to describe one's approach to practice. In addition, this volume refers to a *science-based* biopsychosocial approach because the term *biopsychosocial* has been widely used within health care over the past few decades but usually in a general, vague manner that typically did not refer to any particular findings regard the scientific understanding of human development and functioning. The approach taken here is quite different. Consequently, the first few chapters focus extensively on the conceptual framework needed to practice behavioral health care in a manner that is firmly grounded in science and ethics.

Obviously, these are very complicated subjects. Human nature is extraordinarily complex, and this volume could include many, many more research findings than it does. There is no question but that a full graduate curriculum is needed to thoroughly address the topics discussed here. For practical reasons, however, and with compassion for the reader, the discussion focuses instead on the most important findings. Nonetheless, the field badly needs an integrated, science-based framework that brings together the disparate bodies of behavioral science knowledge and resolves the conceptual confusion associated with the traditional theoretical orientations. The historical reasons for that confusion are quite understandable and are discussed in Chapter 2. Indeed, it is critical for the future of the profession that that confusion be resolved; we can now do that because in recent years the behavioral, biological, and social sciences have progressed dramatically. The aim of this volume is to outline the framework for behavioral health care that is based on a unified scientific understanding of human psychology.

ORGANIZATION OF THE BOOK

The four parts of this book lay out a logical approach to conceptualizing behavioral health care. The first part comprises three chapters that address the basic conceptual framework needed to place the profession on firm scientific and ethical foundations. Chapter 1 provides an overview of these foundations and notes the recent scientific progress that compels a paradigm shift away from outmoded practices and toward a solidly scientific approach to clinical practice. It then goes on to outline a basic metatheoretical approach that can be used to conceptualize human development, functioning, and behavior change in a comprehensive scientific manner as well as the essential implications of that approach. Chapter 2 then reviews the complicated historical development of theory and research in psychology and the scientific reasons for the irreconcilable differences between the theoretical orientations and schools of thought in psychology. The chapter goes on to explain some of the essential characteristics of an integrated science-based approach to understanding human psychology and behavioral health care. Chapter 3 discusses why ethics must be included in the basic conceptual foundations of behavioral health care before outlining a current scientific perspective on moral reasoning and behavior. The chapter then examines why an appreciation of ethical theory and current research on moral reasoning is necessary for a full understanding of the critical roles that ethics play in human behavior and in health care. It concludes with a summary of the most influential approach to biomedical ethics in the United States and Europe.

Part II includes three chapters that provide an overview of the psychological, sociocultural, and physical functioning of the American general public, followed by a fourth chapter that provides a developmental perspective. These topics are viewed as necessary background for appropriately applying the biopsychosocial approach to behavioral health care. Knowledge of the biopsychosocial circumstances of the public is critical for a holistic understanding of individuals, conducting thorough assessments, and developing treatment plans and delivering interventions that maximize the likelihood of treatment effectiveness. The topics in Part II are also necessary background for understanding the prevention of behavioral health problems, promoting health and well-being, and effectively interacting with other health care and human service professionals, family members, and others who play important roles in patients' lives.

The chapters in Part III describe the implications of applying the scientific and ethical foundations of the biopsychosocial approach to the behavioral health care treatment process. The four chapters in this part of the volume address the four general phases of the treatment process, namely, assessment, treatment planning, implementing treatment, and evaluating its effectiveness. There are sometimes no clear demarcations between these four phases. For example, the treatment process begins with assessment, but assessment continues throughout, and assessing treatment outcomes is just the last phase of the ongoing assessment that continues across treatment. Treatment also occurs throughout, from the beginning of the development of a therapeutic relationship during the initial interactions with patients on through the discussion of treatment termination at the end. There are normally clear shifts in purposes and activities across the four phases of treatment, however, and there are clear implications of taking a science-based biopsychosocial approach for each of them.

Part IV addresses additional implications of taking a science-based biopsychosocial approach to behavioral health care. Chapter 12 presents an overview of a public health and preventive approach to behavioral health. The health and well-being of a population cannot be understood without this perspective; it should receive more attention in behavioral health care education, practice, research, and policy than it currently does. Chapter 13 then discusses integrated primary care models of health care where behavioral health needs are addressed along with physical health needs in single primary care settings. These sorts of models are quickly gaining interest within the field and are likely to play major roles in health care settings in the future. Chapter 14 discusses several conclusions that derive from the science-based biopsychosocial approach to behavioral health care along with several exciting possibilities for the field that become more likely as a result of taking a unified science-based approach.

AUDIENCE

The intended audience for this volume includes students and faculty in behavioral health care training programs as well as practicing clinicians across the behavioral health care field. The scope includes both general and specialized practice. Although the breadth and depth of the topics are aimed at the doctoral level of education in professional psychology and psychiatry, the perspective taken is appropriate for readers at the master's level as well as those enrolled in advanced undergraduate courses. Behavioral and social scientists across specializations may also appreciate the integrative, holistic approach to understanding human development, functioning, and behavior change that is described here.

TERMINOLOGY

A note on the terminology used in this volume is needed to avoid potential misunderstandings. The individuals served by behavioral health care professionals are often referred to as *clients*, *patients*, or sometimes *consumers* or even *customers*. The term *patient* is used throughout this book, however, for many reasons. The term is firmly ingrained in health care generally, and it is important that behavioral health care use the same term if the profession is to become better integrated into the greater health care field. The term *client* does have the advantage of avoiding the connotations of the "sick role" in the traditional medical model, where ill patients were expected to be relatively passive recipients of services provided by expert health care professionals as opposed to being active participants in the treatment process. On the other hand, the term *client* also evokes a business relationship in which individuals purchase a desired or needed service and in which the ethical obligations of the seller are normally viewed as being lower (i.e., at the level of commerce) than they are in health care. As discussed in Chapters 1 and 3, professional ethics play a critically important role in behavioral health care, and referring to the individuals whom we serve as *patients* helps convey the importance of that role.

This volume also refers to *behavioral health care* rather than *mental health care* because the former term generally has a broader meaning. The mental health field has historically tended to focus on intrapersonal psychological functioning, whereas substance use disorders, health psychology, family functioning, and other issues have often fallen outside the main focus of mental health. Behavioral health, on the other hand, typically includes all those issues. This volume is explicitly focused on the broad range of psychological functioning and its interaction with physical health and social functioning. Indeed, psychological, physical, and social health and functioning are inextricably intertwined, and so this volume consequently focuses on behavioral health and biopsychosocial functioning broadly. Finally, the reader should note that all of the clinical examples discussed here are amalgamations of actual cases in which all identifying information has been thoroughly changed.

I

CONCEPTUAL FOUNDATIONS OF THE BIOPSYCHOSOCIAL APPROACH TO BEHAVIORAL HEALTH CARE

1

THE FOUNDATIONAL FRAMEWORK OF THE BIOPSYCHOSOCIAL APPROACH

The biopsychosocial approach to behavioral health care is based on a comprehensive scientific understanding of human development, functioning, and behavior change. From this perspective, human psychology and behavioral health care are understood by integrating scientific knowledge of the inextricably intertwined biological, psychological, and sociocultural influences on development and behavior. Based on that understanding, a variety of safe and effective evidence-based psychotherapies and other interventions can be used to alleviate individuals' distress and improve their functioning in all biopsychosocial areas.

This approach to behavioral health care may sound like the standard approach the field has been following for years. It is likely that almost all behavioral health care professionals at some level endorse a biopsychosocial approach to understanding human psychology because the evidence is overwhelming that biological, psychological, and sociocultural factors all have important influences on development and behavior. In addition, very few

DOI: 10.1037/14441-002
Biopsychosocial Practice: A Science-Based Framework for Behavioral Health Care, by T. P. Melchert
Copyright © 2015 by the American Psychological Association. All rights reserved.

would disagree that research supports the effectiveness of a range of biologically, psychologically, and socially oriented interventions for relieving distress and symptomatology and improving functioning for a wide variety of behavioral health issues.

The science-based biopsychosocial approach to behavioral health care is actually quite different, however, from many traditional approaches. Traditional approaches to mental health education and practice often involve learning one or more of the well-accepted theoretical orientations such as psychodynamic or cognitive behavior therapy and then applying that approach to conceptualize clinical cases and deliver treatment. Individual graduate programs might emphasize a particular orientation, whereas the various mental health specializations have generally tended to support certain orientations. In the first half of the 20th century, American psychiatry came to strongly endorse psychoanalytic approaches and later a biological approach in the 1980s, whereas clinical psychology often adopted behavioral and later cognitive approaches. Counseling psychology was heavily influenced by humanistic theories, as was mental health counseling. Social work and marriage and family therapy were influenced by systemic approaches, whereas the substance abuse treatment field often used mutual aid support groups. When students or practicing therapists apply for clinical positions, they normally expect to be asked to explain their adopted theoretical orientation; for example the Association of Psychology Postdoctoral and Internship Centers (2009) uniform application includes the required essay question "Please describe your theoretical orientation and how this influences your approach to case conceptualization and intervention" (p. 22). It is well known that some faculty and supervisors accommodate a variety of orientations whereas others require the adoption of their approach as a precondition to working with them. Navigating these theoretical allegiances is one of the well-known and important tasks of graduate education in the field.

One's adopted theoretical orientation clearly has a major influence on case formulation and treatment as well. If one ascribes to cognitive therapy, for example, a patient's depression is likely to be conceptualized as being caused by depressogenic cognitions or irrational beliefs, and treatment would likely involve replacing those cognitions and beliefs with more rational ones. If one ascribes to a biological psychiatry model of depression, one is likely to conceptualize the same depressive symptoms as resulting from a serotonin deficiency in the brain, and the treatment plan would likely include antidepressant medication that blocks the reuptake of serotonin in the synaptic spaces between neurons. If one ascribes to psychodynamic theory, one is likely to focus on the patient's developmental history, whereas solution-oriented therapists would show much less interest in identifying the causes of one's problems than in identifying solutions to those problems; a behavioral, feminist, family systems, client-centered, or eye-movement desensitization and reprocessing therapist would focus on still other issues. An integrative therapist might combine behavioral and psychodynamic principles (e.g., along the lines of Wachtel, 1977), and an eclectic therapist would try to identify whatever was most likely to work in a given situation.

Students and practitioners in the field are very familiar with the array of diverging conceptualizations of personality, psychopathology, and psychotherapy. Throughout the history of the field, there has been deep disagreement among the various theoretical camps regarding the nature of healthy personality functioning, the development of psychopathology, and the appropriate methods for changing maladaptive behavior. It has also been widely recognized that the fundamental differences between psychodynamic, behavioral, humanistic, systemic, biological, and various postmodern constructivist approaches to these issues could not be reconciled (Messer & Winokur, 1980; A. Wood & Joseph, 2007). Clearly, these perspectives could not all be correct, and they all appeared to be incomplete as well. The integrative and eclectic movement in the field offered a solution to the problem; however, combining some number of the existing theoretical orientations, when each appeared to be incomplete or only partly valid, did not represent a satisfactory solution either. Conflicts regarding these issues came to a head in the 1990s when major controversies arose regarding repressed memories of child sexual abuse and the development of lists of empirically supported psychotherapies (e.g., Task Force on the Promotion and Dissemination of Psychological Procedures, 1995).

A science-based biopsychosocial perspective, however, takes a very different approach to these issues. A great deal is now known about the interactions between biological, psychological, and sociocultural influences on human growth and development. Much remains to be learned, to be sure, but enough is now known about the human mind and brain that behavioral health care education and practice can be informed by a unified scientific perspective on human psychology. The precision and rigor of behavioral science research has increased significantly, and research findings have accumulated rapidly. Personally endorsing a theoretical orientation for understanding psychological phenomena, rather than evaluating theories based on the weight of the scientific evidence, runs counter to the scientific method. Endorsing a theoretical orientation in this way is more akin to selecting a political or religious orientation than it is to using the scientific method.

It is now time to leave that era behind. The behavioral health care field has been highly fractured, offering a diverse array of competing theoretical orientations for understanding the phenomena involved. Substantial time and energy have been spent on competition and controversy instead of finding more complete explanations of human psychology and better approaches to improving mental health and well-being. Using Kuhn's (1962) terminology, the field has been *pre-paradigmatic*. As Chapter 2 demonstrates, there are clear historical and scientific reasons for how and why this situation developed; it is argued here, however, that it is now time to move beyond that era. Behavioral science has advanced to the point where a unified science-based framework should replace the diverse array of competing and conflicting theoretical orientations that historically dominated the field. It is time for behavioral health care to embrace the paradigmatic era.

RECENT SCIENTIFIC PROGRESS: A PARADIGM SHIFT

All of the sciences have undergone dramatic progress recently, and psychology and related behavioral and biological sciences have made especially rapid progress. The psychological research literature has grown substantially, and new scientific tools allow researchers to observe the actual operation of the human brain, genome, and other phenomena at levels that were simply impossible until recently. In the past, many psychological phenomena could be observed only indirectly because experimental techniques for directly examining cognition, emotion, and other processes were unavailable. Psychologists could speculate about the mechanisms involved in more intricate and complex aspects of human psychology, but discovering even whether particular mechanisms existed had to wait for the development of more precise scientific tools. (These issues are discussed in detail in Chapter 2, but an overview is presented here to introduce the science-based biopsychosocial approach.)

One new scientific tool that has had a revolutionary impact on psychological research is functional magnetic resonance imaging, which began to be used for human research and clinical practice in the early 1990s. Prior to that, the electroencephalogram, which uses electrical leads placed on the outside of the skull, had been the primary tool available for gaining access to what was actually happening inside intact human brains. Though its use led to many important discoveries, its limited spatial resolution prevents locating precisely where particular neural activity is taking place. The emergence of functional magnetic resonance imaging allowed scientists to observe the location of brain activity much more accurately, which has led to a far more detailed understanding of how the brain actually works.

Another area of research that has dramatically changed the understanding of brain development and functioning involves genetics and neural plasticity. Over the past two decades, the view that genetically determined psychological characteristics and most neural circuitry were hardwired and essentially fixed has been overturned. As discussed in Chapter 2, scientists have discovered that genetically controlled traits can be expressed or silenced depending on one's life experience such as the type of caregiving one receives as a child. The brain has also been found to be a highly adaptive organ and the neural processing of experience can change significantly, as the result of life experience, across the life span. These discoveries represent entirely different views than what was generally believed to be the case throughout the 20th century.

These and other scientific discoveries are transforming the understanding of human psychology. Hypotheses about the nature of various psychological phenomena that in the past had to remain speculations can now be tested with precision and rigor. For example, Freud's notions about the nature and role of the subconscious could not be directly tested for nearly a century, but subconscious mental activity is now being experimentally examined from multiple perspectives. These advances also allow behavioral health care to be practiced on the basis of scientific knowledge at a level that was simply not possible in the past. Indeed, recent progress in the scientific understanding of the human mind and brain is so great that one is reminded of the quantum revolution that physics underwent at the start of the 20th century that led to a far more detailed understanding of the physical world.

The question of whether the scientific understanding of human psychology has advanced sufficiently to justify a transition away from traditional conceptualizations of behavioral health care to a unified science-based approach involves several complicated issues that are discussed in the chapters that follow. The conclusion derived from those discussions is that there is now overwhelming scientific support for a unified biopsychosocial understanding of human psychology, and it is time for the field to systematically transition to this new scientific framework. As a science-based profession, behavioral health care must update its theoretical and conceptual foundations to be consistent with the latest science on human psychology. This volume provides a description of what that approach might look like.

OVERVIEW OF BIOPSYCHOSOCIAL BEHAVIORAL HEALTH CARE

The science-based biopsychosocial approach to behavioral health care is based on conceptual foundations that are quite different from most of the traditional frameworks that are used in the field, and yet these foundations are not particularly controversial. Instead of relying on the traditional theoretical orientations for explanations of personality, psychopathology, and psychotherapy, the biopsychosocial approach is founded squarely on scientific knowledge regarding human psychology and on professional ethics. These basic conceptual foundations are discussed in detail in Chapters 2 and 3, whereas the basic rationale for the biopsychosocial approach to behavioral health care is outlined below so that the topics discussed in subsequent chapters can be placed in context.

Science Based

The behavioral health care field has always been committed to basing clinical practice on science. A major obstacle for a unified scientific perspective on human psychology, however, was the sheer complexity, subtlety, and intricacy of the phenomena involved. This was clearly recognized by the original founders of the field. William Wundt, the German scientist generally acknowledged as the founder of scientific psychology, only allowed his graduate students to investigate elemental processes involved in sensation, perception, and attention, not because he believed that higher levels of consciousness were unimportant, but because he believed the scientific tools for reliably investigating such complex phenomena were simply unavailable at the time (Benjamin, 2007). William James was also very aware of the limitations of experimental techniques for investigating the tremendous depth and complexity of human experience (e.g., the constantly changing stream of human consciousness; James, 1890). Nonetheless, Sigmund Freud, John Watson, Carl Rogers, and others soon proposed a wide variety of sweeping explanations for human psychology. Each of these diverse theories arguably contributed important insights into the human condition, but they were also irreconcilable with each other and were eventually found to be incomplete and unable to withstand scientific scrutiny (see Chapter 2).

The behavioral health care field is now ready to leave behind the era of many conflicting and competing explanations for human development and functioning. When the field was young, psychological science could shed only limited light on the tremendous complexity of human psychology; over the last decades, however, the behavioral and biological sciences have progressed dramatically. As noted in the following chapters, there is now broad agreement regarding the scientific understanding of many psychological phenomena, even though the understanding of many processes is still limited.

At the level of metatheory, there appears to be no disagreement that a scientific approach to understanding human psychology requires a comprehensive systemic framework that fundamentally recognizes the interactions between the biological, psychological, and sociocultural levels of natural organization. The evidence for this type of framework is overwhelming. It may be impossible, for example, to find an introductory psychology textbook that does not cover the interacting psychological, biological, and social bases of human behavior. Conceptualizations of personality, psychopathology, intelligence, behavior change, and other important psychological constructs that are not based on all three of these interacting levels of natural organization are simply not supported by the evidence.

The basic dimensions of the biopsychosocial approach can be illustrated graphically. A cube can represent the three intertwined psychological, sociocultural, and biological dimensions of influence on human psychology. In addition, human development, functioning, and behavior change necessarily take place across time—human beings are living, adaptive organisms with a very long period for maturation to adulthood, and they continue to change and evolve across the life span. Therefore, a fourth dimension, time, can be represented by an arrow running through the biopsychosocial cube (see Figure 1.1). The cube with the arrow through it also represents the inextricably intertwined nature of these dimensions that cannot be disaggregated without destroying the holistic nature of the living, adapting organism. This fundamental conceptualization of human psychology is analogous to the three spatial dimensions (up–down, left–right, and forward–backward) plus the dimension of time that together are necessary for conceptualizing the physical world.

The biopsychosocial approach was first described by George Engel in 1977 and has become widely known and accepted throughout the health care and human services fields. It has been incorporated into medical education throughout the United States and Europe (Frankel, Quill, & McDaniel, 2003). It also has been incorporated into the accreditation standards for master's and doctoral education in the mental health specializations (e.g., the biological, psychological, and social bases of behavior must be covered in American Psychological Association [APA]–accredited doctoral programs; the accreditation standards for mental health counseling incorporate the biopsychosocial perspective; APA Presidential Task Force on the Future of Psychology Practice, 2009; Council for the Accreditation of Counseling and

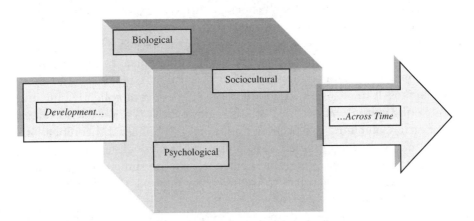

Figure 1.1. Understanding human psychology as the integration of inextricably intertwined biopsychosocial dimensions across time. From *Foundations of Professional Psychology: The End of Theoretical Orientations and the Emergence of the Biopsychosocial Approach* (p. 104), by T. P. Melchert, 2011, London, England: Elsevier. Copyright 2011 by Elsevier. Adapted with permission.

Related Educational Programs, 2009). It has been adopted within several of the clinical specializations in professional psychology (e.g., in child, school, health, and addiction psychology; neuropsychology; and geropsychology; see Martin, Weinberg, & Bealer, 2007; Seagull, 2000; Shah & Reichman, 2006; Suls & Rothman, 2004; W. H. Williams & Evans, 2003). It has also been endorsed by 23 health care and human services professional organizations (APA, 2006).

It is critical to distinguish between the science-based biopsychosocial approach described in this volume, however, and theoretical integration and eclecticism. Some have argued that the biopsychosocial approach is essentially a laissez-faire eclecticism that provides no rationale for selecting one theory or behavioral health care treatment over another (e.g., Ghaemi, 2010). Eclecticism in mental health treatment has been defined as selecting what is likely to work best for a particular person and problem, based primarily on what has worked best in the past for others with similar problems and characteristics (Lazarus, Beutler, & Norcross, 1992). In addition to this commonsense approach to treatment selection, eclecticism has often been viewed as being uncritical, unsystematic, arbitrary, and based on personal preference rather than scientifically supported theory (e.g., Eysenck, 1970). Simply trying to find what works best in a particular situation is often an effective strategy—across human history, this undoubtedly was an effective approach for dealing with life's challenges and accounted for our remarkable growth and eventual dominance as a species. In the context of modern health care, however, eclecticism based on an array of competing, irreconcilable theoretical orientations is not a science-based approach. When science advances to the point where the safety and effectiveness of health care can be systematically evaluated and improved through the application of experimental methods, then eclecticism is no longer justified.

The biopsychosocial approach also is not theoretical integration. Integration is usually referred to as *syncretism* when it is applied to the merging of different beliefs in religion or politics. In those realms, it may also be an effective approach to dealing with many of the challenges of collective life and competing cultures. As with eclecticism, however, it is not a science-based approach. Combining two or more traditional psychological theoretical orientations, when each is based on assumptions, first principles, or worldview instead of accumulated scientific evidence, is more similar to political or religious syncretism than it is to the scientific method. (See Chapter 2 for detailed discussions of these issues.)

A science-based biopsychosocial approach is quite different from eclecticism or integration. Eclecticism and theoretical integration (syncretism) may have been essential to human survival and progress in the past and may have been the basic approaches to medical and mental health care as practiced throughout human history up until recently. Science can now explain many psychological phenomena, however, from the level of our evolutionary origins to the level of specific psychological, biological, and sociocultural processes and mechanisms. This knowledge can also be used to improve the safety and effectiveness of behavioral health care intervention and to enhance biopsychosocial functioning.

Ethics Based

The scientific understanding of human psychology requires the metatheoretical perspective outlined in the preceding section, but it is also essential to appreciate the applied nature of behavioral health care as a clinical profession. Science provides the perspective and authority for understanding the phenomena involved, but science does not necessarily explain how to apply that understanding appropriately in health care practice. The proper application of scientific knowledge and tools with human beings in the context of their families, society, and governmental and health care systems fundamentally requires an ethical perspective to balance all the interests involved. Another way to appreciate the critical importance of both science and ethics in health care is to note the importance of science for understanding *health* and the importance of ethics for understanding *care*. When these two concepts (i.e., health and care) are combined in modern health care systems, then science and ethics both are essential for the responsible, appropriate, and effective practice of health care. Science alone cannot answer many questions related to the fair and appropriate way to care for the health needs of individuals and the general public, and ethics cannot answer many questions related to understanding illness, dysfunction, and health.

There is no question that professional ethics and related legal issues are critical to all human services fields as well as in health care specifically. Science informs the understanding of many issues that are important in education, criminal justice, social services, and health care, but how individuals are treated in all these systems often centrally involves ethical questions. Not infrequently, the ethical and legal issues seem more difficult than the scientific ones, particularly in behavioral health care. For example, when emergencies occur in medicine, the ethical obligations to provide care to prevent harm or death are usually straightforward—patients may have limited ability to make informed decisions and may even be unconscious, but the ethical obligations to provide emergency care are typically straightforward nonetheless. In the case of psychiatric emergencies, however, which normally involve risks of harm to self or others, the ethics involved can be quite complicated—decisions about detaining individuals against their will when they have committed no crimes in order to minimize risks of harm to self or others are frequently very difficult. Balancing the considerations involved in respecting people's autonomy and privacy, not causing harm, attempting to prevent harm, and doing this all in a manner that is fair to the individual and to others is often a complicated process that requires the balancing of numerous complex ethical and legal considerations.

Psychologists have always been sensitive to the ethical implications of their work and highly committed to professional ethics. It is also evident that science alone is insufficient for the decision making involved in delivering behavioral health services. Therefore, professional ethics have always been fundamental to clinical training and practice in the field. It is further argued in Chapter 3 that the field's commitment to ethics training should be broadened and deepened. Too often the teaching of ethics focuses on ethics codes, policies, and laws that are relevant to clinical practice but with insufficient attention on the foundational theories and principles on which the codes, policies, and laws are based. The research on the complicated biopsychosocial nature of moral reasoning and behavior also must be considered in order to thoroughly understand ethical behavior (including one's own). Behavioral health care therefore requires a solid grounding in ethics and moral reasoning in order to be practiced in a responsible and appropriate manner.

The Basic Structure: A Unified Framework

This volume is based on the conclusion that psychological science and professional ethics are now sufficiently well developed to allow the field to proceed under a unified foundational conceptual framework. Obviously neither the scientific nor the ethical foundations are yet fully worked out—many psychological mechanisms and processes are still not well understood, and fairer and more effective health care and human service systems must be developed. Nonetheless, theory and research in both areas have progressed sufficiently that they can provide a common unified framework for understanding human psychology and behavioral health care practice.

To clarify the basic structure of a unified approach to behavioral health care, a specific definition is offered that identifies its essential components. As medical health care focuses on meeting the medical needs of the population, the behavioral health care professions likewise focus on meeting the behavioral health needs of the general public. Because behavioral health and functioning are necessarily intertwined with sociocultural and biological functioning, behavioral health professionals also do not focus on mental health alone but instead address biopsychosocial functioning more generally. The following definition captures these basic definitional issues:

> *Behavioral health care* involves the clinical application of behavioral science and professional ethics to address behavioral health needs and promote biopsychosocial functioning.

This conceptualization of behavioral health care can also be depicted graphically. Figure 1.2 portrays an edifice representing the practice of behavioral health care that rests on two pillars: scientific knowledge of human psychology and professional ethics. Together, science and ethics form the foundation for the practice of behavioral health care—if either one is removed, the structure immediately fails. In addition, behavioral health care practice as well as the underlying science and ethics all must be understood within the biopsychosocial context.

It is important to note that the science-based biopsychosocial approach is entirely consistent with other basic and applied sciences and clinical professions. Its scientific foundations are based on levels of natural organization where knowledge is linked across levels of increasing complexity and builds in a cumulative, integrative manner. Knowledge from biochemistry and molecular biology is used to understand the functioning of organelles, cells, and tissues that comprise organs and organ systems. Knowledge of organ systems, including of course the brain and nervous system, is integrated to understand the functioning of whole individual organisms, and this knowledge is then integrated with knowledge of the social behavior of the organism to understand populations. Though other animals also demonstrate complicated social behavior and have cultures (van Schaik, 2007), culture plays

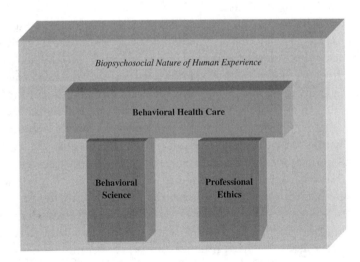

Figure 1.2. Behavioral health care is founded on scientific knowledge of human psychology and professional ethics. All three of these must be understood within the context of the biopsychosocial nature of human experience. From *Foundations of Professional Psychology: The End of Theoretical Orientations and the Emergence of the Biopsychosocial Approach* (p. 105), by T. P. Melchert, 2011, London, England: Elsevier. Copyright 2011 by Elsevier. Adapted with permission.

a uniquely important role in the development and functioning of human individuals and groups. The understanding of groups and species further leads to understanding communities, the ecosystem, and ultimately the biosphere. All these levels of organization must be appreciated to understand the interactions with and constraints imposed by adjacent levels; in other words, human anatomy, physiology, psychology, and social behavior are all constrained by lower level biological and higher level ecosystemic processes. Scientific knowledge builds as explanations of phenomena grow in power, precision, and detail and as explanations are linked across levels of natural organization. (E. O. Wilson, 1998, described the exquisite interconnectedness of scientific knowledge as *consilience*.)

The relationship between science and practice in the biopsychosocial approach also functions the same way as it does in other clinical sciences. In health care, this approach is now commonly referred to as *evidence-based practice* and involves the integration of research evidence, clinical experience and judgment, and patient preferences and values (APA, 2006; Institute of Medicine, 2001). Consider the relationship between biology and medicine. Although knowledge regarding many aspects of biological phenomena is incomplete, medicine uses the knowledge that is available to develop many safe and effective solutions to problems with health and disease. There is clear scientific knowledge regarding many pathological processes but limited knowledge of the causes or cures for others, particularly regarding idiopathic diseases such as Alzheimer's disease, Parkinson's disease, Type 1 diabetes, multiple sclerosis, and many cancers and seizures. (Most psychiatric illnesses are idiopathic as well.) Nonetheless, medicine is very useful for treating a wide range of medical problems, curing some though only partially ameliorating symptoms in others. Despite limited knowledge of many medical issues, there are very few individuals who would choose not to rely on modern medicine and public health measures to manage physical health problems.

In medicine, physicians using the evidence-based approach do not use a personally selected theoretical orientation to conceptualize the evaluation and treatment of injury or disease. Instead, they consider the relevant research, combine that with knowledge gained from prior clinical experience, and then discuss that information with the patient in the context of the patient's preferences, values, behavior, and lifestyle. In some cases, research provides very clear guidance for diagnosing and treating problems, although the assessment and treatment of other problems can be very complicated. Consider cardiovascular disease, the leading cause of morbidity and mortality in the United States and increasingly throughout the world. A wide variety of medications are available to treat heart disease (e.g., anticoagulants, beta blockers, diuretics, statins), along with a variety of surgeries (e.g., angioplasty, bypasses, stents) and implantable devices (e.g., pacemakers, defibrillators). Lifestyle changes are typically prescribed as well (e.g., diet, exercise and physical activity, stress management, smoking or alcohol use reduction). Predicting the onset and course of heart disease for individuals, or how particular individuals respond to treatment after they develop disease, is often highly imprecise, and effect sizes for many treatments are actually relatively small (G. J. Meyer et al., 2001). A stepped approach is often used where less intensive and invasive treatments are tried first (Bonow, Mann, Zipes, & Libby, 2012). Competent, ethical physicians would not recommend treatments eclectically without a rationale, nor would they base decisions on personal preferences regarding theoretical orientation, amount of financial reimbursement, or other factors unrelated to scientific knowledge regarding the disease—doing so would suggest the possibility of malpractice. Instead, the focus is on developing a treatment plan that minimizes risks while maximizing the likelihood of successful outcomes.

The diagnosis and treatment of mental illness are similar in many respects. Whether it be a psychotic or mood disorder or substance abuse, knowledge of the relevant research (e.g., regarding precipitating events, family history, trauma history, current social support, level of functioning, mental status, other risk and protective factors) is combined with clinical judgment and expertise along with patient preferences and values to conduct the assessment and develop a treatment plan. A variety of treatment options are available, many with impressively large effect sizes, and these are often considered in a stepped fashion that minimizes risks of harm while maximizing the likelihood of successful outcomes over the short and long term. (These issues are discussed in detail in Part III of this book.)

MAJOR IMPLICATIONS OF BIOPSYCHOSOCIAL BEHAVIORAL HEALTH CARE

Before proceeding to discuss detailed aspects of the science-based biopsychosocial approach to behavioral health care, some of the general implications of this approach are noted. As mentioned above, some areas within behavioral health care already use a biopsychosocial approach to case conceptualization and treatment. This is especially true in the specializations where the interactions between physical health, mental health, and social functioning are highly evident, and dealing with all of them in treatment is often unavoidable (e.g., in child psychology, neuropsychology, health psychology, addictions, geropsychology). The general practice areas tend to rely less on a biopsychosocial approach and have often relied more heavily on the traditional theoretical orientations to guide clinical intervention. For the field as a whole, these varied and conflicting approaches have resulted in substantial confusion and conflict.

Systematically implementing the science-based biopsychosocial approach across behavioral health care will provide a unified framework for education, practice, and research in the field, but it will also result in significant changes to some common practices. As part of this overview of the biopsychosocial approach, the main implications of this approach are noted here while more specific implications are discussed in the chapters that follow.

1. *Only one theoretical orientation for conceptualizing behavioral health care practice would be taught.* Many educational programs in professional psychology take a survey approach to teaching the most influential of the traditional theoretical orientations, whereas other programs emphasize the theoretical orientations of their faculty. A science-based biopsychosocial approach to understanding human psychology and behavioral health care results in a very different curriculum, however. From this perspective, neither individuals nor demographic and diagnostic groups can be understood without taking a comprehensive biopsychosocial approach. Therefore, students would no longer learn to conceptualize cases according to a selected theoretical orientation but would instead learn to conceptualize cases according to a science-based biopsychosocial approach.

2. *The traditional theoretical orientations would generally be reconceptualized as therapies.* When taking a science-based biopsychosocial approach to understanding human psychology, the term *theory* and related terms would normally be used in their scientific sense to refer to explanations of phenomena that have survived experimental tests aimed at verification and falsification. As a result, the traditional theoretical orientations would generally no longer be referred to as *theoretical* orientations because of their inadequacies as scientific theories (see Chapter 2). It must be recognized, however, that the treatments based on many of these orientations provide demonstrably effective therapies for addressing behavioral health needs. Therefore, a single unified biopsychosocial approach would be used to understand human development and functioning, but there is a wide range of evidence-based psychologically, socially, and biologically oriented therapies and other interventions (e.g., support groups, physical exercise and diet) that therapists can safely and effectively use to treat behavioral health problems and improve biopsychosocial functioning.

3. *The scientific and ethical foundations of the field would be taught in a systematic, integrative manner.* Because science and ethics are

foundational in the biopsychosocial approach, the curriculum needs to ensure a solid grounding in both these areas. The amount of material in these areas is impossible to cover thoroughly, but some breadth and depth are needed to gain a proper appreciation of the subjects and as a foundation for learning new information as it emerges.

The biopsychosocial approach to behavioral health care takes a holistic approach to understanding human development and functioning. A comprehensive understanding of human psychology therefore requires the perspectives of physical health and disease; genetics; the neurosciences; the influence of childhood, families, relationships, neighborhoods, vocational and educational achievement, culture, and religion; and the psychological emphasis on cognition, affect, and behavior. Omitting any of these important biopsychosocial influences on personality, intelligence, moral reasoning, psychopathology, or behavior change can result in a seriously limited perspective on those phenomena. Though educational programs often do not cover these topics systematically, students and practitioners typically learn a significant amount about them because of their importance in clients' lives. Their learning about these topics is often haphazard, however, and consequently inadequate. It is important to note that the same issue applies to physical health and medicine, a comprehensive understanding of which spans all the way from molecular biology to behavioral and sociocultural levels. Medical care that does not emphasize all these levels is likewise limited in its ability to treat and prevent disease and promote health.

4. *Behavioral health care would be conceptualized as a health care profession and would be better able to integrate into health care generally.* In the past, mental health care was frequently conceptualized as a service industry where clients interested in obtaining psychological treatment chose a therapist whose orientation and practices fit their preferences and needs. In contrast, governments license psychotherapists as health care providers responsible for meeting the behavioral health needs of the public, and insurers reimburse therapists for providing needed health care services. Viewing behavioral health treatment as part of the greater health care field emphasizes its role as a clinical profession that is based on science and ethics and addresses patients' behavioral health needs using interventions that have been evaluated for safety and effectiveness.

Integrating behavioral health care into primary health care has become a priority for many psychologists recently (APA, 2013; APA Presidential Task Force on the Future of Psychology Practice, 2009; Goodheart, 2010, S. B. Johnson, 2013). This is occurring at the same time that medicine is increasingly recognizing the importance of behavior and lifestyle to physical health and disease (e.g., Institute of Medicine, 2004). Improving the overall health of the general population will require that mental health, addiction, and lifestyle issues are more effectively addressed in health care generally. This may in turn require that psychologists become better integrated into primary health care (see Chapter 13).

Taking a science-based biopsychosocial approach to behavioral health care education and practice not only facilitates this type of integration but is probably necessary for psychologists to be able to effectively integrate into primary health care. Traditional approaches that revolve around delivering psychotherapy based on a particular theoretical orientation are often not easily understood by medical professionals or the public and do not fit well in medical clinic or hospital practice. The biopsychosocial approach, on the other hand, is familiar to health care professionals, insurers, and other stakeholders. Sharing a general conceptual framework is important to the successful integration of behavioral health into primary health care.

5. *Many long-standing conflicts within the field will become largely irrelevant.* The historical practice of selecting a theoretical orientation to guide one's clinical practice naturally led to competition between the theoretical camps. The biopsychosocial approach, on the other hand, quickly renders much of that competition obsolete. The biopsychosocial approach builds on scientific knowledge regarding human development and functioning, which is very different from the foundations of most of the traditional theoretical orientations. The biopsychosocial approach also integrates scientific knowledge regarding all the important influences on human development and functioning at the macro level of the whole person, rather than focusing on particular midlevel psychological mechanisms and processes as do many of the traditional theoretical orientations (e.g., cognitive therapy for depression, behavior therapy for anxiety, client-centered therapy for low self-worth). From this perspective, all levels of natural organization are important, and all research that explains psychological processes is valued; so too are all

therapies and other interventions that have been demonstrated to safely and effectively relieve distress and improve biopsychosocial functioning. Traditional conflicts about the superiority of particular theoretical orientations, the relevance of research to practice, the superiority of qualitative versus quantitative research, or untested claims regarding the etiology of psychopathology or the mechanisms that account for behavior change all quickly fade in importance when a science-based biopsychosocial approach is applied.

DISCUSSION: EXCITING NEXT STEPS FOR THE PROFESSION

Psychology has entered a very exciting time in its development as a science and clinical profession. Historically, the field has been remarkably successful as both a basic and applied science. It grew quickly in size and influence and has had a major impact on the sciences, health care and human services, business and industry, and even culture generally. The pre-paradigmatic era of the field, however, was also marked by major competition and conflict as many different theoretical orientations and schools of thought were proposed to explain psychological phenomena. Those conflicts and competition are largely outdated at this point, because science has shown that the biopsychosocial complexity of human psychology is simply far greater than what the traditional theoretical orientations, even when combined, are able to explain. Those conflicts and competition caused a great deal of distraction and inefficiency within the field. Leaving them behind allows time and energy to be focused more productively on improving our understanding of human psychology and improving behavioral health care effectiveness.

Psychology and the behavioral and biological sciences generally have advanced dramatically in recent years. Despite the very large amount that remains to be discovered, the evidence currently available overwhelmingly points to a comprehensive, integrative biopsychosocial approach for understanding human psychology. Behavioral health care as a whole has not yet systematically adopted this perspective and often continues to rely on past practices associated with adopting one or more of the traditional theoretical orientations. The time has come to discontinue those practices and replace them with a unified science-based biopsychosocial approach. The chapters that follow will explain the critical components of this approach as applied across education, practice, and research in the field.

The expertise of behavioral scientists and behavioral health care professionals spans all of the biopsychosocial domains of functioning. Our discipline as a whole is naturally situated at the intersection of these three levels of natural organization, and we hold expertise regarding the interplay of mental and physical health, of family and sociocultural influences on physical and mental health, and the myriad other interactions between biopsychosocial processes. As a result, the behavioral health care profession is in a natural position for leading efforts to improve health and well-being in the general population. Entering the paradigmatic era in behavioral health care will not only facilitate this type of leadership, it is likely necessary for the field to be able to move ahead effectively in this direction. This is an exciting time for the profession.

2

SCIENTIFIC FOUNDATIONS OF BEHAVIORAL HEALTH CARE

The science underlying behavioral health care has been advancing rapidly in recent years. Major advances have been made in many areas, and some conventional thinking about important psychological processes has been overturned as new, more powerful scientific tools have allowed observations and experimental tests of psychological processes that were simply not possible before. As mentioned in the previous chapter, the increasing power and sophistication of research tools are having a revolutionary impact on the understanding of human psychology, the significance of which compares in some ways with the quantum revolution in physics at the beginning of the last century that led to a far more detailed understanding of the physical world. This truly is an exciting time for the behavioral sciences.

These scientific advances have major implications for behavioral health care practice as well. In the past, there often were no consensus explanations for understanding many important aspects of personality, psychopathology,

DOI: 10.1037/14441-003
Biopsychosocial Practice: A Science-Based Framework for Behavioral Health Care, by T. P. Melchert
Copyright © 2015 by the American Psychological Association. All rights reserved.

and psychotherapy. Indeed, one could select from a diverse array of explanations based on the different theoretical orientations that had been proposed. Reliable, verified answers to many questions are now available, however. Of course, much remains to be discovered—many aspects of human psychology are still only understood in broad outline form or only at a descriptive level. Nonetheless, the findings that have emerged provide a scientific understanding of psychology that is substantially more detailed and complete than what was available even just a decade ago.

A science-based biopsychosocial approach to understanding human development and functioning is fundamentally different in some important ways from traditional approaches to education and practice in the field. This chapter explains the basis for these differences and why it is vital for the field to systematically transition to a unified science-based biopsychosocial approach. After establishing the rationale for this transition, this chapter outlines the basic features of a current science-based perspective on human psychology and behavioral health care. A full graduate curriculum is needed to cover all of the topics that are incorporated by this perspective, but the initial outline presented here illustrates the paradigmatic approach that allows the field to move forward under a unified, scientific theoretical framework. The chapters that follow then show how the biopsychosocial approach informs the different aspects of behavioral health care intervention.

THE HISTORICAL DEVELOPMENT OF RESEARCH AND THEORY IN PSYCHOLOGY

Psychology has been remarkably successful as both a basic and applied science since its founding as a scientific discipline in the late 19th century. The field has grown into an important behavioral science discipline that has had a significant influence on education, health care, human service fields, research methodology and statistics, business and industry, public policy, and even culture in general. The field has helped transform society's understanding of mental health and psychological functioning, and psychosocial treatments have provided relief to countless individuals suffering from distress and impaired functioning.

Despite its remarkable growth and many achievements, the field has also experienced major conflict and controversy. There has been little consensus regarding many explanations of personality, psychopathology, and behavior change, and there has been perennial disagreement regarding the scientific basis for clinical intervention. Scientifically verified explanations have emerged regarding many psychological phenomena, though explanations for other aspects of the tremendous complexity of human psychology are much less complete. This is particularly true for higher level processes that are often the focus of psychosocial intervention. Many basic processes of sensation, perception, cognition, affect, learning, and development are well understood, but explanations are less complete for complex phenomena such as the nature and development of personality or intelligence, the nature and causes of psychopathology, and the mechanisms that account for behavior change and treatment effectiveness.

Historically, the standard approaches to learning about and understanding personality, psychopathology, and psychotherapy within the field have been based on the traditional theoretical orientations. Textbooks that cover this material frequently take a chronological approach to reviewing the most important of these orientations, starting with Freudian theory and progressing through a selection of psychodynamic, behavioral, humanistic, cognitive, systemic, multicultural, postmodern, and eclectic and integrative approaches. Some theories focus primarily on the development of personality and psychopathology with little emphasis on the process of psychotherapy (e.g., existentialism, multicultural approaches), while others focus primarily on therapy process and methods (e.g., interpersonal therapy, eclectic approaches). The number of theories that have been proposed is simply staggering: Pearsall (2008) identified more than 500 different theoretical perspectives. The earliest of these theories, Freudian psychoanalysis, still remains the most comprehensive and thorough attempt to explain personality, psychopathology, and psychotherapy. Indeed, Freud's theory was the basis for one of the most influential intellectual movements of the last century. It also ended up being the most controversial of the theoretical orientations in psychology, however.

It is obviously not possible to learn a large number of these theories in detail. Learning one or more of them is nonetheless considered required training in the field. For example, the Application for Psychology Internship, used by nearly all psychology internship programs in the Association of Psychology Postdoctoral and Internship Centers (2009), requires that applicants complete the following essay question: "Please describe your theoretical orientation and how this influences your approach to case conceptualization and intervention" (p. 22). The conclusions of the American Psychological Association (APA) Assessment of Competency Benchmarks Work Group (Fouad et al., 2009) also support this approach. They noted the following as an "essential component" for demonstrating clinical intervention planning skills: "Formulates and conceptualizes cases and plan interventions utilizing at least one consistent theoretical orientation" (p. S19).

Given the central role that the traditional theoretical orientations have played in behavioral health care education and practice, it is remarkable how controversial they have remained throughout the history of the field. The criticisms and weaknesses of these various orientations are well known—standard undergraduate and graduate textbooks routinely discuss them when presenting the theories. Even what is currently the single most influential approach, cognitive behavior therapy, is considered inadequate as an explanation for psychotherapy change (e.g., Kazdin, 2007).

The traditional theoretical orientations in behavioral health care are widely considered to provide incomplete explanations of personality, psychopathology, and behavior change, but they continue to play important roles in the field nonetheless. Indeed, it would be difficult for many faculty, students, and practicing therapists to imagine case conceptualizations that are not based on these orientations. The appropriateness of this practice from a scientific perspective, however, is clearly questionable. If these orientations are widely viewed as incomplete and inadequate, is it appropriate for clinicians to select one or more of them to guide their approach to clinical practice? Has behavioral health care failed to update its basic theoretical foundations as scientific knowledge of human psychology has grown? If so, this would appear to conflict with the basic tenets of practice as a clinical science.

THEORETICAL CONFLICT AND CONFUSION IN THE DISCIPLINE

There are clear scientific and historical reasons for the complicated development of research and theory in the behavioral health care field. These reasons must be understood to appreciate the theoretical confusion that has characterized much of the history of the field and to evaluate the current status of theory and research that can guide clinical practice.

Right from the founding of psychology as a scientific discipline, there was controversy regarding the appropriate approaches to understanding psychology. Wilhelm Wundt, who established the first scientific psychology laboratory in 1879, argued that higher cognitive processes should not even be investigated because they were simply too complex to understand using the available experimental methods—explanations of higher level psychological phenomena would not be reliable until more powerful and precise experimental tools became available. Consequently, he allowed his students to study only elemental experiences such as basic sensations, associations, and feelings. By the turn of the century, Sigmund Freud was advocating for a radically different approach to understanding human psychology. Instead of revolving around what appeared to be the obvious importance of conscious phenomena, Freud's theory emphasized the role of the unconscious. In 1913, John Watson presented another radically different perspective, urging his colleagues to abandon their interest in consciousness and instead focus on behavior. Remarkably varied alternative approaches to understanding human psychology including humanistic, systemic, cognitive, and various postmodern perspectives continued to proliferate over the decades.

New theoretical systems for understanding personality, psychopathology, and psychotherapy continue to be developed. New eclectic and integrative approaches have been presented (see Norcross, 2005) as well as entirely new approaches, such as positive psychotherapy (M. E. P. Seligman, Rashid, & Parks, 2006), attachment therapy (Wallin, 2007), personality-guided relational psychotherapy (Magnavita, 2005), coherence therapy (Ecker & Hulley, 2006), unified psychotherapy (Magnavita & Anchin, 2014), and a new "unified theory of psychology" (Henriques, 2011). In addition, no individual approach has become dominant. Surveys typically find that the largest number of adherents to any one orientation, even an eclectic or integrative approach, still remains a minority, usually less than one-third of the sample (Prochaska & Norcross, 2013). Although the intensity of contention and conflict between the theoretical camps has diminished in recent years (Goodheart & Carter, 2008; Magnavita, 2008; Norcross, 2005), disagreements between adherents of the different approaches still remain strong.

In addition to conflicts between theoretical camps, other controversies and schisms have divided the field in recent decades. In 1988, a large number of psychological scientists broke off to form the American Psychological Society after they had become disillusioned with the practice emphasis of the APA. The empirically supported treatment movement in professional psychology quickly became controversial after the Task Force on Promotion and Dissemination of Psychological Procedures (1995) of APA Division 12 (Society of Clinical Psychology) developed a list of "empirically validated treatments" that were identified as having received research support regarding their efficacy, implying that the use of treatments not on the list may be a questionable practice. Disagreements between scientists and practitioners regarding the reliability of recovered memories of child sexual abuse became so intense in the 1990s that they became known as the "memory wars" (Loftus & Davis, 2006, p. 470), one of the most conflictual periods ever in the history of psychology. Concern has also grown regarding the use of discredited or potentially harmful therapies. Norcross, Koocher, and Garofalo (2006) conducted a survey listing dozens of treatments and asked experts about the degree to which they believed each of them had been discredited. The experts rated 25 of the treatments as somewhere between "probably discredited" and "certainly discredited" (e.g., sexual reorientation therapy, rebirthing therapies, thought field therapy, reparenting therapy).

Controversies and conflicts between the theoretical camps and schools of thought in psychology have been so pervasive and persistent over the decades that many psychologists accept them as a normal, almost natural characteristic of the field, similar to the way that politicians of different parties or clergy from different religions are often able to accept fundamental differences between groups. By the turn of the century, however, many leaders in psychology were concerned that the field had become so conflictual and fractured that it might not be able to continue as a scholarly discipline (e.g., Benjamin, 2001; Gardner, 2005; Kendler, 2002; Rychlak, 2005; Staats, 2005; Sternberg, 2005). For example, Benjamin (2001) noted that "a common lament among psychologists today, particularly among those with gray hair, is that the field of psychology is far along a path of fragmentation or disintegration" (p. 735).

Though the theoretical and conceptual confusion in psychology has been deep and intractable, there is actually a great deal of consensus regarding the underlying reasons for the confusion. Four issues in particular are critical for understanding why theoretical development in the discipline has been so complicated. These reasons also help clarify the direction the field needs to take to move beyond this confusion.

Philosophical Underpinnings of Many Theoretical Orientations

The two primary historical forerunners of scientific psychology were physiology and philosophy. Physiology became increasingly focused on the nervous system after discoveries such as Helmholtz's measurement of the speed of nerve conduction in 1849 caused scientists to realize that aspects of brain functioning could be measured precisely and the operation of the brain and mind consequently could be studied empirically. The other primary forerunner to the discipline of psychology was mental philosophy, including the works of John Locke, Thomas Hume, and John Stuart Mill (Benjamin, 2007). The field of physiology was strongly empirical in nature whereas mental philosophy was not, and psychological theory has often taken one or the other of these divergent approaches.

The philosophical underpinnings of many of the historically important theoretical orientations in professional psychology are well known. The details involved are highly complex, but the basic issues can be summarized easily. Many of these orientations are based on foundational assumptions or first principles that take widely varying perspectives on human nature (e.g., biologically based drives in Freudian theory, the *blank slate* of nearly complete malleability in behaviorism, an optimistic self-actualizing tendency in humanistic theories, and a postmodern constructivism in solution-focused therapy). These philosophical starting points often conflict in fundamental ways that lead to irreconcilable differences in the understanding of human psychology and behavior change (Messer & Winokur, 1980; A. Wood & Joseph, 2007). Adherence to these orientations consequently often involves acceptance of their underlying philosophical assumptions or worldview as opposed to being convinced by the weight of the scientific evidence supporting their validity. As a result, disagreements between adherents of the different theories frequently resemble philosophical or political disputes more than scientific ones.

Nonfalsifiability of Psychological Theories

From a scientific standpoint, many of the traditional psychological theoretical orientations suffer from a second critical weakness. The purported mechanisms involved in the development of personality and psychopathology or in behavior change obviously differ greatly across the theories (e.g., developmental fixations, one's learning history, imposed conditions of worth, depressogenic cognitions, a constructed phenomenological worldview). Nonetheless, many of these theories have been used to explain virtually all outcomes that occur in individual cases, and it is consequently difficult to disprove that a particular theory could account for any particular outcome (Popper, 1963). Instead of evaluating these issues on the basis of logical scientific analysis and experimental data, students learning the profession are often advised to choose a theoretical orientation based on the fit between the orientations and their personality and worldview (e.g., Corsini & Wedding, 2008; Truscott, 2010).

The philosopher Karl Popper (1902–1994) is credited with first explaining the nature of this problem. As a young student in Vienna in 1919, Popper heard both Freud and Einstein present their work and was very impressed with both of them. He also noticed a fundamental difference between their theories, however (Popper, 1963). Freud presented his theory in terms that made it amenable to confirmation, whereas Einstein's theory had testable implications which, if false, would prove the theory wrong. Popper noted that many theories such as Freudianism, Adlerianism, and Marxism were only amenable to confirmation and could not be refuted, and he therefore judged them to be poor theories. Popper argued that scientific theories must be falsifiable and that genuine tests of theories are attempts to refute them.

Complexity of Human Psychology

The complicated evolution of theory and research in psychology also cannot be understood without appreciating the tremendous complexity of the subject matter involved. The extraordinary intricacy, subtlety, range, and complexity of psychological phenomena make psychology a fascinating but very challenging field of study. The human brain is almost unfathomably complex. In just a 3-pound organ, roughly 100 billion neurons each with an average of 1,000 synaptic connections carry an individual's personal history, family's history, and even the evolutionary history of the species, while also constantly interacting with, being shaped by, and even creating one's environment, at co-occurring subconscious and conscious levels. Indeed, the human mind appears to be the most complex system in the known universe. The biologist Richard Dawkins (1976) noted that "we animals are the most complicated and perfectly-designed pieces of machinery in the known universe" (p. xxii). E. O. Wilson (1998), another leading biologist, observed that "the most complex systems known to exist in the universe are biological, and by far the most complex of all biological phenomena is the human mind" (p. 81).

Appreciating the complexity of the human mind and brain is critical to understanding the complexity of behavioral science as well as the practice of behavioral health care. As emphasized in Chapter 1, human psychology is located at the intersection of three complex levels of natural organization. No explanation of human development and functioning is complete if it does not recognize the interactions between biological (e.g., genetics, neurophysiology, physical health and disease), psychological (e.g., cognition, emotion, behavior), and sociocultural influences on human psychology (e.g., family, community, socioeconomic factors, ethnicity, culture). Many of the traditional psychological theoretical orientations were not designed to provide comprehensive explanations of human psychology that incorporated the interactions between the three general levels of natural organization that comprise human experience. Instead, these theories often relied on philosophical assumptions about the nature of human life, and many focused on only particular midlevel psychological mechanisms and processes (e.g., behavior therapy for fear, cognitive therapy for depression, and client-centered therapy for low self-worth).

Power and Precision of Scientific Tools

Another critical perspective for understanding progress in science involves the power and precision of the scientific tools available for investigating phenomena. The role these tools play in the development of the physical sciences is well known, but their importance is often underappreciated in the social sciences. Scientific progress is directly dependent on these tools, and some of the most important tools have been conceptual rather than technological. For example, mathematics in Europe was largely written out in words prior to the publication of *Liber Abaci* in 1202 by the Italian Fibonacci, whereby he introduced the Hindu-Arabic numeral system to Europe. Vastly more complex calculations could then be performed, and science and commerce were transformed as a result. Four centuries later, Newton's invention of calculus proved to be so useful that science was again transformed. The use of calculus quickly led to major advances in understanding the nature of gravity, heat, light, sound, fluid dynamics, electricity, and magnetism (Crump, 2001). The more recent development of statistics and advanced mathematical modeling again transformed the kinds of phenomena that could be investigated and explained from a scientific perspective.

Scientific progress is also critically dependent on the development of technological tools. For example, Copernicus hypothesized in 1543 that the earth revolved around the sun, but his hypothesis could not be confirmed until Galileo started building telescopes in 1609. His first telescope had about 3 × magnification, but he kept perfecting his instruments and by December of that same year had achieved 20 × magnification. This allowed him to be the first person to observe that the Milky Way consists of thousands of stars, the known planets are nearby, they reflect sunlight, and the earth rotates around the sun; these and several additional discoveries completely transformed the understanding of the physical world (Crump, 2001). Each further advance in telescope technology over the centuries, such as the Hubble Space Telescope more recently, has led to significant advances in understanding the cosmos (Dar, 2006).

The microscope has been one of the most versatile and transformative scientific instruments ever invented. Van Leeuwenhoek (1632–1723) made the best early instruments, capable of 270 × magnification, and became the first person to observe protozoa, bacteria, blood corpuscles, and blood circulation through capillaries. He was the first person to observe spermatozoa and then found them in the males of all species that reproduce sexually. Biology was transformed as a result. The next revolutionary advance in microscopes occurred in the 1930s and used beams of electrons instead of beams of light, allowing very small objects such as viruses, chromosomes, and nucleic acids (including DNA) to be observed, and biology was transformed once again. The rise of fluorescence microscopy in the postgenomic era is currently leading to further important advances in biology.

Many recent scientific advances obviously would be impossible without the electronic computer, the steadily growing power and usefulness of which results from improvements in both technological tools (hardware) and conceptual tools (software). Advances in brain imaging, genetics, and particle physics, for example, require massive amounts of data processing in addition to highly sophisticated technological equipment. Recent "big science" projects such as the Human Genome Project and the Large Hadron Collider will actually generate more scientific data by several orders of magnitude than what has been collected throughout human history (Hey & Trefethen, 2003). Such capabilities are even transforming the way science is conducted in these areas. Instead of the traditional approach, which can be summarized as "hypothesize, design and run experiment, analyze result," the new approach involves "hypothesize, look up answer in data base" (Lesk, 2004, p. 1).

A technological advance that has been particularly important in psychological research is functional magnetic resonance imaging (fMRI). Before the development of clinically useful fMRI in the early 1990s, the electro-encephalogram, which uses electrical leads placed on the outside of the skull, had been the primary tool available for measuring what was actually happening inside intact human brains. Though its temporal resolution was very good (within milliseconds), its spatial resolution was poor; it could place neural events only within centimeters, which can be the difference between different lobes within the brain. The higher spatial resolution of fMRI allows for far more precise observations of actual brain activity. Further improvements in scanning technology are leading to even more precise measurements of neuronal activity. For example, magnetoencephalography (MEG) has high spatial resolution (in millimeters) as well as very high temporal resolution (less than one millisecond). The difference between MEG and fMRI has been described as analogous to watching brain activity with a high resolution video camera compared to a series of poorly focused still photos.

The development of these and other scientific tools has transformed psychological research in recent years. Hypotheses about the nature of psychological phenomena that in the past had to remain speculations can now be tested with precision and rigor—for example, Freud's notions about the importance of subconscious mental activity could not be thoroughly tested for nearly a century but are now being investigated from many different perspectives with rigorous experimental procedures. In the past, psychological phenomena often had to be investigated with either "bottom–up" techniques, such as examining the connections from one neuron to the next, or "top–down" techniques, such as investigating the organization of intelligence through the factor analysis of IQ test data. It is now becoming possible, however, to investigate comprehensive, detailed, multilevel models that simultaneously combine both bottom–up and top–down approaches in one model (C. C. Wood et al., 2006).

Given the complexity of psychological phenomena and the limitations of the scientific tools that were available to study them, it is completely understandable that science is only now beginning to unravel the nature of highly complex psychological processes. In hindsight, it was perhaps inevitable that many different explanations would be offered to explain the tremendous biopsychosocial complexity of human psychology, just as there were many diverse explanations offered to explain gravity, electricity, magnetism, heat, light, and sound when the physical sciences were young. Because of the lack of a single scientific paradigm for understanding psychological phenomena, the philosopher of science Thomas Kuhn (1962) concluded that psychology was an "immature," pre-paradigmatic science. No paradigm, or major scientific achievement or school of thought, had yet emerged that could convincingly explain phenomena in the field and unite the scientific community in that area. Characterizing psychology in this way may correctly capture the underdeveloped state of theory in the field, but it failed to note that the reasons for that underdevelopment primarily involved the complexity of the subject matter and the limitations of the scientific tools that were available. Less complex phenomena naturally are described and explained before more complex phenomena. If the human mind and brain truly are the most complex systems in the universe, it is only natural that they are understood in less detail than other less complicated types of natural phenomena. The difficulty of uncovering the nature of phenomena in the behavioral sciences is well known—Von Foerster (1972) famously noted that it is harder to explain phenomena in the so-called "soft sciences" (i.e., the social sciences) than it is in the "hard sciences" (i.e., the physical sciences).

The previously described issues are critical for understanding why the traditional theoretical orientations and the behavioral sciences as a whole had difficulty providing comprehensive, scientifically valid explanations of the tremendous complexity of human psychology. The behavioral sciences have been advancing steadily, however, and much more comprehensive and detailed explanations of many psychological phenomena are now available. These explanations are providing a completely different scientific foundation for behavioral health care than what was available in even just the recent past.

A SCIENCE-BASED BIOPSYCHOSOCIAL FRAMEWORK FOR BEHAVIORAL HEALTH CARE

A comprehensive understanding of human development and functioning requires knowledge of all the relevant levels of natural organization. These include numerous biological and psychological factors as well as proximal environmental factors (e.g., family, school, work, and neighborhood) and distal ones (e.g., community, society, culture, historical and evolutionary context). Omitting relevant levels of influence can result in seriously incomplete explanations of personality, psychopathology, intellectual functioning, neuropsychological or physical disorders, or any of the other issues that are commonly addressed in behavioral health treatment.

There are many possible starting points for developing an understanding of this very large and complex body of knowledge. Perhaps the most logical place to start, however, is with evolutionary theory. It is often said that human anatomy and physiology are unintelligible without an understanding of evolution, and the same is true of human psychology as well. Evolutionary theory is particularly useful, in the biological as well as the behavioral sciences, because of its focus on *ultimate* explanations of behavior, of the origin and function of behavior, or why organic life is *designed* the way it is (Tinbergen, 1963). The renowned ethologist Niko Tinbergen noted that the study of animal behavior can focus on different levels of questions, from ultimate explanations regarding the origins and functions of behavior to proximate explanations regarding the detailed operation of mechanisms underlying behaviors. Psychotherapists often focus on mechanisms because facilitating changes in the mechanisms that control behavior, cognition, or emotion can lead to desired outcomes in terms of decreased symptomatology or improved functioning. Focusing only on mechanisms, however, misses the larger questions of how and why particular mechanisms and behavior patterns developed, the adaptive value they may have, their associated weaknesses, and the interventions that are more likely to be successful in achieving desired outcomes. A full understanding of human development and functioning requires both ultimate and proximate explanations of behavior.

Another benefit of evolutionary theory is that it highlights relationships between phenomena and even scientific disciplines that may otherwise appear disconnected. For example, a century ago biology comprised several separate disciplines that interacted relatively little (e.g., zoology, botany, anatomy, physiology, genetics, microbiology, biochemistry). The gradual acceptance of evolutionary theory as a central organizing principle led these disciplines to appreciate the web of interrelationships between biological domains that had previously seemed largely unrelated (Dunbar & Barrett, 2007a). An evolutionary perspective does the same thing for psychology because it shows how biological, psychological, and sociocultural processes interact in producing psychological characteristics and mechanisms as a result of evolutionary adaptation. It shows how not only the subdisciplines within psychology are all related, but "it integrates psychology theoretically with the rest of the natural sciences in a unified causal framework" (Buss, 2005b, p. xxv).

The importance of the simple fact that humans are evolved organisms has been seriously underappreciated in psychology. For much of the 20th century, evolution was not thought to play a major role in the development of important human psychological characteristics because humans were so different from other species and culture plays such an important role in our mental life and development (Mameli, 2007). Evolution was seen as responsible for basic innate mental abilities such as sensation, perception, classical and operant conditioning, imitation, and basic logical and probabilistic reasoning. All of our more sophisticated traits, however, were viewed as categorically different from these basic evolved abilities. Humans may have inherited from our evolutionary ancestors basic mental abilities, but their operation within the context of highly developed human culture resulted in characteristics that were viewed as completely different from those in our evolutionary past. Evolution was consequently seen as not particularly relevant to understanding human psychology and so received little attention in the social sciences.

Noam Chomsky, however, overturned this view of human development in terms of language acquisition. He noted that human children in all cultures learn the language of their communities so quickly and reliably that classical and operant conditioning could not possibly account for it (Chomsky, 1959, 1987). He further argued that this learning could occur only if children possessed innate knowledge of a universal grammar. The genetic and neural mechanisms involved in the universal grammar are still being investigated, but understanding the basic nature of language acquisition represented a milestone for psychology. The evolution of human language was essential for the development and transmission of culture and is one of the most significant developments in the entire history of the evolution of life on earth (Maynard Smith & Szathmary, 1997).

W. D. Hamilton and E. O. Wilson expanded on the idea that biological evolution results in psychological traits and mechanisms by noting that behavioral variations can confer higher fitness to a group of organisms. Behavioral differences, like all other types of differences, can lead to genetic adaptations that are passed down to later generations because they confer higher inclusive fitness to the group that possesses them, not just to the individual that possesses them (Hamilton, 1963, 1975; Wilson, 1975, 1978). This is true for all animals, not just humans (as seen, for example, in the social behavior of ants, bees, or chimpanzees). It is apparent that some of our past evolved adaptations are ineffective for dealing with contemporary biological, psychological, or social circumstances (e.g., modern human diets, activity levels, threats and stressors; Roberts, 2012). Assessing which current human adaptations confer evolutionary advantages into the future is difficult, however, because the extraordinary pace of evolution in human culture and technology in recent centuries and decades has dramatically changed the conditions under which we live (e.g., in terms of foods eaten, size and nature of social groups, dwellings, nature of work, daily and yearly rhythms of life). What is clear is that the genetic inheritance of biological and psychological traits interacts with culture in both directions, resulting in gene–culture coevolution (Lumsden & Wilson, 1981).

Humans have evolved truly extraordinary abilities in many areas of cognition, affect, and behavior (e.g., all of our sensory, perceptual, and motor systems; our ability to detect others' emotions and "read their faces"; the ways we often make very quick, almost automatic, and frequently very effective decisions in response to events in life). These abilities, however, are all constrained by our evolutionary history in ways similar to that of language acquisition. Evolution accounts for our ability to learn the extraordinary repertoire of truly amazing human skills very quickly and with relative ease. It is also responsible for the universality of human characteristics found around the world. However, it also accounts for the striking limitations and weaknesses associated with these abilities (e.g., high concern and trust for members of one's ingroup and fear and stereotyping for members of outgroups; strong confirmatory information processing biases; see Buss, 2005a; Diamond, 2012; Dunbar & Barrett, 2007b; Kahneman, 2012; Roberts, 2012; Swami, 2011).

Evolution, therefore, is just as essential to understanding human psychology and culture as it is for understanding human biology. None of these levels can be properly understood without an evolutionary perspective. Evolution consequently provides a good starting point for gaining a comprehensive science-based understanding of human psychology. To illustrate how knowledge of human evolution informs our understanding of human psychology—or, indeed, transforms our understanding of human psychology—consider the current science on human evolution. Recent paleoanthropological findings have several truly remarkable implications for understanding the human experience.

THE EVOLUTION OF HUMANS AND
HUMAN PSYCHOLOGICAL CHARACTERISTICS

The splitting off of the earliest humans from other hominids (upright bipedal primates) appears to have resulted from changing environmental conditions. The earth underwent a general cooling and drying about 6.5 million years ago. At about the same time, roughly 6 million years ago, the earliest humans split from the chimps and were able to survive in the savannahs that had emerged in Africa (Johanson & Wong, 2009; Stringer, 2012a; Wade, 2006). The chimps were well adapted to live in the rain forests, whereas the early humans were suited for scavenging and hunting in the open grasslands—neither one was well suited for the other environment. (DNA changes at a regular rate over time, and so it is possible to date evolutionary events with some precision. Each nucleotide [the sequence of A, G, C, and T that constitute the genome] in each gamete [i.e., fertilized egg] in each generation has about one chance in a billion to mutate into another nucleotide. As a result of this regular rate of mutation, the finding that living chimps and humans share 98.8% of their DNA indicates that the early humans split off from the older chimp species roughly 6 million years ago.)

Many hominid lines have evolved in Africa since that time. The first more modern species was *Homo erectus*, which evolved about 2 million years ago. They dispersed out of Africa about 1.7 million years ago in an event that has become known as "Out of Africa 1" (Stringer, 2012a). Although they had successfully made the transition to life in the open, scavenging and later hunting over long distances, none of that species lived on into the modern era. The Neanderthals split off from *Homo erectus* about 300,000–400,000 years ago and lived north of the Mediterranean Sea, but they disappeared about 30,000 years ago. The recent sequencing of an intact sample of Neanderthal

DNA made possible the discovery that about 2.5% of the DNA in all modern humans living outside of Africa comes from Neanderthal genes. This clearly suggests that there was intermating between the Neanderthals and Homo sapiens, although researchers have noted that it is unlikely that the very small amount of Neanderthal DNA that remains in our genomes is responsible for our current appearance or traits (Stringer, 2012b).

Homo sapiens, our species, are the only hominids that survived to the modern era. By comparing the DNA from living humans from all the continents, it is apparent that all humans now alive are actually related—we have all descended from the same parents. (All of the descendants of the other early *Homo sapiens* died off because of disease, infertility, famine, warfare, or other reasons.) Analyses of mitochondrial DNA, which is passed down intact from mothers to daughters, indicates that all *Homo sapiens* now alive on earth are descendants of a woman (popularly known as "Mitochondrial Eve") who lived in East Africa about 200,000 years ago (Cann, Stoneking, & Wilson, 1987). The common male ancestor of all human beings, dubbed "Chromosomal Adam," is estimated to have lived more recently, about 142,000 years ago in central or northwestern Africa (Cruciani et al., 2011). This could be due to the practice of polygamy whereby fewer males than females end up passing along their genes to their offspring (i.e., females in polygamous groups are more likely to bear children than are males, some of whom do not get the opportunity to reproduce).

The first *Homo sapiens* to leave Africa left about 100,000 years ago in a fairly small group estimated to include roughly 4,000 individuals. They migrated into the Middle East and from there migrated to Asia and eventually to Australia about 60,000 years ago. They did not enter Europe until about 35,000 years ago and then replaced the Neanderthals who were living there at the time. They migrated to the Americas 15,000 to 20,000 years ago (during the last Ice Age, when the oceans were much lower and Asia and Alaska were connected by land; Stringer, 2012a; Wade, 2006).

The reason that scientists know that the human community that left Africa was so small is that the genetic variation of the peoples who ended up on the various continents outside of Africa is small. Everyone whose continent of origin is outside Africa is genetically similar, and so the community that left that continent had to have been relatively small (Johanson & Wong, 2009; Stringer, 2012a; Wade, 2006). Within Africa, on the other hand, there is great genetic variation among the various groups who live there (e.g., the very tall Masai and the very small pygmies within Africa, while groups living in the rest of the world are relatively similar in height).

Examining the relatedness of people around the world from the perspective of genetic variation gives a very different view of race than what has normally been accepted at cultural levels. For example, skin color has often been used as an identifier of race or the continent of one's origin, but skin color in fact has a very different biological origin (Omi, 2001). Humans need dark skin to survive in equatorial regions of the earth in order to avoid dying from skin cancer (e.g., albinos in Nigeria seldom live more than 30 years; Yakubu & Mabogunje, 1993). On the other hand, those living far from the equator need to have light skin in order to avoid dying from a lack of vitamin D. In other words, skin color is not associated with one's continent of origin, but instead with the distance one lived from the equator.

Genetic analyses further clarify the meaning of race in biological terms. Humans around the world are 99.9% genetically identical. Of the remaining variance between individuals, however, very little is attributable to one's continent of origin (Bonham, Warshauer-Baker, & Collins, 2005). In fact, as little as 2.8% of the remaining variance is attributable to the continents, while another 2.5% is attributable to large groups within continents. The vast majority of our genetic differences, perhaps as much as 95%, is actually attributable to differences between local populations. As mentioned before, there is enormous genetic variation between local populations within Africa, which is actually far greater than that found in all the rest of the world (Tishkoff & Kidd, 2004). As a result, many Africans are more similar genetically to Europeans than they are to other Africans. The term *race* certainly has had extremely important meaning culturally, but it has little biological meaning (Montagu, 1942; Omi, 2001).

Additional perspectives for gaining insight into the nature of our common humanity are provided by anthropological studies of native peoples around the world who still live largely outside of modernity. It is thought that these peoples may live similarly to our shared ancestors of archaic times (Diamond, 2012; Lewis-Williams, 2002). Learning about these peoples before they no longer exist in their original states allows us to understand more about how all humans, throughout existence, have thought, felt, behaved, and lived out their lives. Their experience adds critical perspectives for understanding the fundamental, universal nature of all of humanity.

The implications of this research are huge. All human beings are Africans in terms of their original continent of origin and are literally descended from the same mother and father. We truly are all members of the same extended family. Racial differences are almost entirely cultural constructions—they have little biological meaning. Despite large cultural differences between us, humans are actually very similar at more fundamental levels. Widespread recognition of these facts might help resolve the conflicts between cultures, races, religions, and nations that have caused and continue to cause so much tragedy and suffering within the human family.

In addition to explaining our common origin as a species, research has documented the evolutionary origins and functions of a variety of important psychological characteristics. A wide variety of processes and mechanisms have been investigated including speech and language acquisition; social development (e.g., attachment); decision making (e.g., the "fast and frugal" heuristic cognitive mechanisms that allow very quick and often very effective decision making); social cognition (e.g., the detection of visual cues and the role of mirror neurons in understanding others' behavior); empathy, cooperation, altruism, and prosocial behavior; aggression and violence; individual differences in personality, intelligence, and psychopathology; reproductive behavior; parenting and family life; and the development and role of religion, art, music, and literature. All of these topics are important for understanding adaptive and maladaptive human behavior. For example, Nettle (2006) argued that each of the Big Five personality traits (i.e., Extraversion, Neuroticism, Openness to experience, Conscientiousness, and Agreeableness) is an adaptation that can maximize fitness in certain contexts. Neuroticism, for example, may result in increased costs involving stress and depression, but it also conveys advantages in terms of vigilance to danger and increased striving and competitive behavior. All of the different personality types may confer a combined set of advantages that together raise the inclusive fitness of the whole group further than if there was only limited personality variation. Reviewing all of this research is impossible here; interested readers are referred to several volumes that review current knowledge in these areas (e.g., Buss, 2005a; Dunbar & Barrett, 2007b; Roberts, 2012; Swami, 2011; Vonk & Shackelford, 2012; for broad, very accessible reviews, see Johanson & Wong, 2009; Stringer, 2012a; Wade, 2006). Chapter 3 also describes the evolutionary origins of human moral reasoning and behavior, the effects of which play critical roles in our lives as well.

All of these areas of research provide essential insights for understanding human psychology. As Buss (1991) explained, "At some fundamental level of description, evolution by natural selection is the process that creates physiological, anatomical, and psychological mechanisms. Therefore the crucial question is not *whether* evolution is relevant to the understanding of human behavior but how it is relevant" (p. 461). In addition to being necessary for a scientific understanding of human development and functioning, evolutionary theory provides a unifying perspective that integrates knowledge from across levels of natural organization as well as across scientific disciplines and subdisciplines. Fully appreciating the role of evolution in human psychopathology also has important implications in terms of understanding the etiology, assessment, and treatment of behavioral health disorders and behavioral health care ethics (Siegert & Ward, 2002). This integrated perspective was lacking in the behavioral sciences and especially in the applied clinical areas until recently. This perspective is critical, however, for the field to move forward under a single paradigmatic framework.

The preceding discussion attempted to show how the evolutionary perspective provides a logical starting point for integrating the tremendous complexity involved in understanding human development and functioning. To further illustrate how recent scientific findings inform behavioral health care, I describe two mechanisms involved in the important question of the role of nature versus nurture in human development. This research helps connect the ultimate explanations provided by evolutionary theory with important proximate explanations of mechanisms that are directly relevant to clinical practice.

NATURE VERSUS NURTURE IN HUMAN DEVELOPMENT

The question of the influence of nature versus nurture on human development and functioning is among the oldest and best known questions in psychology. This question has been answered in different ways over the history of the field. The eugenics movement, which started in the 1880s and was very influential through World War II, focused on the importance of genetically inherited traits. It was used as the rationale for the severe neglect and abuse of the mentally ill in the United States and several European countries (including the extermination of 70,000 mental patients at the beginning of the Holocaust; Dowbiggin, 2008; Whitaker, 2010). Many of the theoretical developments in psychology focused instead on the influence of the environment. Though Freud noted that biological drives provided the psychic energy behind psychological functioning, he also emphasized environmental factors as important influences that shaped one's personality and the development of psychopathology. Behaviorism emphasized the influence of one's environment even more as exemplified by Watson's (1925) famous statement:

> Give me a dozen healthy infants, well-formed, and my own specific world to bring them up in and I'll guarantee to take any one at random and train him to become any type of specialist I might select—a doctor, lawyer, artist, merchant-chief and, yes, even into a beggar-man and thief, regardless of his talents, penchants, tendencies, abilities, vocations and race of his ancestors. (p. 82)

More precise answers to the question of the role of nature and nurture in the development of important human characteristics have emerged in recent decades. First, it became clear that evolution helped shape the structure and function of the human brain just as it did for all the other organs in the body. The work of Noam Chomsky (1959), W. D. Hamilton (1963), E. O. Wilson (1975), and others demonstrated the importance of the interaction of genetic inheritance, culture, and experience in producing evolved psychological characteristics. The field of behavioral genetics also showed how genomic variation was related to personality characteristics, psychopathology, and intelligence. Comparisons of concordance in specific traits between identical (monozygotic) and fraternal (dizygotic) twins suggested a pervasive genetic influence on a range of psychological characteristics.

The understanding of the interplay between nature and nurture has been extended significantly by recent research in neural plasticity and epigenetics. This research has dramatically changed commonly accepted views regarding the roles of nature and nurture on development and behavior and has important implications for clinical intervention as well.

Neural Plasticity

Knowledge of brain structure and function has evolved dramatically over the past 150 years. The popular conception of brain function that involved a one-to-one correspondence between particular brain structures and specific functions dates to 1861 when Pierre Broca identified the brain region that was responsible for producing speech (which became known as *Broca's area* toward the back of the left frontal lobe). Over the ensuing decades, researchers found that many bodily functions were associated with specific brain areas. The neurosurgeon Wilder Penfield conducted extensive explorations of the point-to-point correspondence between the surfaces of the body that were represented in specific areas of the somatosensory cortex. His pictorial representation of the cortical homunculus, also popularly known as "the body within the brain," indicated very large neural areas devoted to sensation and motor control for the thumb, lips, and tongue, and small areas for the shoulders and back (Jasper & Penfield, 1954). This research had a large impact in the field. Until relatively recently, the relationships between brain structures and psychological and bodily functions were believed to be strongly hardwired.

The view that the structure and function of the brain were largely fixed by adulthood remained largely intact until the 1990s when it was discovered that the brain functioning of rhesus macaques changed dramatically after the nerves leading from their arms were cut (in studies of possible treatments for stroke). These monkeys' brains no longer received input from their arms, and the area formerly responsible for arm sensation was found to be processing sensations from the face instead (Pons et al., 1991). Similar findings were soon discovered in humans. For example, it was discovered that individuals who were blind at birth and became proficient at reading Braille were using their visual cortex for processing tactile signals from their reading fingers (Sadato et al., 1996). It was also found that blind individuals used their visual cortex for hearing, which allows them to be able to locate the source of sounds more effectively than sighted individuals (Röder et al., 1999).

Many neuroscientists were skeptical of these findings because belief that the neural structure of the brain was largely hardwired was so strong. They argued that these findings must be the result of abnormal neural development until it was found that the brain also changed in healthy, normal individuals. One study found that the somatosensory cortex devoted to the four fingers of the left hand in master violinists who had started playing in childhood was far larger than in nonmusicians, but it was also somewhat larger in individuals who took up the instrument as adults (Elbert et al., 1995). The brain was also found to change over very short time periods. For example, Pascual-Leone, Amedi, Fregni, and Merabet (2005) discovered that asking volunteers to merely imagine practicing a simple musical piece on a keyboard for one week, without ever actually touching any piano keys, resulted in an expansion of the motor cortex responsible for moving those fingers. An even more remarkable demonstration of this phenomenon was found when Pascual-Leone and Hamilton (2001) blindfolded volunteers with normal vision for 5 days to detect possible changes in the primary sensory regions, areas believed to be especially hardwired. The volunteers underwent fMRIs at the beginning of the experiment, then practiced learning Braille and distinguishing small differences in the pitch of sounds for 5 days, and then underwent fMRIs again. It was discovered that the visual cortex in these individuals, which had stopped receiving visual stimulation, had switched over to processing tactile and auditory information in just 5 days.

These discoveries of neural plasticity demonstrated that the brain could indeed break the bonds of its own genome. The brain is in fact capable of remarkable malleability that can result in healthy regions substituting for areas that are destroyed, some regions to grow in response to intensive practice, or areas that are no longer being used to assume other functions (as in blind individuals or in blindfolded volunteers; Raskin, 2011). These discoveries also led to clinical treatments for problems that previously appeared to be untreatable. Building on the research with the macaque monkeys mentioned two paragraphs above, researchers found that patients who had become paralyzed in one arm after a stroke in a particular region of the motor cortex could regain function in the paralyzed arm. By forcing patients to use their paralyzed arms (i.e., by putting their "good" arm in a sling and their "good" hand in an oven mitt), motor control of the paralyzed arm was gradually taken up by brain areas adjacent to the stroke, or sometimes even the corresponding region in the other hemisphere of the brain, opposite of where the stroke had occurred (Taub et al., 2006). Even those who suffered a stroke years before improved enormously, regaining the ability to drink from a glass, comb their hair, and brush their teeth.

If individuals with different forms of psychopathology change their behavior as the result of psychotherapy, corresponding changes should also be observable in the brain. Indeed, this has been demonstrated numerous times. Schwartz (Schwartz & Begley, 2002) treated individuals with obsessive-compulsive disorder (OCD) with mindfulness instruction, teaching them to not react emotionally to an OCD symptom and instead treat it simply as a faulty OCD circuit in their brains (specifically, hyperactivity in the orbital frontal cortex and the striatum, also known as the *worry circuit*). Compared with pretreatment, neuroimaging found that activity in the prefrontal cortex fell dramatically (Baxter et al., 1992). Very similar effects were observed following cognitive behavior therapy treatment for depression—reduced activity in the frontal cortex and increased activity in the limbic system were clearly evident at posttreatment and, in most cases, it remained that way (Goldapple et al., 2004). (As discussed in Chapter 10, a major benefit of psychotherapy for depression and several other disorders is that treatment gains tend to endure posttreatment, which is typically not the case with psychopharmacological treatment.)

Meditation and "mindfulness" therapies such as acceptance and commitment therapy and dialectical behavior therapy have become popular treatment approaches in the past two decades. In the first randomized controlled trial of the effects of mindfulness-based stress reduction training, R. J. Davidson et al. (2003) examined several outcomes associated with an 8-week meditation program. They found that anxiety symptoms in the meditation group fell about 12%, left-side frontal activation (associated with a sense of well-being and resilience) had tripled, and right frontal activity (associated with negative mood) had decreased; blood tests showed that their immune systems were producing more antibodies to a flu vaccine. Since then, dozens of clinical trials have found that mindfulness training is associated with reduced distress in breast cancer patients, improved coping in pain patients, reduced side effects in organ transplant recipients, and reduced anxiety and depression in patients with social anxiety disorder (D. J. Davidson & Begley, 2012). The brain is indeed highly malleable and changes as the result of mental activity (e.g., psychotherapy, meditation) as well as behavior (e.g., practicing a skill).

Epigenetics

Another area of research that has overturned conventional ideas about the role of nature vs. nurture in human development concerns epigenetics. The Greek *epi* means "upon," and *epigenetics* refers to physical modifications to the genome that result in a functional modification of the DNA but no change in the genetic sequence itself (Waddington, 1957). Although individuals inherit genetic instructions for many types of human characteristics, epigenetics can determine whether those instructions are expressed or silenced.

Cells throughout the body generally share exactly the same genes. Though different cells in the body perform very different functions, they generally all share the same DNA. The discovery of stem cells that can develop into any cell within the body, when their development is specifically manipulated, has tremendous potential for curing disease. The process whereby cells develop specialized functions depends on which regions of the genome are silenced, and the regions that remain active then determine the specialized functions of those cells. Genomic silencing that underlies cell specialization was thought to occur very early in development and thereafter remain highly stable throughout the life span, and it was believed that the loss of the silencing and specialization often resulted in organ dysfunction. Evidence has now accumulated, however, showing that the silencing of specific genomic functions is a dynamic process that extends across the life span and that this process is heavily determined by environmental experience (e.g., Gilbert, 2006; Jablonka & Lamb, 2005; Zhang & Meaney, 2010). There is a clear interdependence of genes and environment such that the expression of genetically controlled functions is often directly dependent on environmental events. Again, the DNA sequence itself is not altered by experience, but the modification of the gene through various epigenetic processes can result in either the expression or the silencing of particular cellular functions.

A dramatic example of this process involves the rearing of infant rat pups. Rat mothers exhibit high variability in their approach to caregiving for their infants. Newborn rat pups that receive high levels of licking and grooming by their mothers have been shown to exhibit lower behavioral and endocrine responses to stress than pups who were licked and groomed relatively little by their mothers (e.g., Champagne, 2008; Meaney, 2001). This is true for rat pups raised by their biological mothers as well as those raised by adoptive mothers—it is the soothing care, not the genetic inheritance, that regulates the endocrine and cardiovascular responses in the pup. Those who received high levels of licking and grooming as infants develop into rats that are less fearful and have lower hypothalamic-pituitary-adrenal reactivity to stress throughout their lives. The effect of maternal care on these characteristic responses to stress results from alterations in the corticotrophin-releasing factor systems in the rat pup brain. The same effect can be achieved by a human gently stroking the infant rat pup with a brush (Jutapakdeegul et al., 2003).

The random assignment of infant animals to the various caregiving conditions in these experiments obviously could not be conducted with humans. Nonetheless, correlational research finds that human infants raised under different caregiving styles develop characteristic behavioral responses to stress. The most important example of this is infant attachment research that finds that early caregiving experience has pervasive and enduring effects on a wide range of socioemotional and other psychological and health outcomes (e.g., Mikulincer & Shaver, 2007; see Chapter 7, this volume).

Further evidence supporting epigenetic effects on human brains comes from cadaver studies conducted on the brains of individuals who died by suicide compared with others who died suddenly from auto accidents, heart attacks, and other causes. A remarkable series of studies was made possible through data from the Quebec Suicide Brain Bank—validated psychiatric evaluations and developmental histories are available for all of the individuals whose brains are in the bank. McGowan et al. (2009) found increased DNA methylation (a process that accounts for the silencing of gene transcription) in a critical region of the hippocampus in only those individuals who committed suicide and had a history of child maltreatment. Furthermore, child maltreatment predicted the level of DNA methylation independent of the psychiatric status of the individuals. These correlational studies prevent causal interpretations regarding the associations found, but the results are consistent with those found in rat pups and suggest that variations in parental caregiving can modify the epigenetic state of the genome in humans and other animals at brain sites that are critical to socioemotional development.

Nature Versus Nurture Reconsidered

The structure and function of both genes and neurons were once considered to be highly fixed and largely unaffected by environmental influences once the human brain had reached particular critical stages of development. That view has been overturned, however. A large body of research now finds that the environment has a major influence on the operation of both genes and neurons. Epigenetic modifications can result in plasticity in the operation of the genome that may be at levels similar to the high plasticity that has been found in the growth and synaptic operation of neurons—Zhang and Meaney (2010) concluded that "it appears that the operation of the genome is indeed subject to environmental regulation in a manner that may be no less dynamic than that of synaptic connections" (p. 456). Further research will provide more details regarding these processes, but it is now clear that the environment has a significant effect on genomic and neural plasticity and that these processes provide the underlying neurophysiological basis for the developmental and psychological changes that are readily observed at behavioral levels. This is an area in which correlation versus causation has sometimes been seriously misconstrued. When neurophysiological effects are found to be correlated with environmental effects, the neurophysiological effects are sometimes simply assumed to be causative because they operate at a lower level of natural organization. It is now apparent that the environment causes some of these biological effects.

This research presents a very different answer to the nature versus nurture question than what was commonly accepted even just a decade ago. The effects of genetic inheritance and environmental influence are continually in dynamic interplay. The effects of each can only be understood within the context of the other, a relationship that continues across the life span. Many years ago, a journalist asked the psychologist Donald Hebb (the originator of the "Cells that fire together, wire together" postulate) about whether nature or nurture was more important in explaining individual differences in personality. Hebb (1958) responded that the question was similar to asking what contributes more to the area of a rectangle, the width or the length. Recent research corroborates how discerning his answer was and provides further evidence of the inextricably intertwined nature of biopsychosocial development and functioning.

THE NATURE OF A UNIFIED SCIENTIFIC PERSPECTIVE FOR BEHAVIORAL HEALTH CARE

Discovering a single, unified theory that successfully explained all of human psychology would obviously bring behavioral health care out of its pre-paradigmatic stage of development and provide a solid scientific foundation for clinical education and practice. There have been many calls for a unified theory that would resolve the pre-paradigmatic theoretical confusion in psychology (e.g., Anchin, 2008; Magnavita, 2006; Sternberg, 2005). Such a theory is extremely unlikely to emerge, at least in the near future, however. The experience of the other sciences indicates why.

Physics is the oldest of the sciences (more than two millennia old) and has been highly successful in explaining a wide range of natural phenomena from the exceedingly small (e.g., subatomic particles) to the very large (e.g., the cosmos). Despite all its achievements, however, physics has not yet discovered a unified theory that explains matter and energy. In fact, there are critically important aspects of the physical world about which very little is known, from the level of the cosmos (e.g., 95% of the universe consists of dark matter and dark energy about which very little is known; Randall, 2011) down to the level of particle physics. (The discovery of the Higgs boson in 2012, the elementary particle that provides critical support for the standard model of physics, was a monumental achievement for science, but there is still much about the subatomic world that remains unknown; CERN, 2012.) Discovering a unified theory of matter and energy is regarded by many as the ultimate goal of physics, but the field may still be a long way from reaching that goal (Mitchell, 2009).

Biology is a much younger science than physics, but it progressed rapidly after the invention of the microscope. Biology was still largely a descriptive science until Darwin published *On the Origin of Species* in 1859, though it took until the 1940s before the full significance of natural selection was appreciated (Quammen, 2006). The discovery of evolution transformed the understanding of plant and animal life on earth and provided a paradigmatic perspective that helped connect the disjointed subfields within the discipline. Nonetheless, there is clearly still a great deal to learn about many biological processes, including evolution itself (Larson, 2004). Science is a long way from identifying a single unified theory that fully explains the biology of life.

Despite being very well established and highly successful disciplines, physics, chemistry, and biology have not yet discovered unified theories for explaining phenomena within those fields. In contrast, scientific psychology is much younger and investigates extraordinarily complex phenomena with scientific tools that have been quite limited for examining the intricacy and complexity of the phenomena involved. Though the power and precision of scientific tools have been advancing steadily, a huge amount of work remains to unravel the tremendous complexity of the human mind and brain. Therefore, there is no reason to expect that a unified theory will be discovered in psychology before one is discovered in physics, chemistry, or biology.

It is essential to recognize, however, that a unified scientific theory of psychology is not necessary for the field to leave behind its pre-paradigmatic past. There are now no unified theories in physics, chemistry, or biology, but those fields are all solidly scientific and paradigmatic in the Kuhnian sense. It is also not necessary to explain all phenomena within a particular area for a field to be scientific—none of the sciences has done that.

The case of medicine is very instructive in this regard. Certainly, the success of the biomedical sciences is impressive, even though a great deal about how the biological world operates remains to be discovered. For example, there are many common idiopathic diseases for which the causes and cures remain unknown (e.g., Alzheimer's and Parkinson's disease, most seizures, multiple sclerosis, rheumatoid arthritis, Type I diabetes). Most psychiatric disorders are idiopathic as well. Indeed, no psychiatric syndrome has yet been found to have a clear biological cause, as evidenced by the lack of a single biological test that is ready to be used as part of the diagnostic criteria for mental disorders (Frances, 2009) that appear in the *Diagnostic and Statistical Manual of Mental Disorders* (5th ed.; American Psychiatric Association, 2013). Currently, there is also significant concern about the safety of many medical interventions and the widespread use of tests, medicines, and other procedures that may cause more harm than benefit (e.g., Goldacre, 2013; Healy, 2012; Institute of Medicine, 2000; U.S. Preventive Services Task Force, 2013).

Medicine in the United States reached the "tipping point" when it most clearly transitioned from primarily an art to a science in 1910 when Abraham Flexner submitted his report on the state of medical education in North America. Biology had been making important advances and the practice of medicine was transforming dramatically at the end of the 19th century. Pasteur introduced the germ theory of infection in 1878 and the following year tested the first vaccination. Sterilization of medical instruments had been introduced and was becoming common toward the end of the century. (Before antiseptic methods were introduced, death rates following amputations, for example, were very high; one Parisian surgeon noted that his death rate was 100%; Porter, 1997.) Out of concern that American medical education was not sufficiently science-based, Flexner visited and rated nearly every one of the 168 medical schools in the United States and Canada. His highly influential report included his ratings and often scathing criticisms of the individual schools, and several of them closed soon after as a result. Over the next decades, 42% of the schools closed, and the schools that remained open significantly increased their admission standards and laboratory and clinical training requirements (Hiatt & Stockton, 2003). Even though very little was known at the time about many medical interventions that we now take for granted (e.g., the first antibiotic, penicillin, was not discovered until 1928 and was not mass produced until the end of World War II), transitioning to a science-based framework for medical education and practice was not viewed as premature.

Psychology as both a basic and applied science has been evolving in a manner similar in some ways to the other sciences. Enough was discovered in physics, chemistry, and biology that those fields long ago reached the point when they became scientific and paradigmatic. Unified theories for explaining phenomena within those disciplines clearly had not been discovered, though enough verified explanations of important phenomena had accumulated that the applied fields of engineering and medicine could be practiced in a significantly safer and more effective manner.

Behavioral health care has reached a similar point. The field can now replace the practice of selecting from a diverse array of competing theoretical orientations for guiding one's clinical practice with a unified scientific framework from which all clinicians can practice. Though we may still be stumbling a bit through the transition from our complicated, contentious pre-paradigmatic period, we are well along the way toward adopting a unified scientific framework for understanding human development, functioning, and behavior change. APA officially endorsed the evidence-based approach to clinical practice in 2005 (APA Presidential Task Force on Evidence-Based Practice, 2006), an emblematic step reflecting the transition to the paradigmatic era. This volume is another reflection of that transition.

TRANSITIONING TO A UNIFIED SCIENTIFIC APPROACH: THE METATHEORETICAL BIOPSYCHOSOCIAL FRAMEWORK

The solution to the historical problem of theoretical confusion in behavioral health care is (naturally) the same as it was in the other sciences. As noted in the preceding section, unified theories that explain all phenomena in physics, chemistry, or biology do not currently exist, and it would be highly unlikely that such a unified theory would emerge in psychology, arguably the most complex of the sciences, before it did in the other fields. In all the sciences, however, explanations of more discrete, less complex phenomena are typically much more complete, whereas explanations of highly complex phenomena involving many variables and dynamic processes are typically less complete. The understanding of weather and climate are good examples of the difficulty of explaining complex phenomena. Predictions regarding the weather become inaccurate very quickly (i.e., the amount of variance explained falls rapidly) such that they are completely unreliable after a week or 10 days (or "chaotic" in terms of complexity theory).

In order to scientifically investigate complex phenomena that are not yet fully understood, metatheoretical frameworks are needed to integrate what is known and provide approximate explanations (Mitchell, 2009; Rogers, 2010). Metatheoretical frameworks identify the most important factors that need to be considered and integrated to understand the theory and research regarding particular phenomena, and specific models built from these metatheories can then be empirically tested and refined. Whether it be the climate, the behavior of galaxies or subatomic particles, or the development of personality disorders, the refinement of these models results in increasingly more complete and accurate explanations of phenomena. Metatheories can be contrasted with scientific theories that involve a principle or body of principles to explain a class of phenomena. Using empirical observations, rules, and scientific laws, theories describe current observations and predict future observations of phenomena (Hawking, 1996; Popper, 1963). A *metatheory*, on the other hand, is "a theory the subject matter of which is another theory" (Encyclopaedia Britannica, 2013). It is a model that organizes what is tentatively or partially known about complex phenomena by referring to other theory and research about the operation and interaction of its component parts.

At the metatheoretical level, the outlines of the framework needed to understand human psychology are clear. At the most general level, there is no disagreement across the sciences and humanities that human psychology is determined by a range of psychological, sociocultural, and biological factors that interact through complex developmental processes. The influence of specific factors varies dramatically depending on the phenomenon and the developmental, environmental, and other contextual factors involved, and more tends to be known about basic processes than more complex ones. Taken together, however, the amount that is known is extensive. Psychologists would generally agree that all the historically important "waves" of theory development in the field (e.g., psychodynamic, behavioral, humanistic, cognitive, systemic, multicultural) have contributed important insights into understanding human psychology and behavioral health care. They would generally also agree, however, that these insights also need to be integrated with those from the biological and neurosciences, the social sciences, and the humanities to gain a comprehensive understanding. (The arts and humanities also provide critical insights into human experience.) The integration of all these perspectives is staggeringly complex (which is, of course, the nature of human phenomena). At the general metatheoretical level, however, there is unanimity that human psychology cannot be understood without taking a developmental perspective that integrates the inextricably intertwined biological, psychological, and sociocultural influences on development and functioning. This perspective is so fundamental that it is analogous to the three spatial dimensions plus the dimension of time that are required to comprehend the physical world. At the metatheoretical level, the developmental biopsychosocial perspective is simply fundamental for understanding human psychology.

DISCUSSION: BEHAVIORAL HEALTH CARE AS A PARADIGMATIC CLINICAL SCIENCE

Achieving a comprehensive scientific understanding of the tremendous complexity involved in human development and functioning has naturally been extremely challenging. This chapter began by explaining why the traditional theoretical orientations were unable to provide comprehensive scientific explanations of human psychology. Science has now advanced to the point, however, where it can provide a solid framework for understanding human psychology and behavioral health care. The basic outlines of the metatheoretical framework that provides a unifying paradigmatic perspective for the field are clear. There is no disagreement that biological, psychological, and sociocultural levels of natural organization interact across time in producing psychological outcomes. There is also no scientific debate regarding the evolutionary origins of psychological characteristics and mechanisms. Starting with an evolutionary perspective is essential because it provides both ultimate explanations regarding the origin and function of psychological characteristics (i.e., it explains why humans and other organisms are "designed" the way they are) as well as proximate explanations regarding the mechanisms and processes involved. Evolutionary theory is also the perspective that links the psychological sciences with the biological and social sciences, thereby reflecting the inherently biopsychosocial nature of the human organism. Obviously, much about human psychology remains to be explained, but the basic structure of the metatheoretical framework for understanding human psychology and behavioral health care is now clear.

It is time for the behavioral health care field to enter the paradigmatic era based on a unified science-based approach to understanding human psychology.

There is no disagreement regarding the ultimate evolutionary explanations for human development and behavior, and the same is true with regard to many proximate explanations of mechanisms and processes. There are disagreements regarding many issues, and particularly regarding more complex processes, but this is the case in all the sciences and will continue to be the case until all phenomena are thoroughly understood. There are many possible starting points for gaining a comprehensive scientific understanding of human psychology, but wherever one begins, that understanding must include evolutionary theory in order to be complete. As was noted earlier, human anatomy and physiology are essentially unintelligible without evolutionary theory, and the same is true not just for human cognition, emotion, and behavior, but social functioning and culture as well. The anatomy, physiology, and psychology of early *Homo sapiens* allowed for the evolution of language, which subsequently gave rise to highly complex social systems, culture, art, and science. None of these biological, psychological, or sociocultural levels of natural organization can be scientifically understood without evolutionary theory.

This volume refers to a *science-based* biopsychosocial approach because it is critical that this approach be differentiated from eclecticism and theoretical integration with which the biopsychosocial approach has sometimes been associated. The biopsychosocial approach has been criticized as advocating an anarchic eclecticism in behavioral health care in which "anything goes" in terms of theoretical orientations for understanding and treating clinical syndromes (e.g., Ghaemi, 2010). It is true that behavioral health care was often practiced this way as biologically, psychologically, and socially oriented theories and interventions have all been applied, not on the basis of their scientific validity, but typically on the basis of personal preference—it was essentially up to individual clinicians to select from an array of competing, irreconcilable theories to guide their clinical practice. This was emblematic of behavioral health care as a pre-paradigmatic field.

A clinical science operates in a very different manner, however. Theoretical integration and eclecticism do not play a role in science-based approaches to understanding natural phenomena. When scientific knowledge accumulates to the point where it can provide a unified, evidence-based approach to understanding phenomena in an area, personally choosing from a diverse array of competing theoretical orientations is no longer justified. The contrast between the current scientific understanding of the structure and function of the human organism and the explanations of human psychology provided by the traditional theoretical orientations is striking—there is relatively little overlap between these two sets of explanations. Therefore, there should be no confusion regarding the difference between the science-based biopsychosocial approach and the pre-paradigmatic eclecticism that was formerly sometimes associated with the term *biopsychosocial*.

Although science can explain increasing numbers of psychological, biological, and sociocultural phenomena, many processes are still only partially or poorly understood. Physical and behavioral health care consequently remain very complicated enterprises. The biopsychosocial complexity of human development and functioning clearly indicates that outcomes are multifactorially determined, the result of multiple mechanisms and levels of influence interacting over time. When multiple mechanisms and levels of influence are involved, in the case of either mental or physical health problems, there may be multiple targets that are appropriate for clinical intervention as well. This is particularly true when treating problems that are chronic and have complex causation (e.g., a range of options is available for treating chronic heart disease or depression, and prognosis is often uncertain in either case). Biological, psychological, and sociocultural factors interact in complex ways that can facilitate or debilitate treatment outcomes, and many medical and psychiatric illnesses cannot be cured (as in idiopathic illnesses where both the cause and cure are unknown). Many illnesses also have a deteriorating course and the most successful treatment may only slow the rate of deterioration. (The issues involved in assessment and treatment planning for cases at all levels of severity and complexity are discussed in Part III of this volume.) So even as the scientific understanding of health and illness steadily advances, health care remains a very complicated clinical practice.

This chapter and the ones that follow include topics that extend beyond the usual graduate curriculum in the behavioral health care professions. In addition, keeping reasonably current with the rapidly expanding scientific knowledge concerning human development and functioning is formidable given how expansive the field is. A science-based approach to learning and practicing behavioral health care is actually much more difficult than learning to practice on the basis of the traditional theoretical orientations because the actual complexity of human beings is much greater than what the traditional orientations describe. The theoretical orientations address only part of the biopsychosocial whole of human experience, and several of them focus only on particular psychological mechanisms. A comprehensive scientific understanding of human development and functioning, however, requires a broad, integrative approach that is much more complex.

The steadily growing body of scientific knowledge regarding human psychology suggests that the behavioral health care field has no alternative but to transition to a unified, science-based approach to education and practice in the field. As a clinical science, the field must keep current with scientific advances regarding human development and functioning. The health care field generally and behavioral health specifically have endorsed an evidence-based approach to practice. At the same time, the limitations of the traditional theoretical orientations as scientific frameworks are now well known. Adopting a personal theoretical orientation to guide one's clinical practice, when that orientation is known to provide only partial explanations or actually conflicts with the scientific understanding of human psychology, is not consistent with evidence-based practice and the foundational principles of a profession based on science.

The science-based biopsychosocial approach to understanding human psychology and behavioral health care suggests a complexity to human experience that truly is amazing. Indeed, the complexity of human existence as viewed from the scientific perspective is far greater than that suggested by any of the traditional theoretical orientations. This makes it all the more exciting as the starting point for learning the practice of behavioral health care as a clinical science.

3

ETHICAL FOUNDATIONS OF BEHAVIORAL HEALTH CARE

Humans have always been deeply concerned about questions of right and wrong, good and evil, and innocence and guilt. The world's religions and philosophies and many of its most important written documents have been centrally concerned with these questions, and our daily thoughts and feelings frequently turn to these issues as well. People often disagree about what is right and wrong, but ethics and morality have been a universal concern to people in all cultures and throughout history.

Scholarly interest in ethics is also as old as history itself. Indeed, philosophers such as Aristotle could probably easily follow current debates regarding the nature of human morality such as the extent to which moral judgments are driven by human emotions compared with objective reasoning. On the other hand, the scientific analysis of human morality is relatively recent. Psychotherapists have always been very concerned about ethics both in terms of their role in guiding professional services as well as the role they play in

DOI: 10.1037/14441-004
Biopsychosocial Practice: A Science-Based Framework for Behavioral Health Care, by T. P. Melchert
Copyright © 2015 by the American Psychological Association. All rights reserved.

patients' lives. But psychologists and evolutionary biologists have focused on the nature and origins of prosocial behavior and altruism for only the past few decades, and extensive experimental investigation of specific aspects of moral reasoning and behavior has been undertaken only relatively recently.

This chapter reviews the reasons why professional ethics is fundamental in the practice of behavioral health care and notes some of the recent research on moral reasoning and behavior as well as the evolutionary origins of human cooperation and ethics. That discussion is followed by a summary of the most influential framework for informing health care ethics in the United States and Europe. These topics demonstrate that ethics are fundamental in behavioral health care practice and that a better understanding of moral reasoning and behavior is critical for gaining a more complete understanding of human psychology in general.

WHY ETHICS IS FOUNDATIONAL IN BEHAVIORAL HEALTH CARE

This volume gives great importance to professional ethics in behavioral health care. Professional ethics, along with the scientific understanding of human psychology, is considered fundamental to the conceptual foundations of the field. The importance of the scientific foundations of behavioral health care should be abundantly clear. Modern expectations and standards require that health care be informed by scientific knowledge and that the safety and effectiveness of interventions be evaluated through scientific research. Ethics, however, is equally as important in behavioral health care. It is of course ethically unacceptable to cause harm to individuals through the use of unsafe or irresponsible behavioral health care practices, and the ethical foundations of health care obligate therapists to contribute to the well-being of patients and appropriately balance the risks and benefits of intervention. The safety and effectiveness of behavioral health care intervention are top priorities from the perspective of both the scientific and ethical foundations of the field.

Another reason that ethics is fundamental in behavioral health care is that clinical practice frequently requires ethical guidance beyond that provided by appealing to empirical evidence and analysis alone. Science is essential for explaining many aspects of assessment and treatment, but many other aspects of health care require a consideration of ethical principles and guidelines to determine how to appropriately apply the scientific knowledge and tools that are available. The same is true in many other areas of life besides health care. Science can often illuminate what will happen if different courses of action are undertaken, but it can be limited in its ability to answer questions about how various social, economic, and political problems and opportunities should be addressed. (See Harris, 2010, for an alternative perspective that elevates science to a higher level of ethical explanatory power.)

Another perspective for appreciating the importance of ethics in health care is to note that science is critical for understanding *health*, whereas ethics plays a major role in understanding *care*. Understanding health, illness, adaptive functioning, and dysfunction requires scientific knowledge, but ethical considerations are also critical for figuring out how to appropriately care for individuals with behavioral and physical health needs. Ethical conduct and moral virtues are essential to carrying out health care responsibilities (T. L. Beauchamp & Childress, 2009). All forms of caring relationships (e.g., parental caregiving of children, elder care, medical and nursing care, mental health care) are seriously diminished when respect, compassion, trustworthiness, integrity, and other moral virtues are compromised. These virtues are especially important in behavioral health care because of the nature and role of the therapeutic relationship, patients' vulnerability when revealing and processing highly personal and private issues, and the stigma that behavioral health issues frequently carry in society (the effects of which can even outweigh the impairments related to the mental illness; Hinshaw & Stier, 2008).

A solid foundation in ethics is also critical at practical levels. Professional ethics and legal issues are strongly emphasized during graduate training and on licensure exams. Ethical behavior is also a high priority for employers. Engaging in unethical behavior as a student or employee is taken very seriously by faculty, supervisors, and managers and can quickly lead to major disciplinary or legal action. Routine aspects of daily practice require solid preparation in professional ethics and legal issues (e.g., maintaining appropriate confidentiality when using electronic medical records; obtaining proper informed consent; handling a second-hand report of child abuse or a subpoena for patient records). Many of the issues that patients deal with in therapy also have important ethical dimensions. These sometimes involve life and death issues (e.g., suicide) as well as many other highly consequential situations (e.g., responding to abusiveness or boredom in one's career or marriage; parenting children who are engaging in risky behavior; dealing with conflicts between personal issues and religious expectations; taking responsibility for one's mental illness, substance abuse, or personality pathology; engaging in behavior that is harming one's partner or family without their knowledge). There are also times when ethical dilemmas encountered in clinical practice become excruciatingly difficult (e.g., a 17-year-old Muslim girl informs you that she acquired a sexually transmitted infection but begs you not to report it because she says she is from a very conservative family and will be subjected to an honor killing if her family learns that she had premarital sexual relations).

The steadily growing research literature on the nature of moral reasoning and behavior provides additional reasons to highlight the role of ethics in behavioral health care. Moral reasoning and behavior are complicated phenomena that are subject to a variety of emotional, intuitive, subconscious, irrational, and social influences. Familiarity with these influences along with solid preparation in ethical theory can help therapists to avoid the shortcomings of our own ethical reasoning as well as help us to better assist clients with the ethical dilemmas they face in their lives.

All these considerations point to the central importance of professional ethics in behavioral health care. Scientific analysis and evidence clarify many important issues encountered in behavioral health care practice, but supplementing that knowledge with solid preparation in ethical theory and principles greatly strengthens therapists' ability to engage in sound clinical decision making. At all levels, from managing the routine responsibilities of daily practice to developing national health care policy, ethics plays a critical role in behavioral health care.

A SCIENCE-BASED BIOPSYCHOSOCIAL PERSPECTIVE ON MORAL REASONING AND BEHAVIOR

Substantial progress has been made recently in understanding the nature of moral reasoning and behavior. A comprehensive review of the literature in this area is not possible here, but highlighting some recent findings will demonstrate the complex dynamics involved and the need for careful attention to this topic. Of particular importance to the present discussion is the finding of substantial irrationality that is involved in human moral reasoning. The evolutionary origins of moral reasoning and behavior also emphasize the importance of a science-based biopsychosocial perspective on the subject.

Irrationality in Human Cognition and Moral Reasoning

Not too long ago, moral reasoning was generally thought to result from reflective, deliberative, logical reasoning. Kohlberg's (1971) well-known stage model of moral development was a dominant approach in psychological theorizing about morality. These models were found to be insufficient, however, as research suggested that moral reasoning was more complex than was suggested by traditional models. For example, Carol Gilligan (1982) pointed out that girls and women were more likely than boys and men to include caring and feelings of responsibility to others in their moral judgments. Haidt (2001) had an especially important impact on the psychological study of morality when he noted that cognitive approaches to morality cannot handle four important observations about moral behavior. First, though conscious reasoning, reflection, and deliberation are important in many moral judgments, other moral judgments are made very rapidly and automatically without conscious reasoning. Second, individuals are often quite defensive about their moral judgments and seek out evidence and arguments to defend their judgments rather than analyze them in an objective, logical manner aimed at finding the "truth" of the matter. Third, evidence suggested that moral reasoning often follows, rather than precedes, judgments and behaviors, and provides post hoc explanations to justify intuitive judgments and moral or immoral actions. Finally, emotion is found to play a larger role than conscious reasoning in many moral judgments and actions. These findings all suggested that major aspects of moral reasoning are not logical or rational (see Mikulincer & Shaver, 2012).

The role of irrationality in human cognition has been studied extensively by Daniel Kahneman, who became the second psychologist ever to win a Nobel Prize in 2002. Kahneman and his colleague Amos Tversky (who died in 1996) began investigating cognitive biases that unconsciously distort our judgments about the world. These biases operate even among highly trained and experienced professionals. (For example, in one study a group of German judges with an average of more than 15 years of experience rolled a pair of dice that were loaded to give either a 3 or a 9, and after rolling the high number they stated that they would give a shoplifter a substantially longer sentence than after they rolled a 3; Englich, Mussweiler, & Strack, 2006.) Kahneman and Tversky's most famous experiment involved telling research participants about an imaginary 31-year-old woman named Linda who was single, outspoken, very bright, and deeply concerned about discrimination and social justice when she was a student. In one of their studies, a group of doctoral students in the decision-making program at the Stanford Graduate School of Business were asked which is more probable: Linda is a bank teller, or Linda is a bank teller and is active in the feminist movement (Tversky & Kahneman, 1983). Despite having completed several courses in statistics, probability, and decision theory, 85% of the students chose "feminist bank teller" as more likely than "bank teller" (which is wrong because every feminist bank teller is a bank teller and adding an additional condition only lowers its probability).

This latter experiment illustrates what Kahneman (2012) and others referred to as *System 1* and *System 2 thinking*. System 1 thinking is fast, automatic, intuitive, and largely unconscious. It produces a "quick and dirty" draft of reality that is often accurate and useful in many situations such as when we have to respond quickly to threats and opportunities in life. System 2 thinking, on the other hand, is slow, deliberate, analytical, and requires conscious effort to reason analytically and explicitly about the world. Though the deliberate and rational System 2 thinking is beneficial in many cases, this system is also lazy and often accepts the easy but unreliable story about the world that is provided by System 1. In the "Linda" experiment, 85% of the doctoral business students, despite their expertise in probability, chose the easy, automatic answer provided by System 1. Kahneman (2012) noted that "The sophisticated allocation of attention [to rely on System 1 thinking] has been honed by a long evolutionary history. Orienting and responding quickly to the gravest threats or most promising opportunities improved the chance of survival" (p. 35). Our reliance on the less effortful cognitive system, however, also reflects that "Laziness is built deep into our nature" (p. 35).

Kahneman also found surprising dynamics in individuals' judgments about their level of happiness. For example, when asked retrospectively how happy they are with various events in their lives (e.g., a vacation or dental visit), people tend to remember their peak level of pain or pleasure, or the way the experiences ended. If they keep an ongoing record of their actual experience, however, sampled from moment to moment, their average level of "experienced" well-being can be quite different from their retrospectively "remembered" well-being. This was demonstrated in a study of patients undergoing colonoscopies (Redelmeier & Kahneman, 1996). One group received a standard colonoscopy that was quite uncomfortable (this was in the 1990s before anesthetic drugs were widely used with this procedure), and a second group received the standard colonoscopy but also received several extra minutes of mild discomfort added on to the end of the exam (without being told). The second group obviously experienced all of the pain that the first group did and then some, but their procedure ended less painfully. The researchers found that the patients in the second group remembered their pain as substantially lower than the patients in the first group. The pain level at the end of the procedure had a large effect and the actual duration of the pain had no effect whatsoever on their reports of the total amount of pain they experienced. Kahneman (2012) wrote, "Odd as it may seem, I am my remembering self, and the experiencing self, who does my living, is like a stranger to me" (p. 390).

Neuroscience research is clarifying the neural basis for some of these unexpected cognitive processes. For example, people often assume that the seemingly natural or strongly felt response to a moral situation is the morally correct response, even though it may be based on automatic processing rather than a deliberate approach to analyzing the issues involved. For example, in one study, research participants were asked to imagine two scenarios described by Greene (2003, p. 848):

- As you are driving through the countryside you hear a man calling for help. You pull over and a man whose legs are covered with blood explains that he had a hiking accident and asks you to take him to the nearby hospital. You want to help because the man is seriously injured, but if you give him a ride, his blood may stain the upholstery in your car. Is it appropriate for you to leave this man on the side of the road in order to keep your upholstery clean?

- You are opening your mail and read a letter from a reputable international aid organization asking for a small donation that they will use to provide much needed medical care to poor people in a country in another part of the world. Is it morally acceptable to not make this donation?

With regard to the first situation, a large majority of people say that it would be horribly selfish to refuse the hiker's request for help (Greene, 2003). The man badly needs medical attention and you are in a position to provide it without great cost. Not to do so would be seriously morally deficient. On the other hand, in the second situation, most people would say it is not morally wrong to ignore the request from the aid organization. It would be admirable to help people in faraway places with life-threatening medical needs, but we are not obligated to provide assistance. The costs involved in these two situations might be similar (i.e., the cost of getting the car upholstery cleaned could be about the same as the donation). Nonetheless, people tend to respond in opposite ways even though only one person in the first situation would be helped while a much larger number of people might be helped in the second.

Functional magnetic resonance imaging studies conducted by Greene and others (e.g., Greene, 2003; Greene, Nystrom, Engell, Darley, & Cohen, 2004; Hauser, 2006) have found that moral dilemmas that are personal in nature, such as the first one above, are associated with greater activity in the emotion and social cognition areas of the brain. In those situations, research participants experienced strong, immediate feelings regarding the appropriate moral response. Impersonal situations, such as the second dilemma, are associated with greater activity in the cortex regions associated with abstract reasoning and cognitive control and less activity in the emotion and social processing areas and no automatic feelings about the morality of the situation. This difference likely has an evolutionary basis because, over the course of human history, a survival advantage was gained by those who were concerned about the well-being of those who were close to them. Indeed, altruism appears to have developed as a characteristic of humans and many other species because of its importance to survival of the group as a whole (see the section "Evolution of Cooperative and Prosocial Behavior"). When examined objectively, however, place of residence may not be a relevant consideration for judging the value of human life and well-being.

There are many psychological responses like the one described in the preceding paragraphs that involve automatic neural processing that may have conferred an evolutionary advantage but are not necessarily based on logical or moral considerations (Greene, 2003; Greene et al., 2004; Hauser, 2006).

For example, if one happens upon a group of delinquent teenagers kicking and beating a cat or dog to death for amusement, most people would immediately judge that behavior to be thoroughly immoral. If one happened upon that event on the way to a restaurant for a steak dinner, however, questions regarding the morality of killing and eating animals may not even enter one's consciousness (Pollan, 2006). The feelings one has about these situations are also typically subjectively felt to be quite natural and correct. Just because the resulting judgments feel so "right" or so "wrong," however, does not necessarily make them correct from an objective moral perspective.

Another fascinating area of research regarding human morality concerns the nature and extent of dishonesty in human interactions. Dan Ariely (2012) and his colleagues have found that individuals commonly cheat in a wide variety of laboratory and naturalistic settings so they can personally benefit. For example, when they can easily get away with it, most college students report solving roughly 15% more problems on a math exercise than they actually did so they are reimbursed more for their research participation. To explain these findings, Ariely and his colleagues proposed a "fudge factor theory" that involves two opposing motivations: individuals want to view themselves as honest, honorable people, but they also want to gain as much money as possible (Mazar, Amir, & Ariely, 2008). Ariely and others have also found that a variety of social and cognitive factors affect the amount of cheating people engage in. For example, people are more likely to steal things than money (e.g., students will take cans of Coke from a dormitory refrigerator though not $1 bills sitting on a plate next to the Coke; Mazar et al., 2008), people cheat more when they are fatigued (Mead, Baumeister, Gino, Schweitzer, & Ariely, 2009), people cheat more after they see others cheat and get away with it (Gino, Ayal, & Ariely, 2009), or they cheat more after they have been given counterfeit sunglasses to try out than people given authentic designer sunglasses to try out (Gino, Norton, & Ariely, 2010). They found that though few people cheat to a maximal degree, large proportions cheat small amounts, and the amount of their cheating can be significantly increased or decreased based on a variety of cognitive and social manipulations (Ariely, 2012).

The research described in the preceding paragraphs shows that a variety of nonconscious factors readily affect human moral reasoning and behavior. These factors obviously affect patients' ethical decision making within their own lives, and so therapists should be familiar with this research so they can evaluate and process ethical issues with their patients from an informed perspective. But therapists' own ethical decision making is also affected by these factors. Familiarity with this research helps individual therapists as well as the profession collectively to deal more effectively with the ethical dimensions of their work.

Evolution of Cooperative and Prosocial Behavior

As with understanding human psychology generally, an evolutionary perspective presents a useful starting point for understanding moral behavior because of its focus on ultimate explanations regarding the origin and nature of cooperation, prosocial behavior, and altruism, as well as proximate explanations regarding the mechanisms involved. The following discussion briefly notes the origins and functions of these characteristics to demonstrate the importance of a science-based biopsychosocial approach to understanding human psychology.

Understanding the nature of cooperative, prosocial behavior and especially altruism among humans has been one of the most problematic questions in all of evolutionary theory. Humans show remarkable proclivities to cooperate in terms of child rearing and family life, economic exchanges, religious and political practices, and military defense. Indeed, these rather amazing levels of cooperation are a defining characteristic of human beings that play an essential role in our success as a species. If not for prosocial emotions and behavior, humans would be self-interested sociopaths pursing their own needs and welfare, and society, culture, and all the institutions that help ensure some level of human security and dignity would not exist. Instead, cooperation, reciprocal altruism, and mutualism are quintessential human characteristics (Krebs, 2005; Price, 2011). Humans evolved to pursue their own self-interest that maximized their personal chances of survival and reproduction as well as collective actions that involved the common good of the whole community. Human culture universally fosters the internalization of norms for promoting self-control and subordinating the interests of the individual to those of the group, as well as for fostering honesty, fairness, cooperation, bravery, and empathy for others' distress (Gintis, Bowles, Boyd, & Fehr, 2007; Mesoudi & Jensen, 2012). These critically important human characteristics were not predicted by Darwin's theory of natural selection and the survival of the fittest.

Darwin (1859) himself was aware that altruism presented a serious challenge to his theory. The primary engine of adaptation by natural selection involves maximizing the fitness of individuals so that they can survive, outcompete rivals, and reproduce. Altruism necessarily benefits others at one's own expense, however, and would promptly be eliminated by the mechanism of natural selection. Darwin noted that "if it could be proved that any part of the structure of any one species had been formed for the exclusive good of another species, it would annihilate my theory, for such could not have been produced through natural selection" (p. 190). Over a century later, E. O. Wilson (1975) regarded altruism as still "the central theoretical problem of sociobiology" (p. 3).

The most important development in explaining altruistic cooperation resulted from switching the focus in evolutionary theory from the reproducing individual to the replicating gene. W. D. Hamilton (1963, 1964) argued that the gene should be the fundamental focus of evolution and that the gene can successfully replicate by not only promoting the reproduction of its carrier but also by promoting the reproduction of any individuals who carry copies of the gene. Based on this concept, Richard Dawkins (1976) noted that genes are "replicators" and individual bodies are the "vehicles" they build in order to enable themselves to replicate. Darwin's theory was primarily a theory about the adaptation of individuals in the competition to survive, whereas Hamilton's insight showed how genes that promoted the survival of genetic relatives increase the *inclusive fitness* of the kin group. This general principle underlying kin selection, which favored genetically related relatives, was eventually broadened to include nonrelated individuals (Dawkins, 1976; Hamilton, 1975). Trivers (1971) hypothesized that cooperation between individuals can evolve if partners engage in mutually beneficial exchanges of altruistic acts. The return altruism may happen far into the future, but as long as one can trust that the altruism will be reciprocated, then engaging in altruistic acts can be highly effective and adaptive. There are many examples of mutually beneficial relationships between individuals and even species in nature (e.g., puppies huddling together to share body heat, the flora that live in the human digestive tract but also provide their hosts with a range of beneficial services; Guarner & Malagelada, 2003).

Humans are unique, however, as a cooperative species. Indeed, we are the best example of a truly reciprocally altruistic species (Brown, 1991; Trivers, 1971). Though there are many species of social mammals that display reciprocal altruism, genuine altruism is primarily a human attribute (Moll, de Oliveira-Souza, & Zahn, 2008). Our ability to cooperate and altruistically reciprocate in very large groups on a wide variety of economic, political, religious, and cultural activities is a remarkable phenomenon that does not occur in the rest of the animal kingdom. In addition, humans have evolved mechanisms for punishing those who violate prosocial cooperative norms (e.g., "cheaters") and those who take advantage of others' altruism but do not reciprocate by giving back ("free riders"; Boyd, Gintis, Bowles, & Richerson, 2003). The ability to internalize norms for prosocial behavior is a nearly universal human characteristic. Groups that evolved mechanisms for internalizing these kinds of cooperative norms outcompete groups with socially neutral or antisocial norms (Gintis et al., 2007). This is a prototypical example of *gene–culture coevolution* (Wilson, 1975).

In one of the most comprehensive reviews of the literature on the neural basis of moral cognition, Moll et al. (2008) hypothesized that the mechanisms underlying the formation of attachment bonds, which are present in virtually all classes of mammals, provide the underlying structures and mechanisms for interindividual bonding and affiliative behaviors and may have evolved to form the more sophisticated realm of human morality. These researchers point to connections between the basic, ancient neural mechanisms associated with attachment bonds and more recently evolved cortical systems associated with abstract reasoning and moral cognition. The gene–culture coevolution of these structures may have allowed humans to form attachment bonds to one another and also to attach motivational significance to abstract ideas, cultural symbols, and beliefs. Without these cultural attachments, the extraordinarily high levels of cooperation and altruism found even among unrelated individuals throughout human societies would not be supported. Moll et al. referred to this as *extended attachment* and concluded:

> Extended attachment may be a key ingredient that allowed our ancestors to develop emotional bonds to cultural artifacts and ideas, promoting social coherence in collective hunting, building shelter, rituals, and other kinds of social exchanges going beyond simple interpersonal reciprocity. Imprinting values to abstract symbols, practices, and beliefs rendered humans capable of developing and internalizing values and virtues. (p. 173)

This commitment to culture-specific shared values, however, may have also promoted intergroup competition and aggression toward outgroups (Bowles & Gintis, 2004). Those who do not share a particular group's culture-specific values have often been treated very harshly across human history. Extended attachment consequently may help explain both our truly extraordinary achievements as a species as well as our darkest tendencies that have haunted humankind throughout our history.

Research finds that humans possess an innate and universal system of moral evaluation (Bloom, 2012; Haidt, 2001). Human babies, for example, respond to morally relevant properties of events. They display empathy and compassion by crying when they hear other babies cry and soothing others in distress. They altruistically help out others, including strangers. They distinguish between "good guys" and "bad guys" and show clear preferences for prosocial behavior and punishment of bad behavior (Bloom, 2012). These findings of an innate moral sense, even in preverbal babies, led Noam Chomsky and others to propose that there exists an innate moral grammar, similar to the innate universal language grammar that allows humans to quickly and easily acquire language (see Hauser, 2006; Mikhail, 2007).

The evolutionary origins of prosocial and cooperative behavior focus on ultimate explanations for understanding human morality. Internalized norms for cooperation, prosocial behavior, and altruism are a defining characteristic of humans and are ultimately responsible for the unique nature of human experience and the truly remarkable accomplishments of human culture.

These prototypical examples of gene–culture coevolution also illustrate the necessity of using a biopsychosocial approach to understanding human psychology. Cooperative prosocial behavior provided humans with a distinct survival advantage. As human communities grew over recent millennia, human relationships became more complex, culture advanced, and these internalized norms were eventually formalized and became the basis for ethical theory and law. The contemporary systems of professional ethics that are discussed in the next section are the most recent incarnations of these archaic qualities of human beings.

IMPORTANCE OF ETHICAL FOUNDATIONS

The science-based biopsychosocial approach taken in this volume emphasizes the scientific understanding of the nature and origins of moral reasoning and behavior, and it further emphasizes the foundational importance of professional ethics in behavioral health care. In addition, this volume takes the position that a grounding in the foundations of professional ethics is necessary for gaining a deep, thorough, and useful understanding of the role of ethics in professional practice. It is clearly essential to be knowledgeable about the many specific ethics codes, laws, rules, and policies that govern mental health practice. But having familiarity with only these codes, rules, and policies, without understanding the foundational principles from which they are derived, can result in an incomplete and superficial analysis of many ethical dilemmas that arise in behavioral health care practice, research, education, and policy.

Being ethical appears to be a straightforward requirement for human relations. For example, some version of the Golden Rule is found in many of the world's religions and secular ethical systems, and it provides reliable guidance even in many difficult circumstances. Upon closer examination, however, it is evident that many ethical questions are far more complex than those that can be addressed by the Golden Rule. This is particularly true in today's increasingly complex and diverse society and interconnected global community that is undergoing rapid technical, scientific, social, and political change. The following three issues help demonstrate the complexity of moral issues and the need to be careful and thorough when approaching ethical questions.

Confusing What *Is* for What *Ought* to Be

There have been many social practices and conventions that were widely accepted in one historical or cultural context but were viewed as thoroughly morally unacceptable in another time or context. For example, after observing the relationship between those with more and less power in society, it was evident to Herbert Spencer, the father of Social Darwinism, that the notion of the "survival of the fittest" applied to human social and economic relations just as it applied to the evolution of animal species. He went on to argue that it would be wrong for government to interfere with nature's tendency to let the strong dominate the weak. Spencer failed to note that just because it was true that the powerful tended to dominate the less powerful, that does not imply that this is the way things ought to be (G. E. Moore, 1903/1959). A cruel mental health example of this from the mid-18th century involves a Louisiana physician who identified a new psychiatric diagnosis, *drapetomania*, a running-away-from-home disorder, to diagnose the pathology of slaves who wished to run away from their masters. The recommended treatment for the disorder was a beating (Szasz, 1971. See the next section for more examples.) The research reviewed above regarding the strongly felt and seemingly natural moral feelings that we automatically have in response to certain types of situations but not others also highlights the need to differentiate between situations that are commonly accepted as morally acceptable versus those that may not be after they are analyzed objectively.

The Universality of Ethics

Questions regarding the universality of ethics arise quickly when working with individuals of diverse ethnic, cultural, and religious backgrounds. Ethical systems vary greatly across cultures and religions regarding the treatment of women, children, animals, and the environment. Do our ethics codes, moral standards, and related legal requirements apply universally, or is morality largely the product of historical and cultural circumstances? That is, are ethics basically relative? If so, then applying one's own moral standards to others can be inappropriate and even harmful. For example, a therapist might be very uncomfortable after being told by a young woman from a conservative Hindu family that she does not want the arranged marriage that her parents are planning for her. However, advising the woman to refuse the arranged marriage may result in the girl being permanently cut off from her family and relatives, social and emotional supports that cannot be replaced. Are there any universal ethical standards that can be applied in a case like this, given our obligation to do no harm?

Many individuals would argue that there is no universal morality that applies across peoples and cultures. There is clearly substantial agreement among ethical authorities, however, that all individuals who are committed to morality, across cultures, time, and place, agree on the basic foundations of ethics, and there consequently does exist a universal common morality (e.g., T. L. Beauchamp & Childress, 2009; Council for the Parliament of the World's Religions, 1993; Gert, Culver, & Clouser, 2006; Universal Declaration of

Human Rights of the United Nations, 1948). Many culturally specific aspects of a universal morality vary significantly across religious groups, institutions, and even professions, but there is general agreement among ethicists and religious and political leaders that a universal, basic morality does exist.

The world's religions diverge greatly regarding many subjects, but even the leaders of these religions have agreed regarding the existence of a basic universal morality. In 1993, the Council of the Parliament of the World's Religions endorsed the following statement in its "Declaration Toward a Global Ethic":

> We are persons who have committed ourselves to the precepts and prac-
> tices of the world's religions. We confirm that there is already a consensus
> among religions which can be the basis for a global ethic—a minimal
> *fundamental consensus* concerning binding *values*, irrevocable *standards*,
> and *fundamental moral attitudes*. (p. 3)

Psychologists from around the world have endorsed a similar view with regard to ethical principles. In 2008, the International Union of Psychological Science approved the "Universal Declaration of Ethical Principles for Psychologists" that explicates a general "common moral framework that guides and inspires psychologists worldwide" (p. 1). It noted that "the objectives of the *Universal Declaration* are to provide a moral framework and generic set of ethical principles for psychology organizations worldwide" but also that "application of the principles and values to the development of specific standards of conduct will vary across cultures, and must occur locally or regionally in order to ensure their relevance to local or regional cultures, customs, beliefs, and laws" (p. 1).

Despite widely diverging viewpoints between cultures and religions on many moral and legal issues, there does appear to be widespread agreement that a universal basis for fundamental ethical principles does indeed exist. Applying these universal principles across diverse cultures and contexts remains complex, but at least many ethicists and religious and political leaders have concluded that there exists a common starting point for approaching these difficult questions.

The Question of Moral Status

A critical issue that has caused tremendous moral confusion throughout human history concerns the moral status of different groups of individuals. Across history, enemies, slaves, animals, women, children, and psychiatric patients have often had lower moral status. Their interests and rights often received lower protection and frequently no protection at all (T. L. Beauchamp & Childress, 2009; Lindsay, 2005). This situation started changing dramatically during the Enlightenment, however, and has evolved substantially in the past century and a half.

Singer (1981) noted that individuals' "moral circle" expanded significantly over the past century. In centuries past, human's moral treatment of others normally did not extend beyond their immediate group. Even as recently as the Civil War, for example, many people were unconcerned about the morality of some people owning others as slaves or the rights of women, minorities, children, or animals in general. The eugenics movement became popular from the turn of the 19th century until the end of World War II, and the rights of psychiatric patients and other "degenerates" were severely curtailed in many localities in the United States and elsewhere. Before the Civil Rights era in the 1960s, the majority of Americans thought interracial marriage was wrong, and now few do. Views regarding the rights of gay and lesbian individuals to marry and have full legal rights have recently changed very rapidly in several parts of the world.

There has been a dramatic increase in the range of individuals to whom moral norms are applied in recent decades and centuries. It might appear that societies and institutions have embraced higher moral standards in recent decades and centuries, particularly with regard to slaves, women, children, and minorities. The bigger difference, however, is that larger numbers of groups of individuals have been extended moral status that previously had been extended to only certain privileged groups.

There remain many fascinating questions about whether comatose patients, anencephalic babies, fetuses, embryos, human eggs, and even animals deserve full moral rights (T. L. Beauchamp, Walters, Kahn, & Mastroianni, 2008; Jecker, Jonsen, & Pearlman, 2007). In addition, mental health care and medicine often involve caring for children and adults who are ill, impaired, disabled, incompetent, or are otherwise vulnerable, and important decisions involving ethical issues often must be made when these individuals are not able to participate fully in the decision making. Psychotherapists also work with individuals who represent some risk of harm to others. These cases raise complex ethical and legal questions regarding whether these individuals can be detained, even if they have not committed a crime, or detained after they have served their criminal punishments (e.g., in the case of child molesters in states that have sexual predator laws), or have their rights restricted in other ways (e.g., in terms of gun ownership).

The preceding discussion was not intended to show how contemporary ethical questions can be resolved, but only to emphasize the complexity of some ethical questions and the difficulty humans have had in applying morality equitably throughout the human community. It should be evident that familiarity with ethics codes and mental health law alone is insufficient for addressing complex ethical questions such as these. A satisfactory application of ethical principles also requires familiarity with ethical theory, norms, and standards. Attempting to address the moral dilemmas faced by individuals, communities, and society by relying on only a particular professional code of conduct can result in a wide range of problems. This overview is also intended to point to the need for a biopsychosocial approach to understanding ethics. Even the preceding brief review illustrates that an examination of ethics that does not incorporate psychological, sociocultural, and biological perspectives is seriously incomplete.

The remaining sections of this chapter provide an overview of the ethical foundations for the laws, policies, and codes that govern health care in the United States and many other countries. These foundations are essential to the basic justification for contemporary behavioral health care intervention and research.

ETHICAL THEORY

Ethics codes communicate to the public, governments, and the legal system various actions that members of a profession are allowed and prohibited from doing. These codes then help to prevent the government or others from holding members of the profession accountable for taking certain actions or not taking other actions (e.g., breaking a patient's confidentiality when he or she threatens another person, refusing to release patient information to an inquiring police officer without appropriate authorization). Requiring a commitment from members of a profession to observe ethics codes is also an attempt by the profession to be self-regulating so that the government does not set policies and make other basic decisions for the profession.

Codes of ethics serve much broader purposes than just these, however. They also serve to raise the moral sensitivity and conduct of a profession. They are also based on ethics, a branch of philosophy that is a very old and well-developed field of scholarship. The field of ethics is concerned with general ethical theories that provide an integrated body of moral principles for addressing ethical behavior comprehensively. The subfield *biomedical ethics* is the primary concern of the present chapter. This term is commonly used to refer to the ethical principles that guide health care research and practice. These principles derive from general comprehensive ethical theories but are applied specifically in the context of health care and biomedical research.

Before examining biomedical ethical principles more specifically, I briefly review the four general ethical theories that have been the most important to the development of contemporary biomedical ethics (T. L. Beauchamp & Childress, 2009). These are the consequentialist or utilitarian, deontological or Kantian, liberal individualist, and communitarian approaches. The following (brief) overview of these theories helps to convey a sense of their strengths, weaknesses, and importance for informing biomedical ethical principles.

Consequentialist Approaches

John Stuart Mill (1806–1873) developed the most influential consequentialist approach to ethics, called *utilitarianism* because of the priority it gives to the principle of utility, which justifies all other principles and rules. Actions are right or wrong according to their balance of good and bad consequences, that is, their utility. This approach is often associated with the maxim "We ought to promote the greatest good for the greatest number" or at least that which results in the least harm when all the options are undesirable. From this perspective, the ends justify the means if the benefits of an action outweigh harms resulting from the action. Mill and Bentham are considered *hedonistic* consequentialists because they emphasized happiness or pleasure as the goals to be maximized. More recently utilitarians have argued that other values such as knowledge, health, success, and deep personal relationships also contribute to individuals' well-being (T. L. Beauchamp & Childress, 2009; Griffin, 1986).

Utilitarianism is not a fully satisfactory theory of ethics, however (T. L. Beauchamp & Childress, 2009; Cohen & Cohen, 1999; Freeman, 2000). For example, some preferences might be considered to be immoral, regardless of any weighing of harms and benefits (e.g., sadism, pedophilia, inflicting pain on animals). This approach also does not answer the question of whether maximizing value is an obligation that must be observed (e.g., is one obligated to donate one of his or her kidneys because one can be fully healthy with just one kidney?). Another problem concerns whether the interests of the majority can override the rights of minorities. Are there cases where the rights and interests of even the smallest minority need to be protected, independent of the weighing of costs and benefits? Should education, police protection, and health care be provided to all individuals in a society, even if it is relatively costly to provide these services to particular groups?

Deontological or Kantian Approaches

Immanuel Kant (1724–1804) emphasized a very different set of obligations than consequentialist theorists. From his perspective, duties (*deon* is Greek for duty), obligations, and rights are the highest authority, and right actions are not determined solely by the consequences of actions. Ends do not justify means if they violate basic obligations and rights, and human beings must always be treated as ends and never as means only (T. L. Beauchamp & Childress, 2009; Donagan, 1977). To find a source of ultimate obligations and rights, religious traditions have appealed to divine revelation (e.g., the Ten

Commandments) and others to natural law (e.g., at the Nuremberg trials). From Kant's perspective, the *categorical imperative* is the highest authority for determining the morality of ethical principles: "I ought never to act except in such a way that I can also will that my maxim become a universal law" (Kant, 1785/1964, p. 96). In other words, morally acceptable decisions are applicable universally, in all situations that are similar in relevant ways.

This approach also has weaknesses. Kant has been criticized for emphasizing reason above all other considerations, including emotion, suffering, and pain, and consequently his arguments against suicide and other issues have been viewed as inadequate (Cohen & Cohen, 1999). Many of the moral obligations we feel are also based on the nature of the relationships we have with family, friends, coworkers, and neighbors—the ethical correctness of our behavior in these situations is significantly affected by the commitments we have to these individuals, not by objective moral obligations to people in general (T. L. Beauchamp & Childress, 2009).

Liberal Individualism

Utilitarian and deontological ethical theories have been very influential in the Western world, but clearly there has been a strong emphasis on protecting individual rights as well. Philosophers such as John Locke (1632–1704) and Thomas Hobbes (1588–1679) emphasized the importance of human rights and civil liberties, and their rights-based theorizing became strongly integrated into the Anglo–American legal system (T. L. Beauchamp & Childress, 2009; Dworkin, 1977). Hobbes famously remarked that without strong government that provides basic protection of individual rights, security, and rule of law, life is "nasty, brutish, and short" (1651/2002, p. xiii).

From this perspective, basic human rights to autonomy, privacy, property, free speech, and worship are foundational to the functioning of civil society. Though these rights are very strong, they are not absolute. For example, one's right to life is perhaps the strongest of the rights an individual can hold, and yet it too can be overridden in cases of war and self-defense. (Whether an exception also applies to those found guilty of capital punishment remains controversial.) Rights are also considered to be prima facie binding; that is, when first considering an ethical situation, rights need to be observed, though they may be overridden depending on the circumstances (T. L. Beauchamp & Childress, 2009; Dworkin, 1977). In health care, patients' rights to informed consent, confidentiality, to refuse treatment, and to lifesaving emergency care all function in this way. Rights are also correlated with obligations. If someone has a right to something (e.g., education, health care), then others have obligations to provide the goods or services needed to provide that right. Tensions between having a right to something and the corresponding obligations of others to help provide for that right are a perennial source of conflict between those who emphasize liberal individualism (i.e., freedom from government intrusions) over those who emphasize government services and controls to provide for an orderly, secure, and efficient economy and society (e.g., those who emphasize government regulation of industry, education for all children, health care for all citizens).

Though protecting human rights is critical to the effective and humane functioning of society, rights are also viewed as providing a limited perspective on morality (T. L. Beauchamp & Childress, 2009; Cohen & Cohen, 1999). For example, rights typically do not account for the moral significance of a person's motives, conscientiousness, or integrity. It is not always moral to do what we have a right to do (e.g., if the free market is allowed to determine prices, is it ethical for health care providers to charge those who pay for services out-of-pocket the full "sticker" price while those who have insurance are given a highly discounted price?). Liberal individualism also focuses on protecting individual rights from government intrusion, whereas the rights and interests of the community as a whole receive less attention. Community life provides many valuable resources such as public health and security, educated citizens, the protection of animals, and culture in general. (Supreme Court Justice Oliver Wendell Holmes remarked, "I like to pay taxes. With them I buy civilization"; 1939, pp. 42–43). Rights-based systems also tend to take adversarial approaches to resolving conflicts after one's rights have been violated. There are aspects of family life, for example, where these adversarial approaches may not serve psychologically healthy purposes; for example, though children have a right to be free from maltreatment, should parents be held responsible for damages caused by their abuse or neglect of a child? When a couple cannot agree to child custody arrangements after they decide to divorce, is an adversarial rights-based approach to defeating one's spouse in court the best way to resolve the dispute?

Communitarian Approaches

Community-based approaches are often critical of the previous approaches. Communitarian approaches consider the common good, communal values and goals, and cooperative virtues as fundamental considerations in ethics. From this perspective, too much emphasis on individuals' rights and autonomy can result in an uncaring society where individuals look out for themselves and have little responsibility for the well-being of others (T. L. Beauchamp & Childress, 2009; Freeman, 2000; Sandel, 2005). This can result in a breakdown of family and civic responsibilities and lead to marital infidelity, neglected children and elders, welfare dependency, and even the disappearance of a meaningful democracy. Carol Gilligan, in her 1982 book, *In a Different Voice*, emphasized that women's "strong sense of being responsible" (p. 21) to family members and loved ones, as opposed to a strong commitment to autonomy and individual rights, was a sign of moral strength, not weakness. Militant communitarian views (e.g., communism) can be hostile to individual rights, whereas moderate communitarianism emphasizes the importance of communal values such as parenting, teaching, governing, healing, and caring for those who are less able to care for themselves. These values are especially important in health care and human services where many individuals are physically and/or psychologically vulnerable. Promoting health and well-being among individuals in general is also in the interests of the common good of society (Callahan, 1990).

Communitarianism has been criticized, however, for presenting a misleading dichotomy between individual rights and the common good: Either we protect individual rights and autonomy or we pursue the welfare of the community as a whole (T. L. Beauchamp & Childress, 2009; Cohen & Cohen, 1999). Such a dichotomy is unnecessary. Individuals are inherently social beings, and so the common good (e.g., functional families, communities, government) is necessary for the individual to thrive. At the same time, the autonomy and rights of the individual need to be protected against oppressive communities that might otherwise intrude upon and control the individual. Communal goals as well as individual autonomy and rights must be protected so that the interdependent individual and community can both thrive.

An Integrative Approach

None of the moral theories summarized in the preceding sections adequately resolves all moral conflicts, and consequently none, by itself, provides a satisfactory foundation for biomedical ethics (T. L. Beauchamp & Childress, 2009; Rawls, 1999). Each has weaknesses and strengths, and some serve some purposes better than others. For example, utilitarianism is useful for setting public policy, liberal individualism has played an important role in establishing legal standards, and deontological and communitarian approaches are useful for guiding many health care practices. There also is no clear evidence that any of these theories should be discarded because each brings a valuable perspective the others lack. There is even neuroscience evidence that the human brain relies on multiple types of information processing when faced with different types of moral dilemmas (e.g., personal vs. impersonal situations), and these may correspond to the different types of priorities associated with the various ethical theories (Greene et al., 2004).

Leading ethicists such as Rawls (1999) and T. L. Beauchamp and Childress (2009) used a combination of deductive and inductive approaches to resolve the problem of developing a coherent system of biomedical ethics that can provide well-justified solutions to the wide range of ethical questions encountered in health care practice and research. These ethicists suggested combining the common sense moral traditions shared by members of a society (inductive) with ethical principles derived from the above theories to provide structure and coherence (deductive). A process called *reflective equilibrium* (Rawls, 1999) is then applied where common moral beliefs, moral principles, and theoretical propositions are analyzed and critiqued so that the resulting system becomes increasingly internally consistent and coherent. New scientific, technological, and cultural developments can get incorporated into the common morality through this iterative process of analysis and critique. It should be noted that behavioral and physical scientists use a similar combination of inductive approaches (e.g., careful observation and verification to develop hypotheses) and deductive approaches (e.g., tests of theory-driven hypotheses) to make improvements in theoretical explanations of phenomena.

T. L. Beauchamp and Childress (1977, 2009) applied this procedure in the case of biomedical ethics and derived four basic ethical principles. Their approach, often referred to as the *four-principles approach* or *principlism*, has become the most influential and accepted approach in biomedical ethics in the United States and much of Europe, and perhaps the world (Gert, Culver, & Clouser, 1997; Schöne-Seifert, 2006). Ethics texts in behavioral health care also rely on the foundational principles advocated by T. L. Beauchamp and Childress (e.g., Corey, Corey, & Callahan, 2003; Kitchner, 1984; Koocher & Keith-Spiegel, 2008). Because this approach involves more than merely a top–down deductive process based on inviolable precepts, experience and sound judgment are very important as well. In this system, the foundational principles are not relative, though particular decisions and judgments can vary according to circumstances. The combination of induction and deduction also means that the application of the general principles is subject to revision based on the evolution of scientific developments as well as social and cultural practices (T. L. Beauchamp & Childress, 2009).

PRINCIPLE-BASED, COMMON MORALITY APPROACH TO BIOMEDICAL ETHICS

The principlism or four-principles approach to biomedical ethics developed by T. L. Beauchamp and Childress (1977, 2009) has been the most influential and widely accepted approach to ethics in health care generally and in behavioral health care specifically. It is important to have an appreciation of these foundational principles so that ethics codes, laws, policies, and rules are not applied in a perfunctory, mechanical manner that is insensitive to the circumstances of particular cases. Therefore, the four principles in the T. L. Beauchamp and Childress approach (i.e., respect for autonomy, nonmaleficence, beneficence, justice) are briefly reviewed in the following sections.

Respect for Autonomy

The word *autonomy* is derived from the Greek words *auto* (meaning self) and *nomos* (meaning rule or governance). The concept originally referred to self-governance of independent city-states but has since been applied to individuals as well. To be fully autonomous (e.g., to be completely free from control by others, the source of one's own values, beliefs, and life plans) is unrealistic. Humans are highly social animals and life in modern democratic societies requires high levels of accommodation, collaboration, and participation. Even factors as personal as one's self-identity, values, and beliefs are highly affected by socialization and relationships. Therefore, the focus here is on being substantially autonomous because absolute autonomy is an unrealistic ideal that has limited practical relevance in the modern world (T. L. Beauchamp & Childress, 2009).

Incorporating autonomy into the social order requires not just allowing individuals to claim a right to autonomy but also a basic respect of others as autonomous beings (T. L. Beauchamp & Childress, 2009). For example, if a woman or ethnic minority individual hopes to be judged on the basis of merit for a job promotion or admission to graduate school, but those making the promotion or admissions decisions demonstrate bias or favoritism based on group membership, the individual's merit may have no impact. Therefore, the emphasis of this principle is on respecting others' rights to autonomy, not just simply claiming a right to autonomy for one's self. One result of this emphasis is the priority on working to overcome barriers and obstacles that prevent people from being autonomous. The efforts of the American Civil Liberties Union (ACLU) to protect the free speech rights of groups such as the American Nazi Party represent examples of this principle, even when these groups express views and values with which the ACLU adamantly disagrees. (The American Nazi Party planned to hold a parade in Skokie, Illinois, in 1977, and the ACLU defended their right to assembly and free speech when the city, where one in six residents was a survivor or directly related to a survivor of the Nazi Holocaust, attempted to stop the parade; Strum, 1999.) This principle also implies that health care professionals have an obligation to provide information and foster autonomous decision making on the part of patients. Because of the unequal distribution of knowledge between professionals and patients, professionals are obligated to provide understandable information and explanations and foster responsible and voluntary decision making by patients.

Many behavioral health care patients are not in a position to act autonomously, however. As a group, children are not considered able to understand and protect their own interests and welfare and consequently are given few of the rights afforded adults. Suicidal individuals in crisis or those with cognitive disabilities or impairments also may not be able to make decisions in their own best interests. As a result, in certain circumstances therapists may themselves determine the best interests of these patients and control their behavior in order to protect them from harm.

The principle of respect for autonomy supports many specific ethical rules, such as tell the truth, help people make important decisions when asked, respect people's privacy, protect confidential information, and obtain informed consent (T. L. Beauchamp & Childress, 2009). The history of violations of informed consent illustrates the importance of this principle and so is briefly reviewed in more detail.

At the Nuremberg trials following World War II, the world was shocked to learn of the horrifying medical experimentation that was conducted on inmates in Nazi concentration camps. Physicians and medical researchers in particular were shocked that the rights of research participants could be so thoroughly and flagrantly violated by medical professionals. This led to the development of the general informed consent guidelines that are still in use today. These include the recognition that health care providers and researchers must minimize risks of harm as well as obtain informed consent to enable autonomous choices by patients and research participants. Researchers and clinicians must also conduct a cost–benefit analysis to help ensure that the benefits of research or treatment outweigh the risks of any harm caused by the research or treatment.

Unfortunately, there have been many other egregious violations of research participants' rights to informed consent over the years. Many dangerous experiments were conducted on prisoners, reform school residents, and other institutionalized individuals (e.g., exposing people to radiation or injecting them with deadly diseases or toxins; Loue, 2000; Washington, 2007). The most famous violation of informed consent in the United States involves the syphilis study conducted in Tuskegee, Alabama from 1932 to 1972 to determine the natural history of untreated latent syphilis (Jones, 1981). The study was fully approved by the U.S. Public Health Service. It included only African American men with 399 in the experimental group and 201 in the control group. The men in the experimental group had previously contracted syphilis—they were not given syphilis by the researchers. But they were lied to for decades about the medical procedures they received to track the progress of the infection (e.g., painful and risky spinal taps) and the effective treatments that became available but were intentionally withheld from them (e.g., penicillin, starting in the 1940s). The researchers met with physicians in the area where the men lived and provided them with the men's names and a directive that they not be given any treatment for their syphilis. The researchers even paid for funeral expenses when the men finally died so they could secretly conduct autopsies on the men's bodies in order to examine the progression of the disease; all of this was done without the knowledge or consent of the patients or their families. Victims of the study included the men who died from syphilis, wives who contracted the disease, and children born with congenital syphilis (Jones, 1981).

The Tuskegee syphilis study is the best-known example in the United States where individuals with less social and political power were exploited by medical researchers. Unfortunately, this has happened many other times. In a 1991 experiment, the long-acting contraceptive Norplant was implanted into uninformed African American teenage girls in Baltimore, a study that was applauded by some community leaders. Dangerous experimental AIDS drugs were also tested on foster children in New York City from 1988 until 2001 without parental consent (Washington, 2007).

Nonmaleficence

The principle of nonmaleficence is commonly associated with the maxim to "Above all, do no harm." This principle is implied in the Hippocratic Oath and is often considered the fundamental principle of the health care professions. The implications of nonmaleficence for intentional harms to patients are generally obvious—intentional harms involving slander, assault, or theft are often prosecuted under criminal law. The implications involving unintentional harms, however, are typically much more complex and subtle.

An important implication of nonmaleficence for psychotherapists concerns incompetence. Harm can be caused by omission as well as commission, often by imposing risks of harm through either ignorance or carelessness (T. L. Beauchamp & Childress, 2009; Sharpe & Faden, 1998; Stromberg et al., 1988). Examples of this include having insufficient training and supervised experience to complete an adequate suicide risk assessment or treatment plan, competently diagnose particular disorders or provide certain interventions, or appropriately manage countertransference. If patients are harmed as a result, the therapist can be judged negligent, which can then be grounds for malpractice. The critical question at issue in these cases involves whether the professional was practicing up to the *standard of care* for the profession. Professionals are not expected to practice at an "expert" level, but they can be found negligent if their practice falls below current professional standards for competent practice (Koocher & Keith-Spiegel, 2008; Stromberg et al., 1988). Therefore, it is critical that therapists obtain sufficient training and supervised experience to be able to competently conduct the assessments and interventions appropriate for the patient populations they work with. The training and clinical experience required for working in a specialization are deeper though narrower compared with the broader training and experience required for general practice. Therapists also need to maintain their competence and keep up with current standards of practice, in part by completing continuing education requirements.

Concern regarding the safety of medical interventions in the United States grew dramatically following the publication of the Institute of Medicine report *To Err is Human* in 2000. This report famously estimated that 44,000 to 98,000 Americans ("a jumbo jet a day") die each year as a result of medical errors. Many of these deaths were caused by misdiagnosis, inappropriate medications, infections acquired while receiving health care, and wrong-site surgery. This report stimulated the development of the modern patient safety movement that resulted in a variety of measures to improve patient safety (e.g., the Joint Commission began unannounced hospital surveys, duty hour limits were established for medical residents, and most U.S. states mandated the reporting of serious adverse events; Wachter, 2009). Attention was also focused on the impact of diagnostic errors. In the first large physician survey regarding this issue, Schiff et al. (2009) found that practicing physicians readily recalled and volunteered information regarding missed or delayed diagnoses, including depression that led to a suicide attempt. Autopsy studies have also found that diagnostic errors are frequent and contributed to patient death in approximately one in 10 cases (Wachter, 2009). Classen et al. (2011) found that a comprehensive approach to detecting medical errors during hospitalization identified a far larger number of adverse events than previous approaches. Errors resulting in injury ranged from those that caused only temporary harm to errors that resulted in death. These adverse events were found to occur in 33.2% of the admissions at three leading hospitals, a rate that was 10 times higher than that found using the usual methods for identifying adverse events (i.e., mandated voluntary reporting or the Patient Safety Indicators used by Medicaid, Medicare, and many other organizations).

The safety of psychotherapy has also long been a concern (e.g., Freud's concern about his role in potentially causing harm in the case of Dora led it to become one of the most famous case studies in the history of psychotherapy). Bergin (1966) conducted perhaps the first empirical investigation of patient deterioration that appeared to be caused by psychotherapy, but little additional empirical attention was given to the issue until the 1990s when the subject of repressed memories of child abuse became highly controversial. Arguments about whether individuals were harmed as the result of therapists using unsafe memory recovery techniques or offering unsupported interpretations of recovered child abuse memories grew into what many consider the most contentious controversy ever in the field (the "memory wars"; Loftus

& Davis, 2006). Other recent interventions for which there is evidence of potential or actual harm include rebirthing attachment therapy (Chaffin et al., 2006), group interventions for antisocial youth (Weiss et al., 2005), conversion therapy for gay and lesbian patients (American Psychiatric Association, 2000b), critical incident stress debriefing (Mayou, Ehlers, & Hobbs, 2000), and grief therapy (Bonanno & Lilienfeld, 2008). Research also indicates that individual therapists vary significantly in their effectiveness (e.g., Ackerman & Hilsenroth, 2001; Lambert, 2010; Wampold, 2001). This finding obligates therapists and their supervisors to ensure that therapist behaviors and practices associated with patient nonimprovement and deterioration are identified and changed. (Procedures that can help meet this obligation are discussed in Chapters 10 and 11.)

Another set of behavioral health care interventions that have become controversial recently involve psychotropic medications. Very few psychologists have prescription privileges, but medication prescribed by other health care providers is now used more frequently than psychotherapy for treating mental health issues (Wang et al., 2006), and therapists are naturally concerned about the safety and effectiveness of the treatments individuals receive for these issues. Concerns about these medications have existed since the first psychotropic medication, Thorazine, was introduced in the early 1950s, because these medications did not address a known cause of a disorder, had limited effectiveness for reducing symptoms or correcting dysfunction, and introduced major side effects. Concern about these medications has grown recently as the number of individuals taking them has risen dramatically (e.g., 11% of Americans age 12 and over took antidepressant medication in 2005–2008, and 23% of women age 40–59 took antidepressants; Pratt, Brody, & Gu, 2011; see Chapter 10 for more discussion of this topic). Many physicians are now questioning the safety and effectiveness of antipsychotic, antidepressant, mood stabilizer, and antianxiety medications, stimulants for attention-deficit/hyperactivity disorder, and sleep medications for children or adults who do not have serious disorders (e.g., Carlatt, 2010; Frances, 2009; Goldacre, 2013; Healy, 2012; Whitaker, 2002, 2010).

Beneficence

The overarching purpose of health care is to provide benefit to individuals and society. Morality requires that health care providers not only respect patients' autonomy and not harm them but also contribute to their well-being. The obligation of beneficence includes providing benefits (i.e., promoting welfare as well as preventing and removing harms) and the balancing of the benefits and risks of treatment in an optimal manner (T. L. Beauchamp & Childress, 2009). Potential risks of psychotherapy include experiencing strong, aversive, painful feelings and memories, or risks of ruptured relationships or loss of employment if individuals become more assertive or change their life goals. On the other hand, another risk for individuals involves the consequences of not addressing problems the individual faces. Without treatment, many problems will not get better or will actually get worse—e.g., emotionally, interpersonally, vocationally, academically, physically, or legally. The Tarasoff case presents a well-known example of how benefits and harms need to be balanced. A major potential benefit could have been provided to Tatiana Tarasoff (i.e., her life potentially being saved) if the confidentiality of the patient who represented a threat to her had been broken (i.e., a violation of respect for autonomy and nonmaleficence). The Supreme Court of California judged that the potential harm caused by breaking the patient's confidentiality in order to warn Tarasoff was outweighed by the potential saving of her life (*Tarasoff v. Board of Regents of the University of California*, 1976).

Even though individual autonomy is highly valued in the United States, Americans commonly accept many limits on their autonomy because it is in the best interests of individuals and the community. For example, traffic laws, air travel security restrictions, drinking water treatments, and medical restrictions are commonly accepted without serious questioning. There is general agreement that some strong forms of beneficence, also known as *paternalism*, are justified in order for society to function in a secure, efficient manner (T. L. Beauchamp & Childress, 2009). A particularly strong form of paternalism in behavioral health care involves suicide intervention. The question here is whether therapists are obligated to control suicidal patients' behavior through involuntary hospitalization in order to prevent them from harming themselves. When individuals are unstable, in serious distress, and at risk for causing irreversible harm to themselves through suicide, are professionals obligated to at least temporarily restrict their rights and control their behavior in order to prevent a serious harm from occurring? (Individuals who decide to end their lives after engaging in careful, logical decision making may represent a different situation, however; T. L. Beauchamp et al., 2008.)

Justice

The principle of justice focuses on approaches to fairness and how to ethically distribute the benefits and responsibilities of society. If there were no limits to resources or opportunities, this would be a far less difficult question to decide. When resources or opportunities are limited, however, these decisions can quickly become controversial. (For example, should prisoners get organ transplants when there is a shortage of organs? Should affirmative action considerations be applied when it comes to making university admissions decisions?) The minimal principle of justice is often attributed to Aristotle who argued that equals must be treated equally and unequals must be treated unequally (T. L. Beauchamp & Childress, 2009). That is, no person should be treated unequally, despite obvious differences between individuals, until it has been shown that there is a difference between them that is relevant to the treatment at stake. For example, most people would agree that all children should be provided a free public education, despite many obvious differences among children, because those differences are not relevant when judging the value of education. The major problem with Aristotle's approach, however, is that the criteria for judging which differences are relevant is not specified (Rescher, 1966). For example, when individuals need behavioral or physical health care but they are not facing a life threatening issue, is their ability to purchase treatment (i.e., their level of income) relevant to the decision regarding whether or not they should receive services?

Societies typically use a variety of methods for distributing the benefits and responsibilities of community life (Rescher, 1966). Everyone is given an equal share of some things, such as an elementary and secondary education for all children. The selection of those who can attend college and graduate school, however, is supposed to be based strictly on merit, as are jobs and promotions. Some benefits of society are decided on the basis of need (e.g., unemployment compensation, disability benefits, welfare services), whereas salaries are generally determined on the basis of the free market. Whether health care should be provided to everyone, regardless of ability to pay, has been controversial in the United States. The question of whether mental health care and substance abuse treatment should be provided has been even more controversial (Cummings, O'Donohue, & Cucciare, 2005). The American Medical Association (1994) took the position that it is the ethical duty of society to provide an adequate level of health care for all citizens, and the passage of the Patient Protection and Affordable Care Act (2010) suggests that American society has been moving in that direction in recent years. The field of public health has its foundations in social justice, and issues related to implementing interventions to prevent physical and behavioral health problems can be controversial as well (see Chapter 12).

Many political disputes center on the approach to deciding the distribution of society's benefits and responsibilities that is viewed as fairest. Communitarian approaches tend to emphasize need and commonalities between individuals, whereas libertarian approaches emphasize liberty and fair procedure. Utilitarian approaches (the ones usually used in the West) emphasize a mixture of criteria so that the public utility is maximized. Societies (and even regions within the United States or within individual states) often differ in the emphasis given to these various approaches but typically use several of these principles when developing law and policy (T. L. Beauchamp & Childress, 2009; Rescher, 1966).

The four principles described in the preceding sections provide the mostly widely accepted approach to biomedical ethics. These principles help form the basis for developing ethics codes, policies, and laws, as well as deciding how to respond to particular ethical dilemmas encountered in daily clinical practice. Balancing these various considerations can be complicated, but together these principles provide a very useful foundation for biomedical ethics. Nonetheless, these principles alone are widely considered to be insufficient. One additional perspective is needed to provide a more thorough and satisfactory approach.

MORAL CHARACTER

Discussions of ethical theory typically revolve around principles, rules, obligations, and rights. These tend to emphasize behavior and the actions one does or does not perform. *Character ethics*, on the other hand, emphasizes the *actor* (T. L. Beauchamp & Childress, 2009; Cohen & Cohen, 1999; Freeman, 2000). Moral character and virtues have received increasing attention in biomedical ethics because principles, rules, and rights can be impersonal and insensitive, whereas the moral character and trustworthiness of professionals are critical in systems intended to care for individuals who are ill, distressed, and vulnerable. As health care became industrialized in recent years, concern has grown about the level of personal commitment of professionals to their patients in contrast to their potential concerns about minimizing costs and maximizing profits for the health care organization. This too has raised interest in the moral character of health care professionals.

There is significant consistency among characterizations of virtuous health care professionals (e.g., Cohen & Cohen, 1999; MacIntyre, 1982). T. L. Beauchamp and Childress (2009) focused on the following five virtues:

- Compassion. Caring and compassion are fundamental to humane health care and are consequently emphasized across health care professions. This does not imply that health care professionals should be overly or passionately involved with their patients. Too much caring can result in a loss of objectivity and sound judgment. Instead, T. L. Beauchamp and Childress (2009) have suggested that an empathic concern mixed with an objective evaluative perspective serves patients' interests most effectively.
- Discernment. *Discernment* refers to the ability to make decisions and judgments without undue influence by extraneous considerations, fears, and personal attachments (T. L. Beauchamp & Childress, 2009). Aristotle defined *practical wisdom* as understanding how to act with the right intensity of feeling, in the

correct manner, at the right time, and with the proper balance of reason and emotion. In the therapeutic context, some individuals are adept at saying just the right thing at the right time and knowing when not to say anything at all. When a therapy patient is very upset, some therapists are very skilled at being able to discern when to provide comfort and reassurance and when to remain silent and allow the patient to access deeper emotions and thoughts.

- Trustworthiness. *Trustworthiness* refers to the confidence that one will act with the right motives and apply the appropriate moral norms when encountering a particular situation. Trust has probably always played a central role in health care, whereas distrust became a significant concern more recently as health care in the United States became industrialized and the motives of for-profit managed care companies were questioned. There is also concern that physicians practice "defensively" as a consequence of the increase in malpractice lawsuits in recent decades. Because of the highly personal nature of psychotherapy, therapists' trustworthiness is an especially important concern in behavioral health care.

- Integrity. Conflicts between one's core moral beliefs and the demands of mental health practice can be wrenching. Some strongly held political or religious beliefs can also impair one's ability to work effectively with certain patients. Patience, humility, and tolerance are all critical in behavioral health care practice, especially in pluralistic, democratic societies and particularly in psychotherapy where therapists often learn a great deal about patients' personal beliefs, values, and behavior. This does not suggest that one must compromise one's values and beliefs—compromising below a certain threshold of integrity means that integrity is lost. Instead, when these types of conflicts arise, therapists can refer patients to other therapists.

- Conscientiousness. Some people are very capable of judging the right course of action in a problematic situation but are not interested in taking the actions needed to correct the situation. *Conscientiousness* refers to figuring out what is the right response to a situation, intending to carry it out, and exerting the appropriate level of effort to ensure the actions are carried out effectively (T. L. Beauchamp & Childress, 2009).

All these virtues fall on a continuum that ranges from ordinary to extraordinary moral standards, from the level of the common morality (that applies to everyone) to the morality of aspiration (T. L. Beauchamp & Childress,

2009). Although we are all bound to the standards of common morality, we are not bound to more excellent, heroic, and saintly ideals than most people have, though perhaps we should aspire to them.

DISCUSSION: THE NECESSITY OF SCIENCE AND ETHICS

In this volume, I argue that psychological science and professional ethics are both essential to the safe, effective, and responsible practice of behavioral health care. One without the other is inadequate for practice in the profession. Psychological science is necessary for understanding human development, functioning, and behavior change, and behavioral health care must be grounded squarely on ethical principles and standards to be practiced in a responsible and just manner. The scientific and ethical perspectives on behavioral health care are also intertwined. The ethical obligations to do no harm and provide benefit cannot be carried out without the scientific evaluation of the safety and effectiveness of interventions.

Research on the nature of moral reasoning and behavior shows that it is a highly complicated phenomenon governed partly by subconscious, automatic reactions that are not based on careful deliberative analysis. Human cognition evolved to be able to respond quickly to threats and opportunities in a highly efficient manner that is necessary for survival in the natural world. But automatic responses sometimes conflict with careful ethical analyses of situations. Just as with evolved physical characteristics that are not optimal for life in the modern world (e.g., physiological reactions to stress, the body's conservation of calories for lean times), there are likely evolved psychological characteristics that are not a good fit for life in the modern world. More detailed knowledge of these characteristics may lead to more effective responses to the challenges of modern life that require collaboration and cooperation among diverse sectors within societies and the human community as a whole.

This discussion provides another illustration of how an integrative biopsychosocial approach is necessary for the scientific understanding of human psychology. Failing to integrate psychological, sociocultural, and biological perspectives on moral reasoning and behavior results in a seriously incomplete understanding of the subject. The genetically inherited evolutionary mechanisms that fundamentally shape our ethical thinking and behavior are critical to understanding the topic, as are the psychological mechanisms involved in cognition in general (e.g., System 1 and System 2 thinking) and with regard to moral reasoning and behavior specifically (e.g., automatic responses to ethical decisions that can differ from logical, explicit analyses of situations). Sociocultural influences also have a major influence in terms of how ethical norms and standards are applied within cultures (e.g., which groups receive moral status within a society) as well as how social factors influence moral and immoral behavior (e.g., with regard to cheating and lying). One or more of these levels may have a larger influence with regard to particular mechanisms or behaviors, but all are essential for a thorough understanding of the topic. Moral reasoning and behavior simply cannot be understood without an integration of all three biopsychosocial perspectives.

It also should be noted that the priorities of the scientific and ethical perspectives on the field converge. The ethical perspective emphasizes health care professionals' responsibilities to not harm, including unintentionally, as well as provide benefit through intervention, reducing and removing harm, suffering, or dysfunction, and by preventing foreseeable harms. The scientific perspective on behavioral health care as a clinical science emphasizes similar factors, with the safety and effectiveness of intervention over the short and long term being top clinical and research priorities. Though the science and ethics underlying behavioral health care have very different starting points, both end up focusing on the ability of interventions to safely and effectively relieve distress and improve functioning.

The topic of ethics in behavioral health care is growing in importance and complexity. Scientific and technological advances are leading to innovations in communication, access to information, and health care delivery. For example, tele-therapy and the centralized storage of electronic health care records (in "the cloud") are now possible as a result of the Internet and other communication technologies. These technologies offer many advantages but also present new concerns about security and one's ability to maintain control over one's privacy. Emerging medical technologies are raising new ethical challenges as well (e.g., enhanced intellectual performance, genetic testing of embryos, maintaining individuals on life-support machines indefinitely; T. L. Beauchamp et al., 2008; Jecker et al., 2007). The increasing diversity of society also introduces additional dilemmas. Many personal and family issues are highly controversial within and across cultures (e.g., divorce, abortion, homosexuality, gender roles, arranged marriages, the control and discipline of children). Harm can result from a lack of familiarity with a patient's culture, the ethical and family values generally observed within that culture, the specific beliefs and values of the individual patient and his or her family, and the interaction of these factors with mental health (Knapp & VandeCreek, 2007; Sue & Sue, 2008). As with difficult situations faced by individuals in any culture, these cases often involve a balancing of benefits and harms (e.g., the autonomy of young people facing an arranged marriage they do not want vs. the alienation from their family, religion, and culture that can result if the marriage is not accepted). Questions regarding the universality of ethics and resolving ethical disagreements also grow in importance as societies become more diverse and interaction between communities increases.

Keeping current with the evolving knowledge of human development, functioning, and behavior change is also more challenging as scientific knowledge advances and ethical and legal guidelines grow in complexity. To illustrate the complexity of cases encountered in clinical practice, a case example is presented in the next section. As noted in the Introduction, all case examples presented in this volume are amalgamations of actual cases where all identifying information has been thoroughly modified.

Living together in a more fully cooperative and collaborative manner is one of humanity's greatest challenges. This is true at all levels, for individuals, families, communities, and societies, as well as for the global community as a whole. A stronger scientific understanding of the nature and origins of moral reasoning and behavior is likely to provide insights for addressing this challenge. These issues involve highly controversial questions, to be sure, and these questions have been top concerns for religious and governmental institutions throughout history. Answers to many of these questions have been elusive, but two things are certain: Humans will continue to be preoccupied with morality, and learning to cooperate effectively will continue to be among the greatest challenges for humankind.

CASE EXAMPLE: A REFERRAL FROM A LOCAL PARENT

A psychologist returned a call from a mother who stated that her 15-year-old son, a high school freshman, needed to be assessed by a licensed therapist or potentially face a suspension hearing at school because of a stated intention to use a date rape drug. The school librarian overheard a group of boys who were looking up information on a school computer about "date rape" drugs. The boy in question was saying that he intended to purchase the drug from another boy at school because one of the most attractive and popular girls in his class agreed to go out on a date with him the coming weekend. The librarian immediately got the school counselor and principal involved because the boy was a member of the junior varsity football team and the school has been dealing with allegations of sexual assault and the use of date rape drugs by members of the team. The players and their parents had been informed that the players would be suspended from school and referred to government officials if the school learned that they used a date rape drug or had any sexual contact with a minor. The principal, school counselor, and librarian met with the boy, who acknowledged saying what the librarian had reported. He said, however, that he and the boys were "just talking—it was totally not serious." He said he would never have gone ahead with actually putting the drug in the girl's drink because "that just wouldn't be right. I would never do that."

The boy's mother asked if the psychologist would meet with her son to follow through with the school's recommendation and help prevent a possible suspension hearing. The psychologist lives in the community, has a daughter in middle school, and knows parents of some of the high school football players. Therefore, she asked to know the name of the girl in question to make sure she didn't have a dual relationship that would prevent her from taking on the case. It turned out that she was friends with the parents of the girl. She decided that there were too many potential risks involved in taking the referral, and so she gave the mother the names of three other therapists in the area who work well with young adults. That ended the psychologist's involvement in that particular case.

The following school year, the psychologist's daughter started high school. The daughter came home one day after school very excited because the quarterback on the high school football team asked her out on a date. The daughter said the boy was really popular and good looking, and all her girlfriends couldn't believe that she was asked out because she was a freshman and the quarterback was a sophomore who was so good at football that he was the starting quarterback on the varsity football team. After asking for the boy's name, it was clear that this was the same boy who had been overheard by the school librarian the previous year talking about using a date rape drug.

The psychologist was extremely concerned that her daughter might be at increased risk of unwanted sexual contact even though she had no specific evidence this was the case. She also realized that she could not prohibit her daughter from going out with the quarterback without risking rebellion by her daughter—her daughter was allowed to date in high school and was now very excited that she was asked out on a date by one of the most popular boys in the school.

The psychologist felt that she could not consult with colleagues in the community because the allegations of inappropriate sexual behavior by the football players had generated intense interest and divisiveness in the community. Several professionals who were involved in the case had been accused of either minimizing and covering up or exaggerating the seriousness of the problems. Needing an objective view regarding her feelings about her personal situation, she decided to contact her former ethics professor from her graduate program in another state because he had always emphasized the importance of consultation when faced with ethical dilemmas. While speaking by phone with him, he said he completely understood her worry about any unwanted or forced sexual contact with her daughter even though she had no specific information about the risks her daughter currently faced. He also agreed that preventing her daughter from going on a date with the quarterback would increase the risk of conflict and rebellion with the daughter. The psychologist further noted that her daughter was not using any form of birth control, at least not to her knowledge, which increased the potential risks further.

The ethics professor suggested that the psychologist could contact the quarterback's mother about the situation, not as a professional but simply as a mother who was appropriately concerned about her daughter's social and romantic involvements. He suggested that she be very careful about not pre-judging the boy's intentions or character but that she was inquiring simply to see if the other mother thought she had a valid concern.

The psychologist went ahead and called the quarterback's mother. Fortunately, the boy's mother was very understanding about the situation. She said that she and her husband had planned to go out to a movie during the time their son was going to have the psychologist's daughter over for the evening. Because of the psychologist's concern, however, she said that they would watch a movie at home that night and make sure that her son was never unsupervised. She said that the school had informed all the football players and their parents that if a school official became aware that any player had sexual contact with a minor, the school would be required to report that contact to the authorities and the boy's eligibility to play on the team could be affected. The mother said that because the psychologist had been so rea-sonable and helpful regarding her son's situation the previous year, she would promise to make sure that her son would not be alone with their daughter unsupervised.

When the psychologist picked up her daughter after the date that week-end, she secretly couldn't have been more pleased that her daughter had not enjoyed her evening with the quarterback at all. She said that he just wanted to talk about sports and play videogames and he said rude things about her girlfriends. She said she wouldn't go out with him again if he asked. The psy-chologist was hugely relieved because she fully realized that the situation could have turned out very differently.

II

THE PUBLIC WE SERVE:
ITS BIOPSYCHOSOCIAL
CIRCUMSTANCES

4

PSYCHOLOGICAL FUNCTIONING

The definition of *behavioral health care* proposed in Chapter 1 notes that "behavioral health care involves the clinical application of behavioral science and professional ethics to address behavioral health needs and promote biopsychosocial functioning" (p. 20). This definition has several important implications. First, it identifies science and ethics as foundational to the field, the starting points for learning the profession. Scientific knowledge regarding human development and functioning and biomedical ethics provide the basic justification and rationale for clinical practice. As the previous two chapters illustrated, these topics are essential for understanding the nature of human psychology and for engaging in responsible and ethical health care practice and research. Together, they provide the necessary conceptual foundations for practicing the profession.

The proposed definition suggests that after aspiring clinicians have integrated these basic conceptual foundations, they should develop expertise

DOI: 10.1037/14441-005
Biopsychosocial Practice: A Science-Based Framework for Behavioral Health Care, by T. P. Melchert
Copyright © 2015 by the American Psychological Association. All rights reserved.

regarding individuals' behavioral health needs and biopsychosocial functioning. Meeting individuals' needs is the fundamental purpose of behavioral health care, and so clinicians should develop familiarity with the research regarding people's functioning and life circumstances across the biopsychosocial domains. This section of the book addresses this topic. There are no clear boundaries between the biological, psychological, and sociocultural domains of functioning—indeed, phenomenologically they often appear to interact seamlessly in providing a unified experience of the world. Nonetheless, these three general levels of natural organization underlie human experience and are discussed in separate chapters (Chapters 4–6). Chapter 7 presents the developmental perspective that addresses growth and development over time and helps integrate the topics covered in the three chapters that precede it.

This approach to learning the profession is different from many traditional approaches to education and training in the field. Students across the behavioral health care fields are required to learn about the biological, psychological, and social bases of behavior, but there is typically also significant emphasis on learning about the traditional theoretical orientations to conceptualizing cases. Students are generally expected to adopt one or some combination of those orientations to structure and organize their approach to clinical practice. Students then learn how their adopted approaches can be used with different types of individuals and disorders. Some of these orientations include specific hypotheses about the nature and development of psychopathology, personality, and behavior change; others address only parts of these topics. The empirical support for these hypotheses also varies greatly. In general, however, these orientations do not systematically integrate current scientific knowledge about the full range of biopsychosocial influences on development and functioning (see Chapter 2). Because of their inadequacies as scientific theories, the traditional theoretical orientations cannot provide the scientific foundations for the field, and so here they are reconceptualized as therapies in the biopsychosocial approach.

The biopsychosocial approach to behavioral health care advocated in this volume relies on a quite different conceptual framework from the traditional approaches. The biopsychosocial approach begins with a firm grounding in the scientific and ethical foundations of the field and this is followed by an examination of the behavioral health needs and biopsychosocial circumstances of individuals. After being well-grounded in these topics, the treatment process is then learned. Learning interventions and how to implement them before being well grounded in the scientific understanding of human psychology and individuals' behavioral health and biopsychosocial functioning is viewed as putting the cart before the horse. Too often, therapists learn how to use therapeutic tools before they have a thorough understanding of what, when, where, how, and why to use them. Therapists who specialize in cognitive therapy, for example, may tend to see a need to address irrational thinking, whereas family therapists may see a need to address dysfunctional family dynamics, and psychopharmacologists may see needs for medicating symptoms. The rationale for providing these treatments is frequently based more on the assumptions of one's adopted theoretical orientation than the particular biopsychosocial circumstances and developmental history of the patient. (Maslow, 1966, famously noted that if all you have is a hammer, then everything looks like a nail, or as Kaplan, 1964, put it, "Give a small boy a hammer, and he will find that everything he encounters needs pounding" [p. 28].)

Traditional approaches involving the application of one's preferred theoretical orientation differ from a comprehensive, scientifically grounded approach to health care assessment and treatment planning. From a science-based health care orientation, one cannot rationally plan how best to intervene before one understands individuals' needs and circumstances in a comprehensive biopsychosocial manner. Treatment plans should address individuals' needs and disorders in the short term as well as the underlying causes and risk factors for psychopathology and promote health, resilience, and optimal functioning to be maximally effective over the long term. This requires a comprehensive, science-based approach to understanding cases. This is true in medicine as well as in behavioral health care. Treatment that is not focused on individuals' health in the context of their behavior and life circumstances as a whole, but instead focuses narrowly on treating symptoms or distress without addressing the underlying causes, is likely to be less effective over the long term.

The chapters in this section of the book summarize the important psychological, sociocultural, physical health, and developmental influences that must be incorporated in a biopsychosocial conceptualization of behavioral health care. Thoroughly reviewing these topics obviously requires extensive study and analysis; the overview presented here is instead intended to demonstrate that a thorough understanding of individuals' behavioral health and biopsychosocial needs and functioning is not possible without a comprehensive perspective that systematically integrates the important factors involved.

To gain a psychological perspective on individuals' behavioral health and biopsychosocial functioning, it is useful to start with a review of the epidemiological research regarding the prevalence of mental disorders. The implications of this research are noted, the prevalence of suicide and substance use and abuse is reviewed, and psychological health and well-being are discussed.

MENTAL DISORDERS

Mental health problems are common in the general population. Surveys consistently find that large proportions of the public currently meet the criteria for a mental disorder or have at some point during their lifetimes. In the largest study of comorbidity ever conducted in the United States, the National Comorbidity Survey, nearly 50% of the respondents reported at least one lifetime mental disorder and nearly 30% reported at least one 12-month disorder (Kessler et al., 1994). The most common disorders were depression, alcohol dependence, social phobia, and simple phobia. In addition, a subgroup of 14% of the respondents accounted for the vast majority of the severe disorders and had three or more comorbid disorders over the course of their lifetimes. This study was replicated a decade later and the National Comorbidity Survey Replication found that the prevalence of mental disorders had changed little from the original survey (Kessler et al., 2005; Wang et al., 2005, 2006). The following findings were noted:

- 50% of all Americans report having symptoms diagnostic of a mental disorder during the course of their lifetimes.
- Many of their symptoms emerged as early as age 11, half of all lifetime cases started by age 14, and three-quarters started by age 24.
- More than one fourth of adults reported having symptoms diagnostic of a mental disorder over the previous year, and most of these disorders could be classified as at least moderate in severity.
- Mental illness is the most prevalent chronic health condition experienced by youth.
- Most people wait years or even decades to seek treatment for their depression, anxiety, or bipolar disorder.
- Fewer than one third of those with mental disorders receive adequate treatment for their mental health problems.

The U.S. Substance Abuse and Mental Health Services Administration (SAMHSA) every other year combines data from numerous sources to obtain estimates regarding the mental health of the American population in general. The 2010 report, *Mental Health, United States, 2010* (SAMHSA, 2012a), included the following findings:

- 19.9% of the U.S. population experienced a mental illness (excluding substance use disorders) in the past year.
- 4.8% had serious mental illness that resulted in serious functional impairment during the past year.
- 6.5% experienced major depressive disorder.
- 3.2% experienced serious psychological distress in the past 30 days, a level of symptomatology that may impair a person's ability to participate in family, community, or work life.
- Serious mental illness was highest among 18 to 25 year olds (7.3%) and lowest among adults ages 50 and older (2.8%).

- Serious mental illness was more likely among women (6.4%) compared with men (3.2%).
- Serious mental illness was particularly prevalent among adults living in poverty (9.1%).
- Of adults with serious mental illness, 25.7% had co-occurring substance dependence or abuse.

Mental disorders are also common among children and youth. One out of eight children ages 8 to 15 (13.1%) met the criteria for a mental disorder in the past year, and 11.3% met the criteria for a mental disorder with severe impairment in the past year (Merikangas et al., 2010).

A more detailed perspective on the mental health issues faced by the general population in the U.S. is provided by the prevalence data reported in the *Diagnostic and Statistical Manual of Mental Disorders* (fifth ed.; *DSM–5*; American Psychiatric Association, 2013). Table 4.1 lists all *DSM–5* diagnoses that were found to have 1% or higher prevalence. The cutoff of 1% is arbitrary but helpful for considering whether a problem might be viewed as relatively common and within the purview of general behavioral health care practice.

These data indicate that the population deals with a wide range of issues, including primarily psychologically and biologically based disorders as well as disorders that have significant social components. The top nine most prevalent concerns involve sexual functioning, addictions, panic attacks, and sleep problems (none of which receive extensive attention in many professional psychology or other behavioral health care education programs).

In the first nationally representative survey on personality disorders, Grant et al. (2004) found that an estimated 14.8% of the adult U.S. population met the criteria for at least one personality disorder. The survey did not assess borderline, schizotypal, and narcissistic personality disorders to reduce interviewing time, and the overall rate of any personality disorder would have been higher if those disorders had been included. In that survey, the following percentages of respondents met the criteria for specific personality disorders:

- 7.9% had obsessive–compulsive personality disorder.
- 4.4% had paranoid personality disorder.
- 3.6% had antisocial personality disorder.
- 3.1% had schizoid personality disorder.
- 2.4% had avoidant personality disorder.
- 1.8% had histrionic personality disorder.
- 0.5% had dependent personality disorder.

All of the personality disorders in the survey except for histrionic were associated with considerable emotional disability and impairment in social and occupational functioning. In general, risk factors for the personality

TABLE 4.1
Psychiatric Diagnoses Rank Ordered by Prevalence as Reported in the *DSM–5*

Diagnosis	Lifetime prevalence unless otherwise noted
Premature ejaculation	20%–30% of males
Female orgasmic disorder	10%–42% report symptoms, 10% do not experience orgasm throughout their lifetimes
Male hypoactive sexual desire disorder	6% ages 18–24, 41% ages 66–74 years
Genito-pelvic pain/penetration disorder	15% report recurrent pain
Tobacco use disorder	13% adults, 12-month
Panic attacks	11.2%, 12-month
Alcohol use disorder	8.5% adults, 12-month
Insomnia disorder	6%–10% point prevalence, 1/3 of adults report symptoms
Obstructive sleep apnea	2%–15% of middle-aged adults, > 20% older adults
Specific phobia	7%–9%, 12-month
Major depressive disorder	7%, 12-month
Social phobia	7%, 12-month
Posttraumatic stress disorder	8.7% (3.5%, 12-month)
Somatic symptom disorder	5%–7%
Illness anxiety disorder	1.3%–10%, 12–24 month
Obsessive-compulsive personality disorder	2.1%–7.9%
Restless legs syndrome	2%–7.2%
Schizotypal personality disorder	4.6%
Learning disorders	5%–15% among children, 4% of adults
Hoarding disorder	2%–6% point prevalence
Borderline personality disorder	1.6%–5.9%
Narcissistic personality disorder	0–6.2%
Conduct disorder	2%–10% of children and adolescents, 12-month
Attention-deficit/hyperactivity disorder	5% of children, 2.5% of adults
Male erectile disorder	13%–21% ages 40–80 occasionally, 2% of males younger than 40–50 frequently
Adjustment disorder	5%–20% of outpatients, up to 50% of inpatients
Acute stress disorder	20%–50% of people exposed to inter-personal traumatic event
Sleepwalking disorder	29.2% of adults, 3.6% past year
Oppositional defiant disorder	3.3%
Paranoid personality disorder	2.3%–4.4%
Generalized anxiety disorder	2.9% adults, 0.9% adolescents, 12-month
Intermittent explosive disorder	2.7%, 12-month
Panic disorder	2–3%, 12-month
Body dysmorphic disorder	2.4%, point prevalence
Cannabis use disorder	1.5% adults, 3.4% adolescents, 12-month
Avoidant personality disorder	2.4%
Separation anxiety disorder	4% children, 1.6% adolescents, 0.9%–1.0% adults 12-month

TABLE 4.1

Psychiatric Diagnoses Rank Ordered by Prevalence
as Reported in the *DSM–5*   *(Continued)*

Diagnosis	Lifetime prevalence unless otherwise noted
Alzheimer's (major dementia)	5%–10% in the 70s, at least 25% thereafter
Circadian rhythm sleep-wake disorder	5%–10% of night shift workers
Dementia (neurocognitive disorder)	1%–2% at age 65, up to 30% by age 85
Premenstrual dysphoric disorder	1.8%–5.8%, 12-month
Depersonalization/derealization disorder	2%
Histrionic personality disorder	1.8%
Bipolar disorder (I, II, or not otherwise specified)	1.8%
Dissociative amnesia	1.8%, 12-month
Antisocial personality disorder	0.2%–3.3%, 12-month
Agoraphobia	1.7%, 12-month
Dissociative identity disorder	1.5%, 12-month
Chronic major depressive disorder	1.5%, 12-month
Trichotillomania	1%–2%, 12-month
Excoriation (skin picking) disorder	1.4%
Obsessive-compulsive disorder	1.2%, 12-month
Binge-eating disorder	1.6% females, 0.8% males, 12-month
Bulimia nervosa	1%–1.5% of young females, 12-month
Disruptive mood dysregulation disorder	2%–5% of children and adolescents
Intellectual disability	1%
Autistic spectrum disorder	1%
Enuresis	1% of individuals age 15 and older

Note. Some disorders that appear in a limited age group are not included (e.g., developmental coordination disorder). Rank ordering is approximate given the nature of the estimates provided. *DSM–5 = Diagnostic and Statistical Manual of Mental Disorders* (fifth ed.; American Psychiatric Association, 2013).

disorders included being Native American or African American; being a young adult; having low socioeconomic status; and being divorced, separated, widowed, or never married.

SUICIDE

Suicide is a very serious and irreversible act that affects large numbers of individuals. The prevalence and seriousness of suicide are often not apparent when focusing on mental disorders alone, however. For example, the literature reviewed in the previous section infrequently refers to suicide or suicide attempts.

Surveys have found that suicide was the 10th leading cause of death in the United States in 2010, accounting for 38,364 deaths, an average of 105 per day, which is more than double the number of homicides (Centers for Disease Control and Prevention [CDC], 2012b). Suicide is the 3rd leading cause of death among young adults 15 to 24 years of age, accounting for 20% of all deaths in that age group annually. It was the second leading cause of death among persons 25 to 34 years old, the fourth leading cause among individuals 35 to 54 years old, and the eighth leading cause of death among persons 55 to 64 years old.

While the number of suicides is high, the number of individuals with suicidal ideation is far higher. It has been estimated that there are 25 attempted suicides for every one completed suicide (Crosby et al., 2011), and that 10% to 12% of U.S. adults report having made at least one suicide attempt (Chiles & Strosahl, 2005). It is also estimated that up to 40% of the general population in the United States has had suicidal ideation at some point in their lives (Chiles & Strosahl, 2005; Hirschfeld & Russell, 1997). A large survey of college students found that slightly more than one-half reported ever having had suicidal ideation (Drum, Brownson, Denmark, & Smith, 2009). Among youth in Grades 9 through 12, a nationally representative CDC survey found that 15.7% reported having seriously considered attempting suicide in the previous 12 months, 12.8% reported having made a suicide plan during the previous 12 months, 7.8% reported attempting suicide at least once in the previous 12 months, and 2.4% reported making a suicide attempt that resulted in injury, poisoning, or an overdose that required medical attention (Schiller, Lucas, & Peregoy, 2012). A smaller survey also found that 40% of youths who reported attempting suicide said they had made their first attempt already in elementary or middle school (Mazza, Catalano, Abbott, & Haggerty, 2011). In 2011, about 487,700 people were treated in emergency departments for self-inflicted injuries (including both suicidal and nonsuicidal behaviors such as self-mutilation), resulting in an estimated $6.5 billion in combined medical and work loss costs (CDC, 2012b).

The National Violent Death Reporting System survey conducted by the CDC is based on data submitted by 16 states (Karch, Logan, McDaniel, Parks, & Patel, 2012). The 2009 survey found that firearms were used in the majority (51.8%) of suicide deaths, followed by hanging, strangulation, or suffocation (24.7%) and poisoning (17.2%). The most common method used by males was a firearm (56.7%); poisoning was the method used most often by females (36.9%). Among the decedents who received toxicology tests, one third (33.3%) tested positive for alcohol and 20.8% tested positive for opiates. Among those who were tested for antidepressants, 23.1% tested positive.

Precipitating circumstances were identified in the survey for approximately 90% of those who committed suicide (Karch et al., 2012). Overall, 41.0% experienced a depressed mood at the time of their deaths, 44.1% were described as having a diagnosed mental health problem, and 31.3% were receiving treatment at the time of their deaths. Of those with a diagnosed mental disorder, 74.1% had a diagnosis of depression or dysthymia (or both), 14.6% had bipolar disorder, and 10.6% had an anxiety disorder. A large proportion (28.3%) had disclosed their suicidal intent before dying, 33.1% left a suicide note, and 19.8% had previously attempted suicide. About 31.4% had an intimate partner problem within the preceding 2 weeks and 26.6% had some other type of crisis. Physical health problems were noted in 21.0% of cases, and job and financial problems were noted in 14.6% and 13.8% of deaths, respectively.

SUBSTANCE USE AND ABUSE

Alcohol Use

The 2011 National Survey on Drug Use and Health conducted by SAMHSA (2012b) found that 51.8% of Americans age 12 or older reported being current alcohol drinkers. The rates for the different categories of drinking alcohol are reported below. These rates were slightly lower than rates reported one decade earlier.

- 51.8% of Americans aged 12 or older reported being current drinkers of alcohol.
- 22.6% reported participating in binge drinking (i.e., at least five drinks on the same occasion on at least 1 day in the past month).
- 6.2% reported heavy drinking (i.e., binge drinking on at least 5 days in the past 30).
- 39.8% of young adults (18–25 years old) reported binge drinking.
- 12.1% of young adults (18–25 years old) reported heavy drinking.
- 13.3% of youths (12–17 years old) reported drinking alcohol.
- 7.4% of youths (12–17 years old) reported engaging in binge drinking.
- 1.5% of youths (12–17 years old) reported engaging in heavy drinking.

The CDC National Health Interview Survey for 2011 (Schiller et al., 2012) found similar rates of alcohol drinking. That survey found that 52% of all American adults ages 18 and over were current regular drinkers, 14% were current infrequent drinkers, 6% were former regular drinkers, 9% were former infrequent drinkers, and 20% were lifetime abstainers. According to the 2011 National Survey on Drug Use and Health conducted by SAMHSA (2012b), 8.0% of the population age 12 or older met the criteria for substance dependence or abuse. Alcohol accounted for the large majority of these cases.

Illicit Drug Use

The 2011 National Survey on Drug Use and Health conducted by SAMHSA (2012b) found that an estimated 8.7% of Americans age 12 or older were current (past month) drug users. Illicit drugs included marijuana/hashish, cocaine including crack, heroin, hallucinogens, inhalants, or prescription psychotherapeutics used nonmedically (e.g., pain relievers, stimulants, sedatives). Particular findings included the following:

- 8.7% of Americans age 12 or older reported being current (past month) users of illicit drugs.
- Marijuana was the most commonly used illicit drug (7.0%), followed by psychotherapeutics (2.4%), cocaine (0.5%), hallucinogens (0.4%), methamphetamines (0.2%), and heroin (0.1%).
- 10.1% of youths ages 12 to 17 were illicit drug users.
- 21.4% of young adults ages 18 to 25 were illicit drug users.

Approximately one in 12 Americans age 12 or older report using illicit drugs within the past month. Marijuana accounts for the large majority of this drug use, followed by the abuse of psychotherapeutic medications. The use of other substances is low in comparison with these first two categories.

Tobacco Use

In the 2011 National Survey on Drug Use and Health conducted by SAMHSA (2012b), an estimated 26.5% of Americans age 12 or older reported using tobacco in the past month (22.1% were cigarette smokers, 5.0% had smoked cigars, 3.2% had used smokeless tobacco, and 0.8% had smoked tobacco in pipes). This was a decrease from 30.4% in 2002. The rate of tobacco use among youth ages 12 to 17 was 10.0% (a decline from 15.2% in 2002). The rate of cigarette smoking among pregnant women ages 15 to 44 was 17.6%.

WELL-BEING AND FLOURISHING

A main feature of the biopsychosocial approach is its comprehensive perspective on human development and functioning. This includes focusing on the full spectrum of functioning across all the biopsychosocial domains. Although individuals' problems, disorders, and vulnerabilities obviously require the attention of health care providers, their strengths and resources have a critical impact on their development and functioning as well. Indeed, people's strengths often appear to have a greater impact on their overall well-being than their disorders and weaknesses. Gaining a complete understanding of people's needs and functioning consequently requires consideration of their strengths, resources, and well-being in addition to their problems, disorders, and vulnerabilities. This is true across all the biopsychosocial domains.

Behavioral health care and medicine have long emphasized problems, disorders, and vulnerabilities. But recently there has been growing interest in wellness and positive functioning as reflected in the growing positive psychology, recovery, and wellness movements. Though some criticize the historical emphasis on problems and vulnerabilities, it is important to recognize that that emphasis was entirely appropriate given the context. Strengths, resources, and assets have always been important in people's lives, but the impact of disease, injury, and disability over most of human history was very serious and frequently even fatal. As a result, health care providers and the public naturally focused attention on problems, disease, and weakness. The primary causes of illness and death have now shifted, however, from acute and infectious disease to chronic diseases associated with behavior and lifestyle (see Chapter 6). This has resulted in a gradual shift from the historical focus on treating pathology and disease to the promotion of physical and mental health and well-being (see Chapter 7).

The research reviewed above clearly indicates that many individuals are not enjoying high levels of happiness and well-being. Keyes (2007) defined a positive state of mental health as "flourishing" and found that functioning at any level lower than flourishing is associated with increased functional impairment and increased physical and mental health problems. Based on national survey data, Keyes estimated that roughly only two in 10 Americans are flourishing, and nearly two in 10 are in poor mental health, which he referred to as "languishing." Most of the rest were in between, a level that was associated with moderate distress, lower social well-being, and a moderate number of chronic physical conditions. (See Chapter 7 for a more thorough discussion of this topic.)

DISCUSSION: THE NECESSITY OF A BROAD PERSPECTIVE ON PSYCHOLOGICAL FUNCTIONING

The topics reviewed in the preceding sections provide an initial overview of the psychological functioning of the general population. Each factor noted significantly influences individuals' development and functioning and each affects the course of treatment as well. As a result, these topics are integrated into commonly accepted approaches to assessment and treatment planning in the mental health field (e.g., the Joint Commission standards for the accreditation of behavioral health care facilities; see Chapter 8). The data reviewed also have important implications with regard to behavioral health care education, policy, and research in addition to clinical practice (e.g., see Chapter 12).

People experience a broad range of issues and disorders. In addition to mood and anxiety disorders, which tend to receive significant attention in traditional behavioral health care, people experience a wide variety of issues involving sexuality, addictions, sleep problems, reactions to major stressors, learning and attention-deficit disorders, and personality disorders. Suicidal ideation and behavior are highly prevalent and co-occurring problems. In addition, only a minority of individuals are flourishing or functioning at an optimal level with high levels of positive emotion and social well-being and few health problems and disabilities. This complicated picture of the biopsychosocial health and well-being of the general public becomes more evident when social and medical functioning are also integrated into the discussion. Addressing this broad range of issues presents a major challenge to specialists as well as general practitioners because so many individuals are experiencing problems in several areas of their lives.

Education and training in the field often do not focus extensively on some of the most prevalent mental health issues noted above. Individuals commonly face problems related to sexual functioning, addictions, sleep, somatic symptoms, personality disorders, learning disorders, suicidality, and lack of positive mental health, but many graduate programs in the field give only limited attention to several of these issues. Chronic and comorbid problems are also prevalent, and these too often receive limited attention. The significant prevalence and consequences of substance use disorders are generally well known, but graduate training on the topic is often limited or sometimes even nonexistent (Harwood, Kowalski, & Ameen, 2004). Many experts believe the topic of suicide should receive far more attention in behavioral health care training as well. A task force of the American Association of Suicidology has concluded that current training in the assessment and management of suicidal patients has serious gaps (Schmitz et al., 2012). Several studies have found that only about one-half of psychology trainees received training on suicide, and the training provided was often very limited. These same trainees nonetheless frequently treat suicidality—one survey of psychologists-in-training found that 97% provided care to at least one patient (and often several) with some form of suicidal behavior or ideation (Kleespies, Penk, & Forsyth, 1993).

The field has a great deal of work to do to address the public's behavioral health needs and promote their biopsychosocial functioning. Before that responsibility can be fully appreciated, however, there are several additional factors that must be considered. Individuals' mental health concerns cannot be understood in isolation—their sociocultural circumstances and physical health also need to be considered to gain a thorough understanding of their development and functioning. Treatment that effectively addresses individuals' problems and promotes their well-being over the long term requires a comprehensive understanding of their circumstances across the biopsychosocial domains.

5

SOCIOCULTURAL FACTORS

Behavioral health care has made major strides in recognizing the importance of sociocultural factors in individuals' development and functioning over the past half century. Since the Civil Rights era, there is far greater recognition of the many ways that gender, race, ethnicity, class, religion, and other sociocultural factors interact with psychological and biological factors in producing psychological outcomes. The interactions among these factors are complex, and there often are no clear boundaries between them. For example, race was once viewed as having an important biological influence on psychological outcomes (as discussed in Chapter 2). It has since been found to have limited biological meaning, but it remains a very important sociocultural variable that significantly affects one's development and functioning. Infant attachment is another important variable. Based on a biologically evolved attachment system, mothers and other caregivers provide patterns of care to infants that result in the infants developing expectations

DOI: 10.1037/14441-006
Biopsychosocial Practice: A Science-Based Framework for Behavioral Health Care, by T. P. Melchert
Copyright © 2015 by the American Psychological Association. All rights reserved.

about self and others (i.e., internal working models) that significantly influence their personality characteristics, psychopathology, and other psychosocial outcomes (see Chapter 7). Neither race nor attachment can be neatly categorized as biological, psychological, or sociocultural phenomena but are instead good examples of biopsychosocial processes.

For practical purposes, however, variables can be placed into relevant categories so that they can be learned in a systematic manner. This chapter reviews variables that are typically viewed as social or cultural in nature. The categories that are reviewed in this chapter—demographic characteristics, educational attainment, vocational and financial status, family and relationship functioning, child maltreatment, elder abuse, criminal victimization and legal involvement, and religion and spirituality—were chosen because they are included in the Joint Commission on Accreditation of Healthcare Organizations (2006) standards for behavioral health care facilities and several other approaches to conceptualizing psychological assessment and intervention (see Chapter 8).

DEMOGRAPHIC CHARACTERISTICS

The United States is steadily becoming a more multicultural society. Indeed, based on current trends, the U.S. Census Bureau projects that individuals from racial and ethnic minority groups will make up the majority of the U.S. population by 2042 and half of all children by 2023 (U.S. Census Bureau, 2008). In order to be relevant to the growing number of individuals who do not fall within the traditional target groups for many psychotherapeutic treatments, behavioral health care providers should develop multicultural competencies so they can work effectively with individuals and families from diverse groups (Sue & Sue, 2008). A review of basic demographic data highlights the necessity of developing these competencies. Selected data from the 2010 U.S. Census reflecting self-identifications of race and ethnicity are provided in Table 5.1.

As can be seen in that table, the Asian population grew at the fastest rate over the previous decade (just slightly more than the Latino population), whereas the White alone population grew the slowest (U.S. Census Bureau, 2011). The Latino population grew the most in number (15.2 million) between 2000 and 2010, accounting for more than one half of the 27.3 million increase in the total U.S. population in those years. Data collected regarding languages spoken show that of individuals at least 5 years of age, 20% reported speaking a language other than English at home, though the majority of these reported that they spoke English "very well." Spanish was the most frequent language other than English spoken at home, but Chinese, Tagalog, French, Vietnamese,

TABLE 5.1

Selected Demographic Results From the 2010 U.S. Census

Race	Number	% of total	% change, 2000–2010
Total population	308,745,538	100.0	9.7
One race	299,736,465	97.1	9.2
White	223,553,265	72.4	5.7
Black or African American	38,929,319	12.6	12.3
American Indian and Alaska Native	2,932,248	0.9	18.4
Asian	14,674,252	4.8	43.3
Native Hawaiian and Other Pacific	540,013	0.2	35.4
Some other race	19,107,368	6.2	24.4
Two or more races	9,009,073	2.9	32.0
Hispanic or Latino	50,477,594	16.3	43.0
Not Hispanic or Latino	258,267,944	83.7	4.9
White alone	196,817,662	63.7	1.2

Note. *Hispanic or Latino* refers to people of Cuban, Mexican, Puerto Rican, South or Central American, or other Spanish culture or origin regardless of race. More people selected the *White race* category than the *White alone* category. Data are from U.S. Census Bureau (2011).

German, and Korean were reported as spoken at home by at least one million individuals (U.S. Census Bureau, 2011).

The Gallup Poll included a question regarding sexual orientation in its national survey for the first time in 2012. In response to the question "Do you, personally, identify as lesbian, gay, bisexual, or transgender?" 3.4% responded "Yes" and 4.4% refused to respond or responded "Don't know" (Gates & Newport, 2012). These results are similar to those found with smaller surveys taken in previous years. Nonwhites were more likely to identify as lesbian, gay, bisexual, or transgender (LGBT; 3.2% non-Hispanic White, 4.6% Black, 4.0% Hispanic, 4.3% Asian) and women were slightly more likely than men to identify as LGBT (3.6% vs. 3.3%). Younger individuals ages 18 to 29 (6.4%) were much more like to identify as LGBT than individuals 65 and older (1.9%).

EDUCATIONAL ATTAINMENT, VOCATIONAL STABILITY, AND SOCIOECONOMIC STATUS

Educational attainment, vocational stability, and socioeconomic status contribute substantially to individuals' development and functioning, and there is wide variability across these measures in the United States. The census data presented in Table 5.2 indicate that more than four out of five

TABLE 5.2
Selected Data From the U.S. Census for 2009

Category	Measure
Educational attainment for U.S. population 25 years and older (%)	
< 9th grade	6.3
9th–12th grade, no diploma	8.5
High school regular diploma	24.6
High school GED or equivalent	3.9
Some college, no degree	21.4
Associate degree	7.5
Bachelor's degree	17.6
Master's degree	7.2
Professional school degree	1.9
Doctoral degree	1.2
High school or more education	85.3
Bachelor's degree or more	27.9
Income by race and head of household ($)	
Median family income	50,054
Asian	65,129
White, not Latino	55,412
Latino (any race)	38,624
Black	32,229
All households	50,054
Family households	62,273
Married-couple	74,130
Female head, no husband present	33,637
Male head, no wife present	49,567
Nonfamily households	30,221
Female householder	25,492
Male householder	35,482
Living in poverty (%)	
Total population	15.0
Total families	11.8
Married couple families	6.2
Female head, no husband present	31.2
Male head, no wife present	16.1
Children < 18 in female-headed household	47.6
Children < 18 in married-couple families	10.9
Children < 6 in female-headed household	57.2
Children < 6 in married-couple families	12.1

Note. Data are from U.S. Census Bureau (2012a, 2012b).

American adults in 2009 reported obtaining at least a high school diploma or equivalency diploma, and more than one in four reported obtaining a bachelor's degree or higher. This represents more than a threefold increase in high school attainment and more than a fivefold increase in college attainment since 1940 when educational data were first collected by the Census Bureau (U.S. Census Bureau, 2012a). Nonetheless, roughly 15% reported not obtaining a high school diploma or its equivalent. It is also estimated that 1 in 7 Americans lack basic English literacy skills such as those needed to read a map, review a paycheck for accuracy, or understand a warning label on a tool or medicine bottle (National Center for Educational Statistics, 2008).

A significant proportion of the total U.S. population (15%) lives in poverty, a significant increase over the period before the 2007 recession. The situation is particularly dire for many children, especially if they live in single-parent female-headed households. Nearly 48% of all children under age 18 living in a female-headed household in 2011 lived in poverty compared to just under 11% of children living in families with married couple parents (see Table 5.2). Young children under 6 years of age living in a female-headed household were even more likely to be living in poverty (57.2%; U.S. Census Bureau, 2012b). Extremely serious problems with financial insecurity are prevalent as well—for example, the lifetime prevalence of homelessness in the United States is estimated to be 6.2% (Toro et al., 2007).

Educational achievement and income are also strongly correlated. The median annual earnings of all Americans ages 25 to 64 in 2006–2008 was $27,455 (U.S. Census Bureau, 2011). For those with less than a high school diploma who worked less than full-time, the median earnings were $11,256, whereas the median annual earnings of full-time workers with a professional degree were $103,411. The unemployment rate is also correlated with educational attainment. For example, in December 2010 (when the United States was in the middle of an economic recession), the unemployment rate for people with less than a high school diploma (or its equivalent) was 15.7%, whereas the unemployment rate for people with an advanced degree beyond the bachelor's was 3.4% (U.S. Census Bureau, 2012a).

Employment and income problems lead to significant stress for large numbers of individuals and families. Indeed, the American Psychological Association's (2012) 2010 Stress in America survey found that the most frequently cited sources of stress are money (76%), work (70%), and the economy (65%). Surveys also find that financial difficulties and stress are the leading cause of marital problems in the United States (Vyse, 2008).

FAMILY AND RELATIONSHIP FUNCTIONING

Families and intimate relationships provide crucial sources of support, structure, resources, and comfort for many individuals; many people flounder or languish without these supports. On the other hand, many people find that families and relationships are major sources of distress. Because the benefits of healthy families and relationships are quite evident, this brief overview of issues in this area focuses on stress and instability associated with unhealthy families and intimate partner relationships.

Divorce and relationship dissolution are common. Divorce is the outcome for roughly half of the ever-married population. Of couples in their first marriage, approximately 33% divorce or separate within 10 years, and the rate of divorce is higher for subsequent marriages (Blaisure & Geasler, 2006). Children are frequently affected by family breakups as well. Over half of divorces occur in families with young children, affecting more than 1 million children each year. Cohabitating couple relationships are even more likely to dissolve than marriages, and 46% of these include young children.

Many relationships are highly dysfunctional as well, and intimate partner violence, sexual violence, and stalking are all major public health problems. The first large national survey of these latter issues was conducted in the United States by the Centers for Disease Control and Prevention in 2010 (Black et al., 2011). The following key findings were reported

- Nearly one in five women (18.3%) and one in 71 men (1.4%) reported being raped at some time in their lives (including completed or attempted forced penetration or alcohol/drug facilitated completed penetration).
- Just over one half (51.1%) of female rape victims reported being raped by an intimate partner, and 40.8% by an acquaintance.
- Roughly one in four women (24.3%) and one in seven men (13.8%) have experienced severe physical violence by an intimate partner at some point in their lifetime.
- Nearly half of all women (48.4%) and men (48.8%) have experienced psychological aggression by an intimate partner in their lifetime.
- About one in six women (16.2%) and one in 19 men (5.2%) reported experiencing stalking at some point in their life where they felt very fearful or believed that they or someone close to them would be killed or harmed.
- About 66.2% of women stalking victims were stalked by a current of former intimate partner; 41.4% of men stalking victims were stalked by a current or former intimate partner.

When rape, physical violence, and stalking by a current or former partner are taken together, the Centers for Disease Control and Prevention survey found that more than one in three women (35.6%) and more than one in four men (28.5%) reported one or more of these types of victimization. Among these individuals, more than one in three women experienced multiple forms of rape, physical violence, or stalking.

CHILD MALTREATMENT

There is extensive evidence regarding the effects of child maltreatment on psychological development and functioning, and rates of child maltreatment are routinely found to be much higher in clinical samples than they are in the general population (Finkelhor, 2008; Myers, 2011). Sadly, the number of children affected by child maltreatment is also very high. The Children's Bureau, an office of the U.S. Department of Health and Human Services, has been collecting data from all 50 states regarding the reports made to Child Protective Service agencies across the country involving suspected child abuse and neglect. Reports based on these data are produced annually. The *Child Maltreatment 2011* report (U.S. Department of Health and Human Services, Administration for Children and Families, Administration on Children, Youth and Families, Children's Bureau, 2012) includes the following findings:

- In the federal fiscal year 2011, 6.2 million children were the subjects of at least one report to a Child Protective Service agency alleging maltreatment.
- 61% of these allegations involving 3.0 million children were screened in for further attention; the remainder were screened out and were not investigated further.
- 57.6% of these reports were made by professionals mandated to make these reports; nearly all of the remainder were reported by parents, other relatives, friends, neighbors, or anonymous sources.
- 681,000 children were found to be victims of child maltreatment.
- 78.5% of these victims suffered neglect.
- 17.6% of these victims suffered physical abuse.
- 9.1% of these victims suffered sexual abuse.
- 80.8% of the perpetrators were parents; 87.6% of these were the biological parents of the victims.
- The unique victim rate (i.e., a child is counted only once regardless of the number of times substantiated abuse was found during the year) was 9.1 victims per 1,000 children in the population; the highest rate of victimization (21.2 per 1,000) was for children from birth to 1 year of age.
- The total number of reported fatalities resulting from maltreatment was 1,545, and 81.6% of them were younger than 4 years old.

In population surveys, much higher rates of child abuse and neglect have been found. Regarding child physical abuse, a nationally representative study of youth ages 10 to 16 years found that 22% reported experiencing a nonfamily assault and 7.5% reported a family assault in their lifetime

(Finkelhor & Dziuba-Leatherman, 1994). After reviewing the available data on emotional and psychological abuse, Binggeli, Hart, and Brassard (2001) estimated that more than one third of the U.S. adult population may have experienced psychological maltreatment and between 10% and 15% experienced a more severe and chronic form of this type of maltreatment.

After reviewing the available data on sexual abuse, Finkelhor (1994) estimated that at least 20% to 25% of women and between 5% and 15% of men had experienced child sexual abuse. In the two largest and most representative national surveys of child sexual abuse in the United States, 8.5% and 9.0% of women reported at least one completed rape prior to the age of 18 (Saunders et al., 1999, and Tjaden & Thoennes, 2000, respectively). The second of these surveys also found that 2% of men reported at least one completed rape prior to age 18.

ELDER ABUSE

The topic of elder abuse is sometimes not included in basic conceptualizations of behavioral health care, not because it is unimportant in any way but because it occurs in a limited segment of the population. A history of child maltreatment is relevant when working with all child and adult populations, whereas elder abuse is restricted to the elderly population. The issue is nonetheless included in the Joint Commission standards for the accreditation of behavioral health care facilities, and clinicians are highly concerned about the abuse and neglect of vulnerable adults just as they are with regard to children. The topic can also arise in all types of clinical practice because even child therapists, through their work with children and parents, may become aware of grandparents or other seniors who are being abused, exploited, or neglected. Therefore, the issue is highlighted here to ensure that it is not overlooked when conceptualizing practice in the field.

In the first systematic review of studies investigating the prevalence of elder abuse, Cooper, Selwood, and Livingston (2008) found widely varying prevalence estimates reported across cultures. They concluded that the best estimate is that more than 6% of the older general population reported experiencing abuse in the last month. In addition, 5.6% of older couples reported that their own relationship had been physically violent in the past year. Seniors who are dependent on caregivers are particularly vulnerable. The researchers found that nearly 25% report significant psychological abuse, 20% are neglected, 1% report physical abuse, and significant numbers (6%–18%) experience financial exploitation. In addition, these researchers found that 33% of family caregivers caring for dependent elders reported perpetrating abuse, 16% of professional caregivers report committing psychological abuse, and 10% of professional caregivers report perpetrating physical abuse. More than 80% of nursing home staff also reported observing abuse by others, though very little of this abuse (2%) was actually reported to management. Cooper et al. concluded that only a small number of these cases are reported to protective service agencies.

CRIMINAL VICTIMIZATION AND LEGAL INVOLVEMENT

Criminal victimization is often highly stressful and traumatic, and adjustment and acute stress disorders frequently result from experiencing these types of stressors and trauma (e.g., the *Diagnostic and Statistical Manual of Mental Disorders, Fifth Edition*, reports that 33% to more than 50% of survivors of rape and military combat develop posttraumatic stress disorder, and 20% to 50% of those experiencing assault or rape or witnessing a mass shooting develop acute stress disorder; American Psychiatric Association, 2013). Large numbers of individuals are victims of crime, though fortunately the numbers have fallen significantly in recent decades in the United States. According to the Department of Justice National Crime Victimization Survey (U.S. Bureau of Justice Statistics, 2012b), 2.3% of individuals ages 12 and older reported experiencing a violent crime in 2011 (which was a dramatic drop from the 1970s when rates were routinely higher than 4.5%); about 0.7% reported experiencing serious violent crimes (which included rape or sexual assault, robbery, and aggravated assault), also a dramatic drop from decades past. An estimated 13.9% of households reported a property crime in 2005 (which was a dramatic drop from the 1970s when rates were consistently above 50%). These included household burglary (2.9%), motor vehicle theft (0.5%), and other types of theft (10.4%).

Other types of legal involvement occur frequently as well. The total number of newly filed, reopened, and reactivated cases of all different types in the nation's state courts in 2006 was 102.4 million incoming cases (U.S. Bureau of Justice Statistics, 2012c); most of these (54%) fell under the category of traffic violations, however, which are typically much less complicated. In addition, at the end of 2011 adult correctional authorities in the United States supervised approximately 6,977,700 offenders who were in prison or jail or on probation or parole—roughly 2.9% of all adults in the United States (U.S. Bureau of Justice Statistics, 2012a).

RELIGION AND SPIRITUALITY

Religion and spirituality (like families and relationships) are frequently critically important sources of support, structure, and comfort in people's lives, though they are sometimes sources of confusion, stress, and conflict as well. In both cases, therapists need to be familiar with the important roles that religion and spirituality play in individuals' development and functioning and in the behavior change process.

Surveys consistently find high levels of religiosity in the United States compared with other industrialized countries. Gallup's 2012 poll (Newport, 2012) found that 40% of American adults reported being very religious, 29% reported being moderately religious, and 31% reported being nonreligious. A Newsweek/Beliefnet ("Newsweek/Beliefnet Poll Results," 2005) poll found that 55% of the respondents reported being religious and spiritual, another 9% reported being religious but not spiritual, and another 24% reported being spiritual but not religious. A third major poll conducted by Financial Times/Harris found that 73% of the American adults surveyed believed in God or some other type of supreme being (Harris Interactive, 2006), and approximately 76% of the adults interviewed in the American Religious Identification Survey identified as Christian (Kosmin & Keysar, 2009). A significant trend in religious belief in America is growth in the percentage of individuals who report no religious affiliation. The Pew Forum (Lugo, 2012) poll found that 20% of U.S. adults reported that they were atheist, agnostic, or "nothing in particular" in 2012, which represents a 5% increase over 2007 and a very large increase over earlier decades. Age was strongly related to reporting being religiously unaffiliated. Although 32% of 18- to 29-year-olds reported being religiously unaffiliated, only 9% of those 65 and older described themselves in that way.

DISCUSSION: THE IMPORTANCE OF SOCIOCULTURAL FACTORS

Sociocultural factors play a critical role in individuals' development and functioning. They frequently also play a significant role in treatment outcomes because sociocultural support, stressors, and other factors commonly have facilitative or debilitative effects on the course of treatment. As a result, all these factors should be integrated into therapists' conceptualization of clinical practice. Indeed, it is not possible to work clinically with patients without dealing with these topics because patients routinely bring these issues with them into treatment. For example, as the U.S. population becomes increasingly demographically diverse, and knowledge and skills for dealing with the cultural influences and challenges faced by individuals who are not members of the mainstream culture need to be incorporated into one's competencies for behavioral health care practice. Financial difficulties and employment stress are common and among the most frequent causes of relationship problems and sources of stress. Relationship and family dysfunction, violence, and abuse are all too common, and large numbers of individuals have experienced child abuse and neglect. Criminal victimization and legal involvements are common, and religion and spirituality are important factors in people's lives as well, often as critically important sources of support though sometimes as sources of stress. Unless therapists develop knowledge and skills related to these various factors, many clients' needs will go unnoticed and many treatment plans will not build what might be critical sources of support in patients' lives. Unless therapists conduct holistic assessments that attend to all these factors, patients are likely to feel less well understood and perhaps view their therapists as being less sensitive and credible.

Some of these topics receive significant attention in behavioral health care education and training, although others receive only limited coverage in many programs. The coverage of these topics in the curriculum is frequently not systematic, and developing familiarity with them often occurs in a haphazard manner, frequently outside formal coursework and clinical training. Multiculturalism is one of the few topics reviewed above that normally receives significant attention in graduate curricula. Even a history of child maltreatment, an issue that is widely viewed as highly influential on socioemotional development, is often not reviewed in a systematic manner in many graduate programs.

A biopsychosocial perspective on behavioral health care systematically integrates all these topics into education and practice. Individuals' development and functioning cannot be thoroughly understood without taking an integrative, holistic perspective that incorporates all these factors, and all of them can affect the behavior change process as well. In addition, building resilience and promoting optimal functioning over the long term often involves building strengths in these areas. When the focus of health care is broadened beyond the treatment of existing disorders to the prevention of maladjustment and the promotion of health and well-being in the population in general, then the importance of these factors becomes even clearer. Sociocultural factors also have a significant influence on individuals' physical health, the topic that is considered next.

6

PHYSICAL HEALTH

Standard approaches to behavioral health care assessment and treatment all note the effect of patients' medical functioning on psychological functioning. Although psychotherapists are not responsible for assessing and treating medical conditions, they are responsible for generally understanding the interaction of physical health and psychological functioning as well as knowing when referrals for medical evaluations may be needed. The biopsychosocial approach further highlights the interactions between biological, psychological, and social functioning. Research is showing in growing detail how these domains are inextricably intertwined. There has also been increasing recognition among all health care professionals of the importance of behavior and lifestyle on physical health and functioning. The Institute of Medicine (2004) concluded that roughly 50% of morbidity and mortality in the United States is caused by behavior and lifestyle factors and that medical schools must increase their coverage of behavioral influences on physical

DOI: 10.1037/14441-007
Biopsychosocial Practice: A Science-Based Framework for Behavioral Health Care, by T. P. Melchert
Copyright © 2015 by the American Psychological Association. All rights reserved.

health if physicians are to increase their effectiveness at treating medical conditions. The growing recognition of the relationship between behavior and disease may result in psychotherapists giving more attention to these factors as well.

This chapter provides an overview of the general medical health status of the U.S. public. It begins with a summary of the data on the prevalence of medical conditions in general and the prevalence of chronic disease, followed by an overview of the primary causes of disease and death and a summary of the general health status of North Americans and their quality of life and well-being. An overview of the physical health of individuals with mental illness is also provided because physical disease and premature death are especially prevalent in this population.

MEDICAL CONDITIONS

The U.S. Centers for Disease Control and Prevention has been monitoring the health status of the nation since 1957 using the National Health Interview Survey. Table 6.1 indicates the percentage of adults ages 18 and older in the latest survey who reported they were told by a doctor or other health care professional that they had the specific medical conditions listed (Schiller, Lucas, & Peregoy, 2012). Conditions are listed in order of decreasing prevalence and for those experienced by more than 1% of adults. Age was correlated with the prevalence of these conditions in many of the cases, although prevalence was elevated across all age groups in other cases.

The data in Table 6.1 indicate large amounts of discomfort, suffering, disease, and activity limitations for large proportions of the population. Many of the conditions listed cause pain or limit the ability to carry out social roles and responsibilities. Virtually all of the conditions have major psychological components in terms of etiology, treatment, and/or consequences. (These psychological components are the major focus of medical psychology as a specialization.)

Somatic symptoms are also the leading reason for outpatient medical visits in the United States, accounting for more than 50% of all visits, and at least 33% of these are medically unexplained (Kroenke, 2003). In addition, somatic symptoms are the predominant reason that 70% to 90% patients with depression, anxiety, or other common mental disorders seek primary care. The implications of these symptoms and conditions for the health and biopsychosocial functioning of the public become clearer when chronic disease prevalence is also taken into account.

TABLE 6.1
Medical Conditions in U.S. Adults

Disorder	Prevalence (%)
Overweight	34
Lower back pain	29 (in the past 3 months)
Chronic joint symptoms	29
Obesity	28
Hypertension	24
Arthritis, rheumatoid arthritis, gout, lupus, or fibromyalgia	22
Restlessness	19
Nervousness	17
Migraine/severe headaches	17 (in the past 3 months)
Hearing difficulty w/o hearing aid	16
Limitations in physical functioning	16
Neck pain	15 (in the past 3 months)
Felt everything was an effort	15
Sinusitis	13
Asthma	13 (8% still have it)
Sadness	12
Heart disease	11
Vision trouble (even with correction)	9
Diabetes	9
Absence of all natural teeth	8
Cancer	8
Hay fever	7
Ulcer	7
Hopelessness	7
Coronary heart disease	6
Worthlessness	5
Face/jaw pain	5 (in the past 3 months)
Chronic bronchitis	4
Stroke	3
Emphysema	2
Kidney disease	2 (in past 12 months)
Underweight	2
Liver disease	1 (in past 12 months)

Note. Rank ordered by prevalence. Data are from Schiller, Lucas, and Peregoy (2012).

CHRONIC DISEASE

In the last part of the 19th century, the world's population in industrialized countries began undergoing an *epidemiological transition* whereby the primary causes of disease and death, for the first time in human history, shifted from acute and infectious diseases to chronic diseases associated with behavior and lifestyle (Gribble & Preston, 1993). Chronic conditions have since become highly prevalent and have become the leading causes of death and disability. Recent research into the health of the U.S. population revealed the following findings:

- Seven out of 10 U.S. deaths each year are from chronic diseases (Kung et al., 2008).
- Nearly 50% of the U.S. adult population lives with a chronic health condition that requires routine adherence to prescribed treatment regimens and/or involves activity limitations (Partnership for Solutions, 2004).
- Approximately 25% of individuals with chronic conditions have one or more daily activity limitations (G. Anderson, 2004).

The prevalence of particular chronic diseases is very high.

- Heart disease is the leading cause of death in the United States, accounting for more than 30% of all mortality, and it is among the leading causes of disability (Kung et al., 2008).
- Cancer is the second leading cause of death, with lung cancer being the leading cause of cancer death in men and women, 80% of which is due to smoking or secondhand smoke exposure (Kung et al., 2008; Centers for Disease Control and Prevention [CDC], 2004).
- Stroke is the third leading cause of death, and 1 million Americans are disabled as a result of stroke (CDC, 2001).
- Nearly 24 million Americans have diabetes, and 57 million have prediabetes (CDC, 2008).
- Diabetes is the leading cause of kidney failure, nontraumatic lower extremity amputations, and blindness among adults ages 20 to 74 (CDC, 2008).
- If current trends continue, one in three Americans born in 2000 will develop diabetes during their lifetime (Venkat Narayan et al., 2003).
- Arthritis is the leading cause of disability, affecting one in every five adults (CDC, 2006).
- One in every three adults is obese, and almost one in five youth ages 6 to 19 is obese (Ogden, Carroll, & Flegal, 2008).

Chronic diseases have also become the leading causes of death worldwide. Trends that started in the United States and other industrialized countries are now affecting societies around the world. The World Health Organization (2008b) estimated that cardiovascular disease, cancer, chronic respiratory disease, and diabetes now account for approximately 60% of all deaths globally.

TABLE 6.2

Leading Causes of Death in the United States, 2011

Cause	Number
Heart disease	596,339
Cancer	575,313
Chronic lower respiratory diseases	143,382
Stroke (cerebrovascular diseases)	128,931
Accidents (unintentional injuries)	122,777
Alzheimer's disease	84,691
Diabetes	73,282
Nephritis, nephrotic syndrome, and nephrosis (kidney disease)	45,731
Influenza and pneumonia	53,667
Intentional self-harm (suicide)	38,285
Septicemia	35,539
Chronic liver disease and cirrhosis	33,539
Essential hypertension and hypertensive renal disease	27,477
Parkinson's disease	23,107
Pneumonia	18,090

Note. Data are from Hoyert and Xu (2012).

PRIMARY CAUSES OF DISEASE AND DEATH

Identifying the causes of disease and death are complicated topics because diseases and injuries often have multiple causes and several factors contribute to death in many cases (Mokdad, Marks, Stroup, & Gerberding, 2004). General conclusions regarding the primary and underlying causes of disease and death are nonetheless possible. The CDC annually collects data from the United States as a whole regarding the causes of death. Table 6.2 shows the 15 leading causes of death in 2011 (Hoyert & Xu, 2012).

Many of these diseases actually share a small number of underlying causes. Overall, the Institute of Medicine (2004) concluded that roughly 50% of morbidity and mortality in the United States is caused by behavior and lifestyle factors. Smoking is the leading cause of preventable morbidity and mortality and has been found to account for 18.1% of all deaths (CDC, 2004). Obesity has become the second leading cause of preventable morbidity and mortality and accounted for 16.6% of deaths (Mokdad et al., 2004). Alcohol consumption is the next most important factor (3.5% of deaths). The World Health Organization (2008c) arrived at very similar conclusions with regard to the health of the worldwide population. It estimated that up to 80% of heart disease, stroke, and Type 2 diabetes and more than one third of cancers worldwide could be prevented by eliminating the shared risk factors of tobacco use, unhealthy diet, physical inactivity, and excessive alcohol use. These four factors appear to be critical for reducing disease and death globally as well as in the United States.

MEASUREMENTS OF QUALITY OF LIFE AND WELL-BEING

Recent efforts to evaluate individuals' health status are extending beyond traditional indicators of disease, disability, and premature death. As the World Health Organization had already noted in 1946, the absence of disease does not imply health (see Chapter 7). Likewise, the presence of disease or disability does not imply poor quality of life. Many individuals with vision loss, difficulty with mobility, intellectual disability, or other significant disabilities live long, productive lives with high levels of quality of life and well-being. On the other hand, many individuals with no disease or disability lead lives with low quality of life and well-being. To gain a more complete assessment of health, quality of life, and well-being, more comprehensive evaluations of health necessarily cross all the psychological, sociocultural, and physical domains.

The Healthy People 2020 project, coordinated by the U.S. Department of Health and Human Services, is a major example of the broadened efforts to measure health and well-being in the United States. The first version of the Healthy People project was initiated by the Surgeon General's 1979 report on the health of the nation as a whole. Each decade since then, a new set of national objectives was developed to improve the health and well-being of the general public. The latest version of this effort, Healthy People 2020 (U.S. Department of Health and Human Services, 2013a), was initiated in 2010 and includes the following four overarching goals:

- attain high-quality, longer lives free of preventable disease, disability, injury, and premature death;
- achieve health equity, eliminate disparities, and improve the health of all groups;
- create social and physical environments that promote good health for all; and
- promote quality of life, healthy development, and healthy behaviors across all life stages (U.S. Department of Health and Human Services, 2013a).

To monitor progress toward these goals, the project uses a variety of measures of health status and quality of life. Some of the primary measures of general health status are listed (U.S. Department of Health and Human Services, 2013b):

- life expectancy (at birth and at age 65; in 2007, the United States ranked 26th and 27th for life expectancy at birth for males and females out of the 33 industrialized countries in the Organization for Economic Co-operation and Development [OECD]; OECD Health Division, 2012]),

- healthy life expectancy (the number of healthy years a person can expect to live, free of activity limitations and selected chronic diseases),
- years of potential life lost (a measure of early death, based on the number of deaths at each age up to some limit, 75 being the most common; early deaths consequently contribute more to this measure; the United States ranked 27th for males and 29th for females compared with 31 OECD countries for which these data were available),
- physically and mentally unhealthy days (based on self-report),
- self-assessed health status (in 2007, 9.5% reported their health to be poor or fair),
- limitation of activity, and
- chronic disease prevalence.

The Healthy People 2020 project is also evaluating several additional measures of health-related quality of life that will provide a more holistic bio-psychosocial assessment of functioning and well-being (U.S. Department of Health and Human Services, 2013c). These include measures of individuals' physical, mental, and social functioning along with assessments of satisfaction with life, positive emotions, resilience, and quality of relationships. Individuals' participation in educational, employment, civic, social, and leisure activities, regardless of physical limitations (e.g., vision loss, mobility difficulty) will also be measured. These additional assessments provide critical information for gaining a comprehensive perspective on health and well-being that extends beyond disease, disability, and life span.

PHYSICAL DISEASE, PREMATURE DEATH, AND MENTAL ILLNESS

There is a growing awareness of the especially serious physical health problems among those with severe mental illness. Individuals with mental illness have significantly higher rates of disease, and their life span is actually 9 years shorter than those without a mental health disorder (Druss, Zhao, Von Esenwein, Morrato, & Marcus, 2011). The most common causes of death for these individuals who self-identified as having a mental health disorder were chronic medical conditions such as cardiovascular disease and cancer (69%), whereas suicide, accidents, and homicide were relatively infrequent causes of death in this population (together accounting for 5% of deaths).

As mentioned in Chapter 4, according to the National Survey on Drug Use and Health an estimated 19.7% of the U.S. population had a mental

TABLE 6.3

Chronic Health Conditions, Emergency Room Use, and Hospitalization
in the Past Year for Adults With or Without Mental Illness

	Any mental illness (%)		Serious mental illness (%)		Major depressive episode (%)	
	Yes	No	Yes	No	Yes	No
High blood pressure	21.9	18.8	21.6	17.7	24.1	19.8
Asthma	15.7	10.6	19.1	12.1	17.0	11.4
Diabetes	7.9	6.6	7.7	6.6	8.9	7.1
Heart disease	5.9	4.2	5.2	4.2	6.5	4.6
Stroke	2.3	0.9	2.6	1.1	2.5	1.1
Emergency room use	38.8	27.1	47.6	30.5	43.3	28.7
Hospitalization	15.1	10.1	20.4	11.6	28.1	10.8

Note. Data are from Substance Abuse and Mental Health Services Administration, Center for Behavioral Health Statistics and Quality (2012).

illness in the past year, 4.6% had a serious mental illness, and 6.5% had major depressive episode (Substance Abuse and Mental Health Services Administration, Center for Behavioral Health Statistics and Quality, 2012). These individuals are at higher risk for some of the most prevalent health conditions and to use an emergency room or be hospitalized within the past year (see Table 6.3).

Individuals in the U.S. public mental health care system with serious mental illness suffer much higher rates of chronic disease and early death. The average life span for Americans in the public health system with serious mental illness is only 53 years, a remarkable 25 years shorter than the general population (Svendsen, Singer, Foti, & Mauer, 2006). In the State of Oregon, individuals with a dual diagnosis of mental illness and substance abuse in the public health system were found to have a life span of only 45 years, 32 years shorter than the general population (Oregon Department of Human Services, Addiction and Mental Health Division, 2008).

For most individuals with serious mental illness who die prematurely, death is the result of preventable conditions. Of individuals with serious mental illness in the public mental health system in the United States, it is estimated that 60% of premature deaths are due to preventable chronic conditions such as cardiovascular and pulmonary diseases and another 30% to 40% are due to suicide and injury (National Association of State Mental Health Program Directors, 2006). Nearly half of all cigarette consumption is by individuals with mental illness or substance use disorders (Lasser et al., 2000), and nearly 75% of people with serious mental illness are tobacco-dependent compared with 22% of the general population (Grant et al., 2004). This is clearly a major public health crisis for this segment of the population. It also presents major costs to society in terms of direct health care costs, lost productivity, impact on economic growth, and stress on public health care systems.

DISCUSSION: THE IMPORTANCE OF PHYSICAL HEALTH

Since the epidemiological transition that started in the late 19th century, the major causes of morbidity and mortality have switched from acute and infectious diseases to chronic diseases associated with behavior and lifestyle. This occurred first in industrialized countries but increasingly characterizes the health of the population globally. Chronic diseases account for the large majority of deaths in the United States and cause major amounts of suffering and disability that also limit daily activities for many individuals. The United States ranks high in morbidity and mortality rates in comparison to similarly industrialized countries (see also Chapter 12).

The underlying causes of disease and death in the United States and recently also around the world frequently involve behavior and lifestyle factors. Smoking and obesity are the leading underlying causes of preventable morbidity and mortality in the United States, and the Institute of Medicine (2004) concluded that approximately 50% of morbidity and mortality in this country is caused by behavior and lifestyle factors. The World Health Organization (2008a) further estimated that up to 80% of heart disease, stroke, and Type 2 diabetes and more than one third of cancers worldwide could be prevented by eliminating the following risk factors: tobacco use, unhealthy diet, physical inactivity, and excessive use of alcohol.

Individuals with mental illness are particularly likely to suffer chronic disease and early death. Indeed, the data regarding this issue are alarming. It appears that individuals with mental illness die nearly 9 years earlier than those without a mental disorder, and individuals in the public health care system with serious mental illness die on average 25 years earlier than the general population. Chronic illnesses have grown among the population in general, but the mentally ill population suffers particularly serious medical problems. There is an epidemic of serious chronic illness and shortened life span among those with serious mental illness. This takes a huge toll in the lives of these individuals and their loved ones and represents a true public health crisis.

In addition to having humanitarian concern about the suffering caused by physical illness, behavioral health care providers are also highly concerned about the impact of physical health on mental health and social functioning. Physical illness, disability, and poor health frequently prevent individuals from participating fully in life and carrying out important responsibilities. Physical health problems certainly have major effects on psychological and social functioning, just as psychological and social functioning have major effects on physical health. Indeed, virtually all of the most prevalent physical health conditions experienced by the U.S. public (see Table 6.1) have major psychological components in terms of etiology, treatment, and consequences. The specialization of health psychology has long focused on these issues, but the interaction and impact of these factors are unavoidable in all types of behavioral health care practice. Physical health conditions affect psychological functioning and the ability to fulfill family and work responsibilities for individuals with all types of mental disorders and for those with no mental disorders at all.

All health care professionals are increasingly recognizing the importance of these issues. Behavioral health care providers should also give more attention to the influence of behavior and lifestyle factors on physical health. When the goal of behavioral health care extends beyond just the treatment of mental disorders and also focuses on preventing disorders, building resilience, and promoting health and biopsychosocial functioning broadly, working to improve individuals' physical health becomes unavoidable. This would require, however, that behavioral health care education gives significant attention to these factors, something that occurs only infrequently at present. Many of the topics reviewed in this chapter do not receive extensive coverage in behavioral health care education programs. Even the major physical health problems of those dealing with serious mental illness are typically addressed in only a limited manner, if at all. According to the biopsychosocial approach to health care emphasized in this volume, all of these issues must be integrated into the knowledge and skills that psychologists bring to clinical practice.

7

BIOPSYCHOSOCIAL FACTORS INTERACTING OVER TIME: A DEVELOPMENTAL PERSPECTIVE

The biopsychosocial conceptualization of human development and functioning that underlies the approach taken in this volume was graphically depicted in Figure 1.1 as a cube intersected by an arrow. The three dimensions of the cube represented the inextricably intertwined biological, psychological, and sociocultural levels of natural organization that comprise the human organism; the arrow depicts the time dimension over which development takes place, the topic of this chapter. Those four dimensions are essential for capturing the basic nature of human development and functioning.

The developmental biopsychosocial perspective is tremendously complex. Indeed, the human mind and brain appears to be the most complex system known to exist. Nonetheless, research advances over recent decades have been steadily unraveling this complexity, and a great deal is now known about how biopsychosocial influences interact across time to produce developmental outcomes. This chapter highlights some of the findings that are essential

DOI: 10.1037/14441-008
Biopsychosocial Practice: A Science-Based Framework for Behavioral Health Care, by T. P. Melchert
Copyright © 2015 by the American Psychological Association. All rights reserved.

to the developmental perspective on human psychology. Development and change continue across the whole life span, but most of the discussion here focuses on childhood because of its importance in establishing the foundation for the interplay of vulnerabilities, dysfunction, strengths, and resources across the life span. Readers are reminded that this subject is very complex and requires extensive study to fully appreciate; here I outline only the basic features of the developmental framework that are necessary for gaining a science-based biopsychosocial understanding of human psychology.

KEY FEATURES OF A DEVELOPMENTAL FRAMEWORK

The development of maladjustment and psychopathology as well as the development of positive health must all be considered in terms of the individual and contextual factors that shape individuals' lives over the life span. There is substantial agreement regarding key features of the developmental perspective that can bring together those factors into a single integrative framework (Cicchetti & Toth, 1992; Kellam & Rebok, 1992; Masten et al., 2008; National Research Council and Institute of Medicine, 2009; Sameroff & Fiese, 1990). The following features are discussed in this section:

- age-related changes in abilities;
- multiple contexts within which development occurs;
- interactions among biological, psychological, and social factors; and
- developmental tasks and competence.

Age-Related Changes in Abilities

Understanding age-related changes in cognitive, emotional, and behavioral abilities is essential for appreciating human development. These change processes are fundamental to the development of health and competence as well as maladjustment and disorder. Biological, cognitive, emotional, behavioral, interpersonal, and other social changes take place throughout life. The earliest period, however, from conception to about age 5, receives special attention because the opportunity to establish a foundation for future development is greater during this stage than at any other time in a person's life (National Research Council and Institute of Medicine, 2000, 2009). Competencies and resilience developed at this stage form the foundation for the development of future competencies throughout later childhood, adolescence, and adulthood. Likewise, the development of dysfunction and vulnerabilities at this stage can lead to repeated challenges across the biopsychosocial domains and across the life span.

Multiple Contexts Within Which Development Occurs

Urie Bronfenbrenner's (1979) ecological perspective on human development is a widely accepted approach to conceptualizing the many levels of environmental influence on human development. This model posits that human development occurs within an ecological system comprising five subsystems: *microsystem* (the immediate environment; e.g., family, school, neighborhood, friends), *mesosystem* (relations between microsystems; e.g., relations between one's family members and school personnel), *exosystem* (relations with settings in which one does not have an active role, e.g., a spouse's work requirements that affect child care and home life), *macrosystem* (one's culture, e.g., socioeconomic class, ethnicity, religion), and *chronosystem* (the historical context, both in terms of how personal events such as a divorce play out over time as well as the sociohistorical context in which one lives). More recently, Bronfenbrenner (2001) added a sixth level that recognizes the importance of *biology*; he labeled his latest version of the model *bioecological theory*. Developmental processes play out within the context of these nested systems, as do behavioral health care interventions and prevention programs.

Interactions Among Biological, Psychological, and Social Factors

The biopsychosocial perspective is essential to the developmental framework. As emphasized throughout this book, human development and functioning cannot be understood without recognizing the interaction among genetic and other biological processes, individual psychological processes, and multiple levels of sociocultural influences from the family to culture and the sociohistorical context. The interplay of these factors is tremendously complex; ongoing research is steadily uncovering how their interaction produces vulnerabilities and dysfunction as well as competence and strengths. Notable examples of the mechanisms underlying these interactions were discussed in Chapter 2 with regard to recent advances in understanding epigenetics and neural plasticity.

Developmental Tasks and Competence

A key feature of developmental frameworks concerns the behavioral expectations that individuals encounter in particular social contexts across their lifetimes. These situations, often referred to as *developmental tasks*, change as one grows older and differ according to culture, gender, and historical period (Kellam & Rebok, 1992; Masten, Burt, & Coatsworth, 2006). Success or difficulty with one developmental task can have major consequences for success in other tasks and for the later development of problems and psychopathology.

Successfully accomplishing developmentally appropriate tasks leads to a positive sense of mastery, self-esteem, social inclusion, well-being, and resilience; failure with these tasks can contribute to maladjustment and psychopathology. The National Research Council and Institute of Medicine (2000) found that accomplishing the developmental tasks of secure attachment, emotional regulation, executive functioning, and appropriate conduct during infancy and early childhood was associated with healthy development and the prevention of behavioral health problems over the long term. Masten et al. (2006) referred to the accomplishment of these tasks as *developmental competence*. In a longitudinal study called Project Competence, they examined the development of three dimensions of competence during childhood (academic, social, and conduct) and five dimensions of competence in late adolescence (academic, social, conduct, job, and romantic).

No attempt is made here to review the many age-related change processes and developmental tasks that take place from the point of conception through the end of life. This is a highly complex subject, and it is difficult even for specialists to keep current with new findings. One of the most important of these processes, however, is attachment. It embodies all of the key features of a developmental framework and has major effects on individuals' personality, psychopathology, and adjustment across the life span. These effects are also the focus of a significant amount of behavioral health care intervention. Therefore, the importance of attachment is highlighted in connection with a prototypical example of a developmental task.

ATTACHMENT AS A PROTOTYPICAL EXAMPLE

Infant attachment provided a good solution to one of the most daunting problems faced by our early hominid ancestors, namely, how to ensure that infants survive during the long years of extreme vulnerability resulting from our long maturation period (Simpson & Belsky, 2008). John Bowlby provided the most thorough explanation of this process. As a result, Bowlby could be considered the first modern evolutionary psychologist (Belsky, 2007). He drew heavily from Darwin when formulating attachment theory (and Darwin himself [1859] predicted that psychology would develop an evolutionary basis). His theory was described in his famous *Attachment and Loss* trilogy of books (Bowlby, 1969, 1973, 1980) and has developed into the dominant approach to understanding early socioemotional development.

Mary Ainsworth and her colleagues developed the classic Strange Situation laboratory procedure for assessing attachment security when infants are 12 months of age (Ainsworth, Blehar, Waters, & Wall, 1978). This procedure involves a series of eight 3-minute episodes involving separations and reunions between the child, the mother, and a female stranger in an experimental room. The child never leaves the room, but the mother and female stranger leave on two occasions. Based primarily on patterns of infant behavior toward their mothers during the second reunion, the infants are classified into the specific classifications of A1 (high avoidance), A2 (low avoidance), B1 (secure with some avoidance), B2 and B3 (secure), B4 (secure with some anxiety), C1 (anxious, angry, and ambivalent), C2 (anxious, passive, and ambivalent), or D (disorganized, highly ambivalent, unpredictable behavior that includes avoidance of the mother).

A large research literature finds that infant attachment is an important predictor of socioemotional adjustment across the life span. Infant attachment has been shown to initiate developmental trajectories that probabilistically lead to differences in important areas of personal and interpersonal functioning. Infant attachment classifications predict behavior problems and psychopathology during childhood and adolescence (e.g., DeKlyen & Greenberg, 2008) as well as the quality of individuals' personal and interpersonal functioning in adulthood (e.g., Berlin, Cassidy, & Appleyard, 2008; Mikulincer & Shaver, 2007). Infant attachment is clearly not deterministic—subsequent developmental experiences such as a change in family circumstances, intimate relationships, or psychotherapy can push developmental trajectories in either positive or negative directions (e.g., Salvatore, Kuo, Steele, Simpson, & Collins, 2011; L. A. Sroufe, Egeland, Carlson, & Collins, 2005). Nonetheless, children's relationships with their early caregivers appear to provide the critical experience that sets these developmental trajectories in motion. Indeed, A. Sroufe and Siegel (2011) concluded that "the emotional quality of our earliest attachment experience is perhaps the single most important influence on human development" (p. 34).

Research finds that one's attachment style is associated with a wide range of outcomes across the psychological, interpersonal, and social realms, including emotional regulation, behavioral self-regulation, psychopathology, interpersonal and relationship functioning, sexual functioning, and behavioral functioning in work and organizational settings (Cassidy & Shaver, 2008; Mikulincer & Shaver, 2007). More serious problems with attachment (e.g., disorganized) that are associated with more adverse early experiences and risk factors (e.g., severe child maltreatment) are also more likely to lead to more serious developmental outcomes (e.g., borderline personality disorder). One's own attachment history appears to have a strong effect on one's parenting as well. Parents' perceptions of their own childhood attachments have been found to predict the attachment classification of their children 75% of the time (Main, Kaplan, & Cassidy, 1985; Steele, Steele, & Fonagy, 1996).

Research finds that attachment style is also relatively enduring. The continuity of attachment from infancy to adulthood is moderately stable, and the continuity of attachment across adulthood is quite stable (approximately 70% of adults receive the same attachment classification across time periods extending up to 25 years; Mikulincer & Shaver, 2007). Given the stability and impact of attachment style, it is disheartening that only about 65% of infants in the general population are found to be securely attached; the remaining 35% are distributed among the three insecure classifications (i.e., avoidant, anxious-ambivalent, and disorganized).

CO-OCCURRING CONDITIONS

Chapters 4 through 6 in this volume highlighted the significant prevalence of psychological, social, and physical health problems in the general population. In addition, large numbers of individuals are dealing with multiple co-occurring problems across multiple areas of their lives. Co-occurring problems can present especially challenging situations for individuals, their families, and health care and human service professionals.

Children commonly have more than one mental, emotional, or behavioral disorder. Angold, Costello, and Erkanli (1999) and Armstrong and Costello (2002) found that the odds of children having attention-deficit/ hyperactivity disorder are 10 times more likely if a child has a conduct or oppositional defiant disorder, the odds of having a substance use disorder are 8 times more likely if a child has a conduct or oppositional defiant disorder, and the odds of having an anxiety disorder are 8 times more likely if a child has depression. They found that there was significant comorbidity among disruptive behavior disorders, attention-deficit/hyperactivity disorder, and substance abuse disorders, and among emotional disorders (anxiety and depression); there was much less comorbidity among the emotional and the disruptive behavioral disorders.

Co-occurring mental disorders are highly prevalent in adulthood as well. In the National Comorbidity Survey (Kessler et al., 1994), 48.0% of the respondents ages 15 to 54 years had one or more mental disorders over the course of their lifetimes, but the vast majority of lifetime disorders (79.0%) were comorbid with at least one other disorder. There were 21.0% who had a lifetime history of just one disorder, 13.0% who had two lifetime disorders, and 14.0% who had three or more lifetime disorders. This latter subgroup of individuals who had a lifetime history of three or more disorders also accounted for the large majority of those with severe disorders within the past 12 months (i.e., that required hospitalization or whose disorder created severe role impairment). In fact, 89.5% of those with severe 12-month disorders also had a lifetime history of three or more disorders. The prevalence of mental disorders remained largely unchanged when the survey was replicated a decade later (Kessler et al., 2005). Though mental disorders are widespread in the United States, the major burden of psychiatric illness appears to be concentrated in a group with highly comorbid conditions who comprise approximately one seventh (i.e., 14%) of the population.

The comorbidity of mental and physical health conditions is also high. More than half of patients with chronic medical diseases meet the criteria for co-occurring mental disorders (Agency for Healthcare Research and Quality, 2009). As noted in Chapter 6, individuals with mental illness have higher rates of disease and a life span that is actually 9 years shorter on average than those without a mental disorder (Druss et al., 2011). Cardiovascular disease and cancer were the cause of death for 69% of these individuals, whereas suicide, accidents, and homicide were relatively infrequently causes of death (together accounting for 5% of deaths). Individuals with serious mental illness in the public mental health system in the United States have alarming rates of serious physical health problems. The life span for these individuals is only 53 years—25 years shorter than the general population (Svendsen, Singer, Foti, & Mauer, 2006). Preventable conditions such as cardiovascular and pulmonary disease account for the majority of the premature death in this population.

RISK AND PROTECTIVE FACTORS

Risk and protective factors play critical roles in the development of dysfunction, disorder, developmental competence, and resilience. *Risk factors* are "characteristics, variables, or hazards that, if present for a given individual, make it more likely that this individual, rather than someone selected from the general population, will develop a disorder" (Institute of Medicine, 1994, p. 6). Some risk factors such as genetic inheritance or gender are generally not malleable to change. Causal risk factors, on the other hand, are factors that can be changed and are associated with a change in outcomes, such as lack of social support, low reading ability, or being victimized by bullying (Durlak & Wells, 1997; Kraemer, Kazdin, & Offord, 1997).

Protective factors are internal or external influences that improve an individual's response to a risk factor (Rutter, 1979). Supportive parents or other adults in the community, for example, are important external protective factors against developing a wide range of maladaptive outcomes in children (National Research Council and Institute of Medicine, 2009). Resilience is an important internal protective factor affecting an individual's response to stressors or traumatic events across the life span (Garmezy & Rutter, 1983). Protective factors sometimes cannot be distinguished from risk factors because they represent the same bipolar variable at the positive end (e.g., effective parenting, high academic achievement) rather than the negative end (e.g., poor parenting, low academic achievement; Luthar, 2003). Attachment insecurity may be the most important risk factor of all in terms of socioemotional outcomes, and it operates in a bipolar manner: Attachment insecurity is a major risk factor while attachment security is protective. Child maltreatment is an important risk factor that is unipolar, however, ranging from none to severe. (The absence of maltreatment is obviously a good thing, but it does not imply positive parenting.)

Risk and protective factors occur at all ecological levels from the biological to the psychological, family, community, and cultural levels. For example, in a synthesis of 18 meta-analytic reviews of the literature, Crews et al. (2007) found that the strongest risk factors for either child internalizing or externalizing problems were comorbid internalizing or externalizing problems, family stress (e.g., divorce, single parenting), corporal punishment, school disengagement, delinquent peers, and poor relations with peers. Risk and protective factors also tend to be inversely correlated. In a sample of 6th to 12th graders, Pollard, Hawkins, and Arthur (1999) found that students in the highest quintile on cumulative risk factors were likely to be in the lowest quintile on protective factors.

Strong Cumulative Effect

Predicting the psychological outcomes that develop in particular individuals is imprecise, just as it is for predicting medical outcomes. Many different developmental pathways may result in the same outcome (*equifinality*), just as one particular developmental starting point can lead to many different outcomes (*multifinality;* Cicchetti & Rogosch, 1996). The cumulative effect of risk and protective factors in predicting maladjustment is quite powerful, however.

Rutter (1979) first proposed the cumulative risk model to show that as the number of risks that children face increases, the developmental status of the child decreases. The following groups of children face an accumulation of risk factors that are associated with a variety of negative outcomes: children with difficult temperaments and low intelligence; children who live in families with serious parental conflict, violence, substance abuse, or behavioral disorder; and children who live in a distressed community with inadequate schools. In a nationally representative sample of children up to 3 years of age who were investigated for child maltreatment, Barth et al. (2008) found that the children as a whole experienced a large number of risk factors, including:

- child maltreatment (100%),
- minority status (58%),

- single caregiver (48%),
- poverty (46%),
- domestic violence (40%),
- caregiver substance abuse (39%),
- caregiver mental health problem (30%),
- low caregiver education (29%),
- biomedical risk condition (22%),
- teenaged caregiver (19%), and
- four or more children in home (14%).

Barth and colleagues (2008) also found that large numbers of these children had measurable developmental delays in their cognitive, language, or emotional functioning that would prevent many of them from being ready to enter kindergarten or first grade. Particularly important was their finding that the number of risk factors present at baseline was strongly associated with having a measured developmental delay. Having one or two risk factors (e.g., maltreatment alone or maltreatment plus one other risk factor) was associated with only a 5% rate of measured delays. The risk of measured delays increased very quickly, however, as the number of risk factors increased, and nearly all children (99%) having 7 risk factors had measured developmental delays (see Figure 7.1).

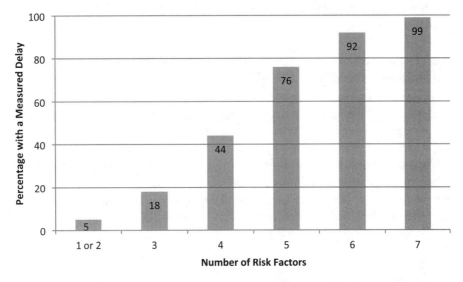

Figure 7.1. Percentage of maltreated children up to 3 years old with a measured developmental delay by number of risk factors present at baseline. Adapted from *Developmental Status and Early Intervention Service Needs of Maltreated Children* (p. 19), by R. P. Barth, A. A. Scarborough, E. C. Lloyd, J. L. Losby, C. Casanueva, and T. Mann, 2008, Washington, DC: U.S. Department of Health and Human Services, Office of the Assistant Secretary for Planning and Evaluation. In the public domain.

An Integrative Framework: Nurturing Environments

Research into the risk and protective factors for healthy and maladaptive development has grown steadily in recent years. The research has been fragmented, however, coming out of a variety of disciplines that examine a wide range of mental and physical health, substance abuse, educational, and criminal justice outcomes. Public health efforts to reduce risk factors and increase protective factors are similarly fragmented, resulting in sluggish progress in understanding how to reduce maladaptive development and improve health and well-being. Biglan, Flay, Embry, and Sandler (2012) recently proposed an integrative perspective to translate developmental research knowledge into a practical framework that can lead to more effective interventions for preventing mental, emotional, and behavioral problems from developing.

Biglan et al. (2012) noted that the available research evidence supports two conclusions: that psychological, emotional, and behavioral problems tend to co-occur, and that these problems derive largely from the same conditions. They further concluded that the available evidence supports the following basic principle: "If we want to prevent multiple problems and increase the prevalence of young people who develop successfully, we must increase the prevalence of nurturing environments" (p. 258). They then argued that nurturing environments can be fostered by focusing on four key features: (a) biologically and socially toxic conditions (e.g., unhealthy diets, child abuse, poverty) must be minimized because they interfere with healthy development; (b) opportunities for young people to engage in problem behavior must be limited through improved monitoring and appropriate enforcement of behavioral expectations and rules; (c) *prosociality* (i.e., the motivation and skills needed to play prosocial roles in society) must be taught, promoted, and reinforced because it increases mental, emotional, and behavioral well-being; and (d) psychological flexibility must be promoted. They conceptualized *psychological flexibility* as "being clear about one's values and mindful of one's thoughts and feelings and acting in the service of one's values even when thoughts and feelings discourage taking valued action" (p. 263; this is very similar to concepts advocated by acceptance and commitment therapy and the mindfulness movements; see Hayes, Strosahl, & Wilson, 1999, and Kabat-Zinn, 2005, respectively).

HEALTH, WELL-BEING, AND FLOURISHING

As noted in Chapter 4, for centuries medicine emphasized the treatment of disorders, pathology, and dysfunction because of the overwhelming impact of disease, injury, and disability on people's survival in the challenging environments that characterized most of human history. Over the past century and a half, however, scientific advances have led to dramatic improvements in understanding and controlling disease, far more children surviving to adulthood, mothers surviving childbirth, and much longer life spans for those who reached adulthood. After remaining fairly constant for most of human history, life span in the United States nearly doubled over the last century and a half, and it rose from 47 in 1900 (the first year for which reliable data are available) to 77 a century later (Arias, 2004). For the first time in human history, the primary causes of illness and death shifted from acute and infectious disease to chronic diseases associated with modifiable lifestyle causes, a shift known as the *epidemiological transition* (Gribble & Preston, 1993).

The dramatic extension of life expectancy over the past century and a half never occurred before in our history as a species. As a result, humans' psychological experience of life is also undergoing a fundamental shift. Focus has shifted from meeting basic biological needs (lower levels in terms of natural organization) to psychological and social ones. John Maynard Keynes (1930/1972) expressed the challenge as how "to live wisely and agreeably and well" (p. 328) once desperation and deprivation are no longer the driving forces of human existence. Abraham Maslow (1943) conceptualized individuals' biopsychosocial needs in terms of a hierarchy where one's basic material and security needs had to be met before the needs for feeling loved, a sense of belonging, and self-esteem could be met. Only after these needs were met could one focus on self-actualization and the full pursuit of meaning and fulfillment in life. Carl Rogers (1961) famously described similar aspirations in terms of becoming a "fully functioning" person. The individuals who met to organize the United Nations following the tremendous devastation of World War II were also concerned with improving health and health care around the world. They formed the World Health Organization (chartered in 1948) and adopted a broad definition of *health* that reads, "Health is a state of complete physical, mental and social well-being and not merely the absence of disease or infirmity" (1948; the definition has not been amended since). For the first time in history, humans in large numbers could look beyond just the absence of disease and infirmity to a more complete state of health that also included psychosocial well-being.

These ideas are now well established in our culture as well as in psychology. Maslow's (1943) hierarchy of needs model is perhaps the best known approach to conceptualizing the relationship of different types of human needs and aspirations. More recently, Martin Seligman's advocacy of positive psychology has also become well known. He recently expanded the focus of his theory and research beyond happiness and life satisfaction to include flourishing more broadly. In his original theory, called *authentic happiness*, M. Seligman (2002) focused on three elements that he argued accounted for happiness: positive emotion, engagement, and meaning. Positive emotion focuses on pleasant feelings, engagement focuses on "flow" and being fully absorbed in activities that are important to a person, and meaning focuses on serving larger purposes in life. M. Seligman (2011) has since added positive relationships and accomplishment to the original three elements. The resulting PERMA model (i.e., positive emotion, engagement, positive relationships, meaning, and accomplishment) is focused on well-being instead of just happiness and has flourishing as its overall goal.

The research reviewed in this and previous chapters clearly indicates that many individuals are not enjoying high levels of the PERMA elements or other indicators of happiness, well-being, and flourishing. Several research programs have investigated this topic (for reviews, see Linley, Harrington, & Garcea, 2009; Lopez & Snyder, 2011; Shaver & Mikulincer, 2012). Keyes took an integrative biopsychosocial approach to this problem and found that anything less than a state of positive mental health (which he referred to as *flourishing*) is associated with increased functional impairment and increased physical and mental health problems. Using nationally representative survey data, Keyes (2007) estimated that roughly only two in 10 Americans are flourishing, whereas nearly two in 10 are in poor mental health (which he referred to as *languishing*). He found that most of the rest were in between, a level that is associated with moderate distress, lower social well-being, and a moderate number of chronic physical conditions. That nearly eight in 10 Americans are not experiencing positive mental health and are instead experiencing moderate to serious distress and dysfunction represents a serious public health issue that is getting insufficient attention from the profession and the public. The proportion of people who are flourishing should be much higher.

DISCUSSION: DEVELOPMENT AS THE CRITICAL FOURTH DIMENSION

The developmental perspective on human psychology provides the time dimension that helps integrate the many biopsychosocial influences on development and functioning into a unified metatheoretical framework. It highlights the connections between these influences in terms of age-related changes and developmental tasks that are occurring at any one time as well as the evolution of developmental outcomes and processes across the life span. It links early experiences with personality and socioemotional processes in childhood, adolescence, and adulthood. It also highlights the importance of the multiple environmental contexts within which psychological developmental occurs.

The integrative developmental biopsychosocial perspective is critical for conceptualizing behavioral health care. Human development and functioning have been investigated from the perspective of numerous psychology subfields, multiple biological specializations, medicine and public health, and several social science disciplines. These fields sometimes use terminology differently, rely on different research methodologies, and focus on different variables and processes. The research literature is consequently fragmented. Research progress is slowed as a result, and practical applications based on this research are also slow to emerge. A scientific integration of these findings is necessary to make this research more useful for behavioral health care and preventive interventions. The work on nurturing environments by Biglan et al. (2012) was noted above to highlight the importance of finding integrative perspectives that can lead to faster progress with research and practical applications.

One of the themes that emerges from the four chapters in Part II of this volume is that many people suffer significant pathology, dysfunction, and distress. The prevalence of problems recounted in these chapters is very high, and many people are dealing with multiple problems across the biopsychosocial domains. The number of individuals who are flourishing is far too low. Research is advancing, however, and interventions to reduce dysfunction and distress are improving. Prevention and health promotion strategies are also improving. Parts III and IV of this book discuss how this research can be applied in clinical practice to treat behavioral health problems and promote biopsychosocial functioning in the population in general.

III

THE BEHAVIORAL HEALTH CARE TREATMENT PROCESS FROM THE BIOPSYCHOSOCIAL PERSPECTIVE

8

ASSESSMENT

The overarching purpose of the science-based biopsychosocial approach to behavioral health care is the application of science and ethics to meet individuals' behavioral health needs and promote their biopsychosocial functioning. Assessment plays the initiating role in the treatment process for reaching this purpose. Assessment occurs continuously throughout treatment—at each patient contact therapists normally engage in some type of assessment of the patient's functioning and the progress of treatment. Therapists also assess the effectiveness of treatment at termination and often afterwards in terms of follow-up. Assessment is therefore important throughout the treatment process. It is critical at the outset, however, because the initial assessment of a patient's concerns and situation significantly affects how the parties involved conceptualize the issues. Decisions about how to proceed are based on this initial evaluation; at this point a decision is made whether any further intervention or contact is even needed.

DOI: 10.1037/14441-009
Biopsychosocial Practice: A Science-Based Framework for Behavioral Health Care, by T. P. Melchert
Copyright © 2015 by the American Psychological Association. All rights reserved.

A wide variety of conceptual frameworks have been applied to understanding the process of psychological assessment over the history of behavioral health care. The dominant approach in the United States in the past three decades has involved the *Diagnostic and Statistical Manual of Mental Disorders* (*DSM*) published by the American Psychiatric Association. There are many issues beyond psychiatric diagnosis that are important in behavioral health assessment, but this manual has played a leading role in how mental disorders are conceptualized. The first two editions of this manual (1952, 1968) were based on a psychoanalytic understanding of personality and psychopathology. However, in the 1970s, the field of American psychiatry took a different direction when it employed an atheoretical, descriptive approach that largely excluded considerations of etiology and development. The third edition (*DSM–III*), published in 1980, reflected this approach and thereby avoided some of the shortcomings of the earlier editions. As a result, the *DSM–III* became much more influential. Its basic conceptualization of psychodiagnosis has also continued through to the latest (fifth) edition, the *DSM–5* (American Psychiatric Association, 2013). Now most psychiatrists primarily prescribe psychotropic medicines based on a biological formulation of assessment and treatment (Mojtabai & Olfson, 2008). (The basic purposes of science are often stated as going from description to explanation, prediction, and control. The *DSM* has been focused on the lowest level of these scientific goals.)

Whereas the *DSM–III* and subsequent editions of the manual have taken an atheoretical, descriptive approach, a wide range of theoretical orientations has emerged within psychology for explaining the nature, etiology, and treatment of psychopathology. Carl Rogers (1951), the founder of humanistic psychology, argued that "psychological diagnosis is unnecessary for psychotherapy, and may actually be detrimental to the therapeutic process" (p. 220). Instead of conducting assessment and treatment planning, Rogers argued that providing empathy, genuineness, and unconditional positive regard within the therapy relationship were "necessary and sufficient" for successful therapy outcome and constructive personality change. Behavior therapists also tended to neglect formal psychological assessment and instead focused on symptoms (Hayes & Follette, 1992). Behaviorists often viewed symptoms as the problem and conducted a functional analysis of behavior to identify the environmental contingencies that reinforced behaviors and that would then be used to guide treatment. Cognitive therapists traditionally relied on general formulations about the causes, precipitants, and maintaining influences of depression (Beck, Freeman, Davis, & Associates, 2004), anxiety (Beck, Emery, & Greenberg, 1985), and other disorders. These general formulations tended to be applied to everyone within a diagnostic category, though recently more individualized cognitive behavior therapy case formulations are also being advocated (Persons & Tompkins, 2007). Like humanistic therapists, postmodern constructivist therapists also generally deemphasized assessment and case conceptualization. Solution-oriented therapists were largely uninterested in the nature or causes of a person's problems (de Shazer, 1985), whereas narrative therapists would argue that objective knowledge is not possible and so the client and therapist together need to co-construct an understanding of the client's life and situation (White & Epston, 1990).

These varied approaches to assessment and case conceptualization present a very complicated picture that is emblematic of the pre-paradigmatic era of the behavioral health field. Therapists could select from an eclectic array of theoretical orientations to guide their clinical work, and the orientation they chose frequently affected the type of information they collected, their understanding of that information, and the type of treatment that would then be recommended and provided. A common question asked by therapists concerns the extensive psychosocial history information that often has to be collected because it is required, for example, in hospitals and clinics accredited by the Joint Commission. In many cases, much of this information goes unused. When operating on the basis of a traditional theoretical orientation, one's adopted orientation may determine the type of assessment information that is needed and the treatment provided. Gathering comprehensive psychosocial history information about a case is consequently often not particularly useful.

A science-based biopsychosocial approach to behavioral health care is oriented very differently from these traditional approaches. Instead of choosing from one of the traditional theoretical orientations in the field, assessment and treatment are based on a unified scientific understanding of development, functioning, and behavior change. This approach recognizes that safe and effective therapies are available for addressing behavioral health needs, and the understanding of which treatment approach is indicated in particular cases is based on a comprehensive biopsychosocial assessment and treatment plan, not on one's preferred theoretical orientation. This approach to assessment and case conceptualization can be complex, particularly when compared with some traditional approaches that focus on a limited set of issues highlighted by a particular theoretical orientation. This chapter clarifies that complexity by discussing the important components and processes involved and placing them in a logical sequence. The overall goal of this process is to produce comprehensive and thoroughly evaluated assessment results for informing the remaining phases of treatment.

This chapter outlines the general conceptual framework for a unified science-based biopsychosocial approach to behavioral health care assessment. The following chapters then show how to use that information to plan and carry out treatment, monitor its progress, and assess its effectiveness at termination and follow-up. Extensive knowledge of human development; psychopathology; the biological, psychological, and sociocultural bases of behavior; legal and ethical issues; and measurement must be combined with strong interviewing, relationship building, and other skills to competently conduct behavioral health assessment. This chapter does not address those subject areas but instead focuses on the conceptualization of the basic purposes and processes of behavioral health care assessment. The discussion encompasses behavioral health care in general. It provides the overarching framework that can be applied across all types of general and specialized practice and behavioral health care settings.

RATIONALE FOR AND CHARACTERISTICS OF THE SCIENCE-BASED BIOPSYCHOSOCIAL APPROACH TO BEHAVIORAL HEALTH CARE ASSESSMENT

The conceptual foundations of the science-based biopsychosocial approach to assessment in behavioral health care are based on the scientific understanding of human psychology and on professional ethics, and the overarching purpose of this approach is to provide health care services that meet individuals' behavioral health needs and improve their biopsychosocial functioning. These foundations and overarching purpose result in several perspectives that are different from many traditional approaches to assessment in the field but are essential in a science-based, health care-oriented approach.

A Unified Scientific Approach to Understanding Behavioral Health Care

The most important characteristic of the science-based biopsychosocial approach to understanding human psychology and behavioral health care is its conceptual foundations in professional ethics and scientific knowledge regarding human development, functioning, and behavior change. This results in a very different perspective on assessment compared with approaches based on the traditional theoretical orientations. In a traditional approach, one's theoretical orientation often dominates the assessment findings; a clinician's orientation frequently determines how an individual's concerns and disorders are diagnosed, conceptualized, and then treated (Garb, 1998). The results of an assessment and treatment plan are often predictable depending on whether one consults a clinician with a biological, psychoanalytic, cognitive, systemic, eye-movement desensitization and reprocessing, or other orientation. This approach developed for logical historical reasons (see Chapter 2), but its assumptions and conceptual foundations are not consistent with a science-based biopsychosocial approach to understanding human psychology and behavioral health care.

The biopsychosocial approach to behavioral health care assessment uses just one unified scientific framework for understanding development, functioning, and behavior change. Therapists might use a variety of evidence-based therapies to treat problems and disorders depending on the circumstances of a case, but there is still just one science-based perspective for understanding human psychology and behavioral health problems. The scientific understanding of human psychology is extraordinarily complex and much remains to be discovered, but the field has evolved to the point where human development, functioning, and the practice of behavioral health care can all be understood from a single unified scientific perspective.

The biopsychosocial approach to behavioral health care is also oriented around its role as a health care profession, the basic purpose of which is meeting the health needs of the public. It is not oriented around being a service industry that offers a range of behavioral health services and consumers taking primary responsibility for making decisions about which services best fit their needs and preferences. Instead, it is oriented around being a health care profession that applies scientific knowledge and health care ethics in an evidence-based manner that integrates the best available research evidence, clinical experience, and information regarding patients' values and preferences to meet individuals' health needs (American Psychological Association Presidential Task Force on Evidence-Based Practice, 2006; Institute of Medicine, 2001). This overriding purpose guides the knowledge, skills, and dispositions that therapists bring to their clinical work.

Reliable and Valid Assessment

The reliability and validity of behavioral health assessment findings are important from the perspective of both the scientific and ethical foundations of behavioral health care. The scientific underpinnings of the field strongly emphasize reliable and valid measurement of human characteristics. Measurement reliability and validity are fundamental in psychology and all of science—science simply does not progress without accurate measurement. Research into the epidemiology and etiology of psychopathology, the effectiveness of treatment for different conditions, and a host of other important behavioral health care questions has limited usefulness without reliable and valid measure of all the predictor and outcome variables. Health care likewise loses its scientific credibility without reliable, valid assessment and diagnosis.

The ethical foundations of behavioral health care also require reliable and valid assessment in terms of the safety and effectiveness of intervention. Unreliable and inaccurate assessments carry major risks of not helping and actually causing harm. Among the clearest examples of the harm that can result are unreliable suicide or homicide risk assessments. As mentioned in

Chapter 3, the patient safety movement in American health care over the past decade resulted in part from concerns about the impact of missed and delayed diagnosis, and depression with subsequent suicide attempt may be among the common missed diagnoses that result in death (Schiff et al., 2009; Wachter, 2009).

Unreliable and inaccurate behavioral health assessments can be unhelpful or harmful in more subtle ways as well. Assessment findings have a major impact on how problems, dysfunction, strengths, and resources are understood by the patient, therapist, and other stakeholders and on the services that are provided as a result. If relevant issues are not pursued or insufficient rapport with patients results in important information not being elicited, problems can easily be missed or misidentified. For example, a child's academic failures in school might be misattributed to a lack of motivation and effort rather than to a learning disability; discrimination the child is facing related to their sex, race, culture, or sexual orientation; or abuse or neglect the child is experiencing at home. When this happens, the child's problems may very well go unresolved, which itself entails a number of negative sequelae. In addition, the child may internalize a negative self-concept and sense of self-efficacy that may remain over his or her lifetime and that is not only inaccurate but also maladaptive. Therapists' ethical obligations to not cause harm, prevent foreseeable harms, and provide benefit clearly can be violated if their assessments are unreliable or invalid.

Incorporation of Biopsychosocial Domains, Strengths, and Weaknesses

A main feature of the biopsychosocial approach is its comprehensive integrative approach to understanding health and functioning. This approach is based on the recognition that psychological outcomes are multifactorially determined from the interaction of the inextricably intertwined psychological, sociocultural, and biological influences on development and functioning. Individuals clearly also have strengths as well as weaknesses across all these domains. Gaining a complete and accurate assessment of an individual's needs and functioning consequently requires the integration of knowledge regarding strengths and resources in addition to problems, disorders, and vulnerabilities.

Behavioral health care assessment that is based on this approach consequently requires a biopsychosocial perspective as well as an assessment of how an individual functions well and poorly across the important areas of their lives. Indeed, what individuals do well or possess in terms of a strength often has as much significance in their lives as what they do poorly or what they lack. For example, a person who has had little success with intimate relationships and has highly conflictual relationships with parents and siblings may have very fulfilling friendships, may be a highly competent and valued employee, and may enjoy excellent physical health as a result of careful attention to diet and exercise. Another individual may suffer from a severe and persistent mental illness but is reliable, caring, and loyal and provides much needed support within the family. These individuals' lives cannot begin to be understood without a holistic approach that recognizes strengths as well as weaknesses and the full spectrum of biopsychosocial functioning. Focusing only on a person's maladaptive characteristics or behaviors or only on particular areas from across the biopsychosocial domains can lead to incomplete and even deleterious assessment results.

BASIC PURPOSES OF BEHAVIORAL HEALTH CARE ASSESSMENT

Building on the underlying rationale for and characteristics of the biopsychosocial approach to behavioral health care assessment, a consideration of the overall purposes of assessment helps inform the processes and procedures that need to be incorporated into assessment practice. Although a wide variety of theoretical orientations historically have been applied to understanding assessment, current guidelines and resources suggest significant consensus regarding the primary purposes of assessment in behavioral health care.

At the most basic level, the treatment process does not proceed without the identification of behavioral health problems that warrant clinical attention. Assessment serves several important additional purposes, however. For example, Maruish (2004b) noted that psychological assessment is important for treatment planning, the provision of baseline data for monitoring the progress of treatment, and as a therapeutic intervention in itself (as feedback to the patient is provided and discussed and the patient and therapist arrive at mutually agreed upon treatment goals).

An examination of major guidelines and resources for conducting behavioral health care assessment reveals significant convergence around its primary purposes (Melchert, 2011). Although their emphases differ, the guidelines significantly overlap regarding several basic purposes for behavioral health care assessment that extend beyond the initial identification of problems and concerns (e.g., see American Psychiatric Association, 2006; Groth-Marnat, 2009; Lezak, 1995; Maruish, 2004b; S. M. Turner, DeMers, Fox, & Reed, 2001; Wiggins, 2003). A synthesis of these guidelines suggests the following basic purposes of psychological assessment:

1. Identify behavioral health problems and concerns that require clinical attention.
2. Gather information regarding a patient's behavioral health and biopsychosocial functioning in order to develop a comprehensive case conceptualization and treatment plan.

3. Engage the patient in the treatment process through a collaborative approach that includes patient self-assessment and a discussion of objective feedback provided back to the patient.
4. Provide ongoing assessment during the course of treatment in order to monitor progress, refine the treatment plan, and refocus interventions as needed.
5. Provide baseline data for an outcomes evaluation and assessment of the effectiveness of treatment.

These overarching basic purposes apply even though the specific purposes of assessment in particular cases may vary substantially. Initial intake assessments with new patients are very different from the reevaluation for ongoing care of chronic issues with patients who are well known to the therapist. Assessments conducted for consultation to others usually do not lead to one performing subsequent treatment or outcomes assessment at all. For behavioral health care assessment in general, however, there is substantial agreement regarding the general purposes listed above.

The sections that follow discuss the issues that must be addressed in clinical practice in order to achieve the basic purposes of behavioral health assessment. A comprehensive health care–oriented approach to assessment is outlined here. Assessment procedures vary significantly depending on the specific purpose and setting (e.g., community mental health center, independent specialty psychotherapy practice, primary health care, inpatient psychiatry, medical, educational, forensic, industrial, organizational, sport, and correctional). The discussion here, however, focuses on the general conceptualization of behavioral health care assessment that can be adapted and applied across professional practice settings. This discussion begins with a consideration of which areas of patients' lives need to be considered to develop comprehensive case conceptualizations that meet their behavioral health and biopsychosocial needs.

AREAS TO INCLUDE IN BEHAVIORAL HEALTH CARE ASSESSMENT

Behavioral health assessment has become much more biopsychosocial in orientation over the last half century. This is clearly reflected in the evolution of the *DSM*. The first two editions, *DSM–I* and *DSM–II*, were published by the American Psychiatric Association in 1952 and 1968 and relied heavily on psychoanalytic theory. Symptoms for specific disorders were not specified in detail, and many were seen as reflections of broad underlying conflicts or reactions to life problems that could be categorized generally as either neurosis or psychosis. Alternative theoretical explanations for psychological development grew in popularity during that time (e.g., humanistic, cognitive, biological, feminist, and multicultural approaches) and weaknesses in the *DSM I* and *II* became obvious. As a result, the third edition of the *DSM* (*DSM–III*), published in 1980, presented a thoroughly revised approach to conceptualizing psychiatric diagnosis. That edition used an atheoretical descriptive approach that did not specify or imply etiology for most of the disorders, and it also introduced the multiaxial assessment system that, with modifications, was used for over three decades until the publication of the *DSM–5* in 2013. The multiaxial system incorporated what is essentially a biopsychosocial approach to assessment by including clinical disorders and conditions on Axis I, personality disorders and pervasive developmental disorders on Axis II, medical issues on Axis III, environmental stressors on Axis IV, and general overall level of functioning on Axis V. In the *DSM–5*, Axes I, II, and III have been combined, and separate notations are to be made for important psychosocial and environmental factors (formerly Axis IV) and disability (formerly Axis V). That is, the same biopsychosocial information is to be documented but in a less differentiated manner than before. The *DSM–5* also recommends that the Z codes of the *International Classification of Diseases* (10th ed., Clinical Modification; *ICD–10–CM*; World Health Organization, 1992) be used instead of the former Axis IV listing of stressors. (Health insurers in the United States are scheduled to begin using *ICD–10* codes for payment and reimbursement in October 2014.) These Z codes do not represent mental disorders but do capture many of the problems individuals experience in the social realm (e.g., those noted in Chapter 5).

The five-axial system of the *DSM–III* greatly expanded the scope of assessment for mental health and biopsychosocial functioning, but it provided little guidance regarding the breadth and specificity of the information that should be evaluated when conducting an assessment. Because the *DSM–III*, *DSM–IV* (American Psychiatric Association, 1994), and *DSM–5* are descriptive systems, they provide little guidance on how to understand the etiology and development of patients' problems. They also leave out level of insight, readiness to change, sense of responsibility, and other factors that greatly affect treatment. Clinical intervention requires much more comprehensive assessment information to identify effective long-term solutions to patients' problems in individual cases (e.g., American Psychiatric Association, 2006; Beutler, Malik, Talebi, Fleming, & Moleiro, 2004; Goodheart & Carter, 2008).

The controversy surrounding the development and release of the *DSM–5* also suggests that more research into the nature and classification of psychopathology is badly needed. For example, Allen Frances (2009), who chaired the committee that revised the *DSM–IV*, noted the lack of research connecting psychiatric syndromes with any underlying neurobiological mechanisms and strongly questioned the loosening of *DSM–5* diagnostic criteria regarding several disorders. Because of the lack of a neuroscience-based classification of mental disorders, the National Institute of Mental Health (2011) announced a major research initiative that shifts away from current *DSM* diagnoses and replaces them with dimensional categories based on advances in genomics, pathophysiology, and behavioral science. This new framework, called the Research Domain Criteria (RDoC), uses a dimensional conceptualization ranging from *normal* to *abnormal*, and classification is based on basic behavioral neuroscience findings rather than existing *DSM* disorders. New RDoC-based research will take years to conduct, but future editions of the *DSM* are likely to evolve considerably as a result.

Virtually all contemporary behavioral health assessment systems indicate that it is important to incorporate all three of the biopsychosocial domains when conducting behavioral health assessment. Many have noted specific areas within these domains to include when conducting assessments. Melchert (2011) found substantial overlap when the specific areas included in six influential behavioral health assessment systems were compared. All of the 26 specific components listed in Table 8.1 were included in at least two of the systems, and 18 of the components were included in at least four of the systems. The overlap in these assessment systems suggests that all 26 of these component areas are considered important in behavioral health care assessment. To evaluate the content-related validity of this set of assessment areas, L. Meyer and Melchert (2011) examined the information contained in 163 individual outpatient therapy files from three different clinics and found that these 26 components captured 100% of the intake information found in the patient files. There was no intake information in any of the patient files that could not be categorized into these component areas, and each of them was necessary to capture all of the information.

Because each of these areas of patients' lives can be important in their development and current functioning, all of them need to be considered when learning to conduct comprehensive biopsychosocial assessment. The depth and detail that one pursues in particular assessments depends on one's specialization, the setting where one practices, and the specific purpose of the assessment. For example, just a small number of these areas might be included when conducting screens and other brief assessments of patients' needs in university counseling centers or primary health care clinics. As the general framework for conceptualizing behavioral health care assessment, however, the above categorization is useful for delineating areas of individuals' lives that can significantly affect their current functioning as well as their growth and development over the life span.

TABLE 8.1

Biopsychosocial Component Areas of Behavioral Health Care Assessment

Domain component	Common issues
Biological functioning	
General medical history	Current medical functioning, recent and past medical history, chronic medical conditions, physical disability, nondiagnosed health complaints, previous hospitalizations, surgery history, seizure history, physical trauma history
Childhood health history	Birth history, childhood illnesses, childhood psychiatric history
Medications	Dosage, efficacy, side effects, duration of treatment, medication adherence
Health habits and behaviors	Diet and nutrition, activity, exercise
Psychological functioning	
History of present problem	Reason for seeking treatment at the present time, recent symptoms, exacerbations or remissions of current illness or presenting problem, duration of current complaint, previous attempts to solve the problem, treatment readiness (e.g., motivation to change, ability to cooperate with treatment)
Level of psychological functioning	Overall mood and affect, level of distress, impairment in functioning
Individual psychological history	Current psychiatric problems, previous diagnoses, treatment history (e.g., format, frequency, duration, response to treatment, satisfaction with treatment)
Substance use and addictions	Types of substances used (e.g., alcohol, tobacco, caffeine, prescribed, over-the-counter, illicit), quantity and frequency of use, previous treatments, other addictive behaviors (gambling, overeating, viewing pornography)
Suicidal ideation and risk assessment	Intent, plan, previous attempts, other self- and other-destructive behaviors (e.g., injury to self, neglect of self-care, homicidal risk, neglect of children or other dependents)
Individual developmental history	Infancy, early and middle childhood, adolescence, early and middle adulthood, late adulthood
Childhood abuse and neglect history	Physical, sexual, emotional, psychological response to abuse or neglect
Other psychological traumas	Traumas and stressful life events, exposure to acts of war, political repression, criminal victimization
Mental status examination	Orientation, attention, memory, thought process, thought content, speech, perception, insight, judgment, appearance, affect, mood, motor activity
Personality style and characteristics	Coping abilities, defense mechanisms, problem-solving abilities, self-concept, interpersonal characteristics, intrapersonal characteristics

(continues)

TABLE 8.1
Biopsychosocial Component Areas of Behavioral Health Care Assessment (Continued)

Domain component	Common issues
	Sociocultural functioning
Relationships and support system	Immediate and extended family members, friends, supervisors, coworkers or other students, previous treatment providers, current parent–child relationship, involvements in social groups and organizations, marital–relationship status and history, recurrent difficulties in relationships, presence of past and current supportive relationships, sexual and reproductive history
Current living situation	Current living arrangements, satisfaction with those arrangements
Family history	Family constellation, circumstances, and atmosphere; recent problems with family; family medical illnesses, psychiatric history and diagnoses; history of suicide in first and second degree relatives, family problems with alcohol or drugs, loss of parent and response to that loss
Educational history	Highest level completed, professional or trade skills
Employment	Current employment, vocational history, reasons for job changes
Financial resources	Finances and income
Legal issues or crime	Current legal issues and legal history, criminal victimization
Military history	Positions, periods of service, termination
Activities of interest or hobbies	Leisure interests and activities, hobbies
Religion	Organized religious practices and activities, active in faith
Spirituality	Personal beliefs, meaning, sense of purpose (which may or may not include a "higher power" or organized religious practices)
Multicultural issues	Race–ethnicity, racial–ethnic heritage, country of origin, sexual orientation (i.e., lesbian, gay, bisexual, or transgender status), class

Note. From *Foundations of Professional Psychology: The End of Theoretical Orientations and the Emergence of the Biopsychosocial Approach* (pp. 124–125), by T. P. Melchert, 2011, London, England: Elsevier. Copyright 2011 by Elsevier. Adapted with permission.

RELIABILITY, VALIDITY, AND THOROUGHNESS
OF ASSESSMENT INFORMATION

The reliability and validity of assessment information are major priorities in behavioral health care from the perspectives of both science and ethics. The legitimacy and credibility of the field as a science-based health care profession are weakened if scientific principles involving measurement and assessment are compromised. Unreliable, incomplete, or inaccurate assessments also have ethical implications: They might be not only unhelpful to patients, their families, and others but also even have negative consequences.

The level of reliability, validity, and thoroughness of assessment information that is needed can vary significantly, however, depending on the purpose of the assessment. Within the clinical context, assessment needs vary greatly depending on whether they are conducted for emergency purposes (e.g., when patients are suicidal or homicidal), consulting purposes (e.g., to assist other treatment providers with complex cases), reevaluation purposes (e.g., to assess the progress of patients in long-term care for the management of chronic conditions), or intake purposes (e.g., to gain an initial assessment of the needs of patients receiving behavioral health care for the first time). Many psychotherapy cases involve individuals who self-refer to address mild or moderate problems regarding their emotional functioning, and they often can personally provide most or all of the information needed to complete the assessment. When the therapist plans to provide ongoing treatment in these cases, establishing an effective therapeutic relationship becomes a priority and may take precedence over the timely gathering of comprehensive assessment information.

The referral question also plays an important role in deciding how to approach the assessment of a particular case. One's assessment approach with psychotherapy patients who self-refer is typically much different from the approach for cases in which parents, spouses, partners, physicians, or educators initiate the referral. In these latter cases, the information provided by third parties is often critical to the reliability and validity of the assessment. Other referrals address legal or administrative questions such as child custody, disability status, readiness to return to employment, or the insanity defense. (An interesting and controversial referral question that has arisen in states with sexual predator laws involves determining whether a convicted child molester who has completed his or her sentence should then be civilly committed and detained indefinitely.) One's approach to obtaining reliable, valid, and thorough assessment information can vary widely across these types of referral questions.

Although the reliability and validity of assessment information are always a priority, limited resources and practicality prevent highly thorough assessments from being conducted in many cases. An overwhelming amount of information from across the biopsychosocial domains can be collected, and using triangulation and other methods to evaluate its accuracy is highly time consuming and costly. Moreover, such a thorough approach is not needed in many situations. Employee assistance programs, crisis hotlines, university counseling centers, and school counseling departments are limited in the services they can provide given the large number of individuals served by a small number of personnel, and so screening and other brief assessment procedures are commonly used to identify cases to refer for more thorough assessment. On the other hand, inpatient psychiatric care routinely requires that medical and psychosocial evaluations be completed in order to thoroughly evaluate the severity and complexity of the issues involved.

The issues addressed in the assessment also play a major role in deciding the type and thoroughness of the information collected. Patient self-report can efficiently provide reliable information regarding some issues; other issues are most reliably and efficiently assessed through the use of questionnaires or psychological tests. For example, one's level of distress, mood, and other subjective states are typically assessed through self-report, which is often the only reliable source of information regarding one's internal subjective state. Variables such as personality characteristics, educational achievement, and intellectual or neuropsychological functioning are often most reliably, validly, and efficiently assessed through the use of test instruments. When an assessment is needed of a patient's performance of responsibilities at work or at home, on the other hand, work supervisors and family members often provide more reliable and complete information than what patients themselves may be aware of or willing to report. Children and cognitively disabled adults are usually unable to provide reliable reports regarding several aspects of their lives. Legal, medical, substance abuse, educational, and child protective service issues also may not be reliably reported by patients themselves. Though patient self-report information is often the most time-efficient to collect, it carries a high risk of being incomplete or inaccurate (sometimes completely inaccurate) for many purposes.

The importance of obtaining reliable assessment information is evident when one considers how often a patient's perception of his or her behavior or performance varies from that of family members, employers, educators, or various public officials (R. C. Miller & Berman, 1983). For example, a husband entering treatment might ask for help with getting along with a "nagging" wife; the wife might report that the husband's violence and alcohol abuse are about to result in a divorce and child custody battle. A patient might report that his or her supervisor at work is angry, unfair, and prejudiced, but the supervisor might report that the employee frequently argues with coworkers, repeatedly makes sexually inappropriate comments, has substandard productivity, and is not responding positively to supervision. Children referred for treatment frequently report circumstances and behaviors that conflict with other reports. The minimization or exaggeration of problems is frequently subconscious or unintentional, but at other times it is not. In either case, relying only on patient self-report can result in inaccurate assessments that might be unhelpful or potentially hurtful for the patient or others.

In general, patients themselves are the primary source for information about their personal distress and other internal states. Therapists often have the most expertise for identifying psychological symptoms and making psychiatric diagnoses. A patient's medical status is ordinarily best understood by his or her medical providers, whereas family members often have the most insight regarding the patient's functioning within the family. Employers or educators often have the best perspective on an individual's functioning at work or school, whereas officials within criminal and legal systems can often provide reliable information regarding a person's legal involvement. Therapists must be conscientious in their decisions about the most reliable sources of information for the purpose as well as adept at collecting data using a variety of sources and techniques. This also requires the ability to communicate and collaborate effectively with other human services professionals, family and community members, and others who play important roles in patients' lives.

A useful model for conceptualizing the reliability of assessment information was proposed by Strupp and Hadley (1977). In their tripartite model of mental health and therapeutic outcomes, at least three different stakeholders hold different perspectives and have different interests in a patient's psychological functioning and treatment. First, the authors argued that the patient is the best judge of his or her own distress and discomfort. Second, the patient's family and particular community members often have the best perspective for judging a patient's functioning in important life roles within the family, at work, or in the community. Third, therapists are normally the best judges of a patient's psychological functioning and psychopathology. Speer (1998) expanded on this model by specifying the sources that are likely to provide the most reliable and useful information regarding these different perspectives. The capitalized bold letters in Table 8.2 indicate those individuals who are likely to provide more reliable information regarding different dimensions of a patient's health and functioning. In this model, significant others could include employers, neighbors, friends, and landlords in addition to family members. Public gatekeepers are those who have professional responsibilities involving the patient but not a social relationship; examples include law enforcement officials, emergency room staff, court officials, and child or adult protective services staff. Independent observers are professionals or specialists who can perform medical, psychiatric, or other evaluations of the patient.

The use of standard intake questionnaires and interview protocol forms can help ensure that the collection of assessment information is reasonably thorough. Standardized screening instruments are also widely recommended because they can provide psychometrically reliable and valid data, and a patient's scores can be compared with normative data that are usually

TABLE 8.2
Reliable Sources of Behavioral Health Assessment Information

Source	Distress	Symptoms, disorder, diagnosis	Functioning, role performance
Patient	**A**	**B**	c
Significant others	d	e	**F**
Public gatekeepers	g	h	I
Independent observers	j	**K**	I
Therapist/provider	m	**N**	o

Note. Bold capital letters indicate sources that are more likely to provide reliable information. From *Mental Health Outcome Evaluation* (p. 50), by D. C. Speer, 1998, San Diego, CA: Academic Press. Copyright 1998 by Elsevier. Adapted with permission.

available. These instruments can also be readministered during and after treatment, providing a useful mechanism for monitoring treatment progress and evaluating outcome (see Chapters 10 and 11).

At a basic level, the adequacy and thoroughness of the assessment information collected for a given case can vary from completely inadequate (e.g., almost nothing is known about important relevant issues) to fully adequate for the purpose. Variation in the purposes of assessment and the uniqueness of each case make it difficult to establish precise guidelines for evaluating the adequacy of assessments, but L. Meyer and Melchert (2011) developed a five-point rubric to rate the general thoroughness of assessment data with regard to each of the biopsychosocial component areas listed in Table 8.1. The descriptors for the five points on the rating scale are noted in Table 8.3. The

TABLE 8.3
Detail and Comprehensiveness Scale
for Assessing Biopsychosocial Components

Score	Rating description
0	Information regarding component area is not present at all.
1	Only a few details or basic data are mentioned, or a check box for this component is marked, but no further information is provided.
2	Most or nearly all basic details or data are present; strengths and weaknesses may be mentioned briefly but are not clearly assessed as a strength or a deficit.
3	Most or nearly all details or data are present, plus one of the following two is also met: (a) strengths associated with this component are described, or (b) deficits associated with this component are described.
4	All of the following criteria are met: (a) most or nearly all details or data are present, (b) strengths associated with this component are described, and (c) deficits associated with this component are described.

Note. From *The Use of a Comprehensive Biopsychosocial Framework for Intake Assessment in Mental Health Practice* (Doctoral dissertation); Appendix F, by L. Meyer, 2008, Milwaukee, WI: Marquette University. Copyright 2008 by L. Meyer. Adapted with permission.

application of this approach is illustrated through examples of intake assessment notes for each of the five levels on the scale (see Table 8.4). Missing important details is typically problematic, with potentially serious consequences, and thereby introduces risks of harm. Comprehensive, detailed information, on the other hand, minimizes those risks while maximizing the likelihood of effective treatment over both the short and long term.

ASSESSMENT OF THE SEVERITY OF PATIENT PROBLEMS AND STRENGTH OF RESOURCES

The information that is gathered through the methods discussed above must be further evaluated at multiple levels to be useful for developing treatment plans that minimize risks of harm and maximize the likelihood of treatment effectiveness. The first of these levels concerns the severity of the patient's problems and needs that have been identified.

TABLE 8.4
Examples of Intake Assessment Notes Documenting
Particular Assessment Issues

Score	Substance use example	Medication example	Religion example
0	[Information regarding this component area is missing.]	[Information regarding this component area is missing.]	[Information regarding this component area is missing.]
1	"Patient states she drinks alcohol."	"Patient takes Prozac."	"Patient is Roman Catholic."
2	"Patient reports drinking alcohol socially, approximately twice per month. She reports not smoking and does not consume caffeine or any illicit drugs."	"Patient currently takes Prozac, 40 mg, once daily for depression."	"Patient is Roman Catholic, is active in her faith, attends church regularly, and was raised Catholic."
3	"Patient reports drinking alcohol socially, approximately twice per month. She reports not smoking and not consuming caffeine or any illicit drugs. Patient reports drinking has a negative impact because when she goes out and drinks with friends, she usually drinks too much and does not want to get out of bed the next day."	"Patient currently takes Prozac, 40 mg, once daily for depression. He states that the medication is helpful because he no longer feels depressed and is more active socially."	"The patient reports that she is Roman Catholic, is active in her faith, goes to church regularly, and was raised Catholic. She states that her religion has helped her by providing a positive support group during her recent difficulties."

(continues)

TABLE 8.4
Examples of Intake Assessment Notes Documenting
Particular Assessment Issues   *(Continued)*

Score	Substance use example	Medication example	Religion example
4	"Patient reports drinking alcohol socially, approximately twice per month. She reports not smoking and not consuming caffeine or any illicit drugs. Drinking on a social basis has been helpful, according to the patient, because she gets to go out with friends and feels more comfortable socializing and meeting new people. Patient reports that drinking also has a negative effect because when she goes out and drinks with friends, she usually drinks too much and does not want to get out of bed the next day."	"Patient currently takes Prozac, 40 mg, once daily for depression. He states that the medication is helpful because he no longer feels depressed and is more active socially. He reports the medication has a downside as well—he strongly dislikes the side effects of dry mouth, insomnia, sexual dysfunction, and weight gain, and he is afraid he will have to take the medication 'forever.'"	"The patient reports that she is Roman Catholic, is active in her faith, goes to church regularly, and was raised Catholic. She states that her religion has helped her by providing a positive support group during her recent difficulties. However, she also states that her religion has had a detrimental effect because she does not always agree with church doctrine and feels a great deal of internal conflict and guilt as a result."

Note. From *The Use of a Comprehensive Biopsychosocial Framework for Intake Assessment in Mental Health Practice* (Doctoral dissertation); Tables 3.3, 3.4, and 3.5, by L. Meyer, 2008, Milwaukee, WI: Marquette University. Copyright 2008 by L. Meyer. Adapted with permission.

The severity of patient problems obviously varies widely and has direct implications for treatment planning. The most severe and urgent problems typically involve emergency issues that must be attended to immediately. Emergency behavioral health problems often involve suicidality or homicidality, as well as family, medical, legal, and other crises that also require immediate attention. Other problems may be quite serious and require intensive intervention but not on an emergency basis. At the other end of the continuum are minor problems and needs that can be addressed through psychoeducation or a referral to external sources of information or support.

Many individuals face a serious problem in just one area of their lives; others face major problems in several areas. Consequently, the severity of the need has to be assessed with regard to particular issues. Many models for assessing the severity of patient problems range from *none* to *severe*. Since the publication of *DSM–III* (American Psychiatric Association, 1980), the terms *mild*, *moderate*, and *severe* have been used to indicate the level of severity of mental disorders, and many other systems have incorporated these same terms and concepts (e.g., Huyse et al., 2001).

In addition to noting the severity of individuals' problems and disorders, the biopsychosocial perspective emphasizes positive functioning and personal resources as well. Behavioral and medical health assessment in the past tended to emphasize deficits and pathology because of their major impact on individuals' lives. A biopsychosocial perspective to health care, on the other hand, emphasizes the whole person and the full continuum of functioning across the biopsychosocial domains. Gaining a holistic assessment of an individual's needs and functioning consequently requires an assessment of strengths and resources as well as problems and vulnerabilities. Strengths and resources include both internal resources (e.g., coping skills) and external resources (e.g., social support), and frequently they serve critically important roles in people's lives, often as important sources of support when facing serious problems and needs in other areas. The U.S. Substance Abuse and Mental Health Services Administration (2011a) initiated a program to focus more attention on developing strengths and resources among individuals with mental illness and substance use disorders. They identified eight dimensions for promoting wellness and recovery: physical, emotional, social, occupational, intellectual, financial, environmental, and spiritual well-being.

The full spectrum of functioning within particular areas of individuals' lives is illustrated in Exhibit 8.1. Rather than conceptualizing problems using a unipolar scale ranging from *no problem* to *severe problem*, a bipolar scale

EXHIBIT 8.1
Assessing the Severity of Problems and Strength of Resources
Within Biopsychosocial Areas

+3	Major strength—A major strength or resource that is an important contributor to the health and well-being of the individual
+2	Moderate strength—A moderate strength or resource that adds significantly to the individual's health and functioning; could be developed or amplified further
+1	Mild strength—A mild strength or resource for the individual; could be developed or amplified further
0	No problem or need—No evidence of problem or need in this area, though not an area of strength; could be developed into an area of strength
−1	Mild problem—Individual is experiencing mild psychological distress and/or impairment in functioning or faces minor risks for a decline in functioning.
−2	Moderate problem—Individual is functioning significantly less than optimally and/or is facing risks for a significant deterioration in level of functioning.
−3	Severe problem—Individual is functioning far below an optimal level and/or risks a major deterioration in level of functioning, with dangerous or disabling consequences possible.

Note. From *Foundations of Professional Psychology: The End of Theoretical Orientations and the Emergence of the Biopsychosocial Approach* (p. 131), by T. P. Melchert, 2011, London, England: Elsevier. Copyright 2011 by Elsevier. Adapted with permission.

incorporates positive functioning as well. This conceptualization, ranging from *severe problem* at the low end to *major strength* at the high end, does not apply neatly to all areas of individuals' lives. For example, if one experienced no significant maltreatment as a child, it is unclear whether that would be best viewed as a strength or simply as having no needs in that area. If a person with a history of severe child abuse worked through the consequences of those experiences and conscientiously developed healthy relationships and strong resiliency and parenting skills as a result, these consequences would be viewed as strengths and not vulnerabilities. These issues would require careful analysis if this scale were used as a measurement model. As a conceptual model, however, which is the main interest here, a bipolar conceptualization of problem severity is very useful as a reminder of the importance of assessing both problems and strengths across biopsychosocial areas.

Table 8.5 illustrates how a bipolar conceptualization of patient needs and strengths can be applied to gain a thorough assessment of patient cases. The dots in the table summarize the assessment of needs and strengths across the biopsychosocial areas for the case of a mildly depressed female hospital administrator who is effective at work, managing a large number of important responsibilities with generally positive appraisals by the chief executive. Many of her subordinates view her as irritable, arrogant, and difficult, though she is widely regarded as efficient in managing the hospital. This patient has distant and perfunctory relationships with her husband and children, however, as well as distant and conflictual relationships with her parents. Her husband has told her that he expects to leave their marriage once their two children graduate from high school. She consumes significant amounts of alcohol when not at work and neglects her physical health. She also privately worries that her life will not be meaningful after retirement because there are few things outside of work that she finds interesting. As another example, the checks in the table refer to the assessment of a homeless man diagnosed with bipolar affective disorder and substance dependence. He has a pleasant and engaging personality, is funny and widely liked, but he has significant needs and problems in most areas of his life. His substance abuse makes him vulnerable to criminal victimization, and he becomes despondent after these incidents. He was severely physically and emotionally abused during childhood and has had difficulty trusting others since then. He is determined to "make it on my own," however, and has a long history of rebounding after experiencing thefts and assaults. Note that even though these individuals' lives differ dramatically, they both were rated as having moderately serious problems in terms of their level of psychological functioning.

Comprehensively assessing patients' problems and strengths is necessary for gaining a thorough understanding of their needs, level of functioning in important areas of their lives, and biopsychosocial circumstances as a

TABLE 8.5

Example of Biopsychosocial Assessment for Two Cases: A Hospital Administrator and a Homeless Person

Biopsychosocial domains and components	−3 Severe problem	−2 Moderate problem	−1 Mild problem	0 No problem or need	+1 Mild strength	+2 Moderate strength	+3 Major strength
Biological functioning							
General physical health		✓		•			
Childhood health history		✓		•			
Medications		✓	•				
Health habits and behaviors	✓		•				
Psychological functioning							
Level of psychological functioning		✓•					
History of present problem	✓		•				
Suicidal ideation and risk assessment	✓	•	•				
Substance use and abuse	✓	•	✓				
Mental status examination			•			•	
Individual psychological history	✓		•				
Childhood abuse and neglect	✓			•			
Other psychological traumas		✓	•				
Effects of developmental history		✓					
Personality style and characteristics		•				✓	
Sociocultural functioning							
Relationships and social support		✓•					
Current living situation	✓	•					
Family history	✓						
Educational history	✓		✓				
Employment	✓				•		
Financial resources	✓						
Legal issues/crime		✓		•			
Military history				✓•			
Activities of interest/hobbies				✓•			•
Religion				•	•		•
Spirituality			✓•		•		
Multicultural issues					•		

Note. Data for the hospital administrator and the homeless person are represented through dots and checks, respectively. From *Foundations of Professional Psychology: The End of Theoretical Orientations and the Emergence of the Biopsychosocial Approach* (pp. 132–133), by T. P. Melchert, 2011, London, England: Elsevier. Copyright 2011 by Elsevier. Adapted with permission.

whole. Identifying problems, needs, and vulnerabilities as well as strengths and resources that can be relied on for support or can be developed even further are important for developing treatment plans that have the maximum likelihood of being effective over the long term. Focusing on strengths along with problems also helps individuals gain a more accurate self-identity and communicates that their therapists are interested in them as whole persons and not just interested in their problems. This in turn helps develop rapport and a stronger therapeutic relationship, both of which are important to positive treatment outcomes as well (see Chapter 10).

OVERALL EVALUATION AND INTEGRATION OF ASSESSMENT INFORMATION

The assessment information collected and evaluated using the guidelines described in the preceding section should be evaluated at two additional levels in order to develop fully informed treatment plans. The problems and needs identified have to be prioritized, and their overall severity and complexity must be evaluated.

Prioritization of Problems and Needs

Patients with emergency needs provide the clearest example of the importance of prioritizing problems and needs. The most common emergencies in behavioral health care involve danger to self or others; in addition, individuals face crises involving family, medical, legal, financial, criminal, or other problems that may require intensive, urgent intervention. In all these cases, failing to address emergency needs as the first priority can have serious consequences. For example, a college student who becomes severely destabilized and suicidal after failing to be admitted into medical school should address the suicidal ideation before exploring educational and career options. Addressing the career and educational decisions before the suicidality may not only be unhelpful but may also increase stress and uncertainty and the chances of a suicide attempt.

Maslow (1943) presented the best-known approach to conceptualizing the prioritization of human needs. In his hierarchy of needs model (depicted in Figure 8.1), the four lowest levels of needs (physiological, safety, love/belonging, esteem) are *deficiency* needs, which, when met, allow one to move up the hierarchy and establish new priorities for personal growth. Research has shown that need fulfillment is more fluid than that suggested by a stepped hierarchical model (Wahba & Bridgewell, 1976), but Maslow's model is nonetheless widely considered useful for categorizing different types of needs and arranging their priority. For example, the suicidal college student has to

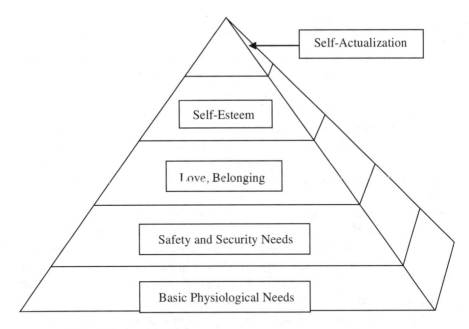

Figure 8.1. Maslow's (1943) Hierarchy of Needs Model.

address his basic safety and security needs (i.e., as a result of being a danger to himself) before he can address issues related to self-esteem, self-identify, meaning, and purpose. Likewise, a homeless person who is worried about basic needs for food, clothing, shelter, and physical safety may find it impossible to focus on higher level needs until some level of basic physical stability is achieved. Focusing on self-esteem and existential issues regarding meaning and fulfillment in life can be very difficult and potentially counterproductive if one's lower level needs have not been met.

Overall Complexity of Problems and Needs

Assessing the severity of individuals' problems and the strength of their resources, along with prioritizing their various needs, allows for another level of evaluation that is critical for planning treatment. This evaluation involves the complexity of patients' problems and needs in the context of their biopsychosocial circumstances as a whole. Significant comorbidity within the psychological domain is common, and coexisting problems across the biopsychosocial domains occur frequently as well. Co-occurring substance dependence; personality disorders; other clinical syndromes; or serious family, medical, or financial problems are common and greatly complicate an individual's life and treatment. The complexity of a patient's situation must be evaluated before a rational and effective treatment plan can be devised to resolve problems and needs over the short and long term.

As with most aspects of behavioral health, the complexity of biopsychosocial problems and needs can be conceptualized as falling on a continuum. Patients without clinically significant mental health problems or concerns would be assessed as having problems of essentially no complexity; those with one or very few problems of lesser severity would be viewed as having problems of very little or mild complexity. Patients with problems of major complexity would include those with multiple problems at moderate or severe levels of need or risk along with strengths that are insufficient to counterbalance the problems (see Table 8.6). Cases of major complexity often involve severe and persistent mental illness or substance dependence; significant comorbidity; a developmental history involving major abuse, neglect, or other trauma; or major personality pathology. Some cases involve a serious problem in just one area, and although the complexity of the problems may be low, the severity of the problems or risks faced may be quite serious nonetheless. For example, a young adult who enjoys strengths and resources in many areas might experience serious destabilization surrounding a humiliating relationship breakup.

More complex and serious behavioral health and biopsychosocial needs often require more comprehensive and detailed evaluation. Patients with serious problems across the biopsychosocial domains may need medical and neuropsychological evaluations, the findings of which are combined with input from family members, employers, teachers, parole officers, or others. Thorough and detailed assessments are more frequent in inpatient psychiatric and substance abuse treatment programs when patients experience highly complex problems. Because the interaction of problems and resources across the many areas of peoples' lives results in a very complex array of combinations, evaluating the interaction of developmental, etiological, risk, protective, sociocultural, and medical factors in patients' functioning can require significant clinical

TABLE 8.6
Overall Complexity of Patient Problems and Needs

Level of complexity	General guideline
None or very little	Minimal or no clinically significant mental health problems or concerns; significant strengths prevent issues from developing into clinically significant problems
Mild	A small number of problems, usually of lesser severity; presence of strengths helps mitigate their effects
Moderate	Intermediate number of problems, usually of intermediate severity, and intermediate number of strengths
Major	Multiple problems of moderate or higher levels of severity and/or risk; strengths insufficient to counterbalance problems

experience. Therefore, case consultation with more experienced and expert clinicians typically increases as severity and complexity of problems increase.

There is some evidence that comprehensive, well-integrated assessment such as that described above is not common. Two studies have included ratings of the adequacy of clinicians' assessment reports from a comprehensive, biopsychosocial perspective. McClain, O'Sullivan, and Clardy (2004) investigated the adequacy of the case formulations completed by a sample of 79 psychiatric residents according to an integrative biopsychosocial framework. The study found that, on average, none of the groups of residents (first through fourth year, from four different institutions) wrote biopsychosocial case formulations that reached what was identified as the basic level of competency. The reports typically included information regarding a wide range of biological, psychological, and sociocultural factors, but the information was not well integrated and was judged to have the potential to lead to problems in treatment.

L. Meyer and Melchert (2011) found similar results. Their study examined the treatment records for a sample of 163 psychotherapy outpatients to evaluate the comprehensiveness of the written assessment documentation and the extent to which that information was integrated and formulated in a manner that would maximize treatment effectiveness. Table 8.7 provides the

TABLE 8.7
Levels of Comprehensiveness and Integration of Behavioral
Health Care Assessments

Score	Rating description
0	Assessment is missing critical biological, psychological, and sociocultural information in the context of the particular case.
1	The clinician obtained information regarding a variety of components across the biological, psychological, and sociocultural domains, but a lack of focus and attention to important concerns could lead to less effective treatment.
2	Basic competency. The clinician obtained comprehensive biological, psychological, and sociocultural information, and there is some evidence of integration of this information to address the patient's most important concerns.
3	The clinician obtained comprehensive biological, psychological, and sociocultural information; obtained information about some of the strengths and weaknesses the patient possesses; and the integration of this information helps to prioritize the patient's concerns and problems.
4	The clinician addressed the patient's strengths and weaknesses comprehensively across the biopsychosocial domains with attention given to individual and sociocultural differences. This information is integrated so that strengths are reinforced and amplified and weaknesses and problems are addressed. Issues are prioritized to reflect the patient's needs, circumstances, and preferences and to maximize treatment effectiveness.

Note. Adapted from "Examining the Content of Mental Health Intake Assessments From a Biopsychosocial Perspective," by L. Meyer and T. P. Melchert, 2011, *Journal of Psychotherapy Integration, 21*, p. 79. Copyright 2011 by American Psychological Association.

rubric used to rate the level of comprehensiveness and integration of assessment information in that study.

The mean rating of the files in the L. Meyer and Melchert (2011) study was only 1.17 ($SD = .45$), and only 14.1% of the files were rated at 2 or higher on the scale, the midpoint indicating basic competency. The findings from this and the McClain et al. (2004) study suggest that assessment information is often reported descriptively, with too little depth and detail, and without an analysis and integration that explains patients' current problems in the context of their strengths, resources, weaknesses, vulnerabilities, and developmental history. Table 8.8 illustrates what comprehensive, integrative assessments look like; it provides examples for each of the five levels of thoroughness in the L. Meyer and Melchert study for three different types of patient cases.

DISCUSSION: ASSESSMENT OF THE WHOLE PERSON

Conducting behavioral health assessment using the guidelines described in this chapter is a very ambitious undertaking. It requires extensive data collection across many areas of biopsychosocial functioning. Clinical interviewing and relationship buildings skills are necessary to develop good rapport with patients so that more reliable and complete information is shared. Strong communication and collaboration skills are needed to work effectively with other parties who can provide information that is important to the assessment. Large bodies of knowledge regarding development; personality; psychopathology; the psychological, sociocultural, and biological bases of behavior; and psychometric measurement need to be learned and applied in order to properly analyze and evaluate the information collected. Professional ethics and legal issues must be handled appropriately throughout the process. Clinical experience is also necessary for the proper evaluation and integration of all the data collected.

The ability to conduct thorough biopsychosocial assessments in this manner represents masterful clinical skill. This type of approach increases the likelihood that individuals' behavior, health, and biopsychosocial needs are accurately identified, that vulnerabilities and risk factors are not missed, and that strengths and resources that are important in people's lives are recognized. This approach also meets all of the basic purposes of assessment that were noted at the beginning of this chapter. It identifies problems and concerns that need clinical attention and provides the information needed for developing comprehensive case conceptualizations and treatment plans. It provides baseline data for conducting ongoing assessment over the course

TABLE 8.8

Examples of Comprehensive and Integrated Behavioral Health Care Assessments

Score	Anxiety example	Depression example	Adjustment example
0	The patient presents with symptoms related to an anxiety disorder and indicates she has been under the treatment of a physician for these concerns for 3 months. She states he prescribed anxiolytics for these symptoms but she does not like taking the medication. Her symptoms have recently gotten worse. In the intake assessment, the therapist does not obtain information related to medication, including what the patient is taking, side effects, efficacy, or medication adherence.	The patient presents with symptoms of depression, but the therapist does not obtain information related to suicidal ideation.	The patient presents with adjustment concerns related to her pending divorce, but the therapist does not obtain sociocultural information regarding the quality of her social support network.
1	The patient presents with symptoms related to an anxiety disorder and indicates she has been under the treatment of a physician for these concerns for 3 months. She states he prescribed anxiolytics for these symptoms but she does not like taking the medication. Her symptoms have recently gotten worse. The therapist notes the medication and dosage the patient has been taking but does not assess side effects and medication adherence.	The patient presents with symptoms of depression, and the therapist obtains some information regarding psychiatric history but does not assess previous diagnoses of mood disorders, previous treatments and their outcome, and past psychological traumas.	The patient presents with adjustment concerns related to her pending divorce and the therapist obtains some information on the quality of her social support network but does not assess the quality of her current relationship with her soon-to-be-ex-husband.

(continues)

TABLE 8.8
Examples of Comprehensive and Integrated Behavioral Health Care Assessments *(Continued)*

Score	Anxiety example	Depression example	Adjustment example
2	The patient presents with symptoms related to an anxiety disorder and indicates she has been under the treatment of a physician for these concerns for 3 months. She states he prescribed anxiolytics for these symptoms but she does not like taking the medication. Her symptoms have recently gotten worse. The therapist notes the medication and dosage the patient has been taking, including important components such as side effects and medication adherence. The therapist notes that these issues may be related to current problems.	The patient presents with symptoms of depression, and the therapist obtains information related to psychiatric and personal history and past traumas. The therapist shows a link between current symptoms and this history.	The patient presents with adjustment concerns related to her pending divorce, and the therapist obtains information regarding the quality of her social support network, and notes how these relationships are stressful and beneficial to her.
3	The patient presents with symptoms related to an anxiety disorder and indicates she has been under the treatment of a physician for these concerns for 3 months. She states he prescribed anxiolytics for these symptoms but she does not like taking the medication. Her symptoms have recently gotten worse. The therapist notes the medication and dosage the patient has been taking, including important components such as side effects and medication adherence. The therapist notes that the medication has helped reduce anxiety symptoms in recent months but has also had undesirable side effects, such as weight gain and tiredness.	The patient presents with symptoms of depression, and the therapist obtains information related to personal history. The therapist shows a link between current symptoms and history. The therapist discusses with the patient detrimental and beneficial patterns of responses to the life events.	The patient presents with adjustment concerns related to her pending divorce, and the therapist obtains information regarding the quality of her social support network. The therapist also obtains information regarding how marriage and divorce have been detrimental to her functioning and have had positive impacts as well.

The patient presents with symptoms related to an anxiety disorder and indicates she has been under the treatment of a physician for these concerns for 3 months. She states he prescribed anxiolytics for these symptoms but she does not like taking the medication. Her symptoms have recently gotten worse. The therapist notes the medication and dosage the patient has been taking, including important components such as side effects, medication adherence, and how the medication has helped ameliorate her anxiety symptoms in recent months but has also had unpleasant side effects, such as weight gain and tiredness. The therapist notes the concern that treatment of the anxiety with medication only has not actually helped manage the effects of her anxiety but merely managed the symptoms. The therapist also notes that the patient believes her anxiety is related to her family of origin issues and developmental history.

The patient presents with symptoms of depression, and the therapist obtains information related to personal history. The therapist shows a link between current symptoms and history. The therapist discusses with the patient detrimental and beneficial patterns of responses to the life events. The therapist makes links between the patient's personal history and current functioning, highlighting recurrent patterns that also appeared in the patient's parent's relationship.

The patient presents with adjustment concerns related to her pending divorce, and the therapist obtains information regarding the quality of her social support network. The therapist obtains information regarding how marriage and divorce have been detrimental to her functioning and have positive impacts as well. The therapist prioritizes the patient's problems in the context of her current resources and takes the patient's religious beliefs and preferences into account in order to maximize treatment effectiveness.

Note. From *The Use of a Comprehensive Biopsychosocial Framework for Intake Assessment in Mental Health Practice* (Doctoral dissertation); Table 3.6, by L. Meyer, 2008, Milwaukee, WI: Marquette University. Copyright 2008 by L. Meyer. Adapted with permission.

of treatment to monitor progress, refine the treatment plan, and refocus interventions as needed. The baseline data also allows for an outcomes assessment that helps measure the effectiveness of treatment. Conducting thorough behavioral health assessments also helps engage patients in the treatment process by helping them gain insight into the nature of their problems. Communicating to patients a thorough understanding of their problems, vulnerabilities, strengths, and resources is important to developing therapeutic relationships and alliances, and there is consistent evidence that the therapeutic relationship and alliance are among the strongest predictors of treatment outcome (see Chapter 10).

It must be noted that behavioral health assessments in many settings do not require the comprehensive, thorough approach described above. As noted, it is not practical to conduct thorough assessments in all cases, and screens and other brief assessment procedures are sufficient for many purposes. Learning a thorough conceptualization of the assessment process is critical, however, for being able to put clinical cases in proper context and appropriately evaluate the information obtained. It is difficult to judge the seriousness and complexity of people's problems if one does not understand the full spectrum of problem severity, the interaction of strengths and vulnerabilities across the biopsychosocial domains, the role of etiological and developmental factors, and the importance of prioritizing issues to minimize risks and maximize the likelihood of treatment effectiveness.

This comprehensive assessment approach is significantly more complex than descriptive approaches that merely gather and report assessment information or approaches conducted on the basis of one of the traditional theoretical orientations that focus primarily on a single domain or area of functioning. The findings of the McClain et al. (2004) and L. Meyer and Melchert (2011) studies suggest that many clinicians do not apply high levels of evaluation and integration to the assessment information they gather. Perhaps many of the therapists in these studies were applying a personally adopted theoretical orientation that focused their attention on particular issues, and they judged that a thorough analysis and evaluation of patients' biopsychosocial circumstances was unnecessary. Clearly, the approach advocated here is different.

The importance and usefulness of comprehensive and thoroughly evaluated assessment information are evident when considering treatment planning, the next general phase of the treatment process. Well-designed treatment plans that effectively resolve problems and address needs while building resources and resilience over the long term as well as the short term require comprehensive, reliable, and valid assessment information that is appropriately evaluated and integrated.

CASE EXAMPLE: A COGNITIVE–BEHAVIORAL VERSUS A BIOPSYCHOSOCIAL APPROACH TO ASSESSMENT WITH A MILDLY DEPRESSED PATIENT

This case example illustrates how behavioral health care assessment can differ when using a traditional orientation compared with the science-based biopsychosocial approach.

Cognitive–Behavioral Approach to Assessment

Maria is a 44-year-old married Latina woman presenting with concerns about depressed mood. The patient first consults a psychologist with a cognitive–behavioral theoretical orientation. The psychologist notes that Maria wrote on the intake questionnaire that "My husband wants me to see a psychologist for mild depression." The patient indicated no concerns about her physical health, marriage, work, or finances. She noted that she has two children, 9 and 11 years old. She denied any suicidal ideation or disturbing thoughts or feelings, and she reported drinking alcohol "socially."

After reviewing the questionnaire and quickly scoring the scales, the psychologist notes that Maria scored in the mild-to-moderate range of depression on the intake questionnaire, and he asks her about her depressed mood. She reports that she is "perhaps a little depressed," but it's really not a problem for her though her husband is concerned. She reports that she probably has a biological predisposition to depression because her mother seemed depressed as long as she can remember. She again denies any suicidal ideation. She reports being a pharmacist who is well respected at work and that her family is financially stable. She says that she is not arguing or fighting more than a normal amount with her husband, children, or coworkers, but she admits that "I am not really enjoying my family life the way I should, or my work, or my friends, or really much of anything except for my kids. I love my kids so much—they're really wonderful. But everything is kind of a chore. I'm not seeing my friends much anymore. I suppose I'm not that much fun to be around either. That's probably why my husband asked me to see a therapist. So here I am."

Maria goes on to explain that she has been married for 12 years to a physical therapist who has a good job at a local orthopedic clinic. She reports that she and her husband have a good marriage and family life, though she feels they have drifted apart since their children started school. She says she was "head-over-heels, totally in love on my wedding day. It was the happiest day of my life! He was interesting, and intelligent, and had a good career. He is funny and positive. And he's incredibly fit and attractive." She says her girlfriends "just love him—they're really jealous of me." She reports that their two children, in third and fifth grade, are both doing well. "They like school, they seem to be above average in their classes, they have nice little friends, and they're well behaved at home." She reports that the children attend an after-school program until she or her husband can pick them up after work and that she spends most of her nonwork time at home with the children. She says that she loves her husband and children a lot but that she doesn't have much enjoyment in her life. "To tell you the truth, I feel guilty. I'm not the best wife, and I'm not the best daughter to my own parents either—I actually avoid them. I hope I'm being a good mom to my kids, though I worry about that. I've just sort of slacked off on things."

At this point, the psychologist explains that he thinks Maria is showing typical signs of mild depression. The psychologist points out that her comments show that she engages in dichotomous thinking, as when she implied that if she isn't really happy with her social life or leisure activities, then she feels like nothing is enjoyable, or that if she has cut back on some of her activities, she has "slacked off on everything." The psychologist also notes that she tends to overgeneralize from some of the less satisfying aspects of her social life and marriage and concludes in a blanket fashion that she has slacked off on everything and that nothing is enjoyable anymore.

Biopsychosocial Approach to Assessment

Maria consults a second psychologist, who takes a biopsychosocial approach to treatment. She completes a similar intake questionnaire, and the psychologist inquires about the same initial topics. She relates the same general information, though the psychologist asks for more details regarding several topics. For example, he asks some follow-up questions about her work, and she reports that she is considered a strong member of the staff and gets very positive evaluations—"I'm a really good worker and I have high standards; I don't make mistakes and am really good with providers and with customers. I get some of the highest merit raises in the region." When she reports that she has good physical health, the psychologist asks about her level of physical exercise and activity. She reports that she used to exercise regularly, nearly as much as her husband, but she gradually stopped after the children were born. She reports that she eats healthy—"I have to! My husband is a health fanatic and he makes most of the meals. And I don't snack between meals. I suppose you don't believe that because I'm kind of heavy now. It's actually kind of disgusting, compared to the way I used to be." When asked how she gained weight if she eats well, she says it's due to alcohol—"I drink a glass of wine or two in the evening to unwind." The psychologist asks about her marital relationship, and she reports that she and her husband gradually stopped going out on dates after their children were born—it was hard finding babysitters, and it cost a lot of money. Her mother babysits for free, but she also criticizes their parenting, so they stopped asking her to babysit. "My mother is a traditional Mexican lady, and she really doesn't approve of me having a job outside the home. She likes my husband and adores our kids. But she doesn't like it that I work." She also notes that her parents are very disappointed that she and her husband do not belong to a church and the kids are not being raised to be religious.

The psychologist asks Maria about their social life, and she reports that she and her husband stopped going out with other couples and she stopped seeing her friends, though her husband still goes out with his friends and is active socially. When asked about the quality of their intimate relationship, she reports that she and her husband used to have an active and satisfying sexual relationship, but that dropped off and she doesn't really enjoy sexual relations a lot anymore. The psychologist asks about her hobbies and interests, and she reports that she used to enjoy reading, music, and film a lot, but now she mostly watches TV. She said that she'd like to be involved in the parent–teacher organization at school but hasn't found the time. When asked about her relationship with her own family, she reports that she has been avoiding her parents mostly because she doesn't like criticism from her mother.

The psychologist explains to Maria that her lack of involvement in social and other activities is common for young parents who begin raising children. The psychologist notes that she and her husband appear to have been very successful with their careers and children, but they have neglected their relationship. He also notes that she sounded quite disappointed about neglecting her exercise and physical health. He asks her whether she is following a pattern similar to her own mother and whether she would like to explore possibilities for improving her relationship with her mother and the rest of the family.

The psychologist explains that there are several different ways to address these issues, but before they decide on the best approach, he would like to hear her husband's perspective on these issues. She agrees to ask him to come in for their next appointment. At the end of the session, the psychologist completes a form (see Table 8.9) with the patient to help summarize Maria's situation. Maria notes that the summary ratings simplify things but give a picture of her life that she never thought about before, and they help her realize that things could be a lot better.

TABLE 8.9
Summary of the Biopsychosocial Assessment for the Case Example

Biopsychosocial domains and components	−3 Severe need	−2 Moderate need	−1 Mild need	0 No need	+1 Mild strength	+2 Moderate strength	+3 Major strength
Biological functioning							
General physical health			✓				
Childhood health history				✓			
Medications				✓			
Health habits and behaviors			✓				
Psychological functioning							
Level of psychological functioning		✓					
History of present problem			✓				
Individual psychological history			✓				
Substance use and abuse			✓				
Suicidal ideation and risk assessment				✓			
Effects of developmental history			✓				
Childhood abuse and neglect				✓			
Other psychological traumas				✓			
Mental status examination						✓	
Personality style and characteristics				✓			
Sociocultural functioning							
Current relationships and social support					✓		
Current living situation		✓					
Family history				✓			
Educational history			✓				
Employment							✓
Financial resources							✓
Legal issues/crime				✓			
Military history		✓					
Activities of interest/hobbies						✓	
Religion				✓			
Spirituality				✓			
Multicultural issues			✓				

9

TREATMENT PLANNING

Individuals whose lives have been filled with distress, confusion, and psychological pain over months and often years, perhaps their whole lifetimes, are sometimes greatly relieved when they receive a psychological diagnosis and assessment that explains their difficult life experience. The explanation alone can provide major relief even though absorbing the significance of the explanation may entail substantial grief for the suffering one and perhaps others have endured. But at least what had been so confusing and frustrating is now understandable, and this often leads to the realization that things can now finally change for the better. Medical diagnoses can provide the same type of relief for symptoms and pain for which no cause had previously been identified.

Most patients want more than just a diagnosis, however. Although it is reassuring to learn that one's problems can be explained as part of known syndromes or one's developmental history, most people also want a resolution to their problems. This is the point when the assessment phase

DOI: 10.1037/14441-010
Biopsychosocial Practice: A Science-Based Framework for Behavioral Health Care, by T. P. Melchert
Copyright © 2015 by the American Psychological Association. All rights reserved.

of treatment generally evolves into the treatment planning phase. At this point, the patient and therapist together agree on a plan to address the problems identified based on the recommendations of their therapists (except in some cases involving children, court mandated treatment, crisis intervention, and other situations in which the treatment process may be less collaborative).

The biopsychosocial approach to treatment planning is based on a holistic understanding of patients' needs that recognizes the full range of interactive psychological, sociocultural, and biological influences on development, functioning, and behavior change. Treatment plans from this perspective are designed to address patients' needs within the context of their unique developmental history and current circumstances. The goal is to relieve psychological distress and reduce symptomatology while also strengthening health and functioning across the important areas of one's life. A range of evidence-based therapies and other interventions are used to resolve problems and build strengths and resources, taking advantage of the synergy that is possible when strengths are bolstered at the same time that problems are lessened across the biopsychosocial domains. From this perspective, the safety and effectiveness of intervention are overarching priorities, and treatment plans are designed to maximize treatment effectiveness and lead to optimal functioning over the long term as well as the short term.

This approach is quite different from some traditional approaches to planning the course of treatment. In traditional approaches, therapists often formulate a conceptualization of patients' personality and psychopathology from the perspective of a particular theoretical orientation and then implement the treatment that is consistent with that orientation. Cognitive–behavioral therapists who conceptualize cases involving patients with major depression, for example, are likely to identify irrational or depressogenic thoughts and beliefs and then develop a therapy plan to replace those thoughts with rational ones. A biologically oriented psychiatrist to whom those same patients are referred is likely to include antidepressant medication in the treatment plan; a solution-oriented therapist might ask the patients how they will know that their problems have been resolved and then focus on creating those conditions.

This chapter examines the basic conceptual issues and process involved in approaching behavioral health treatment planning from a biopsychosocial perspective. It covers the treatment planning process from beginning to end, emphasizing the important decisions that must be made and the important contextual issues that must be kept in mind to help ensure treatment effectiveness. It also covers the full range of patient problems from minor adjustment issues to severe mental illness.

TREATMENT PLANNING FROM A
BIOPSYCHOSOCIAL PERSPECTIVE

The science-based biopsychosocial approach to behavioral health care treatment planning includes three essential characteristics. First, its conceptual foundations rest squarely on science and ethics. Like the rest of the treatment process, treatment planning is based on the scientific understanding of human development, functioning, and behavior change, and its overarching purpose is to apply science and ethics to meet the needs of patients and promote their biopsychosocial functioning. These conceptual foundations and primary purposes guide the whole treatment process, including the specific procedures and practices involved in treatment planning.

A second essential characteristic that follows from the conceptual foundations of the biopsychosocial approach is the priority given to the safety and effectiveness of treatment. Professionals in all areas of health care must ensure the safety and effectiveness of their interventions by relying on rigorous research findings, clinical experience and expertise, careful clinical procedures and practices, and patient preferences and values (American Psychological Association Presidential Task Force on Evidence-Based Practice, 2006; Institute of Medicine, 2001). As discussed in Chapter 3, the ethical obligations of nonmaleficence and beneficence require that health care professionals provide care that benefits individuals and does not introduce disproportionate risks of side effects or harm. Patients need to be able to trust that the treatment they receive is safe and effective. (The safety and effectiveness of behavioral health care intervention are discussed in Chapters 10 and 11.)

A third essential characteristic of the biopsychosocial approach to behavioral health care is its comprehensive perspective on human development and functioning. Treatment planning builds directly on the findings of the psychological assessment, addressing patients' unique problems, needs, and circumstances within the context of their particular developmental history, problems, vulnerabilities, strengths, and resources. It takes a comprehensive and long-term perspective on treatment effectiveness and promoting biopsychosocial functioning across the important areas of individuals' lives. Treatment plans are consequently designed to maximize the likelihood of treatment effectiveness not only in terms of relieving distress and symptoms in the short term but also in terms of making changes that are effective over the long term. It incorporates a developmental perspective that addresses the causes of individuals' problems, disorders, and vulnerabilities to the extent possible based on existing scientific knowledge. It also focuses on bolstering strengths and resources along with reducing vulnerabilities in order to build resilience for facing challenges and taking advantage of opportunities in the future.

INITIAL DECISIONS

Behavioral health care practice encompasses a wide range of types of cases and interventions. It is conducted in a variety of settings and with individuals at many levels of functioning and psychopathology. In some cases, individuals have severe problems in multiple biopsychosocial areas and few resources. Some cases also involve critical needs that require immediate attention (e.g., suicidality, the safety of the children of an unstable parent). At the other end of the spectrum are individuals who have relatively minor developmentally appropriate questions within the context of substantial strengths and resources. For example, they may only need to be reassured that their approach to parenting or a career decision is responsible and appropriate and that they do not need treatment at all. In other cases, over the course of a long-term therapy relationship, individuals face an absence of meaning in life or gradually learn to replace deep dysfunctional personality characteristics with more adaptive ones. Sometimes therapy is delayed for a time because certain issues must be addressed (e.g., substance abuse, employment problems) or resources must be strengthened (e.g., personal coping resources, external social supports) before it is appropriate to examine particularly difficult personal or family issues.

Depending on people's particular problems, vulnerabilities, strengths, resources, and developmental history, intervention obviously can take many different forms. In all cases, however, the first treatment planning decision that must be made is normally at a very basic level. Given the findings of the assessment that was conducted regarding the particular case, is there a clinically significant problem or concern that needs professional attention? Is intervention warranted at this time? It is clearly inappropriate to assume that treatment is indicated whenever someone raises a concern or presents a problem—therapists instead must evaluate whether intervention is the best way to address the concern or problem and, if so, the basic approach that addresses the issues most effectively. This evaluation revolves around the severity and complexity of the issues that were identified in the psychological assessment. At this first, most basic level of evaluation, four options typically are considered (see Exhibit 9.1).

Patients sometimes have questions or concerns that do not rise to the level of clinical concern because the problems or concerns have no significant implications for their behavioral health or functioning. For example, many individuals have questions about experiences that have no significant implications for their development and functioning (e.g., they may wonder whether a particular emotional, cognitive, behavioral, or sexual response they experience is healthy). After learning that their experience is normal and does not signify psychological dysfunction, many individuals are reassured

EXHIBIT 9.1
Initial Decision Making Options Regarding Proceeding With Intervention

1. Do not intervene because the problem or concern does not warrant clinical intervention.
2. Postpone a decision about intervening because it is unclear whether a clinically significant problem currently exists, but do observe and monitor the patient in the meantime ("watchful waiting").
3. Intervene with clinically significant problems.
4. Refer to another professional for more assessment or to provide the needed intervention.

that no further assessment or intervention is needed. (Of course, these individuals should always feel free to return if these or other issues become concerning at a later point.)

Many individuals have questions or concerns that do not indicate a clinically significant problem at present although the issue will become problematic if it worsens. Others have questions or concerns that are likely to resolve on their own, perhaps after receiving minimal guidance or some resources (although intervention is needed if the issues are not resolved). These sorts of situations sometimes arise when individuals enter a developmental stage that is new and unfamiliar (e.g., when first dating, entering a committed relationship, having children, having children leave the home, approaching retirement). When it is unclear whether a patient has a clinically significant problem and the issue may resolve on its own, there is a middle option between providing and not providing intervention that can be very useful. Rather than proceed with intervention, therapists may judge that it is appropriate to postpone formal intervention and instead monitor the patient to observe the progression of the issues and the patient's response. "Watchful waiting" is common in medicine because many developing conditions are near the boundary of clinical significance and/or there is a reasonable likelihood that they will resolve on their own with no intervention. It is very important in both physical and behavioral health care to intervene early to prevent problems from developing or increasing in severity. It is also important, however, not to waste resources, identify normal questions or minor issues as clinically significant disorders that require professional intervention, or risk other undesirable side effects if there is a reasonable likelihood that an issue will resolve on its own.

When patients have clinically significant problems and therapists are competent to treat those problems within the context of patients' background characteristics and life circumstances, then therapists often provide the needed services themselves. Sometimes therapists are fully competent to provide the needed services but are unable to do so because of factors largely unrelated to the patient (e.g., a dual relationship through a third party, having too many suicidal patients in one's caseload to responsibly take on another one). In these cases, referring to other qualified therapists is the usual practice.

Referring clients to other professionals is the normal practice when therapists have not had sufficient training and clinical experience to safely and effectively provide the needed interventions or when they practice in agencies that do not provide the types of intervention or level of care that a patient needs (e.g., employee assistance programs, college counseling centers). It is also common for therapists to possess the experience and expertise to diagnose a problem (e.g., substance abuse, parent–child conflicts) but not have the expertise for providing the treatment that is needed (e.g., substance abuse treatment, family therapy). Consequently, therapists frequently refer patients to other qualified professionals as well as work together with a variety of professionals (e.g., other therapists, neuropsychologists, physicians, psychiatrists, law enforcement officials, educators, social workers) to collaboratively meet patients' needs.

ADDRESSING THE SEVERITY AND COMPLEXITY OF PROBLEMS AND NEEDS

A basic principle of behavioral health care treatment planning is that the particular problems and needs of the individual patient must be addressed at the appropriate level and intensity of intervention. In general, the severity and complexity of a problem are correlated with the intensity of the intervention. Less serious problems require less intensive interventions; whereas complex, serious problems require intensive interventions addressing multiple biopsychosocial needs. Interventions should be sufficient to achieve a positive outcome, but they also should not waste resources, interrupt people's lives or restrict their autonomy unnecessarily, or introduce undesirable side effects that are not justified by the benefits of intervention.

Identifying the appropriate type, level, and intensity of intervention for individuals with different problems and needs is critical in treatment planning. After a clinically significant problem or disorder has been identified, decisions about how to proceed with treatment planning are based on the severity and complexity of the problems identified in the psychological assessment. The complexity of patients' problems taken as a whole must be considered along with the severity of the individual problems. Treatment planning can become very complicated depending on the severity of the problems and their interaction with each other and also with an individual's vulnerabilities, strengths, and resources.

General treatment planning guidelines for identifying the type, level, and intensity of intervention that maximizes the likelihood of treatment effectiveness with regard to individual behavioral health care problems are found in Table 9.1. (The levels of problem severity listed were identified in Exhibit 8.1.) Additional considerations also must be applied depending on the number, type, and overall complexity of the problems involved. As the

TABLE 9.1

Basic Treatment Planning Guidelines Associated With Level of Problem Severity for Individual Areas of Biopsychosocial Functioning

Severity of problem or strength of resource	Basic treatment planning guideline
+1 Mild, moderate, or to major area of +3 strength or resource	• Reinforce strengths, amplify assets, and build resources (internal as well as environmental) so as to build resilience over the long term.
0 No evidence of problem	• Do not intervene. • Build this area into a source of strength or a resource for the patient. • Refer patient back to referral source with opinion that no significant problem exists and provide suggestions for future monitoring or prevention.
−1 Mild problem	• Provide support, psychoeducation, and/or brief treatment for making changes. • Postpone interventions until other higher priority needs are addressed. • Observe and monitor the problem or concern, make decision about intervening at later point.
−2 Moderate problem	• Provide intervention oneself. • Refer to other professional(s) to provide intervention. • Collaborate with other professional(s) on providing intervention(s). • Postpone intervention until other higher priority needs are addressed. • Provide aftercare and follow-up as needed.
−3 Severe problem	• Immediate and/or intensive interventions are generally needed; monitor with extra care. • Provide intervention oneself. • Refer to other professional(s) to provide intervention. • Collaborate with other professional(s) on providing intervention(s). • Plan ongoing care, aftercare, and follow-up as needed.

Note. From *Foundations of Professional Psychology: The End of Theoretical Orientations and the Emergence of the Biopsychosocial Approach* (p. 154), by T. P. Melchert, 2011, London, England: Elsevier. Copyright 2011 by Elsevier. Adapted with permission.

number of co-occurring problems across the biopsychosocial areas increases and the clinical picture becomes more complex, treatment planning also becomes more complex. Within individual problems areas, however, the following basic guidelines apply.

It is important to note that the treatment planning process is frequently dynamic as a result of the evolution of the therapeutic relationship or challenging events and obstacles that arise in patients' lives. In addition to significant external events, new issues often emerge during the course of treatment as therapeutic rapport and trust develop and patients are willing to reveal more sensitive aspects of their histories. Individuals frequently assess whether their therapists are trustworthy in terms of handling sensitive subjects before they are willing to reveal them (e.g., compulsive behaviors, sexual orientation, a personal history of child abuse or neglect). Other patients realize connections between past experiences and current issues only after they gain greater insight into how past events affected their personality development and psychopathology. In all cases, therapists should continually assess the progress of treatment and modify treatment plans appropriately when it becomes evident that the nature, severity, and complexity of patients' problems have changed.

Treatment planning can be particularly dynamic in cases of greater severity and complexity. For example, intensive and immediate interventions are often needed when severe biopsychosocial problems are present and when significant risks of harm to self or others exist. When immediate, intensive care is needed, the target for achieving the most urgent treatment goals may be just hours or days (e.g., to achieve stabilization following a suicidal crisis). The target for achieving less urgent medium-term goals may be several weeks, whereas other goals for achieving stable biopsychosocial functioning may become part of a long-term plan. In the case of severe alcoholism, for example, immediate treatment for detoxification and medical stabilization may be needed acutely. This might be followed by relatively intensive substance abuse treatment, which is followed by family therapy and vocational counseling to address various medium-term goals. Mutual support group involvement with Alcoholics Anonymous may also become a permanent part of an individual's plan to maintain long-term sobriety and improved levels of biopsychosocial functioning.

Extensive graduate coursework and supervised clinical experience are required to gain all the knowledge and skills needed to develop treatment plans for addressing a full range of behavioral health cases. Treatment planning can be particularly complicated for cases of high problem complexity and severity. Many different types of interventions are available for use in these cases, however. A listing of interventions that might be applied to address a full range of biopsychosocial issues is provided (see the section "Identifying Alternative Interventions") to illustrate the options that are available to address cases at all levels of severity and complexity. Before one can develop safe and effective treatment plans for addressing a full range of patients' behavioral health problems in the context of their life circumstances, several additional issues also must be integrated into one's conceptualization of cases.

Crisis Intervention

The most common types of emergency situations in behavioral health care involve suicidality and homicidality. Other issues that may rise to the level of a crisis situation involve serious substance abuse; severely disordered eating; self-harming behaviors such as cutting; severe panic episodes; major sleep disturbance; and the abuse or neglect of children, vulnerable adults, or dependent older adults. Accidents and criminal victimization can also be life threatening, and individuals may face other types of serious family, medical, financial, or legal problems that may require immediate attention to address problems that already occurred or to end a crisis that may be developing. Therapists also need to remain alert to the possibility that third parties are affected by a patient's crisis (e.g., when an unstable parent is responsible for the care of dependent children or elderly, dependent parents).

When severe biopsychosocial problems or risks are identified, intensive and immediate interventions are often needed to treat the harm that occurred or to prevent further harm from taking place. In these situations, interventions addressing other issues are often postponed altogether until the emergency needs are satisfactorily resolved. These are frequently complicated situations that require extensive knowledge and experience to manage effectively, and so students and less experienced clinicians generally rely on the assistance of more experienced supervisors and colleagues. These situations can occur in all types of general and specialized practice, and so all practitioners should be proficient with crisis intervention. Graduate training in this topic is frequently insufficient (e.g., a task force of the American Association of Suicidality found significant shortcomings in current training on suicide risk assessment and management; Schmitz et al., 2012). Therefore, students and practicing clinicians should make special efforts to ensure that their preparation in this area is adequate.

General Level of Care

After emergencies or other crises are evaluated and managed and a patient's individual problems are evaluated for the types of interventions that may be needed, the next consideration typically involves the level of care that is required to most effectively and efficiently address the patient's problems. The goal, once again, is to resolve individuals' problems while also developing strengths, resources, and resilience to optimize their biopsychosocial functioning to the greatest degree possible. Individuals' problems and circumstances obviously vary greatly. At one end of the continuum are patients with limited and circumscribed problems and significant strengths and resources who may need limited psychoeducation, referral to a support group, or a small number of therapy sessions to resolve their issues. At the other end, however, are patients with serious mental illnesses and co-occurring problems in multiple biopsychosocial areas who need comprehensive multidisciplinary treatment to achieve stabilization and rehabilitation. These cases can require the collaboration of psychologists, psychiatrists, medical providers, rehabilitation counselors, occupational therapists, social workers, legal professionals, patients' family members, and others who together provide the different types of care and support needed to assist patients in achieving the highest levels of functioning and quality of life possible.

The need to identify appropriate levels of care to effectively meet patients' needs grew quickly in the 1960s following the deinstitutionalization of the chronically mentally ill in the United States. A major principle underlying that movement was the legal requirement to provide patients with treatment that restricts their liberty the least while still remaining efficient and effective (*Project Release v. Prevost*, 1983). This resulted in attempts to increase the involvement of patients and their families in managing the care so that effective care could be provided in the least restrictive manner possible (Durbin, Goering, Cochrane, Macfarlane, & Sheldon, 2004). On the one hand, clinicians need to maximize the chances of positive outcomes by providing enough treatment to ensure a positive response. On the other hand, professionals need to be as efficient as possible and avoid the wasteful use of resources that could be used to help the many other individuals who need services.

Several approaches for evaluating the level of care needed by behavioral health care patients have been developed (e.g., R. L. Anderson & Lyons, 2001; Durbin et al., 2004; Srebnik et al., 2002). One of the most widely used systems is the Level of Care Utilization System for Psychiatric and Addiction Services (LOCUS) developed by the American Association of Community Psychiatrists (Sowers, George, & Thompson, 1999). Like most level of care models, this system was developed to match patients' behavioral health needs with the appropriate intensity of service and level of care needed to address and manage those needs. The system includes six assessment scales that measure (a) level of risk of harm to self or others; (b) level of general functioning (e.g., ability for self-care, appropriate interaction with others); (c) medical, addictive, and psychiatric comorbidity; (d) level of stress and level of support in the patients' environment; (e) the patients' treatment and recovery history; and (f) the patients' level of acceptance of responsibility for maintaining their health and their engagement with helping resources. Scores on these scales are then summed to help guide treatment recommendations. A modified version of the LOCUS was also developed for use with children and adolescents (i.e., the CALOCUS: Sowers et al., 2003). It follows the same format as the LOCUS but incorporates considerations that are relevant for children (e.g., the sixth assessment scale focuses on the primary caretaker's acceptance and engagement as well as the child's).

To help identify the general level of care needed to plan treatment for behavioral health care patients at all levels of problem severity and complexity, the LOCUS and CALOCUS include six levels of care that represent increasingly intensive (and expensive) use of services: (a) recovery maintenance and health management personally managed by the patient; (b) outpatient services; (c) intensive outpatient services; (d) intensive integrated service without 24-hour psychiatric monitoring; (e) nonsecure 24-hour services with psychiatric monitoring; and (f) secure 24-hour services with psychiatric management. Since the deinstitutionalization movement began a half century ago, these types of level of care principles are particularly important for meeting the needs of patients with all levels of behavioral health care needs.

Stepped Models of Intervention

The level of care models discussed in the preceding section were developed primarily to respond to the needs of individuals with severe mental illness and substance dependence and to identify the general level of care needed to address their problems as a whole. Other stepped models of care have been developed to address particular behavioral health issues. For example, treatment planning for suicidality involves deciding the appropriate level of intervention needed to address the level of suicide risk that has been identified. Because these models address particular behavioral health issues, they typically also address the full range of functioning in a more detailed manner. This section describes several stepped models of intervention that were developed to address some of the most prevalent behavioral health issues, namely, suicidality, substance abuse, depression, anxiety, and problems related to sexuality. These models are critical to developing treatment plans that address patients' problems and concerns at all levels of severity and complexity.

Suicidality

Appropriately conducting assessments and developing treatment plans for suicidal ideation and behavior are critical competencies for all behavioral health care professionals, given the prevalence and significance of suicidality (see Chapter 4). Understanding and implementing graduated, stepped level of care approaches are necessary for intervening in these cases. More immediate and intensive interventions for managing and treating suicidality are indicated as the risk for suicide increases. For example, Rudd (2006) recommended different interventions for five levels of suicide risk (i.e., none, mild, moderate, severe, and extreme). For patients at no or mild level of risk for suicide, no particular changes in ongoing treatment are recommended, but suicidal ideation should be monitored on an ongoing basis. For those at a moderate risk level, increasing the frequency or duration of outpatient visits may be recommended. The need for inpatient hospitalization must be evaluated immediately for those at higher levels of risk.

Substance Abuse

Given the high prevalence of substance abuse and major economic cost of associated medical, mental, and social problems, the U.S. Substance Abuse and Mental Health Services Administration (SAMHSA) initiated the Screen, Brief Intervention, Brief Treatment, and Referral to Treatment (SBIRT) program in the 1990s to expand treatment capacity and early intervention for substance abuse. This program is used in a variety of inpatient and outpatient medical settings to provide early intervention for those who are not dependent on substances but who may be engaging in problematic substance use or abuse (SAMHSA, 2008, 2011b). In the SBIRT program, brief substance abuse screening instruments are incorporated into routine medical practice. If a moderate risk for substance abuse is indicated when patients complete a screening instrument, brief interventions are provided to try to increase awareness of substance use patterns and consequences and to motivate behavior change to reduce harmful drinking and substance misuse. If moderate to high risks are identified, then more comprehensive brief treatment is provided. If severe risk or dependence is indicated, a referral for specialty treatment is then provided.

Depression and Anxiety

The United Kingdom has undertaken a pioneering effort to implement a comprehensive stepped level of care model to decrease depression and anxiety disorders. In 2007, the Department of Health instituted the National Institute for Health and Clinical Excellence treatment guidelines in two pilot programs to improve the availability of evidence-based psychological treatments for depression and anxiety throughout the United Kingdom (Clark et al., 2009). The pilot programs were effective, and a full national implementation is currently underway. This program involves systematic assessment and ongoing measurement of depressive and anxiety symptoms to inform the intervention and care that are provided. At lower levels of depression symptoms, self-help activities with guidance from a psychological well-being practitioner are available along with computer-assisted cognitive behavior therapy, psychoeducational groups, and structured physical activity. Also available are behavior therapy, couples therapy, and short-term psychodynamic therapy. Higher intensity services are available for moderate to severe depression and may include cognitive behavior therapy, interpersonal therapy, and medication (Clark, 2011).

Concerns Related to Sexuality

One of the early stepped approaches was developed to assist with concerns specific to sexuality. The permission, limited information, specific suggestions, and intensive treatment (PLISSIT) model, developed by Annon in 1976, suggests providing individuals with assurance ("permission") or limited answers for common, less complicated questions and concerns about one's sexuality. More specific guidance and finally intensive treatment are recommended for more complicated issues and problems.

Conclusion

These models illustrate the basic principle of treatment planning that the severity and complexity of patients' problems drives the intensity, type, and level of interventions that are planned to address those problems. Stepped models of care and intervention are necessary aspects of this approach. Individuals commonly have problems or concerns across several areas of their lives, whether they are just minor problems in a few areas or serious problems and co-occurring disorders in several areas. In all cases, stepped models help ensure that those concerns are addressed in an appropriate and efficient manner that matches the severity and complexity of individuals' problems and concerns.

Collaborative Care

Health care has become increasingly specialized as the scientific understanding of disease, health, and illness has grown. As a result, there has been growing interest in the benefits of and need for interprofessional treatment teams for evaluating cases, planning and implementing treatment, and monitoring patients' health status. In the 1970s, the Institute of Medicine (1972) and the World Health Organization (1978) began emphasizing the importance of teamwork and collaborative care, and the Institute of Medicine (2000, 2001) and the Interprofessional Education Collaborative Expert Panel (2011) more recently recommended collaborative care to improve the quality and effectiveness of health care in the United States.

The 2010 Patient Protection and Affordable Care Act, which represents the most significant change in health care delivery in the United States in decades, strongly encourages the development of new interprofessional team-based delivery systems such as Accountable Care Organizations and Patient-Centered Medical Homes (Nordal, 2012). These new health care delivery models take a biopsychosocial approach to meeting the behavioral as well as the physical health needs of patients in general. These models involve health professionals from multiple disciplines working in integrated collaborative teams to address the full range of health care patients seen in primary care. An integrated team approach is particularly important when caring for individuals with serious mental illness and substance dependence. It is frequently necessary to also involve family members and sometimes employers, landlords, religious leaders, or others who can play a significant role in planning and implementing treatment plans that effectively meet these patients' needs. This topic is discussed more extensively in Chapter 13.

INCORPORATING PSYCHOTHERAPY AND SUPPORTIVE COUNSELING IN THE TREATMENT PLAN

Psychotherapy is often part of the treatment plan in behavioral health care cases, and many behavioral health care providers obviously have practices that provide psychotherapy exclusively. Supportive counseling is also routinely provided across human service settings. It is important to note, however, that many psychologists, psychiatrists, and other therapists provide very little formal psychotherapy. Psychotherapy is uncommon in many neuropsychology and medical, school, forensic, and correctional psychology settings. Psychotherapy is a highly effective intervention (see Chapter 10), but it is not part of the treatment plan for many individuals. Therefore, it is important to note some basic indicators for the consideration of supportive counseling and psychotherapy in treatment plans.

Much of the history of the behavioral health care field has centered on the different theoretical orientations for understanding human development and conducting psychotherapy, and these orientations are frequently viewed as the starting point for conceptualizing cases and planning treatment. The biopsychosocial perspective on behavioral health care takes a different approach, however. From this perspective, the traditional theoretical orientations do not comprise the conceptual foundations for practicing the profession. Instead, case conceptualization is based on scientific knowledge of human development, functioning, and behavior change. In this approach, the traditional theoretical orientations remain very important in their capacity to inform empirically supported treatments, but they are generally viewed as therapies because of their inadequacies as scientific theories. These therapies are often remarkably effective (see Chapter 10), but there are also other interventions that are available to address the full range of behavioral health and biopsychosocial issues. Formal psychotherapy is very appropriate in many cases, but other interventions may be preferable depending on the patient's presenting problem, the setting, and the purpose of intervention.

Decisions about recommending psychotherapy as opposed to some other form of intervention are based on the findings of the assessment considered within the context of the best research evidence available, the therapist's clinical experience, and patient preferences and values. Treatment plans for many patients will focus on short-term symptom relief or problem-solving to improve functioning or adjustment regarding circumscribed issues. Supportive counseling and problem solving are often very appropriate for these patients. The goal of treatment in many other cases, however, is to find comprehensive, long-term solutions to maladaptive patterns of emotional, cognitive, or behavioral functioning and to improve adjustment and functioning in important areas of a person's life. In these cases, psychotherapy is often the treatment of choice. Psychotherapists frequently attempt to identify underlying sources of distress and dysfunction and correct both proximal and distal sources of that dysfunction so that problems and psychopathology can be resolved on an enduring basis. For these patients, the focus is often on fundamental changes in maladaptive personality characteristics, emotional and behavioral responses, and cognitive distortions.

RECOGNIZING AND ANTICIPATING COMPLICATING FACTORS

In addition to addressing the severity and complexity of patient's biopsychosocial problems and circumstances, carefully constructed treatment plans anticipate challenges and obstacles that the patient is likely to face during the treatment process. In the ideal case, treatment plans are developed with complete and reliable information through a collaborative process involving the patient, therapist, and other relevant stakeholders in patients' lives (e.g., family members, medical providers), with no major challenges or obstacles that arise and interfere with treatment progress. Many cases do not proceed in this ideal manner, however. Some challenges that arise during treatment are the result of events outside of a person's control or are a part of behavior patterns that had not been revealed. Many of these situations are impossible to anticipate and must be dealt with after they arise. The following examples illustrate the variety that can arise in these cases:

- Automobile accidents, criminal victimizations, job losses, major medical illnesses.
- A patient informs you that he cannot pay his copay for treatment because the bank is foreclosing on his unpaid house mortgage and he lost all his past month's salary in gambling.

- A patient who has not worked outside the home in many years reports that her husband, a physician with whom she has an extremely difficult relationship, has been arrested for driving a vehicle while intoxicated and was immediately terminated from his position in the clinic where he practiced.

Many issues that complicate the treatment process are predictable, however, and should be incorporated into treatment planning. For example, a common, predictable difficulty involves the termination process for individuals with dependency issues and abandonment histories. Challenges and obstacles can take many forms, however, and can occur in any of the biopsychosocial areas of functioning. The following contextual factors often complicate treatment and frequently can be anticipated:

- a patient's insight into her or his own problems, acceptance of responsibility for her or his own problems and own recovery stage of change;
- a patient's level of family, peer, and other support;
- a patient's level of stress;
- instability in a patient's psychosocial environment;
- co-occurring medical, psychiatric, and substance use disorders;
- a patient's level of risk to self or others;
- strength of the therapeutic alliance;
- dissolution of romantic or family relationships;
- a patient's coping style and related personality characteristics (e.g., resilience, impulsivity);
- lack of finances, insurance restrictions, transportation or geographic barriers;
- cultural factors;
- disagreement among stakeholders in a patient's treatment;
- legal or administrative issues affecting treatment (e.g., involuntary hospitalization, mandated treatment, evaluation for disability benefits);
- a patient's decision making capacity is questionable;
- a patient's treatment history and previous attempts to solve problems; and/or
- loss of employment.

Identifying and effectively managing these issues requires substantial clinical knowledge and skill, but the success of treatment also often depends on anticipating and working through and around these issues. In addition, it is important to recognize and incorporate facilitative factors that may arise during the course of treatment such as newly developed resources or strengths (e.g., a reestablished relationship with a parent, sibling, or friend that had been ruptured in the past; the initiation of a new, healthy, romantic relationship; a job promotion resulting from improved work performance). These can result in more comprehensive, meaningful, and enduring improvements in treatment outcomes as well. For these reasons, treatment planning must remain dynamic and accommodate significant changes that frequently occur during the treatment process.

PROVIDING ONGOING CARE AND FOLLOW-UP

Many patients have severe need and chronic conditions and are often unable to maintain their treatment gains without ongoing monitoring, support, and care. For example, ongoing care and follow-up interventions are critical considerations in cases involving suicide risk (e.g., Joiner, 2005; Rudd, 2006), and parts of the substance abuse treatment field are shifting from an acute to an ongoing care model (Hazelton, 2008). Relapse is common in depression and anxiety and many other disorders, and the treatment of personality disorders typically requires ongoing attention and care as well. Emphasis on the ongoing management of chronic medical conditions is also growing steadily in medicine as chronic diseases have become widespread, and behavior and lifestyle factors are central features of the treatment plans for many patients with chronic conditions. When behavioral health care is focused on meeting patients' health and biopsychosocial needs, follow-up and plans for ongoing support and care become routine considerations in treatment planning.

IDENTIFYING ALTERNATIVE INTERVENTIONS

Significant coursework is needed to address the topic of the evaluation and selection of interventions that are most likely to be effective with particular patients with particular behavioral health and biopsychosocial issues. Many different psychologically, socially, and biologically oriented behavioral health interventions have been developed over the past century. The safety and effectiveness of many of these have been thoroughly tested though many others have not received this type of evaluation (see Chapter 10). The number of alternative treatments available is also growing. For example, a range of complementary and alternative medicine procedures are gaining increasing acceptance in behavioral health care and medicine in recent years (Barnett & Shale, 2012). In a national survey, 38% of adults and 12% of children in the United States reported using some form of complementary and alternative medicine practices and products in the preceding year (Barnes, Bloom,

& Nahin, 2008). Most frequently used were dietary supplements, meditation, chiropractic, aromatherapy, massage therapy, and yoga.

Table 9.2 provides examples of the wide variety of interventions that are available and might be incorporated into a comprehensive biopsychosocial approach to behavioral health care treatment of issues within particular areas of biopsychosocial functioning. This listing is provided only to illustrate the wide range of interventions that are available for addressing problems and disorders at varying levels of intensity. In general, the intensity and level of care of the interventions listed increases as the severity and complexity of the problems increases. The table does not provide an exhaustive listing of interventions that can be integrated into treatment, nor does it evaluate the empirical evidence regarding the effectiveness of the interventions. (More complete discussions of these issues are available from Barnett & Shale, 2012; Dziegielewski, 2010; S. L. Johnson, 2003; Jongsma, Berghuis, & Bruce, 2008; Jongsma, Peterson, & Bruce, 2006; Jongsma, Peterson, McInnis, & Bruce, 2006; L. Seligman & Reichenberg, 2007).

DISCUSSION: TREATING THE WHOLE PERSON

Mastering treatment planning for a wide range of issues encountered in behavioral health care practice is a highly complex process that requires extensive study and clinical experience. The basic guidelines and principles discussed in the preceding sections are necessary, however, in the general conceptualization of the treatment planning process from a comprehensive biopsychosocial perspective. Clearly, this approach is more complex than many traditional approaches that involve implementing the psychotherapy dictated by one's adopted theoretical orientation. A science-based, health care–oriented biopsychosocial approach involves a comprehensive, holistic perspective for evaluating treatment needs that addresses concerns across all the biopsychosocial domains and at all levels of severity and complexity.

A basic principle of treatment planning from the health care–oriented biopsychosocial approach is addressing the severity and complexity of need with appropriate intensity, types, and levels of intervention. Some questions and concerns require watchful waiting or no treatment at all, whereas emergency needs require immediate attention. Level of care and stepped care models are frequently used to address the many issues that fall between these extremes. Carefully crafted treatment plans also anticipate barriers and obstacles to treatment, and working through and around these issues helps maximize the likelihood of positive outcomes. This comprehensive approach to treatment planning allows therapists to address the full range of issues that individuals bring with them into behavioral health care.

TABLE 9.2

Examples of Possible Interventions Across the Biopsychosocial Domains and Levels of Severity or Need

Domains and components	Strengths (mild, moderate, or major, +1 to +3)	No problem (0)	Mild problem severity (−1)	Moderate problem severity (−2)	Severe Problem (−3)
		Biological functioning			
General medical history	• Reinforce healthy eating, exercise, and lifestyle	• Reinforce healthy eating, exercise, and lifestyle	• Persuade client to engage in healthier lifestyle	• Refer for a physical exam • Help monitor compliance with prescribed treatments	• Refer for immediate physical evaluation or emergency care • Help monitor compliance with prescribed treatments
Childhood health history	• Reinforce healthy coping, adjustment, and treatment adherence if problems were overcome	• Same	• Same	• Same	• Same
Medications	• Reinforce healthy habits and healthy use of medicines and substances	• Reinforce healthy habits and healthy use of medicines and substances	• Refer for medical evaluation • Help monitor effectiveness and side effects of medications	• Refer for psychiatric or medical evaluation • Help monitor effectiveness and side effects of meds • Coordinate family members to supervise patient medicine use	• Refer for immediate psychiatric or medical evaluation or hospitalization • Coordinate family members to supervise client medicine use

(continues)

TABLE 9.2
Examples of Possible Interventions Across the Biopsychosocial Domains
and Levels of Severity or Need   (Continued)

Domains and components	Strengths (mild, moderate, or major, +1 to +3)	No problem (0)	Mild problem severity (−1)	Moderate problem severity (−2)	Severe Problem (−3)
		Psychological functioning			
History of present illness or problem	• Reinforce positive mental health and role functioning • Amplify resources and strengths where helpful	• Reinforce positive mental health and role functioning • Recommend helpful psycho-educational interventions and online resources	• Individual therapy • Group therapy • Support group • Bibliotherapy • Further develop strengths and resources • Meditation, yoga • Online resources and apps	• Individual therapy • Group therapy • Develop compensating strengths and resources • Meditation, yoga • Online resources and apps	• Evaluate need for hospitalization • Refer for evaluation for psychotropic medicine • Develop compensating strengths and resources • Meditation, yoga
Individual psychological history	• Reinforce positive mental health and role functioning • Amplify resources & strengths where helpful	• Reinforce positive mental health and role functioning • Recommend helpful psycho-educational interventions • Further develop strengths and resources	• Conduct neuro-psychological screening • Individual therapy • Group therapy • Support group • Bibliotherapy • Further develop strengths and resources • Meditation, yoga • Online resources and apps	• Refer for neuro-psychological evaluation • Consider intensive long-term therapy (e.g., psychodynamic, ACT, DBT) • Develop compensating strengths and resources • Meditation, yoga • Online resources and apps	• Refer for neuro-psychological evaluation • Consider residential or intensive out-patient treatment • Refer client for vocational rehab., social services, etc. as needed • Refer family members for support group

Substance abuse history	• Reinforce positive mental health and role functioning • Amplify resources & strengths where helpful	• Reinforce positive mental health and role functioning • Recommend helpful psycho-educational interventions	• Discuss substance use and its consequences • Work on reducing substance misuse • Online resources and apps	• Refer for brief substance abuse treatment • Engage client in mutual support group • Online resources and apps	• Consider detox hospitalization • Refer for intensive substance abuse treatment
Suicidal ideation	• Reinforce positive mental health and role functioning	• Reinforce positive mental health and role functioning	• Outpatient therapy • Ongoing monitoring of suicidality	• More intensive outpatient therapy • Ongoing monitoring of suicidality	• Evaluate need for hospitalization • Refer to specialist • Ongoing monitoring of suicidality
Individual developmental history	• Reinforce positive mental health and role functioning • Amplify resources and strengths where helpful	• Reinforce positive mental health and role functioning • Recommend helpful psycho-educational interventions	• Reinforce positive mental health and role functioning • Reinforce and further develop strengths and resources • Online resources and apps	• Reinforce positive mental health and role functioning • Reinforce and further develop strengths and resources • Refer to mutual support group • Online resources and apps	• Reinforce positive mental health and role functioning • Reinforce and further develop strengths and resources • Refer to mutual support group
Childhood abuse history	• Reinforce positive mental health and role functioning • Amplify resources & strengths where helpful	• Reinforce positive mental health and role functioning • Recommend helpful psycho-educational interventions	• Individual therapy • Bibliotherapy • Meditation, yoga • Online resources and apps	• Individual therapy • Group therapy • Family therapy if appropriate • Meditation, yoga • Online resources and apps	• Consider intensive long-term therapy (e.g., psycho-dynamic, ACT, DBT) • Meditation, yoga

(continues)

TABLE 9.2

Examples of Possible Interventions Across the Biopsychosocial Domains and Levels of Severity or Need   (Continued)

Domains and components	Strengths (mild, moderate, or major, +1 to +3)	No problem (0)	Mild problem severity (-1)	Moderate problem severity (-2)	Severe Problem (-3)
Other psychological traumas	• Reinforce positive mental health and role functioning • Amplify resources and strengths where helpful	• Reinforce positive mental health and role functioning • Recommend helpful psychoeducational interventions	• Individual therapy • Bibliotherapy • Further develop strengths and resources • Meditation, yoga • Online resources and apps	• Consider exposure and related therapies • Meditation, yoga • Online resources and apps	• Consider exposure and intensive long-term therapies (e.g., psychodynamic, ACT, DBT) • Meditation, yoga
Personality style and characteristics	• Reinforce positive mental health and role functioning • Amplify resources and strengths where helpful	• Reinforce positive mental health and role functioning • Recommend helpful psychoeducational interventions	• Social skills training groups • Bibliotherapy • Recommend helpful psychoeducational interventions and online resources	• Individual therapy • Group therapy • Online resources and apps	• Consider intensive long-term therapy (e.g., psychodynamic, ACT, DBT)
Mental status examination	• Reinforce positive mental health and role functioning • Amplify resources and strengths where helpful	• Reinforce positive mental health and role functioning • Recommend psychoeducational interventions if it would be helpful	• Conduct neuropsychological screening	• Conduct psychological testing • Refer for neuropsychological exam	• Refer for psychiatric or neuropsychological exam

	Sociocultural functioning			
Relationships and social support	• Reinforce healthy relationships	• Couple session to assess nature and severity of relationship issues	• Individual therapy • Couple therapy • Communication skills training • Develop safety plan if relevant • Refer client to anger management program if relevant	• Individual therapy • Couple therapy • Develop safety plan if relevant • Refer client to anger management program if relevant
Family history	• Maintain positive family relationships	• Family session to assess nature of family issues • Bibliotherapy	• Family therapy • Support group	• Family therapy
Current living situation	• Reinforce positive living situation	• Invite in roommates to conduct assessment session	• Facilitate temporary move to family member or friend	• Refer for evaluation of need for shelter and social services
Employment	• Maintain positive work history and vocational development	• Assist client with planning job search • Refer for career counseling • Reinforce strengths and resources	• Refer for career counseling • Develop strengths and resources	• Psychological testing to determine reasons for employment problems • Refer for vocational rehabilitation
Educational history	• Anticipate future educational and training needs	• Refer for GED program, vocational training, job retraining, career counseling • Recommend online resources	• Complete psychological testing to determine nature and extent of cognitive deficits • Recommend online resources	• Refer for neuropsychology evaluation of cognitive deficits

(continues)

TABLE 9.2

Examples of Possible Interventions Across the Biopsychosocial Domains and Levels of Severity or Need   (Continued)

Domains and components	Strengths (mild, moderate, or major, +1 to +3)	No problem (0)	Mild problem severity (−1)	Moderate problem severity (−2)	Severe Problem (−3)
Financial resources	• Reinforce responsible financial planning	• Reinforce responsible financial planning	• Review client's budget • Bibliotherapy • Online resources	• Refer for financial counseling • Family sessions to assess nature of problems • Online resources	• Coordinate application for welfare, SSDI • Refer for financial counseling • Pursue guardianship for finances
Legal issues	• Reinforce responsible approach to legal and safety issues	• Reinforce responsible approach to legal and safety issues	• Individual therapy • Obtain copies of legal proceedings or reports	• Monitor attendance and performance at school or work • Monitor client's appointments with court officials	• Enlist legal aid • Invite probation officials to periodic meetings • Refer client to ex-offender programs
Military history	• NA	• NA	• Individual therapy	• Refer to Veterans Affairs	• Refer to VA • Refer to veterans support group
Activities of interest/ hobbies	• Maintain activities and interests • Maintain healthy balance of work and leisure	• Encourage engagement in past interests • Explore new interests and hobbies	• Facilitate involvement in community activities • Explore new interests and hobbies	• Individual therapy regarding enjoyment and meaning in life	• Refer for occupational therapy • Meet with family or friends to coordinate activities

Religion	• Maintain meaningful religious involvements	• If interested, encourage engagement in past interests • If interested, explore new religious involvement	• Bibliotherapy • If interested, explore new religious involvement	• Consult with religious leader	• Refer to specialist
Spirituality	• Maintain meaningful spiritual involvements	• If interested, encourage engagement in past interests • If interested, explore new spiritual involvement • Meditation, yoga	• Bibliotherapy • If interested, explore new spiritual involvement • Meditation, yoga	• Refer to spiritual leader or community	• Refer to specialist
Multicultural issues	• Maintain meaningful cultural involvements	• If interested, encourage engagement in past interests • If interested, explore new cultural involvements	• Bibliotherapy • Refer to community organizations	• Refer to community organizations • Refer to specialist	• Refer to specialist

Note. ACT = acceptance and commitment therapy; DBT = dialectical behavior therapy; NA = not applicable. From *Foundations of Professional Psychology: The End of Theoretical Orientations and the Emergence of the Biopsychosocial Approach* (pp. 159–164), by T. P. Melchert, 2011, London, England: Elsevier. Copyright 2011 by Elsevier. Adapted with permission.

CASE EXAMPLE: A BIOPSYCHOSOCIAL APPROACH TO TREATMENT PLANNING WITH A MILDLY DEPRESSED PATIENT

The case example involving Maria, the 44-year-old married Latina woman who was discussed in Chapter 8, is revisited here in terms of treatment planning from a biopsychosocial approach. In her first session with the psychologist, Maria reported that she had disengaged from multiple activities that used to be important to her. She reported that she used to exercise regularly and had been in good physical condition before her children were born, and that regularly drinking wine in the evening contributed to her moderate weight gain. She reported that her diet was healthy, however, and that she was not overeating. She also reported that she and her husband had gradually stopped going out on dates together after their two children were born. The psychologist thought that Maria might be willing to address each of these issues and that doing so could be helpful for maintaining long-term improvement in her mood and functioning. Therefore, he suggested that she begin exercising again, decrease her alcohol consumption, and begin having weekly dates with her husband. She agreed with this plan. He also noted that Maria's work situation appeared to be going very well and that this was an area of major strength in her life, and they both agreed that no changes were needed or desired in that area at this time.

Maria had reported that she had disengaged from her own family of origin and was avoiding her mother because she disliked her mother's criticism. Maria said she was uncomfortable with this situation but that more contact with her mother was not worth the criticism that came with it. She did agree, however, to explore possibilities for improving her relationship with her mother. After noting how much Maria cared about her two children and how interested she was in their education, the psychologist suggested that getting more involved with her children's schooling would help her feel good about her parental guidance around their education. Maria agreed to explore this possibility by attending a parent–teacher organization meeting at her daughters' school.

After the psychologist and Maria discussed each of these topics, Maria's initial treatment plan was developed, and it included the following elements:

1. monitor level of depression;
2. stop drinking altogether during weekdays for the next 2 months;
3. schedule dates out with her husband a minimum of once per week;
4. begin a regular exercise routine;
5. go to parent–teacher organization meetings at the children's school to see whether there are good ways to get more involved in her daughter's education and to support the school in general; and

6. explore the possibility of improving the relationship with her mother and the rest of her family of origin.

The plan focused on making changes in terms of physical health and her involvement with her husband and children, the most important people in her life at the time. It was less clear how to address the issues with her mother and the rest of her family of origin at this initial stage of treatment, though it was judged that addressing the other issues first was more likely to result in productive processing later on of her relationship with her own family.

10

TREATMENT

The behavioral health care field as a whole has relied on a remarkably eclectic set of diverse theoretical orientations for conceptualizing the treatment process. Although allegiance to these orientations appears to have declined in recent years, they still play a major role in case conceptualization and treatment. Students learning the profession are expected to adopt a theoretical orientation to guide their clinical practice, and the Association of Psychology Postdoctoral and Internship Centers's (APPIC) uniform application for applying to an American Psychological Association (APA)-accredited or APPIC-listed psychology internship includes the following required essay item: "Please describe your theoretical orientation and how this influences your approach to case conceptualization and practice" (APPIC, 2009).

The science-based biopsychosocial perspective takes a very different approach to understanding behavioral health care treatment. It is essentially oriented around being a clinical science. It begins with a systematic approach

DOI: 10.1037/14441-011
Biopsychosocial Practice: A Science-Based Framework for Behavioral Health Care, by T. P. Melchert
Copyright © 2015 by the American Psychological Association. All rights reserved.

to learning and applying the scientific and ethical foundations of the field, and its primary focus is on meeting the behavioral health and biopsychosocial needs of patients. Chapters 8 and 9 outlined how patients' behavioral health needs and functioning can be assessed and a treatment plan can be developed that addresses their needs in the context of their biopsychosocial circumstances. Those chapters were relatively technical, emphasizing the information needed and the decisions that have to be made as part of the assessment and treatment planning processes. This chapter discusses treatment from a more conceptual perspective, emphasizing the implications of a science-based, health care–oriented approach to behavioral health treatment. It begins by discussing the overarching framework for approaching behavioral health treatment from the biopsychosocial approach and then outlines a thorough approach to evaluating the safety and effectiveness of treatment.

COMPREHENSIVE SCIENCE-BASED APPROACH TO BEHAVIORAL HEALTH CARE TREATMENT

The science-based biopsychosocial approach takes a very different perspective on behavioral health care than most traditional approaches to learning and practicing the profession. Traditional approaches typically involve learning one or more of the traditional schools of psychotherapy (e.g., psychodynamic, behavioral, humanistic, cognitive, systemic). The theoretical model and its associated techniques, methods, and processes are then learned and applied in supervised clinical practice. The science-based biopsychosocial approach, on the other hand, has a very different starting point. After reviewing current scientific knowledge regarding human psychology along with the ethical foundations of the field, attention shifts to research on the behavioral health and biopsychosocial functioning of the population so that therapists understand the nature of health, dysfunction, and biopsychosocial well-being in general. This background allows therapists to then put the biopsychosocial needs of individual patients in proper context. Building on this foundational knowledge, the treatment process for addressing behavioral health needs is then learned. So rather than start by learning a theoretical orientation that can be applied and adapted to work with some range of individuals, therapists begin by focusing on scientific knowledge of human psychology and biopsychosocial functioning, and then they learn about the treatment process and interventions that can be used to address behavioral health problems and improve biopsychosocial functioning.

Understanding individuals as whole persons in the context of their biopsychosocial life circumstances presents a very broad perspective for understanding human psychology and behavioral health treatment. Chapters 4 through 7 noted the wide range of biopsychosocial issues that are common in the general population. For example, the most common psychiatric disorders listed in the *Diagnostic and Statistical Manual of Mental Disorders* (fifth ed.; American Psychiatric Association, 2013) are sexuality concerns, addictions, panic attacks, and sleep problems (see Table 4.1). A substantial proportion of the population (approximately 15%–20%) meets the criteria for a personality disorder as well. In the sociocultural domain, large proportions of the population deal with relationship problems, parenting problems among those with children, financial stress and vocational instability, criminal involvement and victimization, single parenthood, and divorce and reconfigured families. All aspects of biopsychosocial functioning occur within the context of cultural, ethnic, and socioeconomic diversity that greatly affect development and functioning as well. In the medical domain, common conditions among American adults include weight gain and obesity, lower back pain and chronic joint symptoms, high blood pressure, arthritis and other pain conditions, and restlessness and nervousness (see Table 6.1). These medical conditions frequently cause substantial distress and impairment, and psychological factors are involved in their etiology, consequences, and treatment. The co-occurrence of problems within and across these domains is common.

Conceptualizing behavioral health care in this manner is ambitious, as it must be to capture the complexity of individuals' lives. The starting point is the recognition that psychological outcomes are multifactorially determined based on interacting biological, psychological, and sociocultural processes. This type of perspective is necessary for understanding personality functioning, psychopathology, intellectual and social functioning, physical health, the nature and etiology of acute and chronic problems, risk factors, strengths and resources, and virtually all the common issues that one encounters in behavioral health care. From career decision-making to serious mental illness, this type of comprehensive, integrative perspective is necessary for understanding problems in context and planning and implementing interventions that maximize the likelihood of treatment effectiveness over the short and long term.

To make matters more complicated still, the biopsychosocial approach also incorporates a health and wellness perspective that includes the goal of optimizing functioning across the biopsychosocial domains. Even when patients have no significant problems that warrant clinical attention in particular areas, converting these to areas of strength helps develop resilience and promotes optimal functioning. This perspective is critical for individuals at all levels of functioning. Even highly vulnerable individuals, such as children or seniors dealing with serious biopsychosocial problems or individuals with serious mental illness, can benefit greatly from stronger internal and external resources and supports. Minimizing vulnerabilities and risk factors while strengthening resources is frequently critical for maximizing treatment effectiveness and optimal functioning over the long term for these populations. This perspective is increasingly being advocated. The New Freedom Commission on Mental Health (2003) concluded that the U.S. mental health care system should be fundamentally transformed around the goals of building resilience and facilitating recovery, and SAMHSA (2011a) initiated a national effort to focus attention on developing strengths and resources among individuals recovering from mental illness and substance use disorders. They advocated that health care providers promote recovery by emphasizing wellness across eight areas of well-being: emotional, physical, social, occupational, intellectual, financial, environmental, and spiritual.

Broad Perspective on Treatment

Traditional approaches to behavioral health care have often used particular theoretical orientations to treat mental disorders. These orientations are certainly still important for informing the methods and processes of empirically supported psychotherapies, but the understanding of human psychology and behavioral health care has now broadened significantly beyond the conceptualizations offered by the traditional theoretical orientations.

The research clearly indicates that a variety of therapeutic interventions can effectively address behavioral health needs and promote biopsychosocial functioning. It is not possible to develop expertise with a large number of these interventions, and current practice guidelines offer no advice on the range of treatments that therapists in different types of general and specialized practice should be able to provide. One's approach to treatment varies greatly depending on one's specialization and practice setting. General practitioners are able to address a broad range of common behavioral health issues, whereas specialists possess extensive knowledge regarding a narrower range of issues. The number of treatments one offers across these practice settings can vary significantly, but in all cases one must be able to conceptualize cases from a holistic biopsychosocial approach. Whether one is a general practitioner treating patients for depression, anxiety, and relationship issues or a specialist in sex therapy or neuropsychological rehabilitation, the general expectation of health care systems is now that one is able to conceptualize care from a biopsychosocial perspective.

Several trends currently underway are likely to continue shaping behavioral health care treatment for psychologists. For one thing, psychologists are increasing the number of treatments they can provide. Psychologists' endorsement of eclectic and integrative approaches to practice has grown steadily in recent decades (Norcross, 2005), and small numbers have even completed psychopharmacology training so that they can provide pharmacological treatment in addition to psychotherapeutic intervention (in Louisiana, New Mexico, Guam, and the U.S. Department of Defense; Fox et al., 2009). Another related trend involves the increasing diversity of settings where psychologists practice. Psychologists now work in a wide variety of medical, educational, industrial and organizational, military, rehabilitation, sport, and correctional settings (APA Center for Workforce Studies, 2011). Providing traditional psychotherapy is often not the first priority in many of these settings, whereas assisting individuals' to function effectively and meet the goals and needs of the institution or organization they are a part of is usually a top priority. Being able to offer a range of interventions beyond traditional psychotherapy is necessary in these settings.

If the Patient Protection and Affordable Care Act of 2010 is implemented as it was originally intended, it is likely to have a significant impact on the future employment of psychologists as well. This law is the largest driver of change in the health care delivery system in the United States for the foreseeable future, and it strongly encourages the development of new delivery systems such as Accountable Care Organizations and Patient-Centered Medical Homes (Nordal, 2012). Integrating behavioral and physical health care in a single setting through interprofessional team-based care has the potential to lead to improved quality of care and reduced costs (see Chapter 13). If psychologists work in these new settings, these new health care delivery models require that they efficiently assess and treat a wide range of behavioral health issues in a collaborative manner with other health care professionals. This requires familiarity with a range of treatment options. Many would also argue that a biopsychosocial approach is necessary to work effectively in these settings (e.g., APA Presidential Task Force on the Future of Psychology Practice, 2009). It may not be possible to apply approaches revolving around one of the traditional theoretical orientations in primary health care settings.

Another trend that is likely to continue, especially among those working in primary health care, is the use of stepped treatment approaches. As noted in Chapter 9, these often include brief screens and a range of minimal to intensive intervention options that match the severity of patients' needs (e.g., Screen, Brief Intervention, Brief Treatment, and Referral to Treatment [SBIRT] and permission, limited information, specific suggestions, and intensive treatment [PLISSIT]). Increasing numbers of psychologists are likely to adopt more of these stepped approaches, deliver the less intensive interventions themselves, and then refer individuals with more severe needs to specialty health care providers (Nordal, 2012).

Another growing trend is the emphasis on health and wellness. The positive psychology movement is now well established within psychology, and the recovery and wellness movements are getting established within the broader behavioral health care delivery systems. The medical community is also increasingly recognizing the importance of behavior and lifestyle in the development and treatment of disease (Institute of Medicine, 2004). These movements continue to focus attention on promoting health and wellness across the biopsychosocial domains in addition to treating disorders and pathology.

Priority on the Safety and Effectiveness of Treatment

The biopsychosocial approach advocated in this volume is grounded in science and ethics. As discussed in Chapter 3, health care ethics is very clear with regard to the obligations to provide safe and effective treatment. The implications of the ethical obligation of nonmaleficence ("do no harm") are obvious when a health care professional intentionally harms others, whereas the implications of unintentional harms are typically more complex and subtle. Harm can be caused by omission as well as commission, by imposing risks through either ignorance or carelessness such as when a therapist has insufficient training and supervised experience to accurately diagnose common disorders, complete an adequate suicide risk assessment and treatment plan, or does not appropriately manage countertransference. If patients are harmed as a result, the therapist can be judged negligent and potentially guilty of malpractice. In addition, the ethical principle of beneficence obligates health care professionals to provide benefits and promote patients' welfare, attempt to prevent harms from occurring, remove them once they do occur, and balance benefits and harms in an optimal manner.

The principles of evidence-based practice also strongly emphasize the safety and effectiveness of treatment. In its landmark report, *Crossing the Quality Chasm: A New Health System for the 21st Century*, the Institute of Medicine (2001) identified safety and effectiveness as core needs in health care. Its authors further concluded that clinical decision making should be based on empirical evidence regarding the safety and effectiveness of interventions as well as one's clinical experience and expertise, in addition to accommodating patient values and preferences. The APA (2006) also adopted a policy of evidence-based practice for psychology that endorsed the same principles.

Although therapists have always been concerned about the safety and effectiveness of their interventions, the safety of psychotherapy received relatively little empirical research attention until recently. Bergin (1966) investigated patient deterioration that appeared to be caused by psychotherapy, but little further attention was given to the issue until the 1990s when repressed memories of child abuse became highly controversial. Other therapies for which there is evidence of potential or actual harm include rebirthing attachment therapy, group interventions for antisocial youth, conversion therapy for gay and lesbian patients, critical incident stress debriefing, and grief therapy (see Chapter 3). Research also indicates that individual therapists vary in their effectiveness, a finding that obligates therapists and their supervisors to monitor the progress of treatment.

Systematic Monitoring of the Progress and Effectiveness of Treatment

Emphasizing the safety and effectiveness of treatment also focuses attention on the systematic monitoring of treatment outcomes. The importance of outcomes measurement is highlighted by both the ethical emphasis on providing care that is safe and effective and the scientific emphasis on measuring outcomes in a reliable and valid manner in order to determine the effects of treatment. The effectiveness and efficiency of health care spending are also rising priorities as recognition grows that current levels of health care spending in the United States are not sustainable.

The biopsychosocial approach to behavioral health care emphasizes outcomes assessment. Monitoring the progress of treatment is important for detecting patients who have not improved or who have deteriorated so that appropriate adjustments can be made. Outcomes assessment at termination and at follow-up is necessary to properly evaluate the effectiveness of treatment. Given their importance, these topics are discussed in more detail below in the section "The Safety and Effectiveness of Individual Psychotherapy" and in Chapter 11.

Communication and Collaboration With Other Professionals and Third Parties

Health care professionals address a wide range of biopsychosocial issues and consequently need to be able to communicate and work collaboratively with health care and human service professionals from all professions. Concern about inadequate communication and collaboration among health care professionals grew quickly as part of the patient safety movement. The 2000 report by the Institute of Medicine, *To Err Is Human*, alarmed policymakers and the public because it reported on widespread safety problems in American health care (see Chapter 3). Problems with communication and collaboration were cited as the root of these problems. In their call for a fundamental redesign of the American health care system to improve quality, the 2001 Institute of Medicine report, *Crossing the Quality Chasm*, found that active collaboration and communication among clinicians and institutions was imperative for improving safety and effectiveness. Their 2003 report, *Health Professions Education: A Bridge to Quality*, further concluded that interdisciplinary teamwork was one of five core competencies for all health professionals. The Interprofessional Education Collaborative Expert

Panel (2011) also included interprofessional communication and teamwork in its *Core Competencies for Interprofessional Collaborative Practice*.

Therapists frequently communicate and collaborate with family members of patients, other health care professionals, educators, employers, criminal justice and social service professionals, and others who can assist with assessment or treatment. Chapter 8 emphasized the importance of collateral contacts for obtaining reliable and valid assessment information in many cases, and collaborating with these individuals can also be critical for treatment effectiveness. For example, collaborative approaches are seen as necessary for effectively treating the many behavioral health problems found among infants, children, and adolescents in the United States (Egger & Emde, 2011; Kazak et al., 2010). Collaborative approaches are typically also necessary when problem severity and complexity are high (e.g., serious substance abuse, psychiatric disorders, medical conditions, relationship and family dysfunction) and when patients are more vulnerable and dependent (e.g., children, many individuals with cognitive or physical disability, many seniors).

The need for psychologists to collaborate with other professionals is also growing as they increasingly work in more diverse settings. Interprofessional collaborative primary care teamwork is necessary for integrating behavioral health, disease management, and preventive interventions in primary care settings (see Chapter 13). Psychologists working in hospital, educational, military, industrial and organizational, rehabilitation, sport, and correctional settings also need to communicate and collaborate effectively with other professionals in order to meet institutional and agency goals as well as patients' individual needs and goals.

THE SAFETY AND EFFECTIVENESS OF INDIVIDUAL PSYCHOTHERAPY

This section examines in detail the safety and effectiveness of treatment, which are clearly of central concern in behavioral health care. A science-based and health care–oriented approach to behavioral health care tends to increase the specificity of the questions asked because practitioners need to know much more than just whether a treatment has been found to be effective.

The discussion of treatment effectiveness focuses on individual adult psychotherapy. Several of the findings discussed also apply with regard to family, child and adolescent, and group therapy, but readers should consult other resources for discussions of those treatment formats. As illustrated in Chapter 9, a variety of additional interventions are useful in behavioral health care such as computer-assisted and online interventions, bibliotherapy, self-help groups, supportive counseling, combined medication and psychotherapy, mindfulness, biofeedback, and diet and physical exercise. Readers also should consult other resources for evaluations of those interventions. The following questions are addressed in this section:

- Is psychotherapy effective?
- Is the effectiveness of psychotherapy clinically significant? How often do patients return to normal functioning following treatment?
- Do the benefits of psychotherapy last?
- How does the effectiveness of psychotherapy compare with the effectiveness of psychotropic medications?
- Does psychotherapy work better for some patients than others? Do some patients get worse following therapy?
- What factors account for the effectiveness of psychotherapy?
- How important are the skills of the individual therapist in explaining therapy effectiveness?
- Given that not all patients in therapy improve, can the number of treatment failures be reduced?

Is Psychotherapy Effective?

In 1952, Hans Eysenck presented a fundamental challenge to the psychotherapy field when he concluded that research data did not provide support for the effectiveness of psychotherapy and specifically that psychotherapy did not result in more improvement beyond what occurred with natural spontaneous remission. It took a quarter century of therapy outcome research before his conclusion was reversed. This question was considered settled by the 1980s as the accumulated data showed that psychotherapy is generally effective for a broad range of mental health disorders and across a wide range of therapy approaches. M. L. Smith and Glass (1977) conducted the first meta-analysis of the therapy outcomes research and found an overall effect size of .85 (M. L. Smith, Glass, & Miller, 1980). Many meta-analyses followed, and eventually it was possible to conduct meta-analyses of meta-analyses. Lipsey and Wilson (1993) reviewed all the meta-analyses they could locate and determined that the mean effect size was .81. Lambert and Bergin (1994) conducted a similar analysis and found an average effect size of .82; Grissom (1996) found an aggregate effect size of .75. Wampold (2001) evaluated the results from these and other meta-analyses and concluded:

> A reasonable and defensible point estimate for the efficacy of psychotherapy would be .80. . . . This effect would be classified as a large effect in the social sciences, which means that the average patient receiving therapy would be better off than 79% of untreated patients, that psychotherapy

accounts for about 14% of the variance in outcomes, and the success rate would change from 31% for the control group to 69% for the treatment group. Simply stated, *psychotherapy is remarkably efficacious*. (italics in the original; pp. 70–71)

The effectiveness of psychotherapy is substantial when compared with that of medical, psychopharmacological, educational, correctional, and other human service interventions (Barlow, 2004; G. J. Meyer et al., 2001; Reed & Eisman, 2006). In fact, the effect size for psychotherapy ($d = .80$, which translates to $r = .37$) far exceeds that of many common medical treatments. For example, G. J. Meyer et al. (2001) found that the correlation between coronary artery bypass surgery for stable heart disease and survival at 5 years is .08; between antibiotic treatment for acute middle ear pain in children and improvement at 2 to 7 days, .07; and between taking aspirin and reduced risk of death by heart attack, .02. These would be categorized as small or exceedingly small effect sizes; ($r = \pm.10$ is considered a small effect following Cohen's (1988) guidelines).

An easily interpreted and increasingly popular metric for measuring the effectiveness of treatment is the *number needed to treat* (NNT). NNT refers to the number of patients who need to be treated (often with a medicine) for one patient to benefit compared with the patients in a control group not receiving the treatment (e.g., receiving a placebo instead of a medicine; Laupacis, Sackett, & Roberts, 1988). A perfect medicine would have an NNT of 1.0, meaning that only one patient needs to receive the drug in order for one patient to benefit. Very few treatments are 100% effective, and placebo controls often have some positive effects as well. Therefore, very effective treatments are usually in the range of 2 to 4, and researchers are often pleased with NNT values of less than 10 for brief treatments of active disease (Kramer, 2008; A. Moore, 2009). Antibiotics sometimes represent an exception because they can be highly effective in some cases. One of the most effective treatments of all are antibiotics to treat h pylori bacteria that cause peptic stomach ulcers, which has an NNT of 1.1—if 11 people receive the medicine, the bacteria will be eradicated in 10 of them (although the NNT to keep the ulcers away for 1 year is 1.8; McQuay & Moore, 1997).

Many medicines are actually found to have very large NNT values. For example, the very small correlation between taking aspirin and preventing death by heart attack ($r = .02$) translates into an NNT of 127 (Wampold, 2007). The statin medicine atorvastatin (Lipitor) for lowering cholesterol, the best selling drug in pharmaceutical history, was found to have an NNT of 99.7 after 3.3 years—that is, 100 patients would need to take the medicine for 3.3 years to prevent one heart attack (Carey, 2008; Sever et al., 2003). This does not mean that treatments with very high NNT values are not indicated in many cases. As long as the risks of taking a medicine are minimal (e.g., the incidence of internal bleeding is low for those taking aspirin) and the costs are reasonable, the benefit of preventing even a very small number of individuals from realizing a devastating event (e.g., death by heart attack) may result in a positive balancing of risks, costs, and benefits. The same rationale applies to suicide intervention. The sometimes limited benefit of many highly marketed medications in comparison to their risks and costs, however, has become a very controversial topic recently (e.g., Goldacre, 2013; Healy, 2012; Whitaker, 2002, 2010).

In contrast to the very large NNT values of many medicines, the NNT for psychotherapy based on an effect size of .80 is 2.7, meaning that 2.7 psychotherapy patients would need to be treated before one of them can be expected to benefit from the treatment. (An effect size of .60 translates into an NNT of 3.5, and an effect size of 1.0 translates to an NNT of 2.2; Norcross & Lambert, 2011.) Although not all patients improve, this is in the range of treatments considered very effective. Therapists, patients, insurance companies, and the general public can all be assured that psychotherapy has been found to be a very effective treatment that compares favorably to many other health care interventions.

Is the Effectiveness of Psychotherapy Clinically Significant? How Often do Patients Return to Normal Functioning?

Psychotherapy is a very effective treatment that has been found to frequently result in a clinically meaningful improvement in patients' functioning and not just a statistically significant improvement. In fact, large numbers of patients return to normal functioning following treatment. Research that examines this question typically uses standardized measures of therapy outcome, and posttreatment scores falling to within one standard deviation of the normative mean suggest a return to normal functioning. In three meta-analyses, patients' average posttreatment scores on outcome measures moved into the range reflecting normal functioning (Abramowitz, 1996; Nietzel, Russell, Hemmings, & Gretter, 1987; Trull, Nietzel, & Main, 1988). After reviewing these and other studies, Lambert and Archer (2006) concluded that approximately three quarters of patients who undergo treatment show positive benefits, and 40% to 60% return to a state of normal functioning.

Do the Benefits of Psychotherapy Last?

The effectiveness of a treatment over the long term is critical to judging how successful it is. Treatments that alleviate symptoms in the short term but do not address the underlying causes and improve functioning over the long term are generally much less valuable. Relapse is a huge problem in the treatment of physical problems (e.g., heart disease, cancer, obesity) as well as psychological ones (e.g., depression, anxiety, substance abuse). Maintaining treatment gains and preventing relapse are consequently high priorities in health care.

In the case of therapy, research finds that treatment gains are frequently maintained over the long term. This question is difficult to research because many patients drop out of follow-up studies or obtain other forms of therapeutic intervention during the follow-up period. Nonetheless, numerous studies have tracked patients up to 5 or more years following the end of treatment and consistently found that therapy improvements tend to endure (Lambert & Archer, 2006). There tends to be some decay in improvements over time for most psychotherapies, though the decay is far less than for psychotropic medications. There is also some intriguing evidence that therapy benefits sometimes increase over time. In five independent meta-analyses, effect sizes for psychodynamic therapy at long-term follow-up (ranging from .75 to 3.2 years) were actually higher than they were at posttreatment—the effect sizes at follow-up ranged from .94 to 1.57, which are very large effect sizes (Shedler, 2010).

Long-term positive treatment effects have been found even with disorders considered among the most difficult to treat. For example, Bateman and Fonagy (2008) were able to follow up 100% of the patients who completed treatment for borderline personality disorder 5 years after they finished a randomized, controlled trial comparing the effectiveness of psychodynamic therapy and treatment-as-usual. The psychodynamic group was found to have much lower rates of suicidality, further outpatient treatment, and use of medication. They also had much improved vocational functioning and higher Global Assessment of Functioning scores (*Diagnostic and Statistical Manual of Mental Disorders*, fourth ed., Text Revision; American Psychiatric Association, 2000a). Only 13% of patients in the psychodynamic group still met the diagnostic criteria for borderline personality disorder at the 5-year follow-up compared with 87% in the treatment-as-usual group. In another study with an even longer follow-up period, Resick, Williams, Suvak, Monson, and Gradus (2012) were able to follow-up three quarters of a sample of female patients 5 to 10 years after they completed cognitive–behavioral and exposure treatment for posttraumatic stress disorder that resulted from rape. They found that only 18% to 22% still met the criteria for posttraumatic stress disorder.

How Does the Effectiveness of Psychotherapy Compare With the Effectiveness of Psychotropic Medications?

The use of psychotropic medications to address behavioral health symptoms has grown dramatically in the United States in recent years. Antidepressants have become the most frequently used medication by Americans ages 18 to 44 years, an increase of nearly 400% since 1988–1994. In 2005–2008, about

11% of Americans ages 12 and older took antidepressant medication, and 23% of women ages 40 to 59 took antidepressants (Pratt, Brody, & Gu, 2011). The use of any psychotropic medication by adolescents 12 to 17 years of age in the United States has increased to 6.6% of the population, an increase of approximately 500% from a decade and a half earlier (Jonas, Albertorio-Diaz, & Gu, 2012). The use of psychotherapy, on the other hand, appears to have decreased during the same time (Wang et al., 2006).

Despite the rapid growth in the use of medications over psychotherapy for many behavioral health concerns, psychotherapy has been shown to be effective when compared to pharmacological intervention. Although medications have often been considered the first line of treatment for mental disorders in the medical community (e.g., Muñoz, Hollon, McGrath, Rehm, & VandenBos, 1994), psychological interventions have generally been shown to be equal or greater in effectiveness than medicines for a range of psychological disorders except for severe conditions such as severe schizophrenia and bipolar affective disorder (Barlow, 2004; Elkin, 1994; G. J. Meyer et al., 2001; Thase & Jindal, 2004).

Recent meta-analytic results are particularly informative for evaluating the effectiveness of antidepressant medication. An analysis of U.S. Food and Drug Administration (FDA) databases found that the overall mean effect size for antidepressants approved by the FDA between 1987 and 2004 was .31 (E. H. Turner, Matthews, Linardatos, Tell, & Rosenthal, 2008). The effect sizes ranged from .26 for Prozac to .31 for Lexapro. Methodological differences between medication and psychotherapy trials may be significant enough to prevent direct comparisons of effect sizes found for these two types of treatment, but the effect sizes for the antidepressants were not large. When the effects of antidepressants are compared with those of a placebo pill, antidepressants have also been found to be no more effective than placebo for mild, moderate, and severe depression (Fournier et al., 2010). Both placebo and antidepressant medication were associated with clinically significant improvements in depressive symptomatology, and the effect of the antidepressant was found to be superior to placebo only for those with very severe depression, which is a relatively small proportion of the total population with depression.

Individuals often prefer psychological interventions over pharmacological approaches. Surveys consistently find that the public prefers psychological to pharmacological interventions when they are given a choice (e.g., Hazlett-Stevens et al., 2002; Hofmann et al., 1998; Zoellner, Feeny, Cochran, & Pruitt, 2003). This is in part due to the unwelcome side effects commonly associated with psychotropic medications (e.g., for antidepressants, sedation, insomnia, headache, fatigue, dry mouth, constipation, gastrointestinal distress, and sexual disturbance; metabolic side effects alone for second-generation antipsychotics include significant weight gain, high cholesterol, and onset of diabetes; Virani, Bezchlibnyk-Butler, & Jeffries, 2009).

Concern regarding the safety and effectiveness of psychotropic medication has grown significantly in recent years. Very few psychologists prescribe psychotropic medications, but large numbers of patients take them. Many psychologists also actively collaborate with psychiatrists and other physicians, physician assistants, and nurse practitioners who prescribe these medications. Therefore, the safety of these medicines is of significant concern to psychologists. Indeed, psychologists are sometimes vocal with their concerns about overprescribing and adverse effects (e.g., Society for Humanistic Psychology, 2011). This is a complicated topic with very important implications (e.g., Goldacre, 2012; Healy, 2012; Whitaker, 2010), and so all health care providers should keep current with the literature in this area.

A critical advantage of psychotherapy over pharmacological interventions is the superior durability of its benefits (Barlow, 2004). In the case of major depression, for example, medicines, placebo, and psychotherapy are all typically helpful in reducing symptoms. Depressive episodes also tend to eventually remit on their own without treatment. The critical problem is that depressive episodes usually recur (Judd, 1997). Consequently, treatments need to prevent recurrence in order to be truly effective. Studies consistently find that psychological treatments often provide durable benefits that last long after therapy is discontinued, whereas depressive symptoms are more likely to return when antidepressants are no longer taken (e.g., Hollon & Beck, 2004; Paykel et al., 1999; Teasdale et al., 2000). A meta-analysis of treatment for depression found a relapse rate of 27% for psychotherapy but a 57% relapse rate for pharmacotherapy (De Maat, Dekker, Schoevers, & De Jonghe, 2006). Similar results have been found for anxiety disorders (Gould, Otto, & Pollack, 1995; Gould, Otto, Pollack, & Yap, 1997; Otto, Smits, & Reese, 2005). An important exception to this trend involves more biologically based disorders such as bipolar and schizophrenia where psychotherapeutic interventions are generally second in effectiveness to pharmacologic ones (Lambert & Archer, 2006; Lambert & Ogles, 2004; however, see Seikkula et al., 2006, for data showing the opposite). Aside from the more biologically based disorders, however, psychotherapy is often considered the treatment of choice for many of the most common forms of psychological distress and disorder.

Does Psychotherapy Work Better for Some Patients Than for Others? Do Some Patients Get Worse Following Therapy?

Although psychotherapy is remarkably effective overall, there is substantial variability in the rate of improvement across patients. On one end of the continuum, a significant proportion of patients improve dramatically in short periods of time. Several studies have found that a significant minority of patients make dramatic improvements after the first few sessions of treatment and that this improvement is maintained at follow-up contacts up to 2 years posttreatment (Agras et al., 2000; Fennell & Teasdale, 1987; Haas, Hill, Lambert, & Morrell, 2002; Ilardi & Craighead, 1994; Renaud et al., 1998). Lambert (2007) estimated that perhaps 25% of patients are early responders who may not need treatment that extends beyond a few sessions. Not surprisingly, low severity of psychopathology is an important predictor of patients who respond quickly to treatment (Haas et al., 2002; Taylor & McLean, 1993).

There also are a significant number of patients who do not appear to benefit from psychotherapy. This is not unexpected given the severity and complexity of many patients' problems. Some individuals are on a steadily declining trajectory of functioning that even the most effective therapies and therapists cannot reverse (this is true in medicine as well). Some patients with serious persistent mental illness, chronic substance dependence, or serious personality disorder have a poor prognosis and suffer a deteriorating course to their conditions. In such cases, slowing the rate of deterioration can be an important beneficial outcome of treatment. As emphasized in Chapter 9, managing chronic mental and physical health conditions is a responsibility of health care providers that is very important in terms of maximizing quality of life and treatment outcomes and minimizing harms and costs.

Beyond the issue of patients with severe psychopathology and a poor prognosis not benefitting from psychotherapy, the possibility of deterioration as a result of being in psychotherapy grew into a significant concern during the controversy in the 1990s regarding potentially harmful consequences from therapy involving repressed memories of child abuse (Barlow, 2010; Lilienfeld, 2007). Treatments such as rebirthing attachment therapy, conversion therapy for gay and lesbian individuals, critical incident stress debriefing, and grief therapy have also been found to be potentially harmful. In addition, there is evidence that differences in therapist skill level affect therapy outcome.

More research is needed regarding the causes of deterioration while in behavioral health care treatment, but clearly a substantial number of patients do not benefit. Lambert and Archer (2006) estimated that the conditions of about 5% to 10% of patients actually deteriorate during treatment and that an additional 15% to 25% do not measurably improve. Though there are several reasons for the deterioration and lack of improvement, it is important that treatment progress is monitored so that patient deterioration and nonimprovement are identified, appropriate adjustments are made, and treatment failures are prevented as much as possible.

What Factors Account for the Effectiveness of Psychotherapy?

The factors that account for the effectiveness of psychotherapy have been debated throughout the entire history of the field. In fact, this issue became very controversial in Freud's inner circle and resulted in the removal of Alfred Adler, who disagreed about the role of sexual instincts in personality functioning and the best approach to treat neuroses (Gay, 1988). Heated disagreements regarding the effective elements and processes of psychotherapy continued and are still being debated. Gradually, however, better controlled research has been providing useful data for addressing some of these issues.

Psychotherapy clinicians and researchers have long hypothesized that several specific factors contribute to the effectiveness of psychotherapy. It appeared obvious that the competence of the individual therapist was a significant factor. It has also long been believed that specific methods and techniques are more effective for certain disorders or personality characteristics than for others. Many researchers also believed that some factors are common across therapies, such as therapist empathy, warmth, acceptance, and encouragement, and that they account for the effectiveness of therapy. To a large extent, that some patients improved while others did not was not because of the quality of the therapist or the treatment being offered, but rather because of characteristics of the patient (especially the severity of the psychopathology) or the patient's environment (e.g., positive and negative aspects of the patient's family, support system, and community; Garfield, 1994).

After reviewing the available research, Lambert (1992) identified four general factors that he believed accounted for the effectiveness of treatment and estimated the contribution of each to therapy outcome (see Figure 10.1).

- *Specific techniques* (15%) refers to the effectiveness of particular treatments or techniques for treating particular disorders.
- *Expectancy* (15%) refers to expectations that one will improve as the result of being in treatment (*placebo effect*).

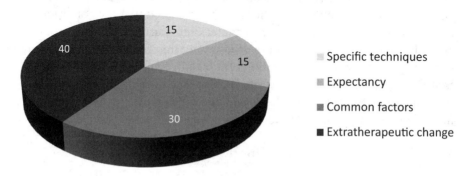

15

40

15

30

- Specific techniques
- Expectancy
- Common factors
- Extratherapeutic change

Figure 10.1. Lambert's (1992) estimates regarding the factors that explain the effectiveness of psychotherapy. Data are from Lambert (1992).

- *Common factors* (30%) refers to factors found across therapies, such as empathy, warmth, acceptance, and encouragement to take risks.
- *Extratherapeutic change* (40%) refers to factors associated with the patient (e.g., severity of psychopathology and level of ego strength) or the patient's environment (e.g., availability of social support)

It is very difficult to empirically measure and determine the contribution of these kinds of factors to the total variance in therapy outcome, and only a few studies have attempted to do so. Wampold (2001) analyzed the findings from several therapy outcome studies and obtained estimates that varied significantly from Lambert's approximations. He concluded that very little of the variance in outcome was attributable to the specific ingredients associated with particular types of therapy but that the competence of the individual therapist had a substantial effect on therapy outcome. Wampold estimated that no more than 8% of the total variance in therapy outcome is accounted for by the specific type of treatment provided, whereas the competence of the therapist accounted for up to 70% of therapy outcomes. The remainder of the outcome variance was not explained by either of these two factors; much of it likely consisted of patient factors such as severity of psychopathology.

A recent meta-analysis of therapy outcomes for depression obtained results between those of Lambert and Wampold. Cuijpers et al. (2012) found that common factors (which in large part might be attributable to the quality of the therapist) accounted for 49% of the variance in depressive symptom improvement, 33% was accounted for by patient characteristics, and 17% was attributable to specific therapy factors. When the original researchers' allegiances to the therapy under investigation were controlled, however, the portion of variance associated with the specific therapy factors fell by nearly one half.

Precise consensus estimates of the proportions of therapy outcome that are attributable to particular factors require further research. The severity of patient psychopathology, the quality of their social support, and other patient variables certainly account for a substantial portion of that variance. The portion attributable to the type of therapy provided, on the other hand, appears to be small. The portion attributable to various aspects of the therapy relationship, or what have often been referred to as *common factors*, however, is substantial. Experts are virtually unanimous in their conclusion that the quality of the therapist–patient relationship is critical to positive therapy outcomes (Lambert, 2013).

A recent project sponsored by the APA Divisions of Clinical Psychology and Psychotherapy involved numerous meta-analyses of therapy outcome to identify factors that are attributable to different components of the therapy relationship. The importance of the therapy relationship and alliance is reflected in the conclusions reached by the panel of experts who reviewed the findings of the project. They concluded that "the therapy relationship makes substantial and consistent contributions to psychotherapy outcome independent of the specific type of treatment" and that "efforts to promulgate best practices or evidenced-based practices without including the relationship are seriously incomplete and potentially misleading" (Norcross & Wampold, 2011, p. 423).

How Important Are the Skills of the Individual Therapist in Explaining Therapy Effectiveness?

It is widely believed across professions that there is substantial variability in the quality of services provided by different service providers. This is true not just in health care and human services but in most if not all areas of life. Indeed, research consistently finds that therapist qualities are important determinants of therapy outcome (for reviews, see Baldwin & Imel, 2013; Horvath & Bedi, 2002; Lambert, 2013; Norcross, 2011; Wampold, 2001). The variance accounted for by therapist effects is consistently found to be similar in size to the best predictors of therapy outcome.

The importance of therapist effects on treatment outcome is illustrated in two large overlapping studies that compared patient outcomes for 71 therapists who each treated a minimum of 30 patients (Okiishi et al., 2006; Okiishi, Lambert, Nielsen, & Ogles, 2003). The therapists were categorized according to the improvement seen in their patients' treatment outcomes. Therapists who were in the middle 50% of the distribution tended to be largely indistinguishable from one another. At the extremes, however, there were distinct differences. The top 10% of the therapists who were associated with the best outcomes had an improved or recovered rate of 44% and a deterioration rate of 5%. The bottom 10% of therapists, on the other hand, had an improved or recovered rate of 28% and a deterioration rate of 11%. One particularly effective therapist who saw more than 300 patients had a deterioration rate of less than 1%; a less effective therapist who saw more than 160 patients had a deterioration rate of 19%.

The evidence clearly indicates that one of the critical elements accounting for therapy outcome is the therapist's ability to create therapeutic alliances and relationships. Even in pharmacotherapy, therapeutic alliance has an important effect on patient outcome. In an analysis of the National Institute of Mental Health Collaborative Depression Study, Krupnick et al. (1996) found that the quality of the therapeutic alliance was the most important factor explaining improvement in patients' depression in both the psychotherapy and pharmacotherapy conditions. The expert panel in the project examining the importance of the therapy relationship to outcomes sponsored by the APA Divisions of Clinical Psychology and Psychotherapy also concluded that "adapting or tailoring the therapy relationship to specific patient characteristics (in addition to diagnosis) enhances the effectiveness of treatment" (Norcross & Wampold, 2011, p. 423). Therapists' sensitivity, flexibility, nondefensiveness, and ability to adapt treatment to the personality and background of the patient are critical to establishing therapeutic relationships, and these clearly make important contributions to therapy outcomes.

Can the Number of Treatment Failures be Reduced?

The evidence suggests that large numbers of psychotherapy cases involving deterioration are due to patient variables such as severe psychopathology or a failure of social support, whereas others are due to therapist characteristics or a failure to tailor the therapy relationship to the personality and needs of the patient. Regardless of the cause, there appear to be practices that can identify patients who are not improving or are deteriorating so that adjustments in treatment can be made and outcomes improved.

An uncomplicated and inexpensive approach to accomplishing this goal is becoming widely recommended. Lambert and his colleagues have investigated the effect of providing therapists, and sometimes their patients, with patient outcome feedback regarding the ongoing progress of treatment. Using a standardized outcome measure to track patient symptomatology and level of functioning, patients were assigned (in four out of the five studies, at random) to either the treatment-as-usual control condition or to the condition where their therapists received feedback regarding the patients' level of functioning scores (Lambert, 2007). In the group of patients who began deteriorating during the course of treatment, the patients of therapists who did not receive feedback had posttest scores that were slightly worse, on average, than when they entered treatment. All of the groups where feedback was provided to the therapists, however, improved significantly by posttest. The effect size between those who received feedback and the treatment-as-usual groups was substantial, approximately .40, and the deterioration rate fell substantially in the groups that received the feedback (Lambert, 2010).

There has been reluctance among therapists to systematically monitor patients' progress during the ongoing course of treatment or at termination. A reluctance to being evaluated is natural, but it should be noted that therapists have always monitored patient progress in nonstandardized ways. Therapy progress is routinely monitored by simply asking patients about how they are doing, and the overall effectiveness of treatment is a normal topic of discussion at termination. Behavioral interventions typically incorporated systematic measurement of treatment progress and sometimes in a detailed manner. Wolpe's (1958) systematic desensitization, for example, monitors the progress of treatment by having patients indicate the success of the counterconditioning on a moment-by-moment basis by raising their finger or verbally indicating their level of distress during the reciprocal inhibition sessions. Sobell and Sobell (2000) noted that an inherent feature of the graduated nature of most substance abuse treatment, where more intensive treatment is provided as the severity of problems increase, is that it is self-correcting. Patients' progress is monitored in an ongoing manner (and urinalyses are frequently used to supplement the unreliability of patient self-report), and treatment strategies are adjusted to match deterioration or improvement in patients' progress.

The safety, effectiveness, and efficiency of treatment will undoubtedly become high priorities in health care. Consequently, techniques that can reliably identify treatment nonimprovement or deterioration will likewise become more widely adopted in behavioral health care. Therapists and their supervisors normally focus special attention on cases where they know that patients are not improving or are worsening (Lambert, 2010). This practice has such great promise that the recent therapy relationship project sponsored by the APA Divisions of Clinical Psychology and Psychotherapy concluded that "practitioners should routinely monitor patients' responses to the therapy relationship and ongoing treatment. Such monitoring leads to increased opportunities to reestablish collaboration, improve the relationship, modify technical strategies, and avoid premature termination" (Norcross & Wampold, 2011, p. 424). The APA Presidential Task Force on Evidence-Based Practice (2006) also noted: "Clinical expertise also entails the monitoring of patient progress . . . that may suggest the need to adjust the treatment" (pp. 276–277; this topic is addressed more extensively in Chapter 11).

DISCUSSION: THE CONTINUING EVOLUTION OF TREATMENT

Behavioral health care treatment has evolved significantly in recent years. The role of the traditional theoretical orientations has declined substantially as the biopsychosocial approach increasingly takes their place. The traditional theoretical orientations are certainly still critical for informing psychotherapy methods, but their role in conceptualizing cases is being replaced by the comprehensive, science-based biopsychosocial perspective. This perspective also focuses attention on strengths, resilience, and well-being in addition to the traditional emphasis on problems, vulnerabilities, and disorders. This is true across all areas and levels of functioning. The focus on health and well-being places more attention on long-term treatment effectiveness. Symptom relief and improved functioning in the short term are certainly important, but these improvements need to be maintained over the long term for treatments to be considered maximally useful and effective.

Several trends in behavioral health care reflect the move toward a unified biopsychosocial approach to practice. Therapists are providing a greater range of treatments as they increasingly endorse integrative and eclectic approaches to practice. Psychologists are also working in more varied settings where they provide a variety of interventions to address a wide range of biopsychosocial issues. In addition to traditional independent psychotherapy practice, many psychologists are working in medical, educational, industrial and organizational, military, rehabilitation, sport, and correctional settings. Psychotherapy is often used infrequently or not at all in these settings, whereas assisting individuals to function effectively and help meet the goals of the institution or agency are often a top priority. The future of professional psychology may also be significantly affected by initiatives to integrate behavioral and physical health care into primary health care settings. That topic is discussed in Chapter 13.

The effectiveness of behavioral health care has become a very important issue in the past three decades. The general effectiveness of psychotherapy for treating behavioral health issues is now well established. The effect size of psychotherapy indicates that it is a very effective treatment that compares favorably with many medical interventions. The effectiveness of psychotherapy is also very meaningful clinically, enabling large numbers of individuals to return to normal functioning. The effects often endure well beyond the end of treatment, unlike the benefits of many psychotropic medications. There is also evidence that even complex, serious disorders can be treated effectively with psychotherapy.

Research examining the factors accounting for the effectiveness of psychotherapy finds that the type of psychotherapy provided appears to account for a small amount of the total variance in outcome. On the other hand, the portion of outcome variance attributable to the quality of the therapy relationship and alliance is large. Research clearly points to the importance of therapist skill in creating therapeutic relationships and alliances as being critical to the overall effectiveness of psychotherapy. This includes the ability to adapt the treatment approach to the personal characteristics and background of the patient. The severity of patients' psychopathology, the quality of their social support, and other patient variables also account for a substantial portion of the variance in outcome. Some individuals have serious psychopathology and a poor prognosis. Although psychotherapy may not resolve their issues, even slowing the rate of deterioration in health and functioning can be a very valuable outcome of treatment in these cases.

Issues related to the safety and effectiveness of health care continue to grow in importance. The research and technology for improving psycho-therapy effectiveness are advancing, and procedures for identifying patients who do not improve or who deteriorate are likely to become more common-place. (Chapter 11 examines these important issues in more detail.)

CASE EXAMPLE: A BIOPSYCHOSOCIAL APPROACH TO TREATMENT WITH A MILDLY DEPRESSED PATIENT

The case example that was discussed in Chapters 8 and 9 is presented again to illustrate the biopsychosocial approach to behavioral health care treatment. The treatment plan discussed in the previous chapter was imple-mented with Maria, the 44-year-old married Latina woman with mild depression. That plan included six components: (a) monitor the depressed mood; (b) stop drinking altogether during weekdays for the next 2 months; (c) schedule dates out with her husband a minimum of once per week; (d) begin a regular exercise routine; (e) go to parent–teacher organization meetings at the children's school to see if there are good ways to get more involved in her daughter's education and supporting the school; and (f) explore the possibility of improving the relationship with her mother and the rest of her family of origin.

Maria had been completing the clinic's standard outcomes question-naire every week before she and her psychologist started their sessions. The psychologist noted that her scores indicated steady improvement with her depressed feelings and in other areas as well. At the fifth session, the psy-chologist asked if Maria would ask her husband to join her once again the following week to reassess how things were going. The couple had a very productive conversation when he came to her second session, though they did not appear to have a close relationship—they interacted respectfully and comfortably but with little affection and limited awareness of each other's feelings or thoughts. Many times they expressed surprise at the other's reac-tions about things. It was clear that they cared about one another, however, and they enjoyed recalling some very happy times together, mostly times preceding the birth of their children.

The wife and husband interacted much more warmly when they came in for her sixth session. They sat closer and their words and gestures suggested more comfort and warmth between them. He was clearly impressed with how she had started exercising again, and Maria was proud to have dropped two pant sizes. They also reported going out on dates once per week as Maria had agreed to and that their sex life had returned in a way they hadn't experi-enced in years. They said their younger child even asked, "Mommy, daddy, why are you so happy?" Maria noted, "This actually made me really sad. I told Mike that they probably couldn't remember me being happy like this because I sort of clammed up, retreated into my shell after they were born. I didn't think anybody realized that. *I* didn't really realize that." Maria said she still wanted to get more involved with the parent–teacher organization at her children's school. She also said that she wanted to improve her relationship with her own mother. Maria and her husband decided to attend Maria's parents' church the following Sunday.

After church the next Sunday, the extended family gathered at Maria's parents' home for a large meal and socializing. People were very happy to see Maria and her family, and they received many compliments about their children. At the next session, Maria and her psychologist discussed how Maria could broach questions she had for her mother. The next Saturday, Maria visited her mother so they could talk. Her mother said she didn't like it that Maria worked outside the home and they weren't attending church regularly, but she also noted that Maria had the best kids and husband among their relatives and maybe she was wrong to judge her as much as she did. They also talked about how Maria's mother was very good at school when she was young and could have done what Maria had in terms of education and career, but instead she did what her parents and culture expected of her. She said that she was beginning to realize that seeing her daughter become so successful actually made her jealous and that was the reason she sometimes criticized Maria. She said she still wanted them to raise their children in the church, but she was trying to accept that that wasn't her decision to make.

At the ninth session, Maria said that she was very happy with how things were going. There was a large drop in her scores on the clinic's outcome assessment questionnaire into the nonclinical range. She said she felt like a huge weight was lifted from her shoulders in terms of the conversation she had with her mother, though she said she couldn't help being skeptical about whether her mother really meant everything she said. After attending just two parent–teacher organization meetings at school, she said she was happy and felt respected to be invited to join the parent advisory committee for her children's school. She noted that she had gotten many compliments about losing weight and that she was committed to staying active and fit. She also noted that she only occasionally felt a desire to drink more than a couple of glasses of wine at special dinners or parties and that she felt better physically as a result. Maria and her psychologist talked about how her mother's criticism and mixed messages to her were understandable given her mother's psychodynamics. After acknowledging major progress with her issues, she agreed to come back for one more session to discuss the nagging feelings she occasionally had about whether she had made the right decisions with her life.

11

OUTCOMES ASSESSMENT

Psychotherapists typically have mixed feelings about outcomes assessment. Many therapists are very concerned about how patient outcome data might be used. Psychopathology and psychotherapy involve complicated issues, and simple outcome measures may not meaningfully capture the complexity of a patient's life and functioning or the complicated process of therapy (Mitchell, 1999). In addition, how can therapists be assured that outcome data are not used in ways that are detrimental to patients? Are safeguards sufficient to prevent these data from affecting patients' future insurability, employability, or their reputations in general? Patients are also sometimes irritated by having to complete questionnaires, and these tests take up valuable therapy time. Therapists are concerned about how the data might be used to evaluate them as well. How might these data affect one's job security, salary, or workload? Although student course evaluations are common in colleges and customer satisfaction surveys are now common in medical settings, these kinds of assessments are not yet common in

DOI: 10.1037/14441-012
Biopsychosocial Practice: A Science-Based Framework for Behavioral Health Care, by T. P. Melchert
Copyright © 2015 by the American Psychological Association. All rights reserved.

behavioral health care. A reluctance to being evaluated is understandable: Therapists already routinely discuss the effectiveness of treatment as part of the termination process, and so why does this need to be supplemented with outcome assessment data?

Despite these concerns, outcomes assessment continues to grow in importance. Patients, therapists, supervisors, managers, insurers, and researchers all have an interest in objective data that demonstrate the effectiveness of intervention. This chapter outlines the conceptual framework for approaching outcomes assessment from the science-based biopsychosocial framework advocated in this volume. It begins by reviewing the rationale for incorporating outcomes assessment into routine behavioral health care practice and then reviews the decision making process for conducting outcomes assessment.

THE BIOPSYCHOSOCIAL FRAMEWORK FOR APPROACHING OUTCOMES ASSESSMENT

The emphases of the biopsychosocial approach to behavioral health care have important implications for outcomes assessment just as they do for all the other phases of the treatment process. First, the science-based orientation of the biopsychosocial approach emphasizes, among other things, the reliable and valid measurement of important variables. If one needs to demonstrate the safety and effectiveness of interventions, reliable and valid measures of treatment outcomes are essential. When the primary purpose of behavioral health care is meeting individuals' needs and promoting their functioning, how can attainment of those goals be evaluated without reliable measurement? Discussions between therapists and patients about the effectiveness of treatment are important, but is it reasonable to rely on those discussions alone, unaccompanied by objective measures of treatment outcomes, for evaluating treatment safety and effectiveness? Both patients and therapists may be unable or unwilling to provide reliable, objective assessments of these factors. A science-based approach to health care requires that important variables are assessed using measures that demonstrate strong reliability, validity, and clinical utility.

Second, the ethical foundations of the approach taken in this volume include obligations of nonmaleficence, beneficence, and justice that place high priority on the safety and effectiveness of treatment and on using resources efficiently and fairly. If the field is conceptualized as primarily a service industry that offers a variety of services that individuals select to meet their own personal needs, then accountability is managed primarily by the market and consumers generally have primary responsibility for the services they purchase. On the other hand, the health care orientation of the biopsychosocial approach emphasizes the ethical obligations of health care professionals to provide services that are safe and effective. Systematic, objective outcomes assessment helps ensure that therapists are meeting these obligations. The ethics codes of the behavioral health care professions also recognize the importance of these issues. Standard 5.02(a) of the Code of Ethics of the National Association of Social Workers (2008) states that "social workers monitor and evaluate . . . practice interventions," and the American Counseling Association (2014) *Ethics Code* states that "counselors continually monitor their effectiveness as professionals" (Code C.2.d). The American Psychological Association (APA; 2002) Ethics Code is less specific, but Standard 10.10 does include the requirement that psychologists terminate therapy when it becomes reasonably clear that the patient no longer needs the service, is not benefitting, or is being harmed.

Third, the biopsychosocial approach to behavioral health care identifies its primary purpose as meeting individuals' behavioral health needs and promoting their biopsychosocial functioning. The emphasis is on whether needs have been met in the individual case. It does not address whether a treatment has been demonstrated to work in general, for treatment group participants on average compared with control group participants on average. Historically, the psychotherapy field has not placed much emphasis on showing that treatments work in individual cases. From Freud's time through the 1960s, major effort was devoted to defining and perfecting theoretical systems of psychotherapy. This was followed by extensive efforts to establish whether therapies worked on average in a treatment group compared to a control group. These efforts were critical, but the field has now advanced to the point where it can focus on ensuring that treatment is effective not just for groups on average but also in the individual case.

A fourth consideration is that systematically monitoring treatment outcomes has become a priority in the evidence-based practice movement in health care. The APA Presidential Task Force on Evidence-Based Practice included the following definition in its 2006 report: "*Evidence-based practice in psychology* (EBPP) is the integration of the best available research with clinical expertise in the context of patient characteristics, culture, and preferences" (p. 273). The Task Force was also explicit that the monitoring of treatment outcomes was an essential component of clinical expertise:

> Clinical expertise also entails the monitoring of patient progress (and of changes in the patient's circumstances—e.g., job loss, major illness) that may suggest the need to adjust the treatment (Lambert, Bergin, & Garfield, 2004a). If progress is not proceeding adequately, the psychologist alters or addresses problematic aspects of the treatment (e.g., problems in the therapeutic relationship or in the implementation of the goals of the treatment) as appropriate. (pp. 276–277)

The therapy relationship project sponsored by the APA Divisions of Clinical Psychology and Psychotherapy also concluded that "practitioners should routinely monitor patients' responses to the therapy relationship and ongoing treatment. Such monitoring leads to increased opportunities to reestablish collaboration, improve the relationship, modify technical strategies, and avoid premature termination" (Norcross & Wampold, 2011, p. 424).

Existing research on treatment outcomes points to the need to monitor treatment progress. Monitoring treatment outcomes is important for identifying treatment successes, of course, but in some ways it is more important for identifying treatment failures, so that something can be done to potentially reverse the deterioration. It was noted in Chapter 10 of this volume that Lambert and Archer (2006) estimated that perhaps 15% to 25% of patients do not measurably improve during treatment and that 5% to 10% of patients actually deteriorate. Certainly, not all individuals in treatment could be expected to improve—many have very serious problems, unhealthy support systems and social environments, and a poor prognosis, and therapists have only limited influence in patients' lives. The amount of treatment that can be provided is also often limited. Nonetheless, therapists may lack full information regarding what is happening in these cases. For example, Hannan et al. (2005) asked 40 therapists whether each of their patients was worse off than when he or she entered treatment and whether they thought the patients would leave treatment in a worse condition. Their judgments were then compared with weekly Outcome Questionnaire–45 (OQ-45; Lambert et al., 1996) data provided by the patients ($N = 550$). The therapists were told that past research would suggest that 8% of their patients are likely to deteriorate (i.e., their OQ-45 score would increase by 14 or more points). The actual deterioration rate found in the sample was 7.3% ($n = 40$). The therapists, however, predicted that only three of the 550 patients (0.55%) would leave treatment worse off than when they began; in fact, the condition of only one of these three patients actually deteriorated. In addition, out of these 40 patients whose conditions deteriorated, the therapists judged that nearly 40% of them had improved.

Another study showing that therapists are not reliable judges of patients' improvement was conducted by Hatfield, McCullough, Plucinski, and Krieger (2009), who found a deterioration rate of 9% (386 out of 4,253 cases) in a midwestern clinic that used the OQ-45 to track patient progress. The patient files for 70 of the deteriorated cases were inspected (an increase of 14 or more points indicated deterioration), and it was found that therapists had noted deterioration for 21% of these cases, no mention of progress in 59% of these cases, and improvement for 3% of these cases. In addition, 41 patients had OQ-45 score increases of at least 30 points, indicating severe deterioration, and only 32% of these files included a note indicating deterioration. Walfish,

McAlister, O'Donnell, and Lambert (2012) found evidence of a positive self-evaluation bias among therapists that may help to explain these findings. They asked 129 private practice therapists to compare their overall skills with others in the profession and to estimate what percentage of their patients improved, stayed the same, or deteriorated. Of these therapists, 25% viewed their skill level at the 90th percentile or higher, 92% viewed their skill level at the 75th percentile or higher, and none viewed their skill as below the 50th percentile. Nearly half (48%) estimated that none of their patients deteriorated; the average deterioration rate estimated by the therapists as a whole was 4%. (This same type of positive self-evaluation bias is found in other professions as well.)

Another reason that outcomes assessment is a growing concern involves accountability. Health care in the United States is very expensive and, by many measures, the outcomes are poor. Society increasingly demands accountability in general, and health care organizations are under growing pressure to ensure that services are effective and efficient. More money is spent on health care in the United States per capita and as a proportion of gross domestic product than any other nation in the world, and yet morbidity and mortality rates are relatively high (see Chapter 12). As discussed in Chapter 10, there is evidence that the effectiveness of psychosocial treatment can be increased when therapists are provided with outcomes assessment scores that identify patients whose conditions are deteriorating or not improving. Several studies have found that many of these patients are then turned around, resulting in a significantly improved effectiveness rate overall. Given growing pressures for accountability, interest in these findings is sure to grow.

As economic pressures and expectations for evidence-based practice grow, interest in the safety, effectiveness, and efficiency of behavioral health care is almost certain to increase. Research advances are providing clinicians with tools that can help ensure that behavioral health care intervention is effective in individual cases. The biopsychosocial approach also emphasizes meeting individuals' needs. In the past, emphasis was typically on providing patients with an empirically supported treatment that had been shown to be effective on average in an experimental group compared with a control group. That practice may need to be supplemented by the demonstration that treatment is effective in the individual case as well.

If current research findings in this area are replicated and acceptance of the arguments delineated in the preceding paragraphs grows, monitoring of treatment outcomes may become as well integrated in behavioral health care as laboratory tests are in medicine (Lambert, 2010). In the treatment of diabetes, high cholesterol, or high blood pressure, for example, most people would consider it inconceivable that there would not be ongoing monitoring of treatment progress—people expect that glucose levels, lipids, or blood pressure are routinely tested, often at every patient contact, when patients have difficulty in these areas. Behavioral health care professionals may some-day view outcomes measurement similarly.

GENERAL OUTCOMES ASSESSMENT IN HEALTH CARE

At the most basic level, *treatment outcomes* simply refer to the results or consequences of treatment. The focus of outcomes assessment is generally on what is most meaningful to patients and other stakeholders. Outcome measures typically assess lessened symptomatology, improvements in func-tioning, improved quality of life, satisfaction with services delivered, or cost-effectiveness.

There are many approaches to assessing health care outcomes. Medical researchers differentiate between two general classes of outcomes (Kane, 2006). Condition-specific measures typically focus on symptomatology that reflects the status of the medical condition a patient has or the consequences that a disease has on a person's life. Generic measures, on the other hand, provide comprehensive assessments of health-related functioning across domains in a person's life that are not specific to a particular disease or condi-tion (Maciejewski, 2006).

Generic or Global Outcome Measures

Generic measures of health are designed to assess a full range of important physical, psychological, and social aspects of health. Consistent with the World Health Organization (1948) definition of health, these approaches focus on the *quality* of health in addition to its *quantity* (i.e., life span and other easily quantified indicators). Measures emphasizing quantity of health generally focus on morbidity, mortality, and life expectancy, whereas measures emphasizing quality of health focus on overall health and functioning. Generic outcome measures (also referred to as *global outcome measures*) tend to focus on patients' perceptions of their physical, psychological, and social functioning and over-all quality of life, factors that patients frequently view as more relevant than condition-specific outcomes (Maciejewski, 2006).

Quality of life is generally considered critical to measures of life satisfac-tion and the overall outcome of health care, but it can be difficult to measure because individuals place very different priority on different aspects of their lives. Therefore, measures of quality of life are typically multidimensional. Eight dimensions have often been included in comprehensive assessments of quality of general life functioning: physical functioning, social func-tioning, emotional functioning, sexual functioning, cognitive functioning, pain–discomfort, vitality, and overall well-being (Maciejewski, 2006; Patrick & Deyo, 1989). The 36-item Short-Form Health Survey (SF-36; Ware & Sherbourne, 1992) measures all eight of these dimensions and has become the most widely used generic measure of functioning in medical research (Maciejewski, 2006).

Condition-Specific Outcome Measures

Condition-specific measures of health care outcome assess specific aspects of functioning that are closely related to a patient's disease or condition. Condition-specific measures are designed to be highly sensitive so that they can detect even small treatment effects. There are two basic types of measures: clinical measures, which focus on the signs, symptoms, or test results associated with a particular disease or condition; and experiential measures, which focus on the impact of the disease or condition on the patient (Atherly, 2006). Clinical measures such as blood tests and blood pressure checks are routinely used to screen for and monitor treatment outcomes for high cholesterol, diabetes, and hypertension because generic or experiential health outcome measures can easily miss clinically important signs of problems in these areas. A successful treatment for hypertension, for example, is often imperceptible to patients because changes in blood pressure are difficult to detect. A generic outcome measure probably will not detect the effect of a successful or a failed blood pressure treatment whereas a blood pressure measurement will. Even when patients cannot detect the effect, a successful or failed treatment for hypertension can have a profound influence on the long-term health of the patient (Atherly, 2006). Therefore, both global and condition-specific measures are needed to thoroughly evaluate the outcomes of medical treatment.

OUTCOMES ASSESSMENT IN BEHAVIORAL HEALTH CARE

Behavioral health care often requires a similar combination of condition-specific and global measures of treatment outcome for the same reasons that medicine does. Individuals' lives and functioning are complex, particularly when viewed from a biopsychosocial perspective, and the outcomes of treatment must be evaluated in a multifaceted manner to begin to capture that complexity. Focusing on single dimensions of functioning (e.g., decreasing the symptoms of a disorder) can simplify an assessment so that its meaningfulness is limited. This is true for intake and well as outcomes assessments. Maruish (2004a) noted that the term *outcomes* is commonly used in its plural form to emphasize the importance of taking a multifaceted approach to outcomes assessment that covers multiple domains of functioning. It is also important to note that outcomes assessment is not limited to measuring outcomes only at the termination of treatment; the same measures can be used throughout treatment to monitor the progress of intervention. Readministering outcome measures throughout treatment may be the only way to reliably detect lack of improvement or deterioration (just as in the case of many medical treatments), which then gives therapists the chance to try alternative interventions that may prevent treatment failures.

It is useful to recall that many psychologists do not work in settings that provide significant amounts of psychotherapy or other psychosocial treatments. Although the principles discussed here apply generally, specific procedures for outcomes assessment for many medical, school, correctional, forensic, or neuropsychology practitioners deviate from the recommendations discussed here. In addition, the large majority of outcome measures used in published research have focused on intrapersonal factors (Froyd et al., 1996). Taking a biopsychosocial approach generally broadens the focus of assessment to interpersonal, behavioral, social role, and physical functioning, and these other factors are often especially relevant when little or no psychotherapy is provided in particular settings.

Content and Focus of Outcome Measures

Global Measures

Global measures that provide information about patients' general level of distress and overall functioning are often the most practical outcome measure for many therapists and agencies. These measures can be used routinely with all patients receiving services except for those needing immediate attention for suicidality or another type of crisis. Several brief, standardized, widely used instruments provide useful measures of overall functioning: (a) Brief Symptom Inventory (Derogatis & Melisaratos, 1983); (b) OQ-45 (Lambert et al., 1996); and (c) SF-36 (Ware & Sherbourne, 1992). The four-item Outcome Assessment Scale is a very brief alternative that is very easy to use in clinical practice (Bringhurst, Watson, Miller, & Duncan, 2006). A widely used instrument for children and youth is the Child Behavior Checklist (Achenbach & Edelbrock, 1983). The Brief Symptom Inventory focuses primarily on psychological symptoms, whereas the SF-36 and the Child Behavior Checklist include scales measuring variables from across the biopsychosocial domains. Many alternatives to these instruments are also available (see Ogles, 2013).

Condition-Specific Measures

When patients have a specific problem or disorder that is the focus of treatment, condition-specific measures may be needed to adequately assess the effectiveness of treatment for that particular problem or disorder. These are often used in conjunction with global measures to evaluate changes regarding particular symptoms or behaviors as well as overall functioning. Condition-specific measures are also often needed as part of intake assessment to obtain information necessary for completing the assessment, making proper diagnoses, and obtaining baseline data to evaluate the progress and effectiveness of treatment. The specific signs and symptoms of individual disorders or problems (e.g., substance abuse, obsessive–compulsive disorder, enuresis, psychotic disorders, eating disorders) are often missed entirely by global outcome measures.

Many standardized instruments with strong psychometric properties are available for assessing specific disorders and problems. Examples widely used in general practice for monitoring specific symptoms include the Beck Depression Inventory (second edition; Beck, Steer, & Brown, 1996), the State–Trait Anxiety Inventory (Spielberger, Gorsuch, & Lushene, 1970), the Fear Questionnaire (Marks & Matthews, 1979), and the Dyadic Adjustment Scale (for measuring relationship satisfaction in couples; Spanier, 1976). Therapists working in specialized areas are normally familiar with the instruments commonly used in their respective areas.

The United Kingdom is currently implementing a nationwide screening and intervention program aimed at depression and anxiety (also noted in "Stepped Models of Intervention" in Chapter 9). To monitor treatment progress, patients are asked at each patient contact to complete very brief outcome measures such as the nine-item Patient Health Questionnaire Depression Scale (Kroenke, Spitzer, & Williams, 2001) or the seven-item Patient Health Questionnaire Anxiety Disorder Scale (Spitzer, Kroenke, Williams, & Lowe, 2006).

Individualized Measures

In addition to standardized instruments, it is sometimes important to use individually tailored measures designed to assess particular symptoms or behaviors (Clement, 1999; Ogles, 2013). A patient's unique experiences, problems, and biopsychosocial circumstances are of course evaluated during intake assessment. When particular or unique aspects of an individual's life become a focus of treatment, individualized measures that can capture changes in those aspects are needed. One individual with substance dependence, depression, agoraphobia, or sexual dysfunction may share few similarities with another person with the same disorder, and it is important to incorporate that individuality into the treatment process.

Several approaches to conducting individualized assessment have been developed. One well-known approach involves the use of target complaints, a system that was included in the National Institute of Behavioral Health

Core Battery initiative (Waskow & Parloff, 1975); this was an important effort to establish a standardized approach to outcome measurement that was never widely adopted. In this system, the patient, therapist, or the patient and therapist together identify targets for treatment and then rate the level of problem severity for each target complaint (e.g., missed work days, shoplifting incidents, arguments with one's mother). This unique list of complaints can then be tracked periodically starting from intake. Goal Attainment Scaling (Kiresuk & Sherman, 1968) uses a similar approach in which treatment goals are established collaboratively by the patient and therapist, and progress toward meeting those goals is assessed across treatment. Behavior therapy that includes identifying target behaviors and performing a functional analysis is also a highly useful approach to intervention and outcomes assessment (e.g., Hersen & Rosqvist, 2008).

The individualized assessment of suicidal behaviors, thoughts, or feelings are frequently important when assessing and treating suicidality and other forms of danger to self or others (Joiner, 2005; Rudd, 2006). A range of additional self- or other-harming behaviors must be closely monitored, such as disordered eating, high-risk sexual behavior, self-mutilation, substance abuse, and the neglect or abuse of children, vulnerable adults, or dependent seniors. Standardized, condition-specific or global measures are often inadequate for monitoring treatment progress or patient deterioration when these issues are a focus of treatment. These measures are often repeated at follow-up as well to help assess whether treatment has been effective over the longer term.

Sources of Outcome Data

The science-based biopsychosocial approach emphasizes reliable and valid assessment, which is also important when conducting outcomes assessment and evaluating the effectiveness of treatment. To obtain reliable and valid information, it is frequently important to rely on a variety of sources when treatment goals involve the patient's functioning in social roles such as at work, home, school, or in the community (see Chapter 8). When treatment focuses on intrapersonal issues (e.g., depression, anxiety), patients themselves are typically the most reliable reporters regarding their internal state. When treatment focuses on externalizing disorders or patient's functioning in social roles, however, patients' perceptions of their behavior or performance can vary significantly from those of family members, employers, educators, or public officials (R. C. Miller & Berman, 1983). The minimization or exaggeration of problems is sometimes not conscious or intentional though sometimes it is. In either case, individuals' perceptions and reports often must be supplemented because people are not always the most objective and reliable reporters for this information.

Engaging significant individuals in the patient's life as collateral reporters on the patient's progress can also be very helpful for building social support for the patient and reinforcing changes he or she has made. This can be critical at treatment termination because patients' ability to maintain treatment gains can depend on the level of social support and reinforcement they receive from significant individuals in their lives who are invested in their functioning at home, work, or in the community. Though clinicians often minimize the involvement of significant others in their treatment of patients because of time pressures, they also should make the effort necessary to help ensure positive patient outcomes over the long term.

Schedule for Collecting Data

Therapists also need to decide on when to gather outcome data. Common practice is, at minimum, to assess patients at intake and then again at termination or discharge (Maruish, 2004a). It is very difficult to quantitatively demonstrate the effectiveness of treatment without baseline data, so administering outcome measures at the initiation and termination of treatment is critical to conducting meaningful outcomes assessment.

On the other end of the continuum are cases where patients are experiencing crises and assessing and monitoring their functioning is done on an essentially continuous basis. When individuals are having serious problems with suicidality or substance abuse or other issues that involve significant risks of harm to self or others, they may require continual observation and monitoring. The monitoring might be done by staff in an inpatient psychiatric unit, outpatient treatment facility, or by family and friends, but continual monitoring and assessment may be needed to ensure the safety and security of the patient until the crisis resolves.

Readministering outcomes assessment measures regularly across treatment is now recommended for routine behavioral health care practice (Andrews & Page, 2005; Lambert, 2010; Ogles, 2013). This practice has important benefits. Monitoring treatment progress continually across treatment, commonly known as *outcomes monitoring* (Sperry, Brill, Howard, & Grissom, 1996), can identify the significant number of patients who do not improve or who actually deteriorate during treatment, something that can be difficult for therapists to identify. Treatment intensity in these cases might be increased, consultations can be obtained or referrals made, or other changes can be implemented that may prevent a significant number of treatment failures (see Chapter 10). When patients are not improving in an expected manner given their diagnoses and circumstances, it is critical to also reevaluate one's assessment of the case. Many factors might account for the lack of treatment progress (e.g., child abuse or other issues the patient has not revealed, medical disorder that is causing the psychological symptoms). Routine outcomes monitoring helps establish when treatment works but can be even more important for identifying cases that are not improving so that the assessment can be reevaluated or the treatment plan revised, and a significant number of treatment failures can be prevented.

The United Kingdom initiative to provide screening and treatment for depression and anxiety on a national basis includes this type of treatment monitoring. The program uses very brief instruments that are readministered at each patient contact. At one of the pilot sites for the program, pretreatment and posttreatment scores were available for 99% of patients who completed at least two sessions in the program while the second pilot site had these scores for 88% of patients (Clark, 2011). This approach to outcome assessment is very useful for evaluating the effectiveness of treatment in individual cases as well as the national effort as a whole (e.g., outcome measures at the two pilot sites indicated very large treatment effect sizes ranging from .98 to 1.26; Clark et al., 2009).

Follow-Up

Posttermination follow-up is essential to appropriate care in many behavioral health care cases, and particularly for patients who have dealt with more serious problems and those characterized by high relapse rates. For example, follow-up, ongoing monitoring of functioning, and repeated evaluations of the need for recurrent treatment can all be critical to quality and appropriate care for individuals who dealt with substance dependence (Hazelton, 2008) or chronic suicidality (e.g., with individuals who have attempted suicide more than once; Joiner, 2005; Linehan & Dexter-Mazza, 2008; Rudd, 2006).

In all behavioral health care cases, maintaining treatment gains for months and years after treatment has ended is generally much more meaningful in patients' lives than making treatment gains that do not last long after termination or discharge. Therefore, follow-up measurement of treatment outcomes after termination can provide the most important and meaningful measurement of the outcomes of therapy (Maruish, 2004a). Mailing or e-mailing patients at 3 or 6 months posttreatment can provide very useful follow-up data, though this request for information alone is likely to result in a low response rate. A mailing can be followed up with a phone call to the initial nonresponders to increase the response rate. Even when patients choose not to respond, it can be important that they know that their therapist is concerned about their well-being and is available to offer support and treatment if needed. If behavioral health care becomes more widely integrated into primary care in this country, it is easier to conduct this type of follow-up assessment on a routine basis.

ADDITIONAL PURPOSES OF OUTCOME ASSESSMENT

Health care outcomes assessment serves additional purposes beyond evaluating the effectiveness of treatment. Employers and managers are often very interested in patient satisfaction with the services provided, and the cost-effectiveness of treatment is a concern to patients, employers who provide medical insurance, and taxpayers, all of whom make large financial investments in these services.

Patient Satisfaction

Satisfaction with the health care services that patients receive began getting research attention in the 1950s when it was noticed that increased patient satisfaction was associated with improved appointment keeping, medication use, and adherence to treatment recommendations (B. Williams, 1994). It was also found to be associated with a decreased likelihood of being sued for malpractice (Hickson et al., 1994). Patient satisfaction with services has grown in importance in the United States as the result of the increased marketing of health care services and is also receiving more attention as an indicator of quality of services. A variety of approaches to measuring patient satisfaction with services can be integrated easily into clinic practice (see M. A. Smith, Schüssler-Fiorenza, & Rockwood, 2006).

Cost-Effectiveness

Concern surrounding the cost-effectiveness of health care in the United States has been growing given the relatively poor health outcomes achieved while spending by far the largest amount per capita in the world (World Health Organization Department of Health Statistics and Informatics, 2012). The cost of U.S. health care also is widely viewed as being unsustainable. Cost-effectiveness analysis is used to determine whether health care treatments are beneficial to society as a whole (Nyman, 2006). The cost-effectiveness of medical treatments can be relatively easily examined in terms of number of lives saved or years of life gained as a result of providing particular treatments. Emphasis has shifted from these simple measures of treatment outcome to measures of quality of life because simply lengthening the life span if quality is not also achieved is not always preferable (T. L. Beauchamp & Childress, 2009). For example, disability-adjusted life years have become widely used to provide a more adequate measure of treatment outcome for use in cost-effectiveness analyses. These measures are discussed more extensively in the next chapter.

DISCUSSION: ENSURING EFFECTIVENESS
AT THE INDIVIDUAL LEVEL

The biopsychosocial approach to behavioral health care does not dictate that outcome monitoring be used throughout the course of treatment. It does, however, emphasize meeting the behavioral health and biopsychosocial needs of patients. Its scientific bases emphasize reliable and valid measurement, and its ethical bases emphasize high quality, safe, and effective treatment. Therapists should be sensitive about not reducing the complexity of people's lives to scores on simple outcome measures. But they also need to be sensitive about scientific requirements involving reliable and valid measurement of important variables, the evidence that therapists may be poor judges of when patients' conditions are not improving or are deteriorating, the evidence that significant numbers of these patients turn around once they are identified, as well as the reasonable expectations for accountability from all the stakeholders involved, including patients. The effectiveness of treatment is very important to therapists and their supervisors—therapists are very committed to helping patients resolve problems and improve their well-being. Treatment effectiveness affects people directly and meaningfully in the real world, where distress, functioning, and well-being matter a great deal. For all these reasons, therapists need to consider the benefits of conducting systematic outcomes assessment as part of routine clinical practice.

Some of the research findings noted above challenge standard clinical thinking. It is clear that a significant number of patients do not improve as a result of treatment, and it also appears that therapists may not be good judges of which patients do not improve or deteriorate. Therapists clearly also vary in their effectiveness, and this can be measured reliably and efficiently. Research suggests that informally discussing the effectiveness of treatment with patients, as has long been standard practice during and at the termination of treatment, is inadequate for evaluating its effectiveness. Large proportions of deterioration and lack of improvement may simply be missed in the absence of the systematic monitoring of treatment outcomes. Therefore, monitoring the progress of treatment through standardized outcome measures may be necessary for identifying and preventing as many treatment failures as possible. Initial research suggests that a large number of these cases can be turned around and improvement rates can be significantly improved. If these findings are replicated in future research, the lack of outcomes monitoring as part of standard treatment may eventually be viewed as substandard practice (Lambert, 2010). Clinicians should all be committed to ensuring quality care, improving clinical practice, strengthening clinical science, and maintaining the profession's ethical commitment to quality services. Therapists therefore need to keep abreast of the research in this area.

The emphasis of much of this chapter (and this whole volume) has been on the effectiveness of behavioral health care intervention. Although high-quality behavioral health care interventions are remarkably effective, and their effectiveness may be increased even further through the use of systematic outcomes assessment, readers should not get the impression that 100% effectiveness is possible. Relapse is common for many psychological conditions (as well as medical ones). Some patients also have very serious behavioral health problems characterized by a progressively deteriorating course of functioning. Many have unhealthy social environments, and many others have deeply entrenched personality dysfunction that is very difficult to treat. Therapists have only a limited amount of influence in people's lives and cannot be expected to reverse all psychopathology. The best that can be hoped for in many cases is to slow the rate of deterioration—the same is true in medicine as well.

Slade, Lambert, Harmon, Smart, and Bailey (2008) illustrated the limits of psychotherapeutic treatment even when extraordinary measures are taken to maximize treatment effectiveness. In their study, outcome monitoring data were provided to therapists so that lack of improvement could be readily identified, and therapists were also provided with clinical problem solving feedback to help make decisions about conducting additional assessment and modifying the treatment plan (e.g., assessing motivation to change, reevaluating the diagnosis, referring for evaluation for medication). The researchers found that the deterioration rate under these conditions was reduced to 4.6%; they considered this the lower limit of what can be achieved in usual practice. Approaching such a low level of deterioration is a remarkable accomplishment. It should also be noted that inpatient and other programs where serious psychopathology is the usual referral would not be expected to achieve such a low deterioration rate.

Therapists should keep current with the research to ensure that they stay informed regarding methods that can improve treatment effectiveness. In the meantime, the current literature suggests a number of recommendations for performing outcomes assessment in routine behavioral health care practice. The following best practices are worth noting:

1. Select global, condition-specific, and individualized outcome measures that provide information that is relevant for the individual case. Global functioning is often a priority whereas focal or target symptoms or behaviors are more likely to be measured with condition-specific or individualized measures.
2. Collect baseline data to aid in interpreting results—outcomes cannot be fully interpreted without baseline data.

3. Use standardized, normed, and psychometrically sound global and condition-specific instruments so that the data obtained are more interpretable and normative comparisons are possible.
4. Brief instruments that are quickly administered and scored are generally preferred—time, cost demands, and clinical utility are important in almost all types of clinical practice.
5. Gaining information from multiple sources is often critical for obtaining reliable data about individuals' behavior and functioning and particularly when treatment focuses on externalizing issues or the patient's functioning in social roles (e.g., at home, work, school, or in the community).
6. Readministering measurements over the course of treatment is very useful for monitoring the progress of treatment. The regular readministration of outcome measures (e.g., weekly) may be needed to reliably identify cases showing no improvement or deterioration, and it appears that many of these cases can be turned around and positive outcomes achieved.
7. Follow-up is generally important but is especially important when patients have dealt with issues involving high rates of relapse or harm to self or others.
8. Aggregate outcome data for quality improvement purposes; it is very difficult to reliably identify strengths or areas for improvement without aggregated data. Therapists should aggregate data from their individual practices, and programs should aggregate at the program level.

Making full use of patient outcome data can significantly improve the effectiveness of behavioral health care. Consistent outcome measurement has already shown promise for preventing treatment failures, and it is likely to prove highly useful for the training and supervision of therapists as well. These data can also be aggregated on a large scale across practice networks and provider systems to allow researchers to examine the characteristics of effective psychological treatment for different types of patients with different disorders, vulnerabilities, circumstances, strengths, and resources. Measurement improvements are likely to result from the use of new psychometric methods such as item response theory, Rasch modeling, and possibly neuroimaging and stress hormone measurement (Ogles, 2013). This will almost certainly lead to a more thorough and detailed understanding of behavior change processes, more effective training and supervision, more effective treatment, greater patient satisfaction with services, and improved cost-effectiveness. The behavioral health care field has moved beyond the point where it mainly focuses on demonstrating the effectiveness of its interventions in general. The field is now ready to also focus on ensuring the effectiveness of treatment in individual cases.

CASE EXAMPLE: ASSESSING TREATMENT OUTCOMES FROM A BIOPSYCHOSOCIAL APPROACH WITH A MILDLY DEPRESSED PATIENT

The case of Maria, the 44-year-old mildly depressed woman, has been discussed over the past three chapters. Maria made significant improvement in several areas in the 2.5 months since treatment began. In her last session, she noted that she was very glad that she got back into better physical shape. She now exercises regularly and has lost 15 pounds. Her alcohol consumption has dropped significantly and she has more energy. She said she also now feels more physically attractive to her husband and has become involved athletically with her children in the way that she had originally imagined before she had children. In addition to improvements in her self-esteem and identity, she also reports that her mild depressive feelings have almost disappeared. She reported enjoying being on the parent advisory committee at her children's school and has met many interesting and talented people in that group. Knowing them has made her feel more connected to the community as well.

Maria reported great improvements in her relationship with her mother. She said that although it is too early to trust that this improvement will last, she and her mother have had very honest conversations about Maria's orientation to her career and approach to parenting. She said that she was especially pleased that her father acknowledged that his wife was too critical of the way Maria managed her life.

Maria reported that she has become interested in the possibility of pursuing management positions with her pharmacy company because she sees a number of services and practices that should be improved. She and her psychologist discussed when she might pursue those interests given that she may be too busy with her kids at least until they are in middle school.

After reflecting on the changes that occurred since her first visit, the psychologist referred back to the original biopsychosocial assessment summary that he and Maria completed during their first session and to her scores across sessions on the clinic outcomes questionnaire. The scores indicate steady improvement into the nonclinical range, where she has remained for the last 3 weeks. The psychologist asked Maria what she would consider to be her current level of functioning in each of the biopsychosocial areas indicated in Table 11.1, and he entered dots into the table to indicate the level of functioning posttreatment as compared with pretreatment (indicated by checks). Following this discussion, the psychologist and patient decided to terminate treatment, though Maria said she would contact him if her progress reverses or questions arise. The psychologist also obtained Maria's consent to call her monthly for the next 3 months to follow up on how she is progressing.

TABLE 11.1
Pretreatment and Posttreatment Assessment of Biopsychosocial Functioning for the Case Example

Biopsychosocial domains and component	−3 Severe need	−2 Moderate need	−1 Mild need	0 No need	+1 Mild strength	+2 Moderate strength	+3 Major strength
Biological functioning							
General physical health			✓				
Childhood health history					✓	●	
Medications				✓		●	
Health habits and behaviors			✓				●
Psychological functioning							
Level of psychological functioning			✓			●	
History of present problem			✓		●		
Individual psychological history			✓ ●				
Substance use and abuse			✓	● ✓			
Suicidal ideation and risk assessment				● ✓			
Effects of developmental history				●			
Childhood abuse and neglect				✓ ●			
Other psychological traumas				● ✓			

Mental status examination

Personality styles and
  characteristics

Sociocultural functioning

Current relationships and
  social support
Current living situation
Family history
Educational history
Employment
Financial resources
Legal issues/crime
Military history
Activities of interest/
  hobbies
Religion
Spirituality
Multicultural issues

Note. Checks represent pretreatment and dots represent posttreatment scores.

IV

ADDITIONAL IMPLICATIONS OF THE BIOPSYCHOSOCIAL APPROACH

12

PUBLIC HEALTH PERSPECTIVE ON BEHAVIORAL HEALTH

The biopsychosocial approach to behavioral health care emphasizes meeting the behavioral health needs and promoting the biopsychosocial functioning of the general public. This includes providing treatment for behavioral health problems that individuals have already developed, but it also involves a public health and preventive perspective both for those who could be prevented from developing problems as well as those who are showing early signs of developing problems but where the course of those problems could be reversed. The difficulty and cost of reversing health problems after they have fully developed is becoming increasingly clear. Public health strategies are needed to prevent illness and dysfunction from developing in the first place and to promote health and resilience in general. These strategies can help reduce the enormous burden that behavioral and physical health problems pose for individuals, their families, and society generally.

DOI: 10.1037/14441-013
Biopsychosocial Practice: A Science-Based Framework for Behavioral Health Care, by T. P. Melchert
Copyright © 2015 by the American Psychological Association. All rights reserved.

The public health field has been extraordinarily successful in reducing the incidence and consequences of infectious diseases and many other health problems. The effects on human life have been transformative. Public health has a long history that spans many disciplines, and the importance of mental health and behavior in that field has grown substantially in recent decades. This chapter presents the basic principles of public health, with a focus on behavioral health.

THE REMARKABLE EFFECTIVENESS OF
PUBLIC HEALTH INTERVENTIONS

For most of human history, disease was essentially synonymous with epidemic (Turnock, 2012). Epidemics of plague, leprosy, cholera, smallpox, typhoid, tuberculosis, and yellow fever devastated communities, were not understood, could not be controlled, and simply had to be accepted. Starting in the Enlightenment, however, diseases began to be understood and the public health field emerged. We are still in the midst of the truly transformative effects that the public health movement has had on the human experience. Our physical, mental, and social lives have been, and continue to be, dramatically transformed as a result of public health interventions.

In 1900, life expectancy in the United States was estimated to be 47 years, having risen only minimally over previous centuries. One century later, however, it had risen to 77 years (Arias, 2004). Infectious diseases were still the dominant threat to human health around the globe in 1900, but the scientific understanding of disease and the implementation of public health measures began to dramatically change that situation. Edward Jenner discovered a vaccine for smallpox in 1797, and John Snow traced an outbreak of cholera to a single water well on Broad Street in London in 1854. That same year, he also noticed that water drawn from the Thames River upstream from London was not associated with cholera, whereas water drawn downstream from London was. As these findings became accepted, public health measures involving sanitary water systems and vaccinations grew and death related to infectious diseases fell precipitously.

The death rate for infectious diseases in the United States fell dramatically over the 20th century. The rate was approximately 800 per 100,000 individuals in 1900 and was steadily declining until the influenza pandemic of 1918 when it rose to nearly 1000 per 100,000. It continued to drop, however, and fell to around 50 per 100,000 individuals by midcentury, where it has stayed since (Centers for Disease Control and Prevention, 1999). Most deaths from infectious disease now involve influenza in elderly individuals. Other infectious diseases have been nearly or completely eliminated. For example, the number of cases of measles in the United States was estimated at 503,282 in 1900 and fell to 43 in 2007; the number of cases of diphtheria was 175,885 in 1900 and fell to 0 in 2007; the number of cases of mumps was 152,209 in 1900 and fell to 800 in 2007; the number of smallpox infections was estimated at 48,164 in 1900 and fell to 0 in 2007; and the number of cases of paralytic poliomyelitis was 16,316 in 1900 and fell to 0 in 2007 (Centers for Disease Control and Prevention, 1999, 2009).

The dramatic improvements in human health over the past century and a half are often mistakenly attributed to improvements in medicine when in fact public health measures have actually played a far larger role. In 1959, the biologist Dubos observed that "no major disease in the history of mankind has been conquered by therapists and rehabilitative modes alone, but ultimately only through prevention" (p. 4). In 1965, McKeown similarly concluded that "health has advanced significantly only since the late 18th century and until recently owed little to medical advances" (p. 9). More recently, Bunker, Frazier, and Mosteller (1994) found that only 5 years of the 30-year increase in life span over the 20th century was the result of improved medical treatment—the rest was attributable to prevention efforts. In a study of years of life gained in England and Wales from 1981 to 2000, 79% of the increase was attributed to reductions in major risk factors, whereas only 21% was attributed to modern medical and surgical treatments (Ünal, Critchley, Fidan, & Capewell, 2005).

Another major concern that heightens the importance of prevention in health involves the very high cost of health care, particularly in the United States. More money is spent on health care in the United States per capita ($8,233 in 2012; the next closest country was $5,388) and as a proportion of gross domestic product (17.6% in 2012; the next closest country was 12.0%) than any of the other 33 nations in the Organization of Economic Co-operation and Development (OECD; OECD Health Division 2012). This level of spending is widely viewed as unsustainable. Despite having the most expensive health care system in the world, outcomes involving population morbidity and mortality are low. Figure 12.1 plots the average life expectancy in the 34 OECD countries against the per capita expenditures on health care in "international dollars" (i.e., purchasing power parity dollars adjusted for relative purchasing power across countries; OECD Health Division, 2012). The average life expectancy across the OECD countries in 2010 was 79.8 years (vs. 78.7 years in the United States). The per capita spending on health care across the OECD countries was $3,265 ($8,233 in the United States). Indicators of long, healthy, and productive lives for the United States are lower than those for many other developed countries. In the *World Health Report 2000*, the United States ranked 37th in overall health among all of the countries in the world (France, Italy, Spain, Oman, Austria, and Japan were the top sizable countries; World Health Organization [WHO], 2000).

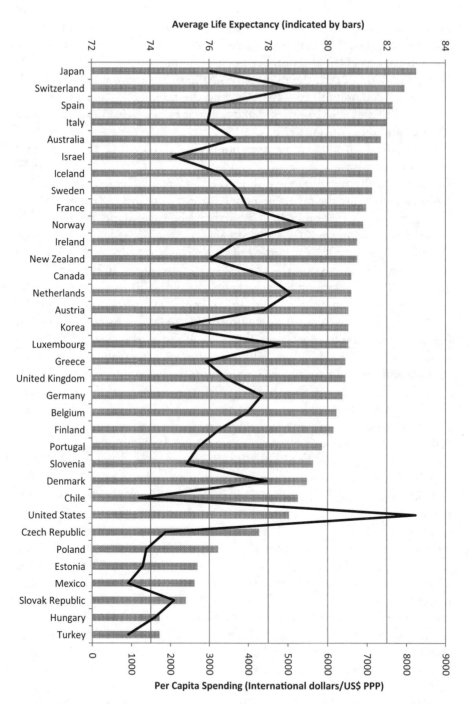

Figure 12.1. Average life expectancy and per capita health care spending in OECD countries. PPP = purchasing power parity; OECD = Organization of Economic Co-operation and Development. Data are from OECD Health Division (2012).

KEY FEATURES OF PUBLIC HEALTH

Public health has several features that make it a unique and complex field. First, it is grounded squarely in science. Unlike medicine or psychology (which was studied as "mental philosophy" for many centuries before the term *psychology* was used), public health did not exist before the 19th century. Epidemiology, the basic science of public health practice (Rothman & Greenland, 1998), emerged out of the quantitative analysis of disease patterns. It was an entirely new science with no history of past practices, conventions, or traditions. Second, its primary purpose has been prevention (Turnock, 2012). Prevention is widely valued and appreciated, but the field also suffers from having no large natural constituency that advocates for prevention. The main beneficiaries of many preventive interventions are very young or have not yet been born.

A third important feature of public health is its foundation in social justice (D. E. Beauchamp, 1976; Krieger & Brin, 1998; Turnock, 2012). A social justice perspective views public health as a public good. As discussed in Chapter 3, justice is concerned with the equitable distribution of the benefits and burdens of society. Health and access to health services are generally considered to be social benefits, and both require collective action on the part of others to provide. This leads to another important feature of public health, which is its inherently political nature. The social justice foundations of public health inevitably lead to political conflict. Public health requires collective action to serve populations, and there are major political differences in how these actions and goals are valued. Public health measures require government to enforce public policies regarding sewage and water systems, pollution control, infectious disease control, drug efficacy and safety, food production and sale, workplace safety, public safety, and many other issues that are frequently politically contentious. Individuals may agree generally regarding principles of greater public health and safety, but disagree strongly regarding the means to achieving those goals.

A fifth feature of public health is its expanding agenda and scope (Institute of Medicine, 1994, 2002). Before 1900, infectious diseases were the focus of public health measures. The health problems and needs of mothers and children were added to that agenda in the early 20th century, and chronic disease prevention and medical care became important foci in the middle of the century. Later, substance abuse, teen pregnancy, mental illness, HIV infection, and violence were added to the agenda. The importance of behavior and lifestyle in public health has grown steadily over the history of the field. After the events of September 11, 2001, including the anthrax scare that followed, bioterrorism preparedness became another public health priority. This expanding scope and agenda of the public field is reflected in a sixth feature, which is its highly diverse interdisciplinary culture. The field relies heavily on epidemiologists and biostatisticians, but a wide variety of other professionals play important roles—physicians, nurses, dieticians, economists, political scientists, lawyers, sociologists, anthropologists, psychologists, social workers, engineers, gerontologists, and disability specialists. The vast majority of professionals working in public health do not hold public health degrees, and so public health could be viewed more as a movement than a profession (Turnock, 2012).

MEASURING PUBLIC HEALTH

Measuring the health of the public is not straightforward. Measuring infectious and acute disease is relatively easy because these diseases typically are objectively defined states. Measuring positive states of health and well-being, however, include subjective components that go well beyond the absence of disease and disability. Both quantity and quality of health are essential considerations from this perspective.

Morbidity and Mortality

Mortality is the most commonly reported indicator of health because these data are usually the most easily obtained. This is ironic, however, in that mortality (i.e., death) is not a measure of health or of disease and is only an indirect indicator of the health of a living population (Turnock, 2012). Data on morbidity (i.e., illnesses, injuries, and functional limitations) provide another important perspective on the health of a population but are not as readily available as mortality data. Though morbidity and mortality data provide critical perspectives on the health of a population, they both provide only indirect indicators of quality of health. As has been mentioned several times before, the absence of disease and disability (and death) does not imply health.

Alternative Measures

Years of Potential Life Lost

A variety of alternative measures of health have been developed to compensate for the limitations of the indirect measures of morbidity and mortality. One of the most common measures involves computing the years of potential life lost. This measure is based on mortality data but gives greater weight to deaths that occur at a younger age. Based on some arbitrary age (75 is now the most commonly used), the years of life lost to different causes of death are computed. An infant death contributes 75 years to the measure, a suicide at age 20 contributes 55 years to the measure, and death by cardiac arrest that

TABLE 12.1
Years of Potential Life Lost (YPLL) Before age 75 in the United States in 2000 by Cause of Death and Ranks for YPLL and Number of Deaths

Cause of death	YPLL	Rank by YPLL	Rank by number of deaths
Cancer	1,698,500	1	2
Heart disease	1,270,700	2	1
Unintentional injuries	1,052,500	3	5
Suicide	343,300	4	11
Homicide	274,200	5	14
Cerebrovascular diseases	226,500	6	3
Chronic obstructive lung disease	190,700	7	4
Diabetes mellitus	181,200	8	6
HIV infection	178,900	9	18
Chronic liver disease and cirrhosis	141,700	10	12

Note. Years lost before age 75 per 100,000 individuals younger than 75 years of age. Data are from National Center for Health Statistics (2002). In the public domain.

occurs at age 73 contributes 2 years to the measure. This measure gives a different perspective on the health of a population than a simple ranking of the most frequent causes of death. As seen in Table 12.1, suicide and homicide rise to the top five using this measure whereas they are not in the top 10 when ranked by a simple count of their occurrence in the population (National Center for Health Statistics, 2002).

Disability-Adjusted Life Year and Burden of Disease

Measures to capture quality of life considerations have been developed that combine additional indicators of health with mortality data. The most common of these is the disability-adjusted life year (DALY), which combines self-reported health status and activity limitations with mortality data. This measure is often discussed in terms of the burden that disease has on a population. This perspective is very useful because many conditions have a serious impact on functioning but do not cause death (e.g., schizophrenia, cerebral palsy, arthritis). Epidemiology commonly did not focus on the burden of behavioral health disorders until American Psychiatric Association published the *Diagnostic and Statistical Manual of Mental Disorders* (third ed.) in 1980 because there was too much disagreement about the measurement and prevalence of mental disorders before that time.

The first major use of the DALY measure was in the Global Burden of Disease Study by Murray and Lopez (1996). This landmark study provided a very different view of the impact of disease and of mental illness in particular. The study was updated by WHO in 2008, and its findings are summarized in

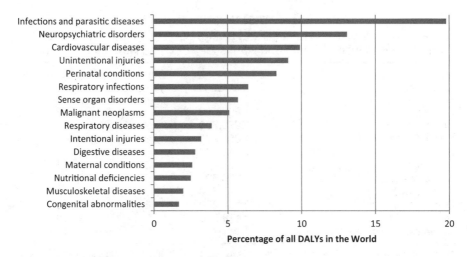

Figure 12.2. Disability-adjusted life years (DALYs) by disease category in the world, 2004. Data are from World Health Organization (2008b).

Figure 12.2 for disease category. For the world as a whole, infectious and parasitic diseases accounted for 19.8% of all DALYs, followed by neuropsychiatric conditions (13.1%). There are neurologic conditions included in this category such as epilepsy (0.5% of all DALYs), but psychiatric disorders account for much more of the total. Figure 12.3 ranks the specific causes of DALYs in the world. Unipolar depressive disorders ranked third, accounting for 4.3% of all DALYs, and several other behavioral health disorders are among the top 30 causes of DALYs. (Not included in these data are personality disorders which, as a group, are much more prevalent than unipolar depressive disorder.)

Another approach to measuring the DALY concept is illustrated using data from the 2006–2007 National Health Interview Survey. For the U.S. population as a whole, Americans on average have a life expectancy of 78, live 9 years with poor health, 12 years with activity limitations, and 35 years with a chronic disease. The same pattern emerged for life expectancy at age 65: Americans who reach age 65 live on average another 19 years, 5 of those years in poor health, 7 with activity limitations, and 16 years with a chronic disease (National Center for Health Statistics, 2012).

RISK AND PROTECTIVE FACTORS

The primary purpose of public health is the prevention of disease and disorders that threaten the health and well-being of the population. Epidemiology is the basic science that provides information about the prevalence and distribution of these problems. But to be useful for prevention, epidemiology also

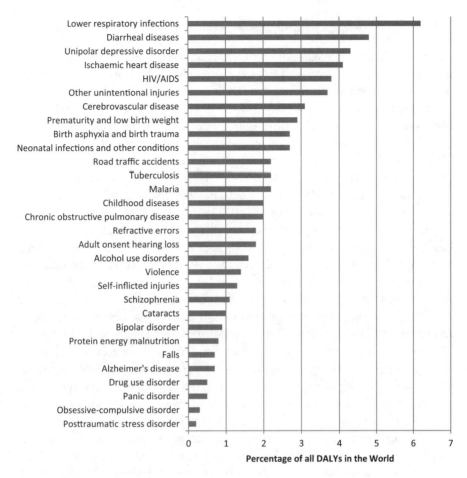

Figure 12.3. Disability-adjusted life years (DALYs) by specific cause in the world, 2004. Data are from World Health Organization (2008b).

must provide information about risk factors that can be targeted for prevention and about the effectiveness of preventive interventions in reducing the prevalence of a disease or disorder.

The term *risk factor* was invented by epidemiology in the 1950s when the Framingham Heart Study found that cardiovascular disease did not have a single cause but rather many different contributing factors that increased risk for disease. As noted in Chapter 7, risk factors are "characteristics, variables, or hazards that, if present for a given individual, make it more likely that this individual, rather than someone selected from the general population, will develop a disorder" (Institute of Medicine, 1994, p. 6). Some risk factors are generally not malleable to change, such as genetic inheritance or gender, whereas some are relatively easily changed such as lack of social support or being victimized by bullying (e.g., Durlak & Wells, 1997). Even disorders with very high heritability are sometimes modifiable as a result of changing the environment. For example, phenylketonuria is one of the few genetic disorders that can be very effectively controlled in this way. Unidentified and untreated phenylketonuria can lead to serious irreversible brain damage including behavioral retardation and seizures, but early detection and avoiding foods high in phenylalanine (e.g., breast milk, dairy products) can be completely successful for avoiding these problems (Centerwall & Centerwall, 2000). Most behavioral disorders, however, have a far more complex etiology, and identifying the causal risk factors involved is much more complicated.

Protective factors are internal or external influences that improve an individual's response to a risk factor (Rutter, 1979). Supportive parents or other adults from the community are important external protective factors against the development of many maladaptive outcomes in children (National Research Council and Institute of Medicine, 2009), and resilience is an important internal protective factor that improves individuals' responses to stressors or traumatic events across the life span (Garmezy & Rutter, 1983). Chapter 7 noted several of the most important risk factors for negative developmental outcomes in children and the important role played by protective factors.

Many behavioral health problems share many of the same risk factors, and experiencing multiple risk factors has particularly negative effects for individuals' development and functioning (see Chapter 7). Rutter (1979) was the first to show that as the number of risks children face increases, their developmental status decreases. In a nationally representative sample of infants and toddlers investigated for child maltreatment, Barth et al. (2008) found that 5% of the children who experienced maltreatment alone or with one additional risk factor had a measured developmental delay in their cognitive, language, or emotional development. As the number of risk factors increased, however, the proportions with developmental delays rose quickly: 44% of those exposed to four risk factors had developmental delays; 76% of those exposed to five risk factors had developmental delays; and 99% of those exposed to seven risk factors had measured developmental delays (see Figure 7.1).

Prevention efforts often aim to reduce risk factors (Institute of Medicine, 1994). After the interaction of risk and protective factors for particular problems has been clarified, research generally focuses on identifying the causal risk factors that are malleable and potentially alterable through intervention. When these factors are identified, preventive interventions can be designed and the effects of those interventions can be evaluated, ideally through preventive intervention trials. A sad implication of the very high prevalence of psychological disorders in both children and adults is that universal prevention programs do not target many risk-free individuals.

BASIC APPROACHES TO PREVENTION

As noted above, the primary purpose of public health is the prevention of disease and problems that threaten health and well-being. The principles of prevention were first applied to control infectious diseases through the use of mass vaccination, water safety, and other public health measures and were later applied to chronic diseases and behavioral disorders (Institute of Medicine, 1994). The prevention of chronic diseases and behavioral disorders is typically much more complicated than preventing infectious diseases, however, because infectious diseases have specific, precise causes, whereas the causes of chronic and behavioral disorders tend to be far more multifactorial and complex.

Definitions of the general categories of public health preventive interventions were developed over a half century ago (Commission on Chronic Illness, 1957). *Primary prevention* refers to the prevention of a disease before it occurs; *secondary prevention* refers to the prevention of recurrences or exacerbations of a disease that has already been diagnosed; and *tertiary prevention* refers to the attempt to reduce the amount of disability that is caused by a disease.

These definitions are less applicable in the case of behavioral health, however, so the Institute of Medicine in 1994 recommended modified definitions of the different levels and types of prevention. It made essentially no change to the definition of *primary prevention*, which referred to interventions that help prevent the initial onset of behavioral disorders. Instead of secondary prevention, however, *treatment* was used to refer to the identification and treatment of individuals with behavioral disorders. In addition, *maintenance* was used to refer to interventions designed to reduce relapse and to provide rehabilitation for those with behavioral disorders. The Institute of Medicine further distinguished between *universal*, *selective*, and *indicated* preventive interventions. These are distinguished by the population groups that are targeted for intervention, namely, (a) the population in general, (b) groups that are at greater than average risk for developing problems, or (c) groups identified through a screening process designed to detect individuals who exhibit early signs of the problem. These different types of prevention strategies and interventions are summarized in Exhibit 12.1.

The first two levels of primary prevention strategies noted above are well known (e.g., a universal prevention program offered to all children in a school to teach problem solving skills or resist substance use; a selective prevention program offered to children who experienced child abuse or parental divorce). Indicated preventive interventions tend to be less well known. Several examples of these were noted in Chapter 5 in terms of stepped models of intervention. One of the best known models used to identify and assist individuals at risk for substance abuse is the screen, brief intervention, brief treatment, and referral for treatment (SBIRT) model. This intervention is

EXHIBIT 12.1
Basic Types of Preventive Strategies and Interventions

Commission on Chronic Illness (1957) definitions:
- **Primary prevention**—interventions to prevent a disease before it occurs
- **Secondary prevention**—interventions to prevent recurrences or exacerbations of a disease that has already been diagnosed
- **Tertiary prevention**—interventions to reduce the amount of disability caused by a disease

Institute of Medicine (1994) definitions applied to behavioral health:
- **Primary prevention**—same as above: interventions to prevent a disease before it occurs
- **Treatment**—the identification and treatment of individuals with behavioral disorders
- **Maintenance**—interventions to reduce relapse and provide rehabilitation for those with behavioral disorders

Types of primary preventive interventions based on target group:
- **Universal**—the population in general
- **Selective**—groups at greater than average risk for developing problems
- **Indicated**—groups identified through a screening process designed to classify individuals with early signs of a problem

National Research Council and Institute of Medicine (2009) addition to the above:
- **Health promotion**—interventions to enhance individuals' ability to achieve developmental competence and well-being

---

being used with all patients in a growing number of inpatient and outpatient medical settings to provide early intervention for those who are not dependent on substances but who may be engaging in problematic substance use or abuse (Substance Abuse and Mental Health Services Administration, 2008). As part of routine medical practice, brief substance abuse screening instruments are used to identify those at moderate risk for substance abuse. Brief interventions are then provided to increase awareness of substance use patterns and consequences and to motivate people to reduce harmful drinking and substance misuse. More comprehensive brief treatment is provided when moderate to high risks are identified, and a referral to specialty treatment is provided when severe risk or dependence is indicated.

As the prevalence of infectious disease dropped dramatically in the first half of the last century, attention began to shift toward health and well-being. Focusing on well-being in addition to the prevention of illness and disorder is becoming more widely accepted, and the National Research Council and Institute of Medicine added *health promotion* in their influential 2009 report to reflect this growing interest in developing competency and resilience and in fostering well-being. They offered the following definition as it applies to behavioral health specifically: "Mental health promotion includes efforts to enhance individuals' ability to achieve developmentally appropriate tasks (developmental competence) and a positive sense of self-esteem, mastery, well-being, and social inclusion and to strengthen their ability to cope with adversity" (p. 67). Health promotion strategies aim to identify and strengthen protective factors such as supportive family, school, and community environments that enhance well-being and help children and adults avoid adverse emotions and behaviors (National Research Council and Institute of Medicine, 2009). As competence and psychological well-being improve, resilience increases and individuals are better able to respond adaptively to stressors and influences that might otherwise lead to dysfunction.

EFFECTIVENESS OF PREVENTIVE INTERVENTIONS

The effectiveness of preventive interventions for reducing mental health disorders and maladaptive behavior was a controversial subject for many years, similar to the controversy surrounding the effectiveness of psychotherapy before the 1980s. Skepticism about the effectiveness of preventive interventions for behavioral health problems persisted until the late 1990s when, like in the case of psychotherapy, meta-analytic results finally answered the question.

Durlak and Wells (1997) conducted the first large-scale meta-analysis of controlled outcome studies of preventive interventions. They examined 177 studies that were designed to reduce adjustment problems and promote behavioral health in children and youth younger than age 18. The interventions that were included focused on parent training, divorce adjustment, school adjustment, awareness and expression of emotions, and interpersonal problem-solving skills. They found that all categories of programs were associated with positive effects (mean effect sizes = .24–.93), which are similar to, and often higher than, those achieved by many educational, medical, and psychotherapeutic interventions. Meta-analyses conducted since then have shown that preventive interventions are effective with diverse problem behaviors including adolescent drug use (Tobler & Stratton, 1997); child sexual abuse (Davis & Gidycz, 2000); depression in children, adolescents, adults, and seniors (Jané-Llopis, Hosman, Jenkins, & Anderson, 2003); and educational failure and criminal behavior (Manning, Homel, & Smith, 2010). After conducting a comprehensive review, the National Research Council and Institute of Medicine (2009) concluded:

> A number of specific preventive interventions can modify risk and promote protective factors that have been linked to important determinants of mental, emotional, and behavioral health, especially in such areas as family functioning, early childhood experiences, and social

skills. Interventions are also available to reduce the incidence of common disorders or problem behaviors, such as depression, substance use, and conduct disorder. Some interventions reduce multiple disorders and problem behaviors as well as increase healthy functioning. (pp. 2–3)

The United Kingdom has undertaken a pioneering effort to decrease depression and anxiety disorders on a nationwide basis (see Chapter 9). The program uses an indicated prevention strategy to screen all individuals entering the health care system and then provide evidence-based psychological treatments to those with depressive and anxiety symptoms (Clark et al., 2009). Systematic assessment and ongoing measurement are used to inform the level of intervention needed using a stepped level of care model. At low levels of depression, for example, self-help activities with guidance from a psychological well-being practitioner, computer-assisted cognitive behavior therapy, psychoeducational groups, and structured physical activities are available. Higher intensity services for moderate to severe depression can include cognitive behavior therapy, interpersonal therapy, and medication (Clark, 2011). Preliminary data on the effectiveness of this initiative are promising (e.g., effect sizes of .98 to 1.26 have been found across a range of outcome measures; Clark et al., 2009). Of those who had at least two contacts with a health care provider (i.e., a first assessment session followed by at least one additional contact, even if they dropped out of treatment after the second contact), 55% were considered recovered in terms of their depression and anxiety test scores, both falling below the clinical cutoff at posttreatment.

MONETARY COSTS OF BEHAVIORAL HEALTH CONDITIONS AND COST-EFFECTIVENESS OF PREVENTION

The suffering and pain experienced by individuals and families dealing with behavioral health disorders are enormous, and these disorders are also very costly in monetary terms. Focusing on only the costs of mental, emotional, and behavioral disorders among young people up to age 24, an analysis conducted for the 2009 National Research Council and Institute of Medicine report found that the total cost of these disorders was approximately $247 billion in 2007. The estimated cost of providing mental health services was $45 billion, and the rest was attributable to costs related to health, productivity, and crime.

Focusing only on lost income, Kessler et al. (2008) used data from the National Comorbidity Survey Replication and found that individuals with serious mental illness had personal incomes far below those with no mental illness. They estimated the loss of personal earnings associated with serious behavioral illness at $193.2 billion in 2002. Considering only the direct costs of treating mental illness and the personal income loss associated with mental illness, these two factors combined equal approximately 2% of the entire gross domestic product of the United States. Using data from the National Comorbidity Survey Replication, Merikangas and colleagues (2007) found that up to one third of illness-related days (when individuals were unable to carry out basic daily activities as usual) is related to mental rather than physical disorders. Musculoskeletal disorders accounted for the largest number of days of role disability, which were followed by anxiety disorders and then mood disorders.

There has been less research on the cost-effectiveness of preventive interventions, but the available evidence suggests they can be very cost-effective. Durlak and Wells (1997) found that preventive interventions focused on physical health promotion, early childhood education, and childhood injury saved from $8 to over $45 for every dollar spent. More recently investigators have found smaller economic benefit from these types of programs. In three fairly rigorous long-term studies of early childhood programs for low-income children, returns of $4 to $9 for every dollar invested were found (Heckman, Moon, Pinto, Savelyev, & Yavitz, 2010; Karoly et al., 2005; Masse & Barnett, 2002). Savings for the public included reduced special education, welfare, and crime costs; participants followed into adulthood had increased earnings. After reviewing the available research, the National Research Council and Institute of Medicine (2009) concluded: "Of those few intervention evaluations that have included some economic analysis, most have presented cost-benefit findings and demonstrate that intervention benefits exceed costs, often by substantial amounts" (p. 259).

DISCUSSION: THE LIMITS OF INTERVENTION AND THE IMPORTANCE OF PREVENTION

The public health field has played and continues to play an enormously important role in the health and well-being of the general public around the world. The remarkable effectiveness of public health measures for reducing acute and infectious disease has resulted in what has been referred to as the *epidemiological transition* (Gribble & Preston, 1993), and the benefit to humankind has been simply transformative. Nothing comparable has ever happened before in human history. This is certainly true with regard to physical health, but the role of public health and prevention may eventually be just as important in behavioral health. No widespread disease or disorder has ever been controlled or eliminated through the individual treatment of those who had the disease or disorder (Dubos, 1959; McKeown, 1965). Given that more than 25% of Americans have a behavioral health disorder in any given year and 50% have one or more disorders over their lifetimes (Kessler et al., 2005), a staggering amount of resources would be needed to treat all those individuals. Even if those resources could be made available, no evidence suggests that behavioral disorders would be controlled or eliminated as a result. Further major reductions in disease and disorders are dependent on the implementation of public health measures.

There was excitement about the potential of public health measures to reduce behavioral health problems in the late 1980s and early 1990s as prevention research advanced and behavioral health prevention became a national priority. That excitement soon abated, however, as prevention became a lower priority for the federal government in the second half of the 1990s (Mrazek & Hall, 1997). Federal funding for prevention research stalled, and the recommendations made in the 1994 Institute of Medicine report and other landmark reports since were not implemented.

The costs and burdens of behavioral and physical illness are enormous, however. Preventing these costs and burdens should be both a humanitarian and economic priority for the health care professions and for society in general. George Albee, the leading researcher and advocate in the behavioral health prevention field, argued this case for a half century. Two years before he died in 2006, Albee addressed the Third World Conference on the Promotion of Mental Health and Prevention of Mental and Behavioral Disorders and presented his conclusions about the importance of behavioral health prevention.

1. One-on-one treatment, while humane, cannot reduce the rate of behavioral disorders . . .
2. Only primary prevention, which includes strengthening resistance, can reduce the rate of disorders. Positive infant and childhood experience are crucial. Reducing poverty and sexism are urgent strategies.
3. Ensuring that each child is welcomed into life with good nutrition, a supportive family, good education, and economic security will greatly reduce emotional distress . . .
4. Cultural differences in diagnoses must be understood and be part of program planning.
5. Strong differences of opinions about causes—particularly brain disease versus social injustice—must be resolved by unbiased scientific judgment before real progress can be made. (Albee, 2006, p. 455)

The moral and economic imperatives for energetically promoting behavioral health prevention are clear. In its landmark 2009 report, the

National Research Council and Institute of Medicine documented the evidence that supports this conclusion. They then went on to note:

> Historically, prevention has received far less attention than treatment in either mental health or physical health. A fundamental paradigm shift needs to occur. The substantial progress in prevention science summarized in this report calls for the adoption of a prevention perspective and a resolve to test and determine the most promising application of specific evidence-based preventive approaches. (p. 378)

Reducing the prevalence and impact of behavioral disorders and promoting positive biopsychosocial functioning are top priorities for behavioral health care professionals. Even though most of them are employed providing treatment and maintenance services, prevention needs to become a higher priority for the field. There is no other way to significantly reduce the prevalence of these problems and make major reductions in the burden they pose for individuals, families, and society. The potential for behavioral health professionals to contribute in this area is great. Cognition, affect, and behavior play crucial roles in health and functioning across the biopsychosocial domains, and behavioral health care professionals are consequently well positioned to take leading roles in promoting health and well-being for the population as a whole. This requires that the field becomes more interdisciplinary in perspective and works more collaboratively with other human services fields. Incorporating a public health perspective into our framework for understanding health and functioning is an important step that can enable this to happen.

13

INTEGRATING BEHAVIORAL HEALTH CARE INTO PRIMARY HEALTH CARE

Previous chapters in this volume have highlighted the serious challenges facing health care in the United States. Simply put, our health care costs are not sustainable, and our health care outcomes are disappointing compared with those of other wealthy nations. The long view puts these challenges within the context of the epidemiological transition that has resulted in the major causes of morbidity and mortality shifting from acute and infectious disease to chronic ones. We are still in the midst of adapting to the much longer life spans afforded by the remarkable success of public health measures for controlling infectious disease, but we have yet to figure out how to maximize the health and well-being of the general public once those diseases have been controlled. The shorter view is that the United States is reaching the point where it is having trouble financing its public and private health care systems, too many people do not have medical coverage, and measures of the health of the American public are poor compared with those for other wealthy countries.

DOI: 10.1037/14441-014
Biopsychosocial Practice: A Science-Based Framework for Behavioral Health Care, by T. P. Melchert
Copyright © 2015 by the American Psychological Association. All rights reserved.

These issues have long been recognized, but the ability to achieve political solutions to the problem has been limited. Despite the tremendous political challenge of reorganizing a sector of the economy that had grown to 17.6% of the gross domestic product (Organization of Economic Co-operation and Development Health Division, 2012), the U.S. government did pass the Patient Protection and Affordable Care Act of 2010, the largest expansion and regulatory overhaul of the U.S. health care system since the passage of Medicare and Medicaid in the 1960s. This legislation has been very contentious politically; if it survives, it will have major effects on the U.S. health care system.

The Affordable Care Act strongly encourages different models of health care delivery that are designed to increase the quality of care that individuals receive as well as the number of people covered by the system. Of particular relevance to the present discussion is the legislation's emphasis on integrated primary health care where behavioral health care is provided as part of comprehensive care in the same setting. Integrated health care has a long history but has had limited influence on much of the health care provided in the United States. This is beginning to change as implementing integrated care on a wide scale is beginning to be viewed as a necessary transition for addressing concerns about cost and effectiveness in the present system. This chapter describes this approach, which could become the way that the large majority of Americans will receive behavioral health care in the future.

ORIGINS OF INTEGRATED CARE IN THE UNITED STATES

The history of integrated care in the United States begins with the Mayo Clinic. A devastating tornado struck Rochester, Minnesota, in 1883, and Dr. Mayo and others in the city realized that the local medical care systems were completely inadequate for meeting the health care needs of the area. To address those needs, a hospital was built over the next several years, and Dr. Mayo's sons, who had entered medicine in the 1880s, began working closely with their father in their new clinic and the new local hospital. The sons later invited several other physicians to join them, and the group eventually developed the world's first integrated, team-based approach to health care focused on providing the best quality care possible. The physicians are salaried to reduce the financial incentive to see large numbers of patients, and their clinics and hospitals went on to provide some of the best quality medical care in the nation (Fye, 2010).

Mental health was not included in early health care plans, however. In fact, up through the 1950s, no health plan in the United States paid for psychotherapy. Kaiser Permanente was a large integrated health care plan that was started in the 1940s in California. That organization instituted the first prepaid psychotherapy benefit in the late 1950s after finding that 60% of patient visits to a physician were for somaticized stress and other emotional factors (Follette & Cummings, 1967). The psychologist Nicholas Cummings wrote that first plan, and Kaiser Permanente later found the plan to be remarkably successful, resulting in a 65% reduction in cost utilization (which became known as the *medical cost offset*; Cummings, 1997). Other plans soon followed, and mental health care became routinely covered in both public and private health care plans across the country.

Mayo Clinic and Kaiser Permanente are very large systems that provide health care to millions of individuals, but the largest provider of integrated health care in the United States has been the Department of Veterans Affairs (Trivedi & Grebla, 2011). As a result of the successes of these integrated care systems, a large number of public and private health care plans began offering integrated care in preparation for the implementation of many of the provisions of the Affordable Care Act in 2014. The sections that follow describe different integrated care models and the opportunities they present for behavioral health care professionals.

PRIMARY CARE AS THE DE FACTO BEHAVIORAL HEALTH CARE SYSTEM

As the data from previous chapters amply show, behavioral health conditions have a major impact on individuals' health and well-being and are a major reason that individuals seek health care services. About 50% of all Americans meet the criteria for a mental disorder during the course of their lifetimes and 25% do so during the year prior to the study (Kessler et al., 2005). Chronic medical conditions are also highly prevalent and are often associated with co-occurring behavioral disorders as well. Nearly 50% of adult Americans have a chronic medical condition, and more than half of these individuals also meet the criteria for co-occurring mental disorders (Agency for Healthcare Research and Quality, 2009; Partnership for Solutions, 2004). The Institute of Medicine (2004) concluded that approximately half of all morbidity and mortality in the United States is caused by behavior and lifestyle. Not only are behavioral health disorders highly prevalent in the general population, but they also are an important part of the clinical picture for many individuals with medical disease as well. From the biopsychosocial perspective, these different domains of functioning are of course inseparable.

Although large numbers of psychotherapists provide therapy in independent offices separate from medical clinics (i.e., specialty mental health care), the majority of individuals with mental health problems who receive treatment actually rely on primary care for meeting their behavioral health needs. As many as 70% of primary care visits in the United States are related to behavioral health needs (Follette & Cummings, 1967; Fries, Koop, & Beadle, 1993), and as many as 80% of all psychotropic medications are prescribed by nonpsychiatric physicians, nurse practitioners, and physician assistants (Mark, Levit, & Buck, 2009). In fact, the role of nonpsychiatric mental health specialists in providing treatment actually declined from the early 1990s to the early 2000s while the proportion of patients with behavioral health problems treated by general medical practitioners increased (Kessler et al., 2005; Wang et al., 2006).

Primary care has long been recognized as the de facto behavioral health care system in the United States (Bray, 1996; Regier, Goldberg, & Taube, 1978). Belar (1996) noted that because physical and behavioral health are intertwined, 100% of medical visits in fact have psychological and behavioral components. Psychologists and other behavioral health care professionals provide relatively little of this care, however, and many patients' behavioral health problems are undiagnosed or undertreated as a result (Blount et al., 2007). Physicians, physician assistants, and nurse practitioners provide the vast majority of the behavioral health care delivered in primary care settings. These professionals are very well-trained in physical medicine, but their training in the evaluation, treatment, and management of behavioral health problems is often limited. Nonetheless, primary care is likely to play an even larger role in providing behavioral health care services in the future. The Mayo Clinic, Kaiser Permanente, the Department of Veterans Affairs, and other integrated care systems have achieved significant success in terms of both quality and cost (Cummings, O'Donohue, Hayes, & Follette, 2001; Fye, 2010; Trivedi & Grebla, 2011). Therefore, interest in expanding integrated care within primary care has grown significantly in recent years.

COLLABORATIVE AND INTEGRATIVE CARE MODELS

Several different approaches to collaborative and integrative health care are used across health care systems. Hunter, Goodie, Oordt, and Dobmeyer (2009) described these as falling on a continuum. At one end is the *coordinated care model*, in which primary care providers and behavioral health specialists work in separate facilities delivering separate care and exchanging information regarding patients as needed. In the middle of the continuum is the *on-site* or *co-located care* model, in which behavioral health and primary care providers deliver separate care but work in the same set of offices or in the same building, sometimes sharing office staff and waiting rooms and communicating with other providers face-to-face regarding patients. In this and the coordinated care models, primary care providers typically refer patients for behavioral health care treatment, and separate records and treatment plans are maintained. These approaches in which care is provided separately by different health specialists are often referred to as *multidisciplinary care*. Diverse professionals bring their expertise to working with patients, communicating and collaborating on a consultative basis, but they do not work as a cohesive team and do not intentionally integrate their care (Kelly & Coons, 2012).

At the high end of the collaborative continuum described by Hunter et al. (2009) is the *integrated care model*, in which behavioral health providers are full members of the primary care team, all of whom communicate, collaborate, and coordinate on all aspects of patient care. The team addresses the full spectrum of the patient's needs, and one treatment plan and medical record are maintained. There has been growing interest in this model as a possible solution for the cost and quality concerns in U.S. health care, and it is also seen as the appropriate model for health care internationally. The World Health Organization, in its 2008 report, *Primary Health Care, Now More Than Ever*, argued that integrated primary care is the best approach to meeting health care needs in developing as well as wealthy countries.

It appears very likely that behavioral as well as physical health care will increasingly be delivered in integrated primary care settings in both the public and private sector in the United States (Belar, 2012; Bray, 2010; S. B. Johnson, 2013; Kelly & Coons, 2012; Nielsen, Langner, Zema, Hacker, & Grundy, 2012; Nordal, 2012; Rozensky, 2011). Patient-centered medical home (PCMH) models are the best known of these models and are being piloted and implemented in a rapidly growing number of health care agencies (Nielsen et al., 2012). Several concerns regarding these models have been raised, and various alternatives are being evaluated (Nordal, 2012), but movement toward PCMH and other models is increasing.

The Patient-Centered Primary Care Collaborative was founded in 2006 to advocate for the primary care PCMH model of health care delivery. After reviewing the available data on the effectiveness of the medical home model, the group issued the following conclusions:

> This report updates our earlier reviews of the cost and quality data from 2009 and 2010, and the findings are clear, consistent, and compelling: Data demonstrates that the PCMH improves health outcomes, enhances the patient and provider experience of care, and reduces expensive, unnecessary hospital and emergency department utilization. The results meet the goals of the Institute for Healthcare Improvement's Triple Aim for better health outcomes, better care, and lower costs. The momentum for transforming the U.S. health system is reaching the tipping point,

and the PCMH and primary care are central to this goal. The current fragmented health system that pays for volume over value is riddled with inefficiencies, has highly variable health outcomes, is not financially sustainable, and is no longer acceptable. (Nielsen et al., 2012, p. 2)

A PARADIGM SHIFT: INTEGRATED PRIMARY CARE

In 2010, the U.S. Congress passed the Patient Protection and Affordable Care Act to address the United States' fragmented and uncoordinated health care delivery system and to improve health outcomes, improve quality and efficiency, and reduce the rate of growth in health care costs. The survival of this milestone legislation over the long term is not clear because of significant political opposition, but the act survived an initial judicial challenge, and the deadline for phasing in its most important provisions was the beginning of 2014.

If the Affordable Care Act is not overturned, it will result in a significant transformation of the U.S. health care system. Although this legislation preserves the U.S. system of private, employer-based health coverage, it includes several major changes, such as government-financed testing of new, more efficient health care delivery models designed to improve patient outcomes; revamped payment systems; expansion of pay-for-performance; wellness and preventive care; and levels of transparency and accountability never before required. The American Psychological Association executive director for professional practice commented that "the [Affordable Care Act] of 2010 will unquestionably be the largest driver of change in our health care delivery system for the foreseeable future" (Nordal, 2012, p. 537).

New health care delivery models are central to the Affordable Care Act. The legislation strongly supports the development of Accountable Care Organizations and PCMHs. Several specific models are allowed under these broad categories, although many experts consider the PCMH model to be the most viable alternative and a major improvement over traditional primary care practice (Nielsen et al., 2012; Nutting et al., 2011). The Agency for Healthcare Research and Quality (2013) described the PCMH as a model of primary care that is (a) comprehensive ("meets the large majority of each patient's physical and mental health care needs, including prevention and wellness, acute care, and chronic care"); (b) patient-centered ("health care that is relationship-based with an orientation toward the whole person"); (c) coordinated ("across all elements of the broader health care system"); (d) accessible ("accessible services . . . responsive to patients' preferences"); and (e) focused on quality and safety ("using evidence-based medicine . . . engaging in performance measurement and improvement"). These components are thoroughly consistent with the emphases of the biopsychosocial approach advocated in this volume.

Views regarding the purpose and nature of primary health care are changing. Though very large numbers of Americans receive behavioral health treatment from their primary care providers, many psychotherapists view primary care as mainly responsible for physical care. Many psychotherapists working in agencies and private practice see themselves as specialists who accept referrals for mental health treatment and provide their services separately from medical care, ordinarily with only limited consultation with primary care providers in some cases. Education and training in behavioral health care typically follow this model as well.

Primary care is increasingly being viewed as a biopsychosocial rather than a biomedical field that is responsible for both behavioral and physical health care needs (Bluestein & Cubic, 2009). Individuals with behavioral health needs would receive their care within the primary care setting unless their problems required more intensive treatment than what is practical to offer there. This represents a paradigm shift for many in the behavioral health care field as well as for health care generally (Nordal, 2012). If this trend continues, the behavioral health care professions may need to dramatically shift their conceptualization of education and practice if they are going to play a significant role in the integrated primary care systems of the future.

The integrated primary care setting also involves a very different approach to practice than specialty mental health care (Bluestein & Cubic, 2009; Bray et al., 2009; Cummings et al., 2001; Hunter et al., 2009; Kelly & Coons, 2012). Caseloads are normally large and involve diverse concerns, including highly complex cases and disorders. Patients are often routinely screened with brief assessment instruments for common issues such as depression, anxiety, and substance abuse, and the results are quickly scored and brief interventions and/or referrals are made. Assessment and treatment sessions may last only 15 minutes, and follow-up sessions may take place when the patient returns for appointments with another member of the team. Sometimes other team members conduct the follow-up sessions. Patients may be seen in examination rooms that are shared between team members instead of in an individual physician's consultation office, and interruptions may be common. Recommendations to patients are often problem focused, and handouts for handling common issues are frequently provided. Interactions between providers are often fast paced, and communication and documentation are typically very succinct and require familiarity with medical terms and abbreviations. The conceptualization of cases is biopsychosocial in orientation with a strong emphasis on evidence-based practice—the traditional conceptualization of cases according to particular theoretical orientations would be quite foreign. This approach to practice is significantly different from the training received in many behavioral health care programs.

INTERPROFESSIONAL TRAINING

Improved teamwork, communication, and collaborative care are widely viewed as essential for improving the safety and effectiveness of American health care in general. The modern patient safety movement arose following the landmark report of the Institute of Medicine (2000), *To Err is Human*, that found that 44,000 to 98,000 Americans die each year as a result of medical errors ("a jumbo jet a day"). The report concluded that the epidemic of avoidable medical errors was largely caused by a fragmented health care delivery system (or "nonsystem" as some view it), where failures of communication, collaboration, and quality assurance processes frequently have fatal consequences. Concerns about the adequacy of interprofessional communication, collaboration, and teamwork extend back several decades, but the 2000 Institute of Medicine report caught the attention of the medical community in a way that previous reports had not. Institute of Medicine reports since then have reinforced the call for improving health care safety and quality through improved interprofessional collaboration (e.g., *Crossing the Quality Chasm*, Institute of Medicine, 2001; *Health Professions Education: A Bridge to Quality*, Institute of Medicine, 2003; see also Chapter 10, this volume).

Effective interprofessional team-based health care is viewed as critical to the success of not only the PCMH and other integrated care models but also to all health care (Institute of Medicine, 2001, 2003). For professionals from a variety of disciplines to effectively collaborate and provide integrated care for patients' physical and behavioral health needs, open communication and true collaboration are essential. This will require improved interprofessional training across all the professions involved. D'amour and Oandasan (2005) emphasized that interprofessional education and practice are distinctly different from interdisciplinary practice. They viewed the latter as reinforcing a "silo-like division of professional responsibilities," while interprofessionalism "is defined as the development of a cohesive practice between professionals from different disciplines" (p. 9).

Given the importance of interprofessional skills to effective integrated care, the Interprofessional Education Collaborative Expert Panel (2011) developed a list of core competencies for all health care professionals. These competencies fall within the domains of values and ethics for interprofessional practice, roles and responsibilities, interprofessional communication, and teams and teamwork. A variety of professions are incorporating these competencies into their accreditation guidelines and standards (Interprofessional Education Collaborative Expert Panel, 2011). For example, the Accreditation Council for Graduate Medical Education (2011) incorporated professionalism, interpersonal communication skills, systems-based practice, and interprofessional teamwork into its standards involving general competencies.

Integrated care is especially important for individuals with severe mental illness. Rates of morbidity and mortality among this group in the United States are high, particularly in the public health system, where the average life span is 25 years shorter than in the general population (see Chapter 4). The National Association of State Mental Health Program Directors (J. E. Miller & Prewitt, 2012) identified integrated health care as a top priority for addressing this alarming state of affairs. They noted:

> Evidence demonstrates that physical and behavioral health problems often occur at the same time. Integrating services to treat both will yield improvement in clinical outcomes and quality of life and the best possible results, and the most acceptable and effective approach for those being served. (p. viii)

They further emphasized that co-occurring substance abuse treatment must be effectively integrated into primary care because of the high prevalence of co-occurring mental health and substance use disorders among individuals with serious mental illness.

DISCUSSION: THE POTENTIAL OF INTEGRATED PRIMARY CARE

The delivery of health care in the United States and around the world is changing. Economic, technological, social, and other pressures on health care systems are growing, and changes are badly needed to contain costs, improve quality, and increase accessibility. These changes are presenting new opportunities as well as challenges. Tens of millions of formerly uninsured Americans may receive coverage. New health care delivery models that provide better coordinated and more effective and efficient care are in high demand. Health care education, research, and practice will all be affected. As primary health care becomes increasingly biopsychosocial instead of biomedical in terms of the treatment provided, the changes will be especially significant for the behavioral health care professions.

At present, it appears almost certain that American health care will increasingly be delivered in integrated primary care settings such as the PCMH (Bluestein & Cubic, 2009; Kelly & Coons, 2012; Nielsen et al., 2012; Nordal, 2012). Even though psychologists have long been involved in integrated health care within Veterans Affairs, Kaiser Permanente, and other organizations, they are often not included in other integrated primary care models that have rapidly expanded in recent years (Kelly & Coons, 2012). It is critical that professional psychology advocate for the interests of our patients and get involved in these systems. Medical professionals are well trained to meet patients' physical health needs but typically receive limited training in behavioral health care. Patients' behavioral health care problems and needs often go unnoticed and undertreated as a result. Behavioral health care professionals can play a very important role in addressing patients' behavioral health problems; improving adherence to medical treatments; and improving overall health, functioning, and well-being. By not getting more involved in these emerging primary care systems, psychologists will almost certainly have a diminished role in health care as other professions take responsibility for providing behavioral health care services. This will result in fewer employment opportunities for psychologists as well.

Training in professional psychology and most of the other behavioral health professions typically has not included preparation for practice in integrated primary care. Many psychologists and other behavioral health care professionals already work in integrated health care settings (e.g., Veterans Affairs), but many psychotherapists work in specialty mental health practice and are not trained in integrated team-based practice. Primary care and integrated care are quite different in nature from independent mental health practice, and the knowledge and skills required for effective team-based practice cannot be easily acquired without systematic training.

As the movement toward integrated care proceeds, psychology needs to reconsider the education of its practitioners so that psychologists develop the interprofessional and biopsychosocial knowledge, skills, and dispositions needed to work in integrated care settings while our unique expertise and perspective are maintained (Belar, 2012; Bray et al., 2009; S. B. Johnson, 2013; Rozensky, 2011). There will likely continue to be an important role for independent specialty psychotherapy practice. As more people receive health care through Accountable Care Organizations and PCMHs, however, these opportunities may decrease. To remain relevant and vital, professional psychology must get involved and adapt to the evolving nature of health care. If professional psychology does not fill the need for behavioral health care professionals in integrated primary care, other specializations will.

The science-based biopsychosocial approach to behavioral health care education and practice advocated in this volume provides the basic conceptual perspective needed for practicing in integrated primary care settings. Adherence to traditional orientations for providing psychotherapy, on the other hand, will make it very difficult to effectively integrate into these settings. Knowledge of health, disease, and dysfunction is growing steadily, and health care is becoming increasingly biopsychosocial in orientation. The behavioral health care field needs to keep current with these developments. The field also has a great deal to offer in terms of preventing health problems from developing, assessing and treating them when they do occur, improving health care quality and efficiency, and promoting the health and well-being of the population in general.

14

THE POTENTIAL AND PROMISE OF BIOPSYCHOSOCIAL BEHAVIORAL HEALTH CARE

The behavioral health care field clearly has reached a very important point in its development. Behavioral science and health care both have advanced dramatically in recent decades. The scientific understanding of human development, functioning, and behavior change has been progressing rapidly, and the ethical foundations of behavioral health care are becoming clearer as well. The era of competing theoretical orientations is giving way as increasing numbers of practitioners are endorsing integrative approaches to practice. Many would argue that the pre-paradigmatic era of the field characterized by irreconcilable theoretical orientations and competing schools of thought is ending and is being replaced by a comprehensive, integrative approach to understanding human psychology.

The inadequacies of the traditional theoretical orientations are not surprising in retrospect. The higher operations of the human mind and brain were simply too complex to explain using the scientific tools that were available at the time. The early researchers could not be expected to unravel the

DOI: 10.1037/14441-015
Biopsychosocial Practice: A Science-Based Framework for Behavioral Health Care, by T. P. Melchert
Copyright © 2015 by the American Psychological Association. All rights reserved.

extraordinary complexity associated with the human mind and brain, a system that is now understood to be the most complicated in the known universe. This would be like expecting Newton and his contemporaries to explain atomic structure or expecting Darwin to explain the human genome. Wilhelm Wundt, William James, and other founders of psychology were well aware of this problem. Nonetheless, numerous theories attempting to explain the nature of human psychology were proposed over the ensuing decades. Many of them provided remarkable insights into human emotion, thought, and behavior, but they were inevitably incomplete because too much was unknown regarding the interacting biological, psychological, and sociocultural processes that determine human development and functioning.

Behavioral science and health care have evolved dramatically in recent decades, however. Knowledge in the field is still quite fragmented, but the preceding chapters illustrate how rapidly knowledge is accumulating and connections are being made across the biopsychosocial domains. Expectations regarding the validity of psychological theory and research are also rising and are actually much higher in some respects than when the traditional theoretical orientations were proposed. Standards for reliable and valid measurement have risen significantly, and theories must now withstand more rigorous experimental tests aimed at verification and falsification. Increasingly it is also expected that psychological theory and research address both ultimate and proximate explanations of psychological phenomena (i.e., evolutionary-based explanations for why we are designed the way we are as well as the operation of the particular mechanisms involved). As the anatomy and physiology of the human body are unintelligible without evolutionary theory, it is now apparent that the same is true for human psychology as well. Scientific knowledge of human psychology is now cumulative and consistent across biological, psychological, and sociocultural levels of natural organization in a way it never was before. E. O. Wilson's (1998) belief in the consilience of scientific knowledge is now coming to pass. Psychology is finally integrating with the other sciences precisely as one would expect of any scientific discipline.

The scientific understanding of human development, functioning, and behavior change is tremendously complex, because human nature is tremendously complex. At the general metatheoretical level, however, the science-based biopsychosocial approach captures the fundamental dimensions that are necessary for understanding psychological phenomena. There appears to be no disagreement that psychological outcomes are multifactorially determined based on complex biopsychosocial developmental processes. Understanding psychological, physical, and social health and functioning requires this basic perspective. Given that psychological outcomes are multifactorially determined, it is also not surprising that multiple psychologically, socially, and biologically oriented interventions have been shown to result in improved psychological functioning.

Despite the remarkable advances in behavioral science in recent years, it is critical not to overstate what is known about many aspects of human psychology. Many basic psychological phenomena are now well understood, but many higher level phenomena are only understood in outline form; it may take decades or longer to fully unravel their complexity. (The same is true of many aspects of biology and medicine as well.) It would, of course, be completely irresponsible to overstate the level of our present knowledge—doing so would violate our ethical obligations of nonmaleficence, beneficence, justice, and respect for autonomy. Humankind has entered into horrible fits of arrogance and hubris many times before, and these have led to violent and barbaric consequences far too often. Claiming to have settled on final explanations for many aspects of human psychology is simply premature at this point. There is too much that remains unknown.

(It could very well be disappointing to eventually develop a complete and detailed understanding of human psychology. That level of understanding would probably lead to the alleviation of huge amounts of distress and suffering, but it would also elucidate what now remain mysteries of human nature. It can be argued that those mysteries hold great value and that critical aspects of human experience would be lost without them. In any case, it is very difficult to even imagine a future when human psychology might be thoroughly described, explained, predicted, and perhaps even controlled. The balancing of the costs and benefits of psychological intervention with that level of knowledge will involve a calculus very different than anything that is familiar to us.)

On the other hand, it is also important not to understate what is currently known about human psychology. A great deal is known about many aspects of development, cognition, emotion, learning, neuropsychological functioning, the factors that give rise to healthy development and to psychopathology, and many other processes. The field has also developed a range of therapeutic interventions that are quite effective for relieving distress and symptomatology and improving functioning. Indeed, their effectiveness compares favorably with many medical and other human service interventions. As long as the safety and effectiveness of interventions can be reasonably assured, biomedical ethics suggests that these interventions should be provided to relieve suffering and improve functioning.

In this volume, the term *science-based biopsychosocial approach* has been used to emphasize the importance of science in the approach being advocated. Over the previous 35 years, the term *biopsychosocial* (by itself) has often been used to acknowledge the biopsychosocial nature of many psychological and medical phenomena, but it often reflected a vague integrative perspective that was not based on particular scientific findings. Because the term was used in such a general manner, it often ended up justifying what was essentially an eclectic approach to case conceptualization and treatment. Scientific knowledge regarding the mind and brain has advanced well beyond the point where a vague integrative perspective and eclecticism are still justifiable. Behavioral health care is now emerging as a true clinical science that needs to be clearly based on the underlying scientific knowledge of human psychology.

A systematic curriculum will be needed to effectively implement a paradigmatic science-based approach to behavioral health care. This approach is fundamentally different from traditional practices involving the personal selection of a theoretical orientation to clinical practice. The starting points for learning the science-based biopsychosocial approach are the scientific understanding of human psychology and the ethical foundations of behavioral health care. Both these areas must be learned in some depth to integrate the concepts and principles involved. As shown in Chapters 2 and 3, both these areas also require a comprehensive, integrative approach to understand the biological, psychological, and sociocultural factors that interact to produce psychological phenomena.

After students gain a solid appreciation of these foundational areas, they are in a position to begin focusing on the basic purpose of behavioral health care, which is to use scientific knowledge and professional ethics to address the behavioral health needs of the public and promote their biopsychosocial functioning. To be able to assess needs and functioning, general knowledge of individuals' problems and functioning across the biopsychosocial domains is needed. (These were addressed in Chapters 4–7.) This background is necessary for understanding the range of individuals' circumstances and experiences, including strengths and co-occurring problems within and across the domains, so that individuals can be understood in a thorough, holistic manner. On the basis of this foundational knowledge, students are then in a position to learn and apply the behavioral health procedures, tools, and methods used in the treatment process. This process begins with assessment and normally progresses to treatment planning, implementing interventions, and evaluating their effectiveness (covered in Chapters 8–11).

To fully appreciate these topics and stay current in the field, one must also learn the principles and procedures of scientific research methodology. This includes an appreciation of the scientific method, verification, falsification, and the importance of reliable and valid measurement. It also requires that one keeps current with the scientific literature. Within just the last decade or two, for example, research on neural plasticity and epigenetics has overturned long-held beliefs about the static nature of the mature brain, and cognitive and evolutionary psychology have provided whole new perspectives on the nature and function of centrally important psychological mechanisms and processes. One must also keep current with systematic, critical reviews of the literature so that the safety and effectiveness of the assessments and interventions used in clinical practice can be assured.

There are many indications that the paradigmatic era in behavioral health care has been reached. It is difficult to know exactly when the tipping point to that era was reached. Transitioning to the paradigmatic era in physics, chemistry, biology, and medicine took place over a period of many years, and there appears to have been no decisive point at which psychology made the same transition, or even whether it has reached that point. Given the well-understood weaknesses of the traditional theoretical orientations, the level and integration of current scientific knowledge regarding human psychology, and the wide endorsement of evidence-based practice in the field, it would appear that the transition to the paradigmatic era in the field is well underway. The appearance of volumes like this one also signals that the field has moved on to a unified science-based approach to understanding human psychology.

As a science-based profession, behavioral health care must update its theoretical and conceptual frameworks so they remain current with the underlying science of psychology. The biological, psychological, and social sciences have now advanced to the point where knowledge of human development and functioning is consistent and coherent across levels of natural organization. The power and precision of recent scientific tools are providing a far more detailed and thorough understanding of psychological phenomena than what was possible even just a decade or two ago. The traditional theoretical orientations that played such an important role in understanding human development and functioning over the last century no longer play key roles in the macro level understanding of human psychology, though they do remain important for informing empirically supported psychotherapies.

Reaching the paradigmatic era in behavioral health care will allow the field to leave behind the perennial confusion and conflict associated with the competing theoretical orientations. With a solidly scientific understanding of human psychology, the field can now move forward with a much more unified voice to take on the challenges facing the profession and humanity in general. Certainly the field of medicine progressed rapidly after reaching the paradigmatic stage in its development, and the potential exists for behavioral health care to do the same.

The question of whether the behavioral health care field has reached the tipping point to a paradigmatic scientific framework may be primarily a question of when that point is (or was) reached rather than if it will be reached. The progress of science has been inexorable and seems to allow no alternative but forward movement. When the fragmented knowledge from across the behavioral sciences is considered in an integrative framework, as this volume attempts to do, there appears to be no doubt that the paradigmatic era has been reached. Psychology as a scientific discipline has already been transformed, and this is allowing behavioral health care for the first time to be practiced as a true clinical science. The benefits of these developments for the public could well be substantial, possibly even transformative.

BENEFITS OF THE PARADIGMATIC ERA

Coming together around a unified scientific perspective on human development and functioning allows behavioral health professionals to address challenges and approach opportunities in a much less fragmented and contentious manner than was ever possible before. The science underlying behavioral health care is also continuing to strengthen, and that will almost certainly lead to improved clinical applications as well. It is very difficult to predict how these developments will translate into clinical practice over the long term. In the short term, however, several trends currently underway have the potential to lead to significant improvements in the effectiveness of behavioral health care and in people's behavioral health and functioning.

Improved Treatment Effectiveness

Recent research has provided several suggestions for how the effectiveness of treatment might be improved. This research needs to be replicated under varying conditions, but the initial results are intriguing. One line of research suggests that treatment effectiveness can be improved through systematic outcomes monitoring. This research (reviewed in Chapters 10 and 11) suggests that providing outcome assessment data to therapists and patients results in more attention being given to cases in which no improvement or deterioration is occurring and that significant numbers of these cases consequently turn around. There is also substantial evidence that therapists' interpersonal and therapeutic skills and qualities affect their ability to form therapeutic relationships and achieve positive outcomes. It appears that a portion of patients who receive therapy are not helped because of negative therapist attitudes or personality characteristics, the inept application of treatment, and other negative therapist factors. This is of major concern to graduate training programs and to supervisors and managers in behavioral health care agencies. Using evidence-based tools and procedures for addressing these issues has the potential to significantly improve the effectiveness of behavioral health care treatment.

The long-term effectiveness of psychosocial treatments should also receive more attention in behavioral health care. As noted in Chapter 10, the superior long-term benefits of psychotherapy compared to pharmacotherapy for most disorders is well established, and several meta-analyses have found that the effect sizes of some therapies were actually larger at follow-up than at treatment termination. Alleviating distress and symptomatology over the short term is certainly important in many cases, but resolving problems and improving functioning over the long term are normally the desired goals of treatment. Identifying the therapy methods and processes that produce positive outcomes that reliably are maintained over the long term should be a research priority. The growing concerns about the safety and effectiveness of psychotropic medications also give more urgency to identifying treatments that reduce relapse and do not have major negative side effects.

Integration Into Primary Care

Primary care is often considered the de facto behavioral health care system because most individuals receive care for both their physical and behavioral health care needs from their primary care providers. Most of the behavioral health care in these settings is provided by medical professionals, however, because behavioral health professionals frequently have not been directly involved in primary care. The behavioral health care provided in these settings could well be significantly improved, however, if more behavioral health care professionals were integrated into primary care teams. Large numbers of individuals whose mental health and addiction problems presently go untreated or undertreated might receive much better care as a result.

The future of professional psychology may be significantly affected by initiatives to integrate behavioral health care into primary health care settings (see Chapter 13). Movement in this direction is increasing as the Patient Protection and Affordable Care Act of 2010 is being implemented. Health care delivery models promoted in this legislation include interprofessional team-based care to treat behavioral health disorders, manage chronic conditions, address medical treatment adherence, and provide preventive interventions. Psychologists have a lot to offer in these models, although many educational programs currently do not provide training in this type of practice. It is probably not possible to implement traditional approaches revolving around adopted theoretical orientations in these settings, whereas the science-based biopsychosocial approach provides the necessary framework and knowledge base for working within integrated primary care teams.

Increase in Prevention and Health Promotion

Prevention has played the central role in improving the physical health of the public over the past century and a half. We have now largely gone through the *epidemiological transition* where the primary causes of disease and death have shifted from acute and infectious disease to chronic diseases associated with behavior and lifestyle. Though the prevalence of acute and infectious disease has declined dramatically, the prevalence of chronic diseases and behavioral health disorders has reached startling levels. Research suggests that intervention after problems have developed may play a relatively small role in reducing the prevalence of those problems within the population. Prevention, on the other hand, can make a large impact. Further improvements in the health and well-being of the public will require major progress in preventing behavioral and physical disorders from developing in the first place.

The National Research Council and Institute of Medicine (2009) called for a paradigm shift toward embracing prevention to reduce the prevalence and impact of behavioral health problems. Research suggests that prevention and health promotion strategies are effective, although there have been few attempts to implement them on a large scale. As the need for these approaches becomes clearer, psychologists could play a major role, including within the context of primary health care. The broad perspective of the biopsychosocial approach easily accommodates the principles of prevention and health promotion, whereas there was not a natural fit between the traditional theoretical orientations and the public health perspective. This is an area of great potential for improving the health and well-being of the general population.

Greater Emphasis on Well-Being and Flourishing

The fundamental changes in human experience associated with the *epidemiological transition* involve fascinating and complicated questions that have not yet received sufficient examination within the field or in society more generally. The challenge noted by John Maynard Keynes (1930/1972), of how "to live wisely and agreeably and well" (p. 328) once desperation and deprivation are no longer the driving forces of human existence, involves questions of daunting importance. They deserve extensive analysis and critique, but some of the initial data that shed light on those questions present a rather bleak picture. The number of individuals who are functioning at optimal levels appears to be low—for example, Keyes (2007) estimated that only two in 10 Americans are flourishing. No matter how one defines *flourishing*, surely there should be more people functioning at higher levels than these data suggest. Keyes (2007) suggested that a reasonable goal would be 66% of the population functioning at the flourishing level.

Each new generation may need to find its own answers to questions regarding the nature of well-being and flourishing. These constructs are necessarily affected by ongoing social changes, scientific and technological advances, and gene–culture coevolution. The nature of well-being and flourishing also differs according to culture and subculture, and aspects are of course determined at the individual level as well. Taking the holistic biopsychosocial approach advocated here is probably necessary for a comprehensive conceptualization of all the issues involved. Even before all these issues are sorted out, however, there is probably little disagreement that 20% functioning at a flourishing level is cause for concern. Over the long term, this is an area that has tremendous potential for improving human functioning.

THE TRULY WONDERFUL INTERCONNECTEDNESS OF LIFE

Human psychology involves truly wonderful though tremendously complicated phenomena. The extraordinary intricacy and complexity of the human mind have given rise to an incredible richness and diversity of human experience while at the same time providing a universality of experience that binds all humans around the world and even across time. The teeming, restless churning of the human mind has resulted in a great deal of misery, tragedy, and suffering, but has also given rise to endlessly fascinating human abilities, including a soaring intellect and exquisite sensibilities, the limits of which are still unknown. The rise of conscious life on this earth is certainly one of the truly wonderful developments in the universe.

The rise of human consciousness has resulted in many amazing accomplishments and the grandest cultural and scientific achievements, but it has not allowed us to escape the massive amounts of human distress and suffering that afflict humankind. As the behavioral health care field enters the paradigmatic era, the field is challenged to alleviate distress and suffering, prevent abuse and exploitation, and promote optimal functioning as effectively and for as many individuals as possible. The research reviewed in Chapter 4 regarding human development suggests that one of the most promising ways to set the stage for the development of optimal functioning is to promote attachment and a sense of belonging and connection. These are among humans' most basic needs and desires (e.g., Bell, 2010; Maslow, 1943; Shaver & Mikulincer, 2012). Starting at birth, nearly all humans develop infant attachment bonds, even though many of them are not secure and are later associated with various types of dysfunction and psychopathology. Nonetheless, needs for belonging and connection continue through the end of life, and interference with those connections at any point can cause significant disruptions in functioning. Psychotherapy can be very effective at healing those disruptions, and primary prevention, early intervention, and health promotion have tremendous potential for preventing the lack of secure and healthy attachment in the first place.

Some of the most remarkable discoveries of science in recent decades concern the interconnectedness of life. At an intellectual level, these interconnections are tremendously meaningful, and they can be meaningful at emotional levels as well. For example, it was evident to Darwin (1859) that all of life must be interrelated, although the precise nature of those interrelationships could not be identified until much later, after more powerful scientific tools were developed. In recent decades it has been verified that all human beings in fact share a common ancestry. This also means that humans consequently share common psychological mechanisms that account for both our remarkable strengths and weaknesses as a species. These mechanisms account for our amazing ability to quickly learn language; navigate a complex social and physical world in a remarkably efficient manner; and develop incredibly complex cultural, economic, and governmental systems. They also account for the biases and irrationality that pervade our personal and social lives and cause confusion, conflict, and sometimes horrible violence and immense suffering as well. Indeed, humanity's brilliance, irrationality, and neuroticism are shared by all peoples across the human family. We may be the first generation of humans to understand human psychology from a scientific perspective, but humans throughout history have shared many of the same psychological experiences, including feelings of intense aloneness and lack of connection and meaning. Fully appreciating these facts about the nature of the human condition should provide some assurance and comfort.

Science has also revealed remarkable connections that extend beyond our fellow human beings. Indeed, science has uncovered relationships among all life forms that have ever existed on this earth. In *Your Inner Fish: A Journey Into the 3.5-Billion-Year History of the Human Body*, Neil Shubing (2008) explained how we in fact carry the whole history of evolution within our bodies and how our genome links us to all life on earth. For example, it is well known that our basic skeletal structures are similar to our mammalian, reptilian, and amphibian forebears: All have the same basic skeletal structures featuring a head at the end of a spine, limbs involving first one large bone followed by two smaller bones, then a bony clump of some type, and then small bones. Even insects like the common housefly share some of these same structural features. Very similar structural elements also appear in ancient and modern fish, though it was not known until recently how their fins (which also feature one large bone, two smaller bones, and a clump followed by small bones) evolved into legs that could support the animals on dry land. In 2004, a 375 million-year-old fossil creature was discovered in northern Canada that had evolved strong fins that enabled it to leave the water to walk on land. The discovery of this creature, named *Tiktaalik*, provided the link that had been missing in the fossil record between fish and four-legged animals. Even fish, it turns out, are among our very distant relatives.

Science has revealed not only that all animals that have ever lived on earth are related to one another but also that all living organisms, plant or animal, are related as well. Research has shown that life's smallest components, such as proteins and nucleic acids, are actually universal components of life on earth. The genetic code is written the same way across living organisms, and all branches of life share the same organelles (i.e., subparts of cells that perform specialized functions) and associated enzymes. Darwin's (1859) prediction that every living creature could trace its lineage back to one source has now been verified to an extremely high degree of certainty (Theobald, 2010). There are no fossil remains of the last universal common ancestor, but scientists believe that that ancestor was very similar to a modern bacteria, lived about 3.5 billion years ago, and split into microbes and later eukaryotes (multicellular organisms) that eventually evolved into the amazing range of plants and animals that now exist. All of life that has ever existed on earth is actually related at this fundamental level. We share the fundamental components that give life with every other living thing that has ever lived, no matter how big or small, whether extinct or still living, all the way back to the point of our common origin 3.5 billion years ago.

And not only is all life on earth descended from a common universal ancestor, science also shows that the whole universe is fundamentally connected. During the Big Bang, tiny particles bound together to form hydrogen and helium. When the early stars became unstable and collapsed, the intense heat and pressure formed heavier particles such as oxygen and carbon that were then spewed out into the universe when the stars exploded. As this process continued, heavier elements such as nitrogen, iron, and all the other elements composing life on earth were eventually formed and dispersed throughout the universe. The most common elements in the universe also turn out to be the most common elements in the human body (Tyson & Goldsmith, 2004). The astrophysicist Neil deGrasse Tyson had this to say when he was asked in an interview in 2008, "What is the most astounding fact you can share with us about the universe":

> The most astounding fact is the knowledge that the atoms that comprise life on Earth, the atoms that make up the human body, are traceable to the crucibles that cooked light elements into heavy elements in their core under extreme temperatures and pressures. . . . When I look up at the night sky, and I know that, yes, we are part of this Universe, we are in this Universe, but perhaps more important than both of those facts is that the Universe is in us. When I reflect on that fact, I look up. Many people feel small, 'cause they're small and the Universe is big, but I feel big, because my atoms came from those stars. There's a level of connectivity. That's really what you want in life, you want to feel connected, you want to feel relevant, you want to feel like a participant in the goings on of activities and events around you. That's precisely what we are, just by being alive.

Science has now revealed the truly amazing interconnectedness of all life on earth and indeed all matter, everything that exists, in the universe. Many religions and philosophical systems have emphasized the interconnectedness of all humanity, all life, or all matter of any kind, but science has now demonstrated this in actual fact. Fully absorbing this knowledge should have a healing effect on humanity. For example, this knowledge almost necessarily forces one to consider how truly precious human consciousness is. The fact that conscious life evolved at all on this earth is astounding. But that human beings eventually used that consciousness to scientifically reveal the extraordinary chain of events that led to the evolution of consciousness in the first place turns our existence into something that truly does border on the miraculous. The significance of these facts strains one's comprehension: that life on earth evolved at all, that humans share our fundamental biological components with all other plant and animal life, that our early human ancestors evolved consciousness, and that all human beings are in fact related to each other and actually descended from the same parents. And, further, that everything that exists in the universe evolved from, and is made of, the very same stardust. We each have our unique personal experience of the world and yet our fundamental components are exactly the same as *everything else*. What an extraordinarily precious thing it is to be aware of these facts!

The human mind is a truly astounding phenomenon. To further understand its nature is one of the great frontiers of science, and to be able to help further realize its potential is a true privilege for the behavioral health care profession. It is very exciting for the behavioral sciences to have reached the point where behavioral health care can now be practiced as a true clinical science that is fundamentally connected to all the rest of science. The potential for the field to increase its effectiveness at improving the human condition also increases significantly as a result. We are embarking on what will likely be a very exciting time for the profession and potentially even for all of humankind.

REFERENCES

Abramowitz, J. S. (1996). Variants of exposure and response prevention in the treatment of obsessive-compulsive disorder: A meta-analysis. *Behavior Therapy, 27*, 583–600. doi:10.1016/S0005-7894(96)80045-1

Accreditation Council for Graduate Medical Education. (2011). *Common program requirements*. Retrieved from http://www.acgme.org/acwebsite/home/Common_Program_Requirements_07012011.pdf

Achenbach, T. M., & Edelbrock, C. S. (1983). *Manual for the Child Behavior Checklist and Revised Child Behavior Profile*. Burlington: Department of Psychiatry, University of Vermont.

Ackerman, S., & Hilsenroth, M. (2001). A review of therapist characteristics and techniques negatively impacting the therapeutic alliance. *Psychotherapy: Theory, Research, Practice, Training, 38*, 171–185. doi:10.1037/0033-3204.38.2.171

Agency for Healthcare Research and Quality. (2009). *Medical expenditure panel survey*. Rockville, MD: Author. Retrieved from http://www.meps.ahrq.gov/mepsweb

Agency for Healthcare Research and Quality. (2013). *Defining the PCMH*. Retrieved from http://pcmh.ahrq.gov/portal/server.pt/community/pcmh__home/1483/PCMH_Defining%20the%20PCMH_v2

Agras, W. S., Crow, S. J., Halami, K. A., Mitchell, J. E., Wilson, G. T., & Kraemer, H. C. (2000). A multicenter comparison of cognitive-behavioral therapy and interpersonal psychotherapy for bulimia nervosa. *The American Journal of Psychiatry, 157*, 1302–1308. doi:10.1176/appi.ajp.157.8.1302

Ainsworth, M. C. S., Blehar, M. C., Waters, E., & Wall, S. (1978). *Patterns of attachment: A psychological study of the Strange Situation*. Hillsdale, NJ: Erlbaum.

Albee, G. W. (2006). Historical overview of primary prevention of psychopathology: Address to the 3rd World Conference on the Promotion of Mental Health and Prevention of Mental and Behavioral Disorders, September 15–17, 2004, Auckland, New Zealand. *The Journal of Primary Prevention, 27*, 449–456. doi:10.1007/s10935-006-0047-7

American Counseling Association. (2014). ACA *Code of Ethics*. Retrieved from http://www.counseling.org/doc/ethics/2014-aca-code-of-ethics.pdf?sfvrsn=4

American Psychiatric Association. (1952). *Diagnostic and statistical manual of mental disorders*. Washington, DC: Author.

American Psychiatric Association. (1968). *Diagnostic and statistical manual of mental disorders* (2nd ed.). Washington, DC: Author.

American Psychiatric Association. (1980). *Diagnostic and statistical manual of mental disorders* (3rd ed.). Washington, DC: Author.

American Psychiatric Association. (1994). *Diagnostic and statistical manual of mental disorders* (4th ed.). Washington, DC: Author.

American Psychiatric Association. (2000a). *Diagnostic and statistical manual of mental disorders* (4th ed., Text Revision). Washington, DC: Author.

American Psychiatric Association. (2000b). *Therapies focused on attempts to change sexual orientation (reparative or conversion therapies): Position statement.* Retrieved from http://www.psych.org/Departments/EDU/Library/APAOfficialDocumentsand Related/PositionStatements/200001.aspx

American Psychiatric Association. (2006). *Practice guidelines for the treatment of psychiatric disorders: Compendium 2006.* Arlington, VA: Author.

American Psychiatric Association. (2013). *Diagnostic and statistical manual of mental disorders* (5th ed.). Washington, DC: Author.

American Psychological Association. (2002). Ethical principles of psychologists and code of conduct. *American Psychologist, 57,* 1060–1073. doi:10.1037/0003-066X.57.12.1060

American Psychological Association. (2006). *Health care for the whole person statement of vision and principles.* Retrieved from http://www.apa.org/practice/hcwp_statement.html

American Psychological Association. (2012). *Stress in America: Our health at risk.* Washington, DC: Author.

American Psychological Association. (2013). *Strategic plan.* Retrieved from http://www.apa.org/about/apa/strategic-plan/default.aspx

American Psychological Association Center for Workforce Studies. (2011). *2011 APA member profiles.* Retrieved from http://www.apa.org/workforce/publications/11-member/index.aspx

American Psychological Association Presidential Task Force on Evidence-Based Practice. (2006). Evidence-based practice in psychology. *American Psychologist, 61,* 271–285. doi:10.1037/0003-066X.61.4.271

American Psychological Association Presidential Task Force on the Future of Psychology Practice. (2009). *Final report.* Washington, DC: Author.

Anchin, J. C. (2008). Pursuing a unifying paradigm for psychotherapy: Tasks, dialectical considerations, and biopsychosocial systems metatheory. *Journal of Psychotherapy Integration, 18,* 310–349. doi:10.1037/a0013557

Anderson, G. (2004). *Chronic conditions: Making the case for ongoing care.* Baltimore, MD: Johns Hopkins University.

Anderson, R. L., & Lyons, J. S. (2001). Needs-based planning for persons with serious mental illness residing in intermediate care facilities. *The Journal of Behavioral Health Services & Research, 28,* 104–110. doi:10.1007/BF02287239

Andrews, G., & Page, A. C. (2005). Outcome measurement, outcome management and monitoring. *Australian and New Zealand Journal of Psychiatry, 39,* 649–651. doi:10.1080/j.1440-1614.2005.01648.x

Angold, A., Costello, E. J., & Erkanli, A. (1999). Comorbidity. *Journal of Child Psychology and Psychiatry and Allied Disciplines, 40*(1), 57–87. doi:10.1111/1469-7610.00424

Annon, J. S. (1976). *Behavioral treatment of sexual problems*. Hagerstown, MD: Harper & Row.

Arias, E. (2004). United States life tables, 2001. *National Vital Statistics Reports, 52*(14), Table 11. Retrieved from http://www.cdc.gov/nchs/data/nvsr/nvsr52/nvsr52_14.pdf

Ariely, D. (2012). *The (honest) truth about dishonesty: How we lie to everyone—especially ourselves*. New York, NY: HarperCollins.

Armstrong, T. D., & Costello, E. J. (2002). Community studies on adolescent substance use, abuse, or dependence and psychiatric comorbidity. *Journal of Consulting and Clinical Psychology, 70,* 1224–1239. doi:10.1037/0022-006X.70.6.1224

Association of Psychology Postdoctoral and Internship Centers. (2009). *APPIC application for psychology internship*. Retrieved from http://appic.org/match/5_3_match_application.html#PREVIOUSAAPI

Atherly, A. (2006). Condition-specific measures. In R. L. Kane (Ed.), *Understanding health care outcomes research* (2nd ed., pp. 165–183). Sudbury, MA: Jones and Bartlett.

Baldwin, S. A., & Imel, Z. E. (2013). Therapist effects: Findings and methods. In M. J. Lambert (Ed.), *Bergin and Garfield's handbook of psychotherapy and behavior change* (6th ed., pp. 258–297). Hoboken, NJ: Wiley.

Barlow, D. H. (2004). Psychological treatments. *American Psychologist, 59,* 869–878. doi:10.1037/0003-066X.59.9.869

Barlow, D. H. (2010). Negative effects from psychological treatments: A perspective. *American Psychologist, 65,* 13–20. doi:10.1037/a0015643

Barnes, P. M., Bloom, B., & Nahin, R. L. (2008, December). Complementary and alternative medicine use among adults and children: United States, 2007. *National Health Statistics Report, 10,* 1–23.

Barnett, J. E., & Shale, A. J. (2012). The integration of complementary and alternative medicine (CAM) into the practice of psychology: A vision for the future. *Professional Psychology: Research and Practice, 43,* 576–585. doi:10.1037/a0028919

Barth, R. P., Scarborough, A. A., Lloyd, E. C., Losby, J. L., Casanueva, C., & Mann, T. (2008). *Developmental status and early intervention service needs of maltreated children*. Washington, DC: U.S. Department of Health and Human Services, Office of the Assistant Secretary for Planning and Evaluation.

Bateman, A., & Fonagy, P. (2008). 8-Year follow-up of patients treated for borderline personality disorder: Mentalization-based treatment versus treatment as usual. *The American Journal of Psychiatry, 165,* 631–638. doi:10.1176/appi.ajp.2007.07040636

Baxter, L. R., Jr., Schwartz, J. M., Bergman, K. S., Szuba, M. P., Guze, B. H., Mazziotta, J. C., . . . Phelps, M. E. (1992). Caudate glucose metabolic rate changes with both drug and behavior therapy for obsessive-compulsive disorder. *Archives of General Psychiatry, 49,* 681–689. doi:10.1001/archpsyc.1992.01820090009002

Beauchamp, D. E. (1976). Public health as social justice. *Inquiry, 13,* 3–14.

Beauchamp, T. L., & Childress, J. F. (1977). *Principles of biomedical ethics*. New York, NY: Oxford University Press.

Beauchamp, T. L., & Childress, J. F. (2009). *Principles of biomedical ethics* (6th ed.). New York, NY: Oxford University Press.

Beauchamp, T. L., Walters, L., Kahn, J. P., & Mastroianni, A. C. (2008). *Contemporary issues in bioethics*. Belmont, CA: Thomson Wadsworth.

Beck, A. T., Emery, G., & Greenberg, R. (1985). *Anxiety disorders and phobias: A cognitive perspective*. New York, NY: Basic Books.

Beck, A. T. Freeman, A., Davis, D. D., & Associates. (2004). *Cognitive therapy of personality disorders* (2nd ed.). New York, NY: Guilford Press.

Beck, A. T., Steer, R. A., & Brown, G. K. (1996). *Manual for the Beck Depression Inventory-II*. San Antonio, TX: Psychological Corporation.

Belar, C. D. (1996). A proposal for an expanded view of health and psychology: The integration of behavior and health. In R. J. Resnick & R. H. Rozensky (Eds.), *Health psychology through the life span: Practice and research opportunities* (pp. 77–81). Washington, DC: American Psychological Association. doi:10.1037/10220-005

Belar, C. D. (2012). Reflections on the future: Psychology as a health profession. *Professional Psychology: Research and Practice, 43*, 545–550. doi:10.1037/a0029633

Bell, D. C. (2010). *The dynamics of connection: How evolution and biology create caregiving and attachment*. Lanham, MD: Lexington Books.

Belsky, J. (2007). Childhood experiences and reproductive strategies. In R. I. M. Dunbar & L. Barrett (Eds.), *Oxford handbook of evolutionary psychology* (pp. 237–254). Oxford, England: Oxford University Press. doi:10.1093/oxfordhb/9780198568308.013.0018

Benjamin, L. T., Jr. (2001). American psychology's struggles with its curriculum: Should a thousand flowers bloom? *American Psychologist, 56*, 735–742. doi:10.1037/0003-066X.56.9.735

Benjamin, L. T., Jr. (2007). *A brief history of modern psychology*. Malden, MA: Blackwell.

Berghuis, D. J., Jongsma, A. E., & Bruce, T. J. (2008). *The severe and persistent mental illness treatment planner* (2nd ed.). Hoboken, NJ: Wiley.

Bergin, A. E. (1966). Some implications of psychotherapy: Negative results revisited. *Journal of Counseling Psychology, 10*, 224–250.

Berlin, L. J., Cassidy, J., & Appleyard, K. (2008). The influence of early attachments on other relationships. In J. Cassidy & P. R. Shaver (Eds.), *Handbook of attachment: Theory, research, and clinical applications* (2nd ed., pp. 333–347). New York, NY: Guilford Press.

Beutler, L. E., Malik, M., Talebi, H., Fleming, J., & Moleiro, C. (2004). Use of psychological tests/instruments for treatment planning. In M. E. Maruish (Ed.), *The use of psychological testing for treatment planning and outcomes assessment* (3rd ed., pp. 111–145). Mahwah, NJ: Lawrence Erlbaum.

Biglan, A., Flay, B. R., Embry, D. D., & Sandler, I. N. (2012). The critical role of nurturing environments for promoting human well-being. *American Psychologist, 67,* 257–271. doi:10.1037/a0026796

Binggeli, N. J., Hart, S. N., & Brassard, M. R. (2001). *Psychological maltreatment of children* (Vol. 4). Thousand Oaks, CA: Sage.

Black, M. C., Basile, K. C., Breiding, M. J., Smith, S. G., Walters, M. L., Merrick, M. T., . . . Stevens, M. R. (2011). *The National Intimate Partner and Sexual Violence Survey (NISVS): 2010 Summary report.* Atlanta, GA: National Center for Injury Prevention and Control, Centers for Disease Control and Prevention.

Blaisure, K. R., & Geasler, M. J. (2006). Educational interventions for separating and divorcing parents and their children. In M. A. Fine & J. H. Harvey (Eds.), *Handbook of divorce and relationship dissolution* (pp. 575–602). Mahwah, NJ: Lawrence Erlbaum.

Bloom, P. (2012). Moral nativism and moral psychology. In M. Mikulincer & P. R. Shaver (Eds.), *The social psychology of morality: Exploring the causes of good and evil* (pp. 71–89). Washington, DC: American Psychological Association. doi:10.1037/13091-004

Blount, A., Schoenbaum, M., Kathol, R., Rollman, B. L., Thomas, M., O'Donohue, W., & Peek, C. J. (2007). The economics of behavioral health services in medical settings: A summary of the evidence. *Professional Psychology: Research and Practice, 38,* 290–297. doi:10.1037/0735-7028.38.3.290

Bluestein, D., & Cubic, B. A. (2009). Psychologists and primary care physicians: A training model for creating collaborative relationships. *Journal of Clinical Psychology in Medical Settings, 16,* 101–112. doi:10.1007/s10880-009-9156-9

Bonanno, G. A., & Lilienfeld, S. O. (2008). Let's be realistic: When grief counseling is effective and when it's not. *Professional Psychology: Research and Practice, 39,* 377–378. doi:10.1037/0735-7028.39.3.377

Bonham, V. L., Warshauer-Baker, E., & Collins, F. S. (2005). Race in the genome era: The complexity of the constructs. *American Psychologist, 60,* 9–15. doi:10.1037/0003-066X.60.1.9

Bonow, R. O., Mann, D. L., Zipes, D. P., & Libby, P. (2012). *Braunwald's heart disease: A textbook of cardiovascular medicine* (9th ed.). Philadelphia, PA: Elsevier Saunders.

Bowlby, J. (1969). *Attachment and loss: Vol. 1. Attachment.* New York, NY: Basic Books.

Bowlby, J. (1973). *Attachment and loss: Vol. 2. Separation.* New York, NY: Basic Books.

Bowlby, J. (1980). *Attachment and loss: Vol. 3. Sadness and depression.* New York, NY: Basic Books.

Bowles, S., & Gintis, H. (2004). The evolution of strong reciprocity: Cooperation in heterogeneous populations. *Theoretical Population Biology, 65,* 17–28. doi:10.1016/j.tpb.2003.07.001

Boyd, R., Gintis, H., Bowles, S., & Richerson, P. J. (2003). The evolution of altruistic punishment. *Proceedings of the National Academy of Sciences of the United States of America, 100,* 3531–3535. doi:10.1073/pnas.0630443100

Bray, J. H. (1996). Psychologists as primary care practitioners. In R. J. Resnick & R. H. Rozensky (Eds.), *To your health: Psychology across the lifespan* (pp. 89–100). Washington, DC: American Psychological Association.

Bray, J. H. (2010). The future of psychology practice and science. *American Psychologist, 65,* 355–369. doi:10.1037/a0020273

Bray, J. H., Goodheart, C., Heldring, M., Brannick, J., Gresen, R., & Hawley, G., . . . Strickland, W. (2009). *2009 Presidential Task Force on the Future of Psychology Practice final report.* Washington, DC: American Psychology Association. Retrieved from www.apa.org/pubs/info/reports/future-practice.pdf

Bringhurst, D. L., Watson, C. W., Miller, S. D., & Duncan, B. L. (2006). The reliability and validity of the Outcome Rating Scale: A replication study of a brief clinical measure. *Journal of Brief Therapy, 5,* 23–30.

Bronfenbrenner, U. (1979). *The ecology of human development.* Cambridge, MA: Harvard University Press.

Bronfenbrenner, U. (2001). The bioecological theory of human development. In N. J. Smelser & P. B. Baltes (Eds.), *International encyclopedia of the social and behavioral sciences* (Vol. 10, pp. 6963–6970). New York, NY: Elsevier. doi:10.1016/B0-08-043076-7/00359-4

Brown, D. E. (1991). *Human universals.* New York, NY: McGraw-Hill.

Bunker, J. P., Frazier, H. S., & Mosteller, F. (1994). Improving health: Measuring effects of medical care. *The Milbank Quarterly, 72,* 225–258. doi:10.2307/3350295

Buss, D. M. (1991). Evolutionary personality psychology. *Annual Review of Psychology, 42,* 459–491. doi:10.1146/annurev.ps.42.020191.002331

Buss, D. M. (Ed.). (2005a). *The handbook of evolutionary psychology.* Hoboken, NJ: Wiley.

Buss, D. M. (2005b). Introduction. In D. M. Buss (Ed.), *The handbook of evolutionary psychology* (pp. xxiii–xxv). Hoboken, NJ: Wiley.

Callahan, D. (1990). *What kind of life.* New York, NY: Simon and Schuster.

Cann, R. L., Stoneking, M., & Wilson, A. C. (1987). Mitochondrial DNA and human evolution. *Nature, 325,* 31–36. doi:10.1038/329111c0

Carey, J. (2008, January 16). Do cholesterol drugs do any good? *Business Week.* Retrieved from http://www.businessweek.com/stories/2008-01-16/do-cholesterol-drugs-do-any-good

Carlatt, D. (2010). *Unhinged: The trouble with psychiatry—A doctor's revelations about a profession in crisis.* New York, NY: Free Press.

Cassidy, J., & Shaver, P. R. (Eds.). (2008). *Handbook of attachment: Theory, research, and clinical applications* (2nd ed.). New York, NY: Guilford Press.

Centers for Disease Control and Prevention. (1999). Public health achievements, United States, 1900–1999. *Morbidity and Mortality Weekly Report, 48,* 621–629.

Centers for Disease Control and Prevention. (2001). Prevalence of disabilities and associated health conditions among adults—United States, 1999. *Morbidity and Mortality Weekly Report, 50,* 120–125.

Centers for Disease Control and Prevention. (2004). *The health consequences of smoking: A report of the Surgeon General*. Atlanta, GA: U.S. Department of Health and Human Services.

Centers for Disease Control and Prevention. (2006). Prevalence of doctor-diagnosed arthritis and arthritis-attributable activity limitation—United States, 2003–2005. *Morbidity and Mortality Weekly Report, 55*, 1089–1092.

Centers for Disease Control and Prevention. (2008). *National diabetes fact sheet, 2007*. Atlanta, GA: U.S. Department of Health and Human Services. Retrieved from http://www.cdc.gov/Diabetes/fact-sheet07.htm

Centers for Disease Control and Prevention. (2009). Summary of notifiable diseases, United States, 2007. *Morbidity and Mortality Weekly Report, 58*, 1–100.

Centers for Disease Control and Prevention. (2012a). *Injury prevention and control: Data & statistics (WISQARS™)*. Retrieved from www.cdc.gov/injury/wisqars/index.html

Centers for Disease Control and Prevention. (2012b). *Suicide: Facts at a glance*. Atlanta, GA: National Center for Injury Prevention and Control Division of Violence Prevention. Retrieved from www.cdc.gov/violenceprevention

Centers for Disease Control and Prevention. (2012c). Youth risk behavior surveillance—United States, 2011. *Morbidity and Mortality Weekly Report, Surveillance Summaries 61*(4). Available from www.cdc.gov/mmwr/pdf/ss/ss6104.pdf

Centerwall, S. A., & Centerwall, W. R. (2000). The discovery of phenylketonuria: The story of a young couple, two affected children, and a scientist. *Pediatrics, 105*, 89–103. doi:10.1542/peds.105.1.89

CERN. (2012). *CERN experiments observe particle consistent with long-sought Higgs boson*. CERN Press Release. Retrieved from http://press.web.cern.ch/press-releases/2012/07/cern-experiments-observe-particle-consistent-long-sought-higgs-boson

Chaffin, M., Hanson, R., Saunders, B. E., Nichols, T., Barnett, D., Zeanah, C., . . . Miller-Perrin, C. (2006). Report of the APSAC task force on attachment therapy, reactive attachment disorder, and attachment problems. *Child Maltreatment, 11*, 76–89. doi:10.1177/1077559505283699

Champagne, F. A. (2008). Epigenetic mechanisms and the transgenerational effects of maternal care. *Frontiers in Neuroendocrinology, 29*, 386–397. doi:10.1016/j.yfrne.2008.03.003

Chiles, A., & Strosahl, D. (2005). *Clinical manual for assessment and treatment of suicidal patients*. Washington, DC: American Psychiatric Publishing.

Chomsky, N. (1959). A review of B. F. Skinner's *Verbal Behavior*. *Language, 35*, 26–58. doi:10.2307/411334

Chomsky, N. (1987). *Language and problems of knowledge*. Cambridge, MA: MIT Press.

Cicchetti, D., & Rogosch, R. A. (1996). Equifinality and multifinality in developmental psychology. *Development and Psychopathology, 8*, 597–600. doi:10.1017/S0954579400007318

Cicchetti, D., & Toth, S. L. (1992). The role of developmental theory in prevention and intervention. *Development and Psychopathology, 4,* 489–493. doi:10.1017/S0954579400004831

Clark, D. M. (2011). Implementing NICE guidelines for the psychological treatment of depression and anxiety disorders: The IAPT experience. *International Review of Psychiatry, 23,* 318–327. doi:10.3109/09540261.2011.606803

Clark, D. M., Layard, R., Smithies, R., Richards, D. A., Suckling, R., & Wright, B. (2009). Improving access to psychological therapy: Initial evaluation of two UK demonstration sites. *Behaviour Research and Therapy, 47,* 910–920. doi:10.1016/j.brat.2009.07.010

Classen, D. C., Resar, R., Griffin, F., Federico, F., Frankel, T., Kimmel, N., . . . James, B. C. (2011). "Global Trigger Tool" shows that adverse events in hospitals may be ten times greater than previously measured. *Health Affairs, 30,* 581–589. doi:10/1377/hlthaff.2011.0190

Clement, P. W. (1999). *Outcomes and incomes: How to evaluate, improve, and market your psychotherapy practice by measuring outcomes.* New York, NY: Guilford Press.

Cohen, E. D., & Cohen, G. S. (1999). *The virtuous therapist: Ethical practice of counseling and psychotherapy.* Belmont, CA: Brooks/Cole Wadsworth.

Cohen, J. (1988). *Statistical power analysis for the behavioral sciences* (2nd ed.). Hillsdale, NJ: Lawrence Erlbaum.

Commission on Chronic Illness. (1957). *Chronic illness in the United States* (Vol. 1). Cambridge, MA: Harvard University Press.

Cooper, C., Selwood, A., & Livingston, G. (2008). The prevalence of elder abuse and neglect: A systematic review. *Age and Ageing, 37,* 151–160. doi:10.1093/ageing/afm194

Corey, G., Corey, M. S., & Callahan, P. (2003). *Issues and ethics in the helping professions* (6th ed.). Pacific Grove, CA: Brooks/Cole.

Corsini, R. J., & Wedding, D. (2008). *Current psychotherapies* (8th ed.). Belmont, CA: Thomson Brooks/Cole.

Council for the Accreditation of Counseling and Related Educational Programs. (2009). *2009 standards.* Retrieved from http://www.cacrep.org/doc/2009%20Standards%20with%20cover.pdf

Council on Ethical and Judicial Affairs, American Medical Association. (1994). Ethical issues in health care systems reform: The provision of adequate health care. *JAMA: Journal of the American Medical Association, 272,* 1056–1062. doi:10.1001/jama.1994.03520130094039

Council for the Parliament of the World's Religions. (1993). *Declaration toward a global ethic.* Retrieved from http://www.parliamentofreligions.org/index.cfm?n=4&sn=4

Crews, S. D., Bender, H., Cook, C. R., Gersham, F. M., Kern, L., & Vanderwood, M. (2007). Risk and protective factors of emotional and/or behavioral disorders in children and adolescents: A mega-analytic synthesis. *Behavioral Disorders, 32*(2), 64–77.

Crosby, A. E., Han, B., Ortega, L. A. G., Parks, S. E., & Gfoerer, J. (2011). Suicidal thoughts and behaviors among adults aged ≥18 years—United States, 2008–2009. *Morbidity and Mortality Weekly Report Surveillance Summaries, 60* (SS13). Available from www.cdc.gov/mmwr/preview/mmwrhtml/ss6013a1.htm?s_cid=ss6013a1_e

Cruciani, F., Trombetta, B., Massaia, A. G., Destro-Bisol, G., Sellitto, D., & Scozzari, R. (2011). A revised root for the human Y chromosomal phylogenetic tree: The origin of patrilineal diversity in Africa. *American Journal of Human Genetics, 88,* 814–818. doi:10.1016/j.ajhg.2011.05.002

Crump, T. (2001). *A brief history of science: As seen through the development of scientific instruments.* London, England: Constable.

Cuijpers, P., Driessen, E., Hollon, S. D., van Oppen, P., Barth, J., & Andersson, G. (2012). The efficacy of non-directive supportive psychotherapy for adult depression: A meta-analysis. *Clinical Psychology Review, 32,* 280–291. doi:10.1016/j.cpr.2012.01.003

Cummings, N. A. (1997). Behavioral health in primary care: Dollars and sense. In N. A. Cummings, J. L. Cummings, & J. N. Johnson (Eds.), *Behavioral health in primary care: A guide for clinical integration* (pp. 3–31). Madison, CT: Psychosocial Press.

Cummings, N. A., O'Donohue, W. T., & Cucciare, M. A. (Eds.). (2005). *Universal healthcare: Readings for mental health professionals.* Reno, NV: Context Press.

Cummings, N. A., O'Donohue, W., Hayes, S. C., & Follette, V. (Eds.). (2001). *Integrated behavioral healthcare: Positioning mental health practice within medical/surgical practice.* San Diego, CA: Academic Press.

D'amour, D., & Oandasan, I. (2005). Interprofessionality as the field of interprofessional practice and interprofessional education: An emerging concept. *Journal of Interprofessional Care, 19*(Suppl. 1), 8–20. doi:10.1080/13561820500081604

Dar, A. (2006). The new astronomy. In G. Fraser (Ed.), *The new physics for the 21st century* (pp. 69–85). Cambridge, UK: Cambridge University Press.

Darwin, C. R. (1859). *On the origin of species.* London, England: John Murray.

Davidson, D. J., & Begley, S. (2012). *The emotional life of your brain.* New York, NY: Hudson Street Press.

Davidson, R. J., Kabat-Zinn, J., Schumacher, J., Rosenkranz, M. A., Muller, D., Santorelli, S. F., . . . Sheridan, J. F. (2003). Alterations in brain and immune function produced by mindfulness meditation. *Psychosomatic Medicine, 65,* 564–570. doi:10.1097/01.PSY.0000077505.67574.E3

Davis, M. K., & Gidycz, C. A. (2000). Child sexual abuse prevention programs: A meta-analysis. *Journal of Clinical Child Psychology, 29,* 257–265. doi:10.1207/S15374424jccp2902_11

Dawkins, R. (1976). *The selfish gene.* New York, NY: Oxford University Press.

DeKlyen, M., & Greenberg, M. T. (2008). Attachment and psychopathology in childhood. In J. Cassidy & P. R. Shaver (Eds.), *Handbook of attachment: Theory,* research, and clinical applications (2nd ed., pp. 637–665). New York, NY: Guilford Press.

De Maat, S., Dekker, J., Schoevers, R., & De Jonghe, F. (2006). Relative efficacy of psychotherapy and pharmacotherapy in the treatment of depression: A meta-analysis. *Psychotherapy Research, 16,* 566–578. doi:10.1080/10503300600756402

Derogatis, L. R., & Melisaratos, N. (1983). The Brief Symptom Inventory: An introductory report. *Psychological Medicine, 13,* 595–605. doi:10.1017/S00332917 00048017

de Shazer, S. (1985). *Keys to solution in brief therapy.* New York, NY: Norton.

Diamond, J. (2012). *The world until yesterday: What can we learn from traditional societies?* New York, NY: Viking.

Donagan, A. (1977). *The theory of morality.* Chicago, IL: University of Chicago Press.

Dowbiggin, I. (2008). *The sterilization movement and global fertility in the twentieth century.* New York, NY: Oxford University Press.

Drum, D. J., Brownson, C., Denmark, A. B., & Smith, S. E. (2009). New data on the nature of suicidal crises in college students: Shifting the paradigm. *Professional Psychology: Research and Practice, 40,* 213–222. doi:10.1037/a0014465

Druss, B. G., Zhao, L., Von Esenwein, S., Morrato, E. H., & Marcus, S. C. (2011). Understanding excess mortality in persons with mental illness. *Medical Care, 49,* 599–604. doi:10.1097/MLR.0b013e31820bf86e

Dubos, R. (1959). *Mirage of health.* New York, NY: Harper & Row.

Dunbar, R., & Barrett, L. (2007a). Evolutionary psychology in the round. In R. I. M. Dunbar & L. Barrett (Eds.), *Oxford handbook of evolutionary psychology* (pp. 3–10). New York, NY: Oxford University Press. doi:10.1093/oxfordhb/9780198568308.013.0001

Dunbar, R. I. M., & Barrett, L. (Eds.). (2007b). *Oxford handbook of evolutionary psychology.* New York, NY: Oxford University Press.

Durbin, J., Goering, P., Cochrane, J., Macfarlane, D., & Sheldon, T. (2004). Needs-based planning for persons with schizophrenia residing in board-and-care homes. *Schizophrenia Bulletin, 30,* 123–132. doi:10.1093/oxfordjournals.schbul.a007057

Durlak, J. A., & Wells, A. M. (1997). Primary prevention mental health programs for children and adolescents: A meta-analytic review. *American Journal of Community Psychology, 25,* 115–152. doi:10.1023/A:1024654026646

Dworkin, R. (1977). *Taking rights seriously.* Cambridge, MA: Harvard University Press.

Dziegielewski, S. F. (2010). *The DSM–IV–TR in action.* New York, NY: Wiley.

Ecker, B., & Hulley, L. (2006). *Coherence therapy practice manual and training guide.* Oakland, CA: Pacific Seminars.

Egger, H. L., & Emde, R. N. (2011). Developmentally sensitive diagnostic criteria for mental health disorders in early childhood: The Diagnostic and Statistical Manual of Mental Disorders–IV, the Research Diagnostic Criteria–Preschool

Age, and the Diagnostic Classification of Mental Health and Developmental Disorders in Infancy and Early Childhood–Revised. *American Psychologist, 66,* 95–106. doi:10.1037/a0021026

Elbert, T., Pantev, C., Wienbruch, C., Rockstroh, B., & Taub, E. (1995, October 13). Increased cortical representation of the fingers of the left hand in string players. *Science, 270,* 305–307. doi:10.1126/science.270.5234.305

Elkin, I. (1994). The NIMH treatment of depression collaborative research program. Where we began and where we are. In A. E. Bergin & S. L. Garfield (Eds.), *Handbook of psychotherapy and behavior change* (4th ed., pp. 114–139). New York, NY: Wiley.

Encyclopædia Britannica. (2013). *Metatheory.* Retrieved from http://www.britannica.com/EBchecked/topic/378037/metatheory

Englich, B., Mussweiler, T., & Strack, F. (2006). Playing dice with criminal sentences: The influence of irrelevant anchors on experts' judicial decision making. *Personality and Social Psychology Bulletin, 32,* 188–200. doi:10.1177/0146167205282152

Eysenck, H. J. (1952). The effects of psychotherapy: An evaluation. *Journal of Consulting Psychology, 16,* 319–324. doi:10.1037/h0063633

Eysenck, H. J. (1970). A mish-mash of theories. *International Journal of Psychiatry, 9,* 140–146.

Fennell, M. J. V., & Teasdale, J. D. (1987). Cognitive therapy for depression: Individual differences and the process of change. *Cognitive Therapy and Research, 11,* 253–271. doi:10.1007/BF01183269

Finkelhor, D. (1994). Current information on the scope and nature of child sexual abuse. *Future of Children, 4,* 31–53.

Finkelhor, D. (2008). *Childhood victimization: Violence, crime, and abuse in the lives of young people.* New York, NY: Oxford University Press. doi:10.1093/acprof:oso/9780195342857.001.0001

Finkelhor, D., & Dziuba-Leatherman, J. (1994). Children as victims of violence: A national survey. *Pediatrics, 94,* 413–420.

Follette, W. T., & Cummings, N. A. (1967). Psychiatric services and medical utilization in a prepaid health plan setting. *Medical Care, 5,* 25–35. doi:10.1097/00005650-196701000-00005

Fouad, N. A., Grus, C. L., Hatcher, R. L., Kaslow, N. J., Hutchings, P. S., Madson, M. B., . . . Crossman, R. E. (2009). Competency benchmarks: A model for understanding and measuring competence in professional psychology cross training levels. *Training and Education in Professional Psychology, 3*(4, Suppl.), S5–S26. doi:10.1037/a0015832

Fournier, J. C., DeRubeis, R. J., Hollon, S. D., Dimidgian, S., Amsterdam, J. D., Shelton, R. C., & Fawcett, J. (2010). Antidepressant drug effects and depression severity: A patient-level meta-analysis. *JAMA: Journal of the American Medical Association, 303,* 47–53. doi:10.1001/jama.2009.1943

Fox, R. E., DeLeon, P. H., Newman, R., Sammons, M. R., Dunivin, D. L., & Baker, D. C. (2009). Prescriptive authority and psychology: A status report. *American Psychologist, 64*, 257–268. doi:10.1037/a0015938

Frances, A. (2009). A warning sign on the road to *DSM–V:* Beware of its unintended consequences. *Psychiatric Times, 26*(8), 1–4.

Frankel, R. M., Quill, T. E., & McDaniel, S. H. (Eds.). (2003). *The biopsychosocial approach: Past, present, and future.* Rochester, NY: University of Rochester Press.

Freeman, S. J. (2000). *Ethics: An introduction to philosophy and practice.* Belmont, CA: Wadsworth. doi:10.1201/9780203325438.ch090102

Fries, J. F., Koop, C., & Beadle, C. (1993). Reducing health care costs by reducing the need and demand for medical services. *The New England Journal of Medicine, 329*, 321–325. doi:10.1056/NEJM199307293290506

Froyd, J. E., Lambert, M. J., & Froyd, J. D. (1996). A review of practices of psychotherapy outcome measurement. *Journal of Mental Health, 5*, 11–16. doi:10.1080/09638239650037144

Fye, W. B. (2010). The origins and evolution of the Mayo Clinic from 1864 to 1939: A Minnesota family practice becomes an international "medical Mecca." *Bulletin of the History of Medicine, 84*, 323–357. doi:10.1353/bhm.2010.0019

Garb, H. N. (1998). *Studying the clinician: Judgment research and psychological assessment.* Washington, DC: American Psychological Association. doi:10.1037/10299-000

Gardner, H. (2005). Scientific psychology: Should we bury it or praise it? In R. J. Sternberg (Ed.), *Unity in psychology: Possibility or pipedream?* (pp. 77–90). Washington, DC: American Psychological Association. doi:10.1037/10847-005

Garfield, S. L. (1994). Research on client variables in psychotherapy. In A. E. Bergin & S. L. Garfield (Eds.), *Handbook of psychotherapy and behavior change* (4th ed., pp. 190–228). New York, NY: Wiley.

Garmezy, N., & Rutter, M. (Eds.). (1983). *Stress, coping, and development in children.* Baltimore, MD: Johns Hopkins University Press.

Gates, G. J., & Newport, F. (2012). *Special report: 3.4% of U.S. adults identify as LGBT.* Princeton, NJ: Gallop. Retrieved from www.gallup.com/poll/158066/special-report-adults-identify-lgbt.aspx

Gay, P. (1988). *Freud: A life for our times.* New York, NY: Norton.

Gert, B., Culver, C. M., & Clouser, K. D. (1997). *Bioethics: A return to fundamentals.* New York, NY: Oxford University Press.

Gert, B., Culver, C. M., & Clouser, K. D. (2006). *Bioethics: A systematic approach* (2nd ed.). New York, NY: Oxford University Press. doi:10.1093/0195159063.001.0001

Ghaemi, S. N. (2010). *The rise and fall of the biopsychosocial model: Reconciling art and science in psychiatry.* Baltimore, MD: Johns Hopkins University Press.

Gilbert, S. F. (2006). *Developmental biology.* Sunderland, MA: Sinauer.

Gilligan, C. (1982). *In a different voice: Psychological theory and women's development.* Cambridge, MA: Harvard University Press.

Gino, F., Ayal, S., & Ariely, D. (2009). Contagion and differential in unethical behavior: The effect of one bad apple on the barrel. *Psychological Science, 20,* 393–398. doi:10.1111/j.1467-9280.2009.02306.x

Gino, F., Norton, M. I., & Ariely, D. (2010). The counterfeit self: The deceptive costs of faking it. *Psychological Science, 21,* 712–720. doi:10.1177/0956797610366545

Gintis, H., Bowles, S., Boyd, R., & Fehr, E. (2007). Explaining altruistic behaviour in humans. In R. I. M. Dunbar & L. Barrett (Eds.), *Oxford handbook of evolutionary psychology* (pp. 605–619). New York, NY: Oxford University Press. doi:10.1093/oxfordhb/9780198568308.013.0042

Goldacre, B. (2013). *Bad pharma: How drug companies mislead doctors and harm patients.* New York, NY: Faber and Faber.

Goldapple, K., Segal, Z., Garson, C., Lau, M., Bieling, P., Kennedy, S., & Mayberg, H. (2004). Modulation of cortical limbic pathways in major depression: Treatment-specific effects of cognitive behavior therapy. *Archives of General Psychiatry, 61,* 34–41. doi:10.1001/archpsyc.61.1.34

Goodheart, C. D. (2010). Economics and psychology practice: What we need to know and why. *Professional Psychology: Research and Practice, 41,* 189–195. doi:10.1037/a0019498

Goodheart, C. D., & Carter, J. A. (2008). The proper focus of evidence-based practice in psychology: Integration of possibility and probability. In W. B. Walsh (Ed.), *Biennial review of counseling psychology* (Vol. 1, pp. 47–69). New York, NY: Taylor & Francis.

Gould, R. A., Otto, M. W., & Pollack, M. H. (1995). A meta-analysis of treatment outcome for panic disorder. *Clinical Psychology Review, 15,* 819–844. doi:10.1016/0272-7358(95)00048-8

Gould, R. A., Otto, M. W., Pollack, M. H., & Yap, L. (1997). Cognitive behavioral and pharmacological treatment of generalized anxiety disorder: A preliminary meta-analysis. *Behavior Therapy, 28,* 285–305. doi:10.1016/S0005-7894(97)80048-2

Grant, B. F., Stinson, F. S., Dawson, D. A., Chou, S. P., Dufour, M. C., Compton, W., . . . Kaplan, K. (2004). Prevalence and co-occurrence of substance use disorders and independent mood and anxiety disorders: Results from the National Epidemiologic Survey on Alcohol and Related Conditions. *Archives of General Psychiatry, 61,* 807–816.

Greene, J. (2003). From neural "is" to moral "ought": What are the moral implications of neuroscientific moral psychology? *Nature Reviews Neuroscience, 4,* 847–850. doi:10.1038/nrn1224

Greene, J. D., Nystrom, L. E., Engell, A. D., Darley, J. M., & Cohen, J. D. (2004). The neural bases of cognitive conflict and control in moral judgment. *Neuron, 44,* 389–400. doi:10.1016/j.neuron.2004.09.027

Gribble, J. H., & Preston, S. H. (Eds.). (1993). *The epidemiological transition: Policy and planning implications for developing countries.* Washington, DC: National Academies Press.

Griffin, J. (1986). *Well-being: Its meaning, measurement and moral importance*. Oxford, England: Clarendon.

Grissom, R. J. (1996). The magical number .7 ± .2: Meta-meta-analysis of the probability of superior outcome in comparisons involving therapy, placebo, and control. *Journal of Consulting and Clinical Psychology, 64*, 973–982. doi:10.1037/0022-006X.64.5.973

Groth-Marnat, G. (2009). *Handbook of psychological assessment* (5th ed.). Hoboken, NJ: Wiley.

Guarner, F., & Malagelada, J. R. (2003). Gut flora in health and disease. *Lancet, 361*, 512–519. doi:10.1016/S0140-6736(03)12489-0

Haas, E., Hill, R., Lambert, M. J., & Morrell, B. (2002). Do early responders to psychotherapy maintain treatment gains? *Journal of Clinical Psychology, 58*, 1157–1172. doi:10.1002/jclp.10044

Haidt, J. (2001). The emotional dog and its rational tail: A social intuitionist approach to moral judgment. *Psychological Review, 108*, 814–834. doi:10.1037/0033-295X.108.4.814

Hamilton, W. D. (1963). The evolution of altruistic behavior. *American Naturalist, 97*, 354–356. doi:10.1086/497114

Hamilton, W. D. (1964). The genetic evolution of social behavior. *Journal of Theoretical Biology, 7*, 1–16. doi:10.1016/0022-5193(64)90038-4

Hamilton, W. D. (1975). Innate social aptitudes in man: An approach from evolutionary genetics. In R. Fox (Ed.), *Biosocial anthropology* (pp. 133–155). London, England: Malaby Press.

Hannan, C. Lambert, M. J., Harmon, C., Nielsen, S. L., Smart, D. W., Shimokawa, K., & Sutton, S. W. (2005). A lab test and algorithms for identifying clients at risk for treatment failure. *Journal of Clinical Psychology: In Session, 61*, 155–163.

Harris, S. (2010). *The moral landscape: How science can determine human values*. New York, NY: Free Press.

Harwood, H. J., Kowalski, J., & Ameen, A. (2004). The need for substance abuse training among mental health professionals. *Administration and Policy in Mental Health, 32*, 189–205. doi:10.1023/B:APIH.0000042746.79349.64

Hatfield, D. R., McCullough, L., Plucinski, A., & Krieger, K. (2009). Do we know when our clients get worse? An investigation of therapists' ability to detect negative client change. *Clinical Psychology & Psychotherapy*. Advance online publication. doi: 10.1002/cpp.656

Hauser, M. (2006). *Moral minds*. New York, NY: Ecco.

Hawking, S. (1996). *A brief history of time*. New York, NY: Bantam Books.

Hayes, S. C., & Follette, W. C. (1992). Can functional analysis provide a substitute for syndromal classification? *Behavioral Assessment, 14*, 345–365.

Hayes, S. C., Strosahl, K. D., & Wilson, K. G. (1999). *Acceptance and commitment therapy: An experiential approach to behavior change*. New York, NY: Guilford Press.

Hazelton. (2008, December). *Research update: The importance of continuing care*. Center City, MN: Butler Center for Research.

Hazlett-Stevens, H., Craske, M. G., Roy-Byrne, P. P., Sherbourne, C. D., Stein, M. B., & Bystritsky, A. (2002). Predictors of willingness to consider medication and psychosocial treatment for panic disorder in primary care patients. *General Hospital Psychiatry, 24*, 316–321. doi:10.1016/S0163-8343(02)00204-9

Healy, D. (2012). *Pharmageddon*. Berkeley: University of California Press.

Hebb, D. O. (1958). *Textbook of psychology*. Philadelphia, PA: Saunders. doi:10.1037/14200-000

Heckman, J. J., Moon, S. H., Pinto, R., Savelyev, P., & Yavitz, A. (2010). A new cost-benefit and rate of return analysis for the Perry Preschool Program: A summary. *IZA Policy Papers, 17*.

Henriques, G. (2011). *A new unified theory of psychology*. New York, NY: Springer. doi:10.1007/978-1-4614-0058-5

Hersen, M., & Rosqvist, J. (2008). *Handbook of psychological assessment, case conceptualization, and treatment*. Hoboken, NJ: Wiley.

Hey, T., & Trefethen, A. (2003). The data deluge: An e-science perspective. In F. Berman, A. Hey, & G. Fox (Eds.), *Grid computing—making the global infrastructure a reality* (pp. 809–824). New York, NY: Wiley.

Hiatt, M. D., & Stockton, C. G. (2003). *The impact of the Flexner report on the fate of medical schools in North America after 1909*. Retrieved from http://www.jpands.org/vol8no2/hiattext.pdf

Hickson, G. B., Clayton, E. W., Entman, S. S., Miller, C. S., Githens, P. B., Whetten-Goldstein, K., & Sloan, F. A. (1994). Obstetricians' prior malpractice experience and patients' satisfaction with care. *JAMA, 272*, 1583–1587. doi:10.1001/jama.1994.03520200039032

Hinshaw, S. P., & Stier, A. (2008). Stigma as related to mental disorders. *Annual Review of Clinical Psychology, 4*, 367–393. doi:10.1146/annurev.clinpsy.4.022007.141245

Hirschfeld, R. M. A., & Russell, J. M. (1997). Assessment and treatment of suicidal patients. *The New England Journal of Medicine, 337*, 910–915. doi:10.1056/NEJM199709253371307

Hobbes, T. (2002). *Leviathan, or the matter, forme, and power of a commonwealth, ecclesiasticall and civil*. Salt Lake City, UT: Project Gutenberg. (Original work published 1651)

Hofmann, S. G., Barlow, D. H., Papp, L. A., Detweiler, M. F., Ray, S. E., Shear, M. K., . . . Gorman, J. M. (1998). Pretreatment attrition in a comparative treatment outcome study on panic disorder. *The American Journal of Psychiatry, 155*, 43–47.

Hollon, S. D., & Beck, A. T. (2004). Cognitive and cognitive–behavioral therapies. In M. J. Lambert (Ed.), *Garfield and Bergin's handbook of psychotherapy and behavior change: An empirical analysis* (5th ed., pp. 447–492). New York, NY: Wiley.

Holmes, O. W. (1939). *Mr. Justice Holmes and the Supreme Court* (F. Frankfurter, Ed.). Cambridge, MA: Harvard University Press.

Horvath, A. O., & Bedi, R. P. (2002). The alliance. In J. C. Norcross (Ed.), *Psychotherapy relationships that work: Therapist contributions and responsiveness to patients* (pp. 37–69). New York, NY: Oxford University Press.

Hoyert, D. L., & Xu, J. (2012). Deaths: Preliminary data for 2011. *National Vital Statistics Report, 61*(6). Retrieved from http://www.cdc.gov/nchs/data/nvsr/nvsr61/nvsr61_06.pdf

Hunter, C. L., Goodie, J. L., Oordt, M. S., & Dobmeyer, A. C. (2009). *Integrated behavioral health in primary care: Step-by-step guidance for assessment and intervention.* Washington, DC: American Psychological Association. doi:10.1037/11871-000

Huyse, F. J., Lyons, J. S., Stiefel, F., Slaets, J., de Jonge, P., & Latour, C. (2001). Operationalizing the biopsychosocial model: The INTERMED. *Psychosomatics, 42,* 5–13. doi:10.1176/appi.psy.42.1.5

Ilardi, H. H., & Craighead, W. E. (1994). The role of non-specific factors in cognitive–behavioral therapy for depression. *Clinical Psychology: Science and Practice, 1,* 138–155. doi:10.1111/j.1468-2850.1994.tb00016.x

Institute of Medicine. (1972). *Educating for the health team.* Washington, DC: National Academy of Sciences.

Institute of Medicine. (1994). *Reducing risks for mental disorders: Frontiers for preventive intervention research.* Washington, DC: National Academy Press.

Institute of Medicine. (2000). *To err is human: Building a safer health system.* Washington, DC: National Academies Press.

Institute of Medicine. (2001). *Crossing the quality chasm: A new health system for the 21st century.* Washington, DC: National Academies Press.

Institute of Medicine. (2002). *The future of the public's health in the 21st century.* Washington, DC: National Academies Press.

Institute of Medicine. (2003). *Health professions education: A bridge to quality.* Washington, DC: National Academies Press.

Institute of Medicine. (2004). *Improving medical education: Enhancing the behavioral and social science content of medical school curricula.* Washington, DC: National Academies Press.

Interactive, H. (2006). *Religious views and beliefs vary greatly by country.* Retrieved from http://www.harrisinteractive.com/news/printerfriend/index.asp?NewsID=1131

International Union of Psychological Science. (2008). *Universal declaration of ethical principles for psychologists.* Retrieved from http://www.am.org/iupsys/resources/ethics/univdecl2008.html

Interprofessional Education Collaborative Expert Panel. (2011). *Core competencies for interprofessional collaborative practice: Report of an expert panel.* Washington, DC: Interprofessional Education Collaborative. Retrieved from https://www.aamc.org/download/186750/data/core)_competencies.pdf

Jablonka, E., & Lamb, M. J. (2005). *Evolution in four dimensions: Genetic, epigenetic, behavioral, and symbolic variation in the history of life.* Cambridge, MA: MIT Press.

James, W. (1890). *The principles of psychology.* New York, NY: Henry Holt.

Jané-Llopis, E., Hosman, C., Jenkins, R., & Anderson, P. (2003). Predictors of efficacy in depression prevention programmes. Meta-analysis. *The British Journal of Psychiatry, 183,* 384–397. doi:10.1192/bjp.183.5.384

Jecker, N. S., Jonsen, A. R., & Pearlman, R. A. (2007). *Bioethics: An introduction to the history, methods, and practice* (2nd ed.). Sudbury, MA: Jones and Bartlett.

Johanson, D. C., & Wong, K. (2009). *Lucy's legacy: The quest for human origins.* New York, NY: Harmony Books.

Johnson, S. B. (2013). Increasing psychology's role in health research and health care. *American Psychologist, 68,* 311–321. doi:10.1037/a0033591

Johnson, S. L. (2003). *Therapist's guide to clinical intervention: The 1-2-3's of treatment planning* (2nd ed.). San Diego, CA: Academic Press.

Joiner, T. E. (2005). *Why people die by suicide.* Cambridge, MA: Harvard University Press.

Joint Commission on Accreditation of Healthcare Organizations. (2006). *Comprehensive Accreditation manual for behavioral health care: 2006–2006, Standards, rationales, elements of performance, scoring.* Oakbrook Terrace, IL: Joint Commission Resources.

Jonas, B. S., Albertorio-Diaz, J. R., & Gu, Q. (2012). *Trends in psychotropic medication use in the noninstitutionalized adolescent population: An NHANES analysis.* Hyattsville, MD: National Center for Health Statistics. Retrieved from http://www.cdc.gov/nchs/ppt/nchs2012/SS-22_JONAS.pdf

Jones, J. (1981). *Bad blood: The Tuskegee syphilis experiment.* New York, NY: Free Press.

Jongsma, A. E., Peterson, L. M., & Bruce, T. J. (2006). *The complete adult psychotherapy treatment planner.* Hoboken, NJ: Wiley.

Jongsma, A. E., Peterson, L. M., McInnis, W. P., & Bruce, T. J. (2006). *The child psychotherapy treatment planner.* Hoboken, NJ: Wiley.

Judd, L. L. (1997). The clinical course of unipolar major depressive disorders. *Archives of General Psychiatry, 54,* 989–991. doi:10.1001/archpsyc.1997.01830230015002

Jutapakdeegul, N., Casalotti, S. O., Govitrapong, P., & Kotchabhakdi, N. (2003). Postnatal touch stimulation acutely alters corticosterone levels and glucocorticoid receptor gene expression in the neonatal rat. *Developmental Neuroscience, 25,* 26–33. doi:10.1159/000071465

Kabat-Zinn, J. (2005). *Coming to our senses: Healing ourselves and the world through mindfulness.* New York, NY: Hyperion.

Kahneman, D. (2012). *Thinking, fast and slow.* New York, NY: Farrar, Straus & Giroux.

Kane, R. L. (Ed.). (2006). *Understanding health care outcomes research* (2nd ed.). Sudbury, MA: Jones and Bartlett.

Kant, I. (1964). *Groundwork of the metaphysics of morals* (H. J. Paton, Trans.). New York, NY: Harper & Row. (Original work published 1785)

Kaplan, A. (1964). *The conduct of inquiry: Methodology for behavioral science*. San Francisco, CA: Chandler.

Karch, D. L., Logan, J., McDaniel, D., Parks, S., & Patel, N. (2012). Surveillance for violent deaths—National Violent Death Reporting System, 16 states, 2009. *Mortality and Morbidity Weekly Report Surveillance Summary, 61,* 1–43. Retrieved from http://www.cdc.gov/mmwr/preview/mmwrhtml/ss6106a1.htm?s_cid= ss6106a1_e#tab6

Karoly, L. A., Kilburn, M. R., & Cannon, J. (2005). *Early childhood interventions: Proven results, future promise*. Santa Monica, CA: RAND Corporation. doi:10.1037/ e475852006-001

Kazak, A. E., Hoagwood, K., Weisz, J. R., Hood, K., Kratochwill, T. R., Vargas, L. A., & Bazez, G. A. (2010). A meta-systems approach to evidence-based practice with children and adolescents. *American Psychologist, 65,* 85–97. doi:10.1037/ a0017784

Kazdin, A. E. (2007). Mediators and mechanisms of change in psychotherapy research. *Annual Review of Clinical Psychology, 3,* 1–27. doi:10.1146/annurev. clinpsy.3.022806.091432

Kellam, S. G., & Rebok, G. W. (1992). Building developmental and etiological theory through epidemiologically based preventive intervention trials. In J. McCord & R. E. Tremblay (Eds.), *Preventing antisocial behavior: Interventions from birth through adolescence* (pp. 162–195). New York, NY: Guilford Press.

Kelly, J. F., & Coons, H. L. (2012). Integrated health care and professional psychology: Is the setting right for you? *Professional Psychology: Research and Practice, 43,* 586–595.

Kendler, H. H. (2002). A personal encounter with psychology (1937–2002). *History of Psychology, 5,* 52–84. doi:10.1037/1093-4510.5.1.52

Kessler, R. C., Demler, O., Frank, R. G., Olfson, M., Pincus, H. A., Walters, E. E., . . . Zaslavsky, A. M. (2005). Prevalence and treatment of mental disorders, 1990 to 2003. *The New England Journal of Medicine, 352,* 2515–2523. doi:10.1056/ NEJMsa043266

Kessler, R. C., Heeringa, S., Lakoma, M. D., Petukhova, M., Rupp, A. E., Schoenbaum, M., . . . Zaslavsky, A. M. (2008). Individual and societal effects of mental disorders on earnings in the United States: Results from the National Comorbidity Survey Replication. *The American Journal of Psychiatry, 165,* 703–711. doi:10.1176/appi.ajp.2008.08010126

Kessler, R. C., McGonagle, K. A., Zhao, S., Nelson, C. B., Hughes, M., Eshleman, H. U., . . . Kendler, K. S. (1994). Lifetime and 12-month prevalence of DSM–III–R disorders in the United States: Results from the National Comorbidity Study. *Archives of General Psychiatry, 51,* 8–9. doi:10.1001/archpsyc. 1994.03950010008002

Keyes, C. L. M. (2007). Promoting and protecting mental health as flourishing: A complementary strategy for improving national mental health. *American Psychologist, 62,* 95–108. doi:10.1037/0003-066X.62.2.95

Keynes, J. M. (1972). Economic possibilities for our grandchildren. In *The Collected Writings of John Maynard Keynes.* London, England: Macmillan. (Original work published 1930)

Kiresuk, T. J., & Sherman, R. E. (1968). Goal attainment scaling: A general method for evaluating comprehensive community mental health programs. *Community Mental Health Journal, 4,* 443–453. doi:10.1007/BF01530764

Kitchener, K (1984) Intuition, critical evaluation and ethical principles: The foundation for ethical decision in counseling psychology. *The Counseling Psychologist, 12,* 43–55. doi:10.1177/0011000084123005

Kleespies, P. M., Penk, W. E., & Forsyth, J. P. (1993). The stress of patient suicidal behavior during clinical training: Incidence, impact, and recovery. *Professional Psychology: Research and Practice, 24,* 293–303. doi:10.1037/0735-7028.24.3.293

Knapp, S., & VandeCreek, L. (2007). When values of different cultures conflict: Ethical decision making in a multicultural context. *Professional Psychology: Research and Practice, 38,* 660–666. doi:10.1037/0735-7028.38.6.660

Kohlberg, L. (1971). *From is to ought: How to commit the naturalistic fallacy and get away with it in the study of moral development.* New York, NY: Academic Press. doi:10.1016/B978-0-12-498640-4.50011-1

Koocher, G. P., & Keith-Spiegel, P. (2008). *Ethics in psychology and the mental health professions: Standards and cases* (3rd ed.). New York, NY: Oxford University Press.

Kosmin, B. A., & Keysar, A. (2009). *American religious identification survey 2008.* Hartford, CT: Institute for the Study of Secularism in Society and Culture.

Kraemer, H. C., Kazdin, A. E., & Offord, D. R. (1997). Coming to terms with terms of risk. *Archives of General Psychiatry, 54,* 337–343. doi:10.1001/archpsyc.1997.01830160065009

Kramer, P. D. (2008). Compared to what? *Psychology Today.* Retrieved from http://www.psychologytoday.com/node/1022

Krebs, D. (2005). The evolution of morality. In D. M. Buss (Ed.), *The handbook of evolutionary psychology* (pp. 747–771). Hoboken, NJ: Wiley.

Krieger, N., & Brin, A. E. (1998). A vision of social justice as the foundation of public health: Commemorating 150 years of the spirit of 1848. *American Journal of Public Health, 88,* 1603–1606. doi:10.2105/AJPH.88.11.1603

Kroenke, K. (2003). Patients presenting with somatic complaints: Epidemiology, psychiatric co-morbidity and management. *International Journal of Methods in Psychiatric Research, 12,* 34–43. doi:10.1002/mpr.140

Kroenke, K., Spitzer, R. L., & Williams, J. B. (2001). The PHQ-9: Validity of a brief depression severity measure. *Journal of General Internal Medicine, 16,* 606–613. doi:10.1046/j.1525-1497.2001.016009606.x

Krupnick, J. L., Stotsky, S. M., Simmons, S., Moyer, J., Watkins, J., Elkin, I., . . . & Pilkonis, P. A. (1996). The role of the therapeutic alliance in psychotherapy and pharmacotherapy outcome: Findings in the National Institute of Mental Health Treatment of Depression Collaborative Research Program. *Journal of Consulting and Clinical Psychology, 64*, 532–539. doi:10.1037/0022-006X.64.3.532

Kuhn, T. S. (1962). *The structure of scientific revolutions.* Chicago, IL: University of Chicago Press.

Kung, H. C., Hoyert, D. L., Xu, J. Q., & Murphy, S. L. (2008). Deaths: Final data for 2005. *National Vital Statistics Reports, 56*(10), 1–120. Retrieved from http://www.cdc.gov/nchs/data/nvsr/nvsr56/nvsr56_10.pdf

Lambert, M. J. (1992). Implications of outcome research for psychotherapy integration. In J. C. Norcross & M. R. Goldstein (Eds.), *Handbook of psychotherapy integration* (pp. 94–129). New York, NY: Basic Books.

Lambert, M. J. (2007). Presidential address: What we have learned from a decade of research aimed at improving psychotherapy outcome in routine care. *Psychotherapy Research, 17*, 1–14. doi:10.1080/10503300601032506

Lambert, M. J. (2010). *Prevention of treatment failure: The use of measuring, monitoring, and feedback in clinical practice.* Washington, DC: American Psychological Association. doi:10.1037/12141-000

Lambert, M. J. (2013). The efficacy and effectiveness of psychotherapy. In M. J. Lambert (Ed.), *Bergin and Garfield's handbook of psychotherapy and behavior change* (6th ed., pp. 169–218). Hoboken, NJ: Wiley.

Lambert, M. J., & Archer, A. (2006). Research findings on the effects of psychotherapy and their implications for practice. In C. D. Goodheart, A. E. Kazdin, & R. J. Sternberg (Eds.), *Evidence-based psychotherapy: Where practice and research meet* (pp. 111–130). Washington, DC: American Psychological Association. doi:10.1037/11423-005

Lambert, M. J., & Bergin, A. E. (1994). The effectiveness of psychotherapy. In A. E. Bergin & S. L. Garfield (Eds.), *Handbook of psychotherapy and behavior change* (4th ed., pp. 143–189). New York, NY: Wiley.

Lambert, M. J., Burlingame, G. M., Umphress, V. J., Hansen, N. B., Vermeersch, D., Clouse, G., & Yanchar, S. (1996). The reliability and validity of the Outcome Questionnaire. *Clinical Psychology & Psychotherapy, 3*, 249–258. doi:10.1002/(SICI)1099-0879(199612)3:4<249::AID-CPP106>3.0.CO;2-S

Lambert, M. J., & Ogles, B. M. (2004). The efficacy and effectiveness of psychotherapy. In M. J. Lambert (Ed.), *Garfield and Bergin's handbook of psychotherapy and behavior change: An empirical analysis* (5th ed., pp. 139–193). New York, NY: Wiley.

Larson, E. J. (2004). *Evolution: The remarkable history of a scientific theory.* New York, NY: Modern Library.

Lasser, K., Boyd, J. W., Woolhandler, S., Himmelstein, D. U., McCormick, D., & Bor, D. H.(2000). Smoking and mental illness: A population-based prevalence study. *JAMA, 284*, 2606–2610. doi:10.1001/jama.284.20.2606

Laupacis, A., Sackett, D. L., & Roberts, R. S. (1988). An assessment of clinically useful measures of the consequences of treatment. *The New England Journal of Medicine, 318*, 1728–1733. doi:10.1056/NEJM198806303182605

Lazarus, A. A., Beutler, L. E., & Norcross, J. C. (1992). The future of technical eclecticism. *Psychotherapy, 29*, 11–20.

Lesk, M. (2004, September). *Online data and scientific progress: Content in cyberinfrastructure*. Paper presented at the Digital Curation Centre, Edinburgh, Scotland. Retrieved from http://archiv.twoday.net/stories/337419

Lewis-Williams, D. (2002). *The mind in the cave*. London, England: Thames & Hudson.

Lezak, M. D. (1995). *Neuropsychological assessment* (3rd ed.). New York, NY: Oxford University Press.

Lilienfeld, S. O. (2007). Psychological treatments that cause harm. *Perspectives on Psychological Science, 2*, 53–70. doi:10.1111/j.1745-6916.2007.00029.x

Lindsay, R. A. (2005). Slaves, embryos, and nonhuman animals: Moral status and the limitations of common morality theory. *Kennedy Institute of Ethics Journal, 15*, 323–346. doi:10.1353/ken.2005.0028

Linehan, M. M., & Dexter-Mazza, E. T. (2008). Dialectical behavior therapy for borderline personality disorder. In D. H. Barlow (Ed.), *Clinical handbook of psychological disorders: A step-by-step treatment manual* (pp. 365–420). New York, NY: Guilford Press. doi:10.4088/JCP.v69n0617

Linley, P. A., Harrington, S., & Garcea, N. (Eds.). (2009). *Oxford handbook of positive psychology and work*. New York, NY: Oxford University Press.

Lipsey, M. W., & Wilson, D. B. (1993). The efficacy of psychological, educational, and behavior treatment: Confirmation from meta-analysis. *American Psychologist, 48*, 1181–1209. doi:10.1037/0003-066X.48.12.1181

Loftus, E. F., & Davis, D. (2006). Recovered memories. *Annual Review of Clinical Psychology, 2*, 469–498. doi:10.1146/annurev.clinpsy.2.022305.095315

Lopez, S. J., & Snyder, C. R. (Eds.). (2011). *Handbook of positive psychology* (2nd ed.). New York, NY: Oxford University Press.

Loue, S. (2000). *Textbook of research ethics: Theory and practice*. New York, NY: Springer.

Lugo, L. (2012). "Nones" on the rise: One-in-five adults have no religious affiliation. In *Pew research center's forum on religion & public life*. Retrieved from http://www.pewforum.org/Unaffiliated/nones-on-the-rise.aspx

Lumsden, C. J., & Wilson, E. O. (1981). *Genes, mind, and culture: The coevolutionary process*. London, England: World Scientific.

Luthar, S. S. (Ed.). (2003). *Resilience and vulnerability: Adaptation in the context of childhood adversities*. New York, NY: Cambridge University Press. doi:10.1017/CBO9780511615788

Maciejewski, M. L. (2006). Generic measures. In R. L. Kane (Ed.), *Understanding health care outcomes research* (2nd ed., pp. 123–164). Sudbury, MA: Jones and Bartlett.

MacIntyre, A. (1982). *After virtue: A study in moral theory.* Notre Dame, IN: University of Notre Dame Press.

Magnavita, J. J. (2005). *Personality-guided relational psychotherapy: A unified approach.* Washington, DC: American Psychological Association. doi:10.1037/10959-000

Magnavita, J. J. (2006). In search of the unifying principles of psychotherapy: Conceptual, empirical, and clinical convergence. *American Psychologist, 61,* 882–892. doi:10.1037/0003-066X.61.8.882

Magnavita, J. J. (2008). Toward unification of clinical science: The next wave in the evolution of psychotherapy? *Journal of Psychotherapy Integration, 18,* 264–291. doi:10.1037/a0013490

Magnavita, J., & Anchin, J. (2014). *Unifying psychotherapy: Principles, methods, and evidence from clinical science.* New York, NY: Springer. doi:10.1037/e605182013-001

Main, M., Kaplan, N., & Cassidy, J. (1985). Security in infancy, childhood and adulthood: A move to the level of representation. In I. Bretherton & E. Waters (Eds.), *Growing points of attachment theory and research* (pp. 66–104). Chicago, IL: University of Chicago Press. doi:10.2307/3333827

Mameli, M. (2007). Evolution and psychology in philosophical perspective. In R. I. M. Dunbar & L. Barrett (Eds.), *Oxford handbook of evolutionary psychology* (pp. 21–34). New York, NY: Oxford University Press. doi:10.1093/oxfordhb/9780198568308.013.0003

Manning, M., Homel, R., & Smith, C. (2010). A meta-analysis of the effects of early developmental prevention programs in at-risk populations on non-health outcomes in adolescence. *Children and Youth Services Review, 32,* 506–519. doi:10.1016/j.childyouth.2009.11.003

Mark, T. L., Levit, K. R., & Buck, J. A. (2009). Psychotropic drug prescriptions by medical speciality. *Psychiatric Services, 60,* 1167. doi:10.1176/appi.ps.60.9.1167

Marks, I. M., & Matthews, A. M. (1979). Brief standard self-rating for phobic patients. *Behaviour Research and Therapy, 17,* 263–267. doi:10.1016/0005-7967(79)90041-X

Martin, P. R., Weinberg, B. A., & Bealer, B. K. (2007). *Healing addiction: An integrated pharmacopsychosocial approach to treatment.* Hoboken, NJ: Wiley.

Maruish, M. E. (2004a). Development and implementation of a behavioral health outcomes program. In M. E. Maruish (Ed.), *The use of psychological testing for treatment planning and outcomes assessment* (3rd ed., pp. 215–272). Mahwah, NJ: Erlbaum.

Maruish, M. E. (2004b). Introduction. In M. E. Maruish (Ed.), *The use of psychological testing for treatment planning and outcomes assessment* (3rd ed., pp. 1–64). Mahwah, NJ: Erlbaum.

Maslow, A. H. (1943). A theory of human motivation. *Psychological Review, 50,* 370–396. doi:10.1037/h0054346

Maslow, A. H. (1966). *The psychology of science: A reconnaissance.* Chapel Hill, NC: Maurice Bassett.

Masse, L. N., & Barnett, W. S. (2002). A benefit–cost analysis of the Abecedarian early childhood intervention. In H. Levin & P. McEwan (Eds.), *Cost effectiveness and educational policy: 2002 Yearbook of the American Education Finance Association* (pp. 157–176). Larchmont, NY: Eye on Education.

Masten, A. S., Burt, K., & Coatsworth, J. D. (2006). Competence and psychopathology in development. In D. Cicchetti & D. J. Cohen (Eds.), *Developmental psychopathology risk, disorder, and adaptation* (Vol. 3, pp. 696–738). New York, NY: Wiley.

Masten, A. S., Faden, V. B., Zucker, R. A., & Spear, L. P. (2008). Underage drinking: A developmental framework. *Pediatrics, 121*(Suppl. 4), S235–S251. doi:10.1542/peds.2007-2243A

Maynard Smith, J., & Szathmary, E. (1997). *The major transitions in evolution.* New York, NY: Oxford University Press.

Mayou, R. A., Ehlers, A., & Hobbs, M. (2000). Psychological debriefing for road traffic accident victims: Three-year follow-up of randomized controlled trial. *The British Journal of Psychiatry, 176,* 589–593. doi:10.1192/bjp.176.6.589

Mazar, N., Amir, O., & Ariely, D. (2008). The dishonesty of honest people: A theory of self-concept maintenance. *Journal of Marketing Research, 45,* 633–644. doi:10.1509/jmkr.45.6.633

Mazza, J. J., Catalano, R. D., Abbott, R. F., & Haggerty, K. P. (2011). An examination of the validity of retrospective measures of suicide attempts in youth. *Journal of Adolescent Health, 49,* 532–537. doi:10.1016/j.jadohealth.2011.04.009

McClain, T., O'Sullivan, P. S., & Clardy, J. A. (2004). Biopsychosocial formulation: Recognizing educational shortcomings. *Academic Psychiatry, 28,* 88–94. doi:10.1176/appi.ap.28.2.88

McGowan, P. O., Sasaki, A., D'Alessio, A. C., Dymov, S., Labonte, B., Szyf, M., . . . Meaney, M. J. (2009). Epigenetic regulation of the glucocorticoid receptor in human brain associates with childhood abuse. *Nature Neuroscience, 12,* 342–348. doi:10.1038/nn.2270

McKeown, T. (1965). *Medicine in modern society.* London, England: Allen and Unwin.

McQuay, H. J., & Moore, R. A. (1997). Using numerical results from systematic reviews in clinical practice. *Annals of Internal Medicine, 126,* 712–720. doi:10.7326/0003-4819-126-9-199705010-00007

Mead, N. L., Baumeister, R. F., Gino, F., Schweitzer, M. E., & Ariely, D. (2009). Too tired to tell the truth: Self-control resource depletion and dishonesty. *Journal of Experimental Social Psychology, 45,* 594–597. doi:10.1016/j.jesp.2009.02.004

Meaney, M. J. (2001). Maternal care, gene expression, and the transmission of individual differences in stress reactivity across generations. *Annual Review of Neuroscience, 24,* 1161–1192. doi:10.1146/annurev.neuro.24.1.1161

Melchert, T. P. (2011). *Foundations of professional psychology: The end of theoretical orientations and the emergence of the biopsychosocial approach.* London, England: Elsevier. doi:10.1016/B978-0-12-385079-9.00006-0

Merikangas, K. R., Ames, M., Cui, L., Stang, P. E., Ustun, T. B., Von Korff, M., & Kessler, R. C. (2007). The impact of comorbidity of mental and physical conditions on role disability in the US adult household population. *Archives of General Psychiatry, 64,* 1180–1188. doi:10.1001/archpsyc.64.10.1180

Merikangas, K. R., He, J.-P., Brody, D., Fisher, P. W., Bourdon, K., & Koretz, D. S. (2010). Prevalence and treatment of mental disorders among US children in the 2001–2004 NHANES. *Pediatrics, 125*(1), 75–81. doi:10.1542/peds.2008-2598

Mesoudi, A., & Jensen, K. (2012). Culture and the evolution of human sociality. In J. Vonk & T. K. Shackelford (Eds.), *The Oxford handbook of comparative evolutionary psychology* (pp. 419–433). New York, NY: Oxford University Press. doi:10.1093/oxfordhb/9780199738182.013.0022

Messer, S. B., & Winokur, M. (1980). Some limits to the integration of psychoanalytic and behavior therapy. *American Psychologist, 35,* 818–827. doi: 10:1037/0003-066x.35.9.818

Meyer, G. J., Finn, S. E., Eyde, L. D., Kay, G. G., Moreland, K. L., Dies, R. R., . . . Reed, G. M. (2001). Psychological testing and psychological assessment: A review of evidence and issues. *American Psychologist, 56,* 128–165. doi:10.1037/0003-066X.56.2.128

Meyer, L. (2008). *The use of a comprehensive biopsychosocial framework for intake assessment in mental health practice* (Doctoral dissertation, Marquette University, Milwaukee, WI).

Meyer, L., & Melchert, T. P. (2011). Examining the content of mental health intake assessments from a biopsychosocial perspective. *Journal of Psychotherapy Integration, 21,* 70–89. doi:10.1037/a0022907

Michell, J. (1999). *Measurement in psychology: A critical history of a methodological concept.* New York, NY: Cambridge University Press. doi:10.1017/CBO9780511490040

Mikhail, J. (2007). Universal moral grammar: Theory, evidence, and the future. *Trends in Cognitive Sciences, 11,* 143–152. doi:10.1016/j.tics.2006.12.007

Mikulincer, M., & Shaver, P. R. (2007). *Attachment in adulthood: Structure, dynamics, and change.* New York, NY: Guilford Press.

Mikulincer, M., & Shaver, P. R. (Eds.). (2012). *The social psychology of morality: Exploring the causes of good and evil.* Washington, DC: American Psychological Association. doi:10.1037/13091-000

Miller, J. E., & Prewitt, E. (2012). *Reclaiming lost decades: The role of state behavioral health agencies in accelerating the integration of behavioral healthcare and primary care to improve the health of people with serious mental illness.* Alexandria, VA: National Association of State Mental Health Program Directors.

Miller, R. C., & Berman, J. S. (1983). The efficacy of cognitive behavior therapies: A quantitative review of the research evidence. *Psychological Bulletin, 94,* 39–53. doi:10.1037/0033-2909.94.1.39

Mitchell, M. (2009). *Complexity: A guided tour.* New York, NY: Oxford University Press.

Mojtabai, R., & Olfson, M. (2008). National trends in psychotherapy by office-based psychiatrists. *Archives of General Psychiatry, 65,* 962–970. doi:10.1001/archpsyc.65.8.962

Mokdad, A. H., Marks, J. S., Stroup, D. F., & Gerberding, J. L. (2004). Actual causes of death in the United States, 2000. *JAMA, 291,* 1238–1245. doi:10.1001/jama.291.10.1238

Moll, J., de Oliveira-Souza, R., & Zahn, R. (2008). The neural basis of moral cognition: Sentiments, concepts, and values. *Annals of the New York Academy of Sciences, 1124,* 161–180. doi:10.1196/annals.1440.005

Montagu, A. (1942). *Man's most dangerous myth: The fallacy of race.* New York, NY: Columbia University Press.

Moore, A. (2009). *What is an NNT?* Kent, England: Hayward Medical Group. Retrieved from http://meds.queensu.ca/medicine/obgyn/pdf/what_is/WhatisanNNT.pdf

Moore, G. E. (1959). *Principia ethica.* Cambridge, England: Cambridge University Press. (Original work published 1903)

Mrazek, P. J., & Hall, M. (1997). A policy perspective on prevention. *American Journal of Community Psychology, 25,* 221–226. doi:10.1023/A:1024670530280

Muñoz, R. F., Hollon, S. D., McGrath, E., Rehm, L. P., & VandenBos, G. R. (1994). On the AHCPR Depression in Primary Care guidelines: Further considerations for practitioners. *American Psychologist, 49,* 42–61. doi:10.1037/0003-066X.49.1.42

Murray, C. J. L., & Lopez, A. D. (Eds.). (1996). *The global burden of disease: A comprehensive assessment of mortality and disability from diseases, injuries, and risk factors in 1990 and projected to 2020.* Cambridge, MA: Harvard School of Public Health.

Myers, J. E. B. (Ed.). (2011). *The APSAC handbook on child maltreatment* (3rd ed.). Thousand Oaks, CA: Sage.

Narayan, K. M., Boyle, J. P., Thompson, T. J., Sorensen, S. W., & Williamson, D. F. (2003). Lifetime risk for developing diabetes mellitus. *JAMA, 290,* 1884–1890. doi:10.1001/jama.290.14.1884

National Association of Social Workers. (2008). *Code of ethics.* Retrieved from http://www.socialworkers.org/pubs/code/code.asp

National Center for Educational Statistics. (2008). *National assessment of adult literacy: State and county estimates of low literacy.* Retrieved from http://nces.ed.gov/naal/estimates/Overview.aspx

National Center for Health Statistics. (2002). *Health, United States, 2002.* Hyattsville, MD: Author.

National Center for Health Statistics. (2012). *Healthy people 2010 final review.* Hyattsville, MD: Author.

National Institute of Mental Health. (2011). *NIMH Research Domain Criteria (RDoC).* Retrieved from http://www.nimh.nih.gov/research-priorities/rdoc/nimh-research-domain-criteria-rdoc.shtml

National Research Council and Institute of Medicine. (2000). *From neurons to neighborhoods: The science of early childhood development* Washington, DC: National Academy Press.

National Research Council and Institute of Medicine. (2009). *Preventing mental, emotional, and behavioral disorders among young people: Progress and possibilities* (M. E. O'Connell, T. Boat, & K. E. Warner, Eds.). Committee on the Prevention of Mental Disorders and Substance Abuse among Children, Youth, and Young Adults, Board on Children, Youth, and Families. Washington, DC: National Academy Press.

Nettle, D. (2006). The evolution of personality variation in humans and other animals. *American Psychologist, 61*, 622–631. doi:10.1037/0003-066X.61.6.622

New Freedom Commission on Mental Health. (2003). *Achieving the promise: Transforming mental health care in American. Final report* [DHHS Pub. No. SMA-03-3832]. Rockville, MD: U.S. Department of Health and Human Services.

Newport, F. (2012). *Seven in 10 Americans are very or moderately religious.* Princeton, NJ: Gallup. Retrieved from http://www.gallup.com/poll/159050/seven-americans-moderately-religious.aspx#1

Newsweek/Beliefnet poll results. (2005). Retrieved from http://www.beliefnet.com/News/2005/08/Newsweekbeliefnet-Poll-Results.aspx

Nielsen, M., Langner, B., Zema, C., Hacker, T., & Grundy, P. (2012). *Benefits of implementing primary care patient-centered medical home: A review of cost and quality results, 2012.* Washington, DC: Patient-Centered Primary Care Collaborative. Retrieved from http://www.pcpcc.net/sites/default/files/media/benefits_of_implementing_the_primary_care_pcmh.pdf

Nietzel, M. T., Russell, R. L., Hemmings, K. A., & Gretter, M. L. (1987). Clinical significance of psychotherapy for unipolar depression: A meta-analytic approach to social comparison. *Journal of Consulting and Clinical Psychology, 55*, 156–161. doi:10.1037/0022-006X.55.2.156

Norcross, J. C. (2005). A primer on psychotherapy integration. In J. C. Norcross & M. R. Goldfried (Eds.), *Handbook of psychotherapy integration* (2nd ed., pp. 3–23). New York, NY: Oxford University Press.

Norcross, J. C. (Ed.). (2011). *Psychotherapy relationships that work: Evidence-based responsiveness* (2nd ed.). New York, NY: Oxford University Press. doi:10.1093/acprof:oso/9780199737208.001.0001

Norcross, J. C., Koocher, G. P., & Garofalo, A. (2006). Discredited psychological treatments and tests: A Delphi poll. *Professional Psychology: Research and Practice, 37*, 515–522. doi:10.1037/0735-7028.37.5.515

Norcross, J. C., & Lambert, M. (2011). Evidence-based therapy relationships. In J. C. Norcross (Ed.), *Psychotherapy relationships that work: Evidence-based responsiveness* (2nd ed., pp. 3–21). New York, NY: Oxford University Press. doi:10.1093/acprof:oso/9780199737208.003.0001

Norcross, J. C., & Wampold, B. E. (2011). Evidence-based therapy relationships: Research conclusions and clinical practices. In J. C. Norcross (Ed.), *Psychotherapy relationships that work: Evidence-based responsiveness* (2nd ed., pp. 423–430). New York, NY: Oxford University Press. doi:10.1093/acprof:oso/9780199737208.003.0021

Nordal, K. C. (2012). Healthcare reform: Implications for independent practice. *Professional Psychology: Research and Practice, 43,* 535–544. doi:10.1037/a0029603

Nutting, P. A., Crabtree, B. F., Miller, W. L., Strange, K. C., Stewart, E., & Jaen, C. (2011). Transforming physician practices to patient-centered medical homes: Lessons from the National Demonstration Project. *Health Affairs, 30,* 439–445. doi:10.1377/hlthaff.2010.0159

Nyman, J. A. (2006). Cost-effectiveness analysis. In R. L. Kane (Ed.), *Understanding health care outcomes research* (2nd ed., pp. 335–349). Sudbury, MA: Jones and Bartlett.

Ogden, C. L., Carroll, M. D., & Flegal, K. M. (2008). High body mass index for age among U.S. children and adolescents, 2003–2006. *JAMA, 299,* 2401–2405. doi:10.1001/jama.299.20.2401

Ogles, B. M. (2013). Measuring change in psychotherapy research. In M. J. Lambert (Ed.), *Bergin and Garfield's handbook of psychotherapy and behavior change* (6th ed., pp. 134–166). Hoboken, NJ: Wiley.

Okiishi, J. C., Lambert, M. J., Eggett, D., Nielsen, S. L., Dayton, D. D., & Vermeersch, D. A. (2006). An analysis of therapist treatment effects: Toward providing feedback to individual therapists on their patients' psychotherapy outcome. *Journal of Clinical Psychology, 62,* 1157–1172. doi:10.1002/jclp.20272

Okiishi, J., Lambert, M. J., Nielsen, S. L., & Ogles, B. M. (2003). In search of supershrink: Using patient outcome to identify effective and ineffective therapists. *Clinical Psychology & Psychotherapy, 10,* 361–373. doi:10.1002/cpp.383

Omi, M. (2001). The changing meaning of race. In N. J. Smelser, W. J. Wilson, & F. Mitchell (Eds.), *American becoming: Racial trends and their consequences* (p. 243). Washington, DC: National Academy Press.

Oregon Department of Human Services, Addiction and Mental Health Division. (2008, June 6). *Measuring premature mortality among Oregonians.* Retrieved from http://www.oregon.gov/oha/amh/Documents/msur_pre_mort_6_2008.pdf

Organization of Economic Co-operation and Development Health Division (2012). *OECD health data 2012—Frequently requested data.* Paris, France: Organization of Economic Co-operation and Development.

Otto, M. W., Smits, J. A. J., & Reese, H. E. (2005). Combined psychotherapy and pharmacotherapy for mood and anxiety disorders in adults: Review and analysis. *Clinical Psychology: Science and Practice, 12,* 72–86. doi:10.1093/clipsy.bpi009

Partnership for Solutions. (2004). *Chronic conditions: Making the case for ongoing care.* Baltimore, MD: Johns Hopkins University Press.

Pascual-Leone, A., Amedi, A., Fregni, F., & Merabet, L. B. (2005). The plastic human brain cortex. *Annual Review of Neuroscience, 28,* 377–401. doi:10.1146/annurev.neuro.27.070203.144216

Pascual-Leone, A., & Hamilton, R. (2001). The metamodal organization of the brain. *Progress in Brain Research, 134,* 427–445. doi:10.1016/S0079-6123(01)34028-1

Patient Protection and Affordable Care Act, Pub. L. No. 111-148, 124 Stat. 119 (2010).

Patrick, D. L., & Deyo, R. A. (1989). Generic and disease-specific measures in assessing health status and quality of life. *Medical Care, 27*, S217–S232. doi:10.1097/00005650-198903001-00018

Paykel, E. S., Scott, J., Teasdale, J. D., Johnson, A. L., Garland, A., Moore, R., . . . Pope, M. (1999). Prevention of relapse in residual depression by cognitive therapy: A controlled trial. *Archives of General Psychiatry, 56*, 829–835. doi:10.1001/archpsyc.56.9.829

Pearsall, P. (2008). *500 therapies: Discovering a science for everyday living.* New York, NY: Norton.

Penfield, W., & Jasper, H. (1954). *Epilepsy and the functional anatomy of the human brain* (2nd ed.). Oxford, England: Little, Brown.

Persons, J. B., & Tompkins, M. A. (2007). Cognitive-behavioral case formulation. In T. D. Eells (Ed.), *Handbook of psychotherapy case formulation* (2nd ed., pp. 290–316). New York, NY: Guilford Press.

Pollan, M. (2006). *The omnivore's dilemma: The natural history of four meals.* London, England: Penguin.

Pollard, J. A., Hawkins, J. D., & Arthur, M. W. (1999). Risk and protection: Are both necessary to understand diverse behavioral outcomes in adolescence. *Social Work Research, 23*, 145–158. doi:10.1093/swr/23.3.145

Pons, T. P., Garraghty, P. E., Ommaya, A. K., Kaas, J. H., Taub, E., & Mishkin, M. (1991). Massive cortical reorganization after sensory deafferentation in adult macaques. *Science, 252*, 1857–1860. doi:10.1126/science.1843843

Popper, K. (1963). *Conjectures and refutations: The growth of scientific knowledge.* London, England: Routledge.

Porter, R. (1997). *The greatest benefit to mankind: A medical history of humanity.* New York, NY: Norton.

Pratt, L. A., Brody, D. J., & Gu, Q. (2011). *Antidepressant use in persons aged 12 and over: United States, 2005–2008* (NCHS data brief, no. 76). Hyattsville, MD: National Center for Health Statistics. Retrieved from http://www.cdc.gov/nchs/data/databriefs/db76.pdf

Price, M. E. (2011). Cooperation as a classic problem in behavioral biology. In V. Swami (Ed.), *Evolutionary psychology: A critical introduction* (pp. 73–106). West Sussex, England: BPS Blackwell.

Prochaska, J. O., & Norcross, J. C. (2013). *Systems of psychotherapy: A transtheoretical analysis* (8th ed.). Belmont, CA: Thompson Brooks/Cole.

Project Release v. Prevost, 722 F.2d 960 (2nd Cir., 1983).

Quammen, D. (2006). *The reluctant Mr. Darwin.* New York, NY: Atlas Books.

Randall, L. (2011). *Knocking on heaven's door: How physics and scientific thinking illuminate the universe and the modern world.* New York, NY: HarperCollins.

Raskin, S. A. (Ed.). (2011). *Neuroplasticity and rehabilitation.* New York, NY: Guilford Press.

Rawls, J. (1999). *A theory of justice* (2nd ed.). Cambridge, MA: Harvard University Press.

Redelmeier, D. A., & Kahneman, D. (1996). Patients' memories of painful medical treatments: Real-time and retrospective evaluations of two minimally invasive procedures. *Pain, 66,* 3–8. doi:10.1016/0304-3959(96)02994-6

Reed, G. M., & Eisman, E. J. (2006). Uses and misuses of evidence: Managed care, treatment guidelines, and outcomes measure in professional practice. In C. D. Goodheart, A. E. Kazdin, & R. J. Sternberg (Eds.), *Evidence-based psychotherapy: Where practice and research meet* (pp. 13–35). Washington, DC: American Psychological Association. doi:10.1037/11423-001

Regier, D. A., Goldberg, I. D., & Taube, C. A. (1978). The de facto U.S. mental health services system: A public health perspective. *Archives of General Psychiatry, 35,* 685–693. doi:10.1001/archpsyc.1978.01770300027002

Renaud, J., Brent, D. A., Baugher, M., Birmaher, B., Kolko, D. J., & Bridge, J. (1998). Rapid response to psychosocial treatment for adolescent depression: A two-year follow-up. *Journal of the American Academy of Child & Adolescent Psychiatry, 37,* 1184–1190. doi:10.1097/00004583-199811000-00019

Rescher, N. (1966). *Distributive justice.* Indianapolis, IN: Bobbs-Merrill.

Resick, P. A., Williams, L. F., Suvak, M. K., Monson, C. M., & Gradus, J. L. (2012). Long-term outcomes of cognitive-behavioral treatments for posttraumatic stress disorder among female rape survivors. *Journal of Consulting and Clinical Psychology, 80,* 201–210. doi:10.1037/a0026602

Roberts, S. C. (Ed.). (2012). *Applied evolutionary psychology.* New York, NY: Oxford University Press.

Röder, B., Teder-Salejarvi, W., Sterr, A., Rosler, F., Hillyard, S. A., & Neville, H. J. (1999). Improved auditory spatial tuning in blind humans. *Nature, 400,* 162–166. doi:10.1038/22106

Rodgers, J. L. (2010). The epistemology of mathematical and statistical modeling: A quiet methodological revolution. *American Psychologist, 65,* 1–12. doi:10.1037/a0018326

Rogers, C. R. (1951). *Client-centered therapy: Its current practice, implications, and theory.* Boston, MA: Houghton Mifflin. doi:10.1037/11505-011

Rogers, C. R. (1961). *On becoming a person.* Boston, MA: Houghton Mifflin.

Rothman, K. J., & Greenland, S. (Eds.). (1998). *Modern epidemiology* (2nd ed.). Philadelphia, PA: Lippincott-Raven.

Rozensky, R. H. (2011). The institution of the institutional practice of psychology: Health care reform and psychology's future workforce. *American Psychologist, 66,* 797–808. doi:10.1037/a0025074

Rudd, M. D. (2006). *The assessment and management of suicidality.* Sarasota, FL: Professional Resource Press.

Rutter, M. (1979). Protective factors in children's responses to stress and disadvantage. *Annals of the Academy of Medicine, Singapore, 8,* 324–338.

Rychlak, J. R. (2005). Unification in theory and method: Possibilities and impossibilities. In R. J. Sternberg (Ed.), *Unity in psychology: Possibility or pipedream?* (pp. 145–157). Washington, DC: American Psychological Association. doi:10.1037/10847-009

Sadato, N., Pascual-Leone, A., Grafman, J., Ibanez, V., Deiber, M. P., Dold, G., & Hallett, M. (1996). Activation of the primary visual cortex by Braille reading in blind subjects. *Nature, 380,* 526–528. doi:10.1038/380526a0

Salvatore, J. E., Kuo, S. I., Steele, R. D., Simpson, J. A., & Collins, W. A. (2011). Recovering from conflict in romantic relationships: A developmental perspective. *Psychological Science, 22,* 376–383. doi:10.1177/0956797610397055

Sameroff, A. J., & Fiese, B. H. (1990). Transactional regulation and early intervention. In S. J. Meisels & J. P. Shonkoff (Eds.), *Handbook of early childhood intervention* (pp. 119–149). New York, NY: Cambridge University Press.

Sandel, M. (2005). *Democracy's discontent: America in search of a public philosophy.* Cambridge, MA: Harvard University Press.

Saunders, B. E., Kilpatrick, D. G., Hanson, R. F., Resnick, H. S., & Walker, M. E. (1999). Prevalence, case characteristics, and long-term psychological correlates of child rape among women: A national survey. *Child Maltreatment, 4,* 187–200. doi:10.1177/1077559599004003001

Schiff, G. D., Hasan, O., Kim, S., Abrams, R., Cosby, K., Lambert, B. L., . . . McNutt, R. A. (2009). Diagnostic error in medicine: Analysis of 583 physician-reported errors. *Archives of Internal Medicine, 169,* 1881–1887. doi:10.1001/archinternmed.2009.333

Schiller, J. S., Lucas, J. W., & Peregoy, J. A. (2012). Summary health statistics for U.S. adults: National Health Interview Survey, 2011. *Vital Health Stat 10(256).* Hyattsville, MD: National Center for Health Statistics.

Schmitz, W. M., Jr., Allen, M. H., Feldman, B. N., Gutin, N. J., Jahn, D. R., Kleespies, P. M., . . . Simpson, S. (2012). Preventing suicide through improved training in suicide risk assessment and care: An American Association of Suicidology task force report addressing serious gaps in U.S. mental health training. *Suicide & Life-Threatening Behavior, 42,* 292–304. doi:10.1111/j.1943-278X.2012.00090.x

Schöne-Seifert, B. (2006). Danger and merits of principlism: Meta-theoretical reflections on the Beauchamp/Childress approach to biomedical ethics. In C. Rehmann-Sutter, M. Duwell, & D. Mieth (Eds.), *Bioethics on cultural contexts: Reflections on methods and finitude* (pp. 109–119). Dordrecht, the Netherlands: Springer. doi:10.1007/1-4020-4241-8_8

Schwartz, J. M., & Begley, S. (2002). *The mind and the brain: Neuroplasticity and the power of mental force.* New York, NY: Regan Books.

Seagull, E. A. (2000). Beyond mothers and children: Finding the family in pediatric psychology. *Journal of Pediatric Psychology, 25,* 161–169. doi:10.1093/jpepsy/25.3.161

Seikkula, J., Aaltonen, J., Alakare, B., Haarakangas, K., Keranen, J., & Lehtinen, K. (2006). Five-year experience of first-episode nonaffective psychosis in open-dialogue approach: Treatment principles, follow-up outcomes, and two case studies. *Psychotherapy Research, 16*, 214–228. doi:10.1080/105033005 00268490

Seligman, L., & Reichenberg, L. W. (2007). *Selecting effective treatments: A comprehensive, systematic guide to treating mental disorders* (3rd ed.). San Francisco, CA: Jossey-Bass.

Seligman, M. E. P. (2002). *Authentic happiness: Using the new positive psychology to realize your potential for lasting fulfillment.* New York, NY: Free Press.

Seligman, M. E. P. (2011). *Flourish: A visionary new understanding of happiness and well-being.* New York, NY: Free Press.

Seligman, M. E. P., Rashid, T., & Parks, A. C. (2006). Positive psychotherapy. *American Psychologist, 61*, 774–788. doi:10.1037/0003-066X.61.8.774

Sever, P. S., et al. (2003). *Statin effectiveness: ASCOT update.* Retrieved from http://www.medicine.ox.ac.uk/bandolier/booth/cardiac/statascot.html

Shah, S., & Reichman, W. E. (2006). Psychiatric intervention in long-term care. In L. Hyer & R. C. Intrieri (Eds.), *Geropsychological interventions in long-term care* (pp. 85–107). New York, NY: Springer.

Sharpe, V. A., & Faden, A. I. (1998). *Medical harm: Historical, conceptual, and ethical dimensions of iatrogenic illness.* Cambridge, England: Cambridge University Press. doi:10.1017/CBO9780511527029

Shaver, P. R., & Mikulincer, M. (Eds.). (2012). *Meaning, mortality, and choice: The social psychology of existential concerns.* Washington, DC: American Psychological Association. doi:10.1037/13748-000

Shedler, J. (2010). The efficacy of psychodynamic psychotherapy. *American Psychologist, 65*, 98–109. doi:10.1037/a0018378

Shubing, N. (2008). *Your inner fish: A journey into the 3.5-billion-year history of the human body.* New York, NY: Pantheon Books.

Siegert, R. J., & Ward, T. (2002). Clinical psychology and evolutionary psychology: Toward a dialogue. *Review of General Psychology, 6*, 235–259. doi:10.1037/1089-2680.6.3.235

Simpson, J. A., & Belsky, J. (2008). Attachment theory within a modern evolutionary framework. In J. Cassidy & P. R. Shaver (Eds.), *Handbook of attachment: Theory, research, and clinical applications* (2nd ed., pp. 131–157). New York, NY: Guilford Press.

Singer, P. (1981). *The expanding circle: Ethics and sociobiology.* New York, NY: Farrar, Straus, & Giroux.

Slade, K., Lambert, M. J., Harmon, S. C., Smart, D. W., & Bailey, R. (2008). *Clinical support tool manual.* Unpublished manuscript, Brigham Young University, Provo, UT.

Smith, M. A., Schüssler-Fiorenza, C., & Rockwood, T. (2006). Satisfaction with care. In R. L. Kane (Ed.), *Understanding health care outcomes research* (2nd ed., pp. 185–216). Sudbury, MA: Jones and Bartlett.

Smith, M. L., & Glass, G. V. (1977). Meta-analysis of psychotherapy outcome studies. *American Psychologist, 32*, 752–760. doi:10.1037/0003-066X.32.9.752

Smith, M. L., Glass, G. V., & Miller, T. I. (1980). *The benefits of psychotherapy.* Baltimore, MD: Johns Hopkins University Press.

Sobell, M. B., & Sobell, L. C. (2000). Stepped care as a heuristic approach to the treatment of alcohol problems. *Journal of Consulting and Clinical Psychology, 68*, 573–579. doi:10.1037/0022-006X.68.4.573

Society for Humanistic Psychology. (2011). *Open letter to the DSM–5 Task Force and the American Psychiatric Association.* Retrieved from http://societyforhumanistic psychology.blogspot.com/2011/10/open-letter-to-dsm-5-task-force-and.html

Sowers, W., George, C., & Thompson, K. (1999). Level of Care Utilization System for Psychiatric and Addiction Services (LOCUS): A preliminary assessment of reliability and validity. *Community Mental Health Journal, 35*, 545–563. doi:10.1023/A:1018767403107

Sowers, W., Pumariega, A., Huffine, C., & Fallon, T. (2003). Best practices: Level-of-care decision making in behavioral health services: The LOCUS and the CALOCUS. *Psychiatric Services, 54*, 1461–1463. doi:10.1176/appi.ps.54.11.1461

Spanier, G. B. (1976). Measuring dyadic adjustment: New scales for assessing the quality of marriage and similar dyads. *Journal of Marriage and the Family, 38*, 15–28. doi:10.2307/350547

Speer, D. C. (1998). *Mental health outcome evaluation.* San Diego, CA: Academic Press.

Sperry, L., Brill, P. L., Howard, K. I., & Grissom, G. R. (1996). *Treatment outcomes in psychotherapy and psychiatric interventions.* New York, NY: Brunner/Mazel.

Spielberger, C. D., Gorsuch, R. L., & Lushene, R. E. (1970). *Manual for the State–Trait Anxiety Inventory.* Palo Alto, CA: Consulting Psychologists Press.

Spitzer, R. L., Kroenke, R., Williams, J. B., & Lowe, B. (2006). A brief measure for assessing generalized anxiety disorder: The GAD–7. *Archives of Internal Medicine, 166*, 1092–1097. doi:10.1001/archinte.166.10.1092

Srebnik, D. S., Uehara, E., Smukler, M., Russo, J. E., Comtois, K. A., & Snowden, M. (2002). Psychometric properties and utility of the Problem Severity Summary for adults with serious mental illness. *Psychiatric Services, 53*, 1010–1017. doi:10.1176/appi.ps.53.8.1010

Sroufe, A., & Siegel, D. (2011). The verdict is in: The case for attachment theory. *Psychotherapy Networker, 35*, 34–39, 52–53.

Sroufe, L. A., Egeland, B., Carlson, E. A., & Collins, W. A. (2005). *The development of the person: The Minnesota study of risk and adaptation from birth to adulthood.* New York, NY: Guilford Press.

Staats, A. W. (2005). A road to, and philosophy of, unification. In R. J. Sternberg (Ed.), *Unity in psychology: Possibility or pipedream?* (pp. 159–177). Washington, DC: American Psychological Association. doi:10.1037/10847-010

Steele, H., Steele, M., & Fonagy, P. (1996). Associations among attachment classifications of mothers, fathers, and their infants. *Child Development, 67*, 541–555. doi:10.2307/1131831

Sternberg, R. J. (2005). Unifying the field of psychology. In R. J. Sternberg (Ed.), *Unity in psychology: Possibility or pipedream?* (pp. 3–14). Washington, DC: American Psychological Association. doi:10.1037/10847-001

Stringer, C. (2012a). *Lone survivors: How we came to be the only humans on earth*. New York, NY: St. Martin's Press.

Stringer, C. (2012b). What makes a modern human. *Nature, 485*, 33–35.

Stromberg, C. D., Haggarty, D. J., Mishkin, B., Leibenluft, R. F., Rubin, B. L., McMillian, M. H., & Trilling, H. R. (1988). *The psychologist's legal handbook*. Washington, DC: Council for the National Register of Health Service Providers in Psychology.

Strum, P. (1999). *When the Nazi's came to town: Freedom for speech we hate*. Lawrence: University of Kansas Press.

Strupp, H. H., & Hadley, S. M. (1977). A tripartite model of mental health and therapeutic outcomes. *American Psychologist, 32*, 187–196. doi:10.1037/0003-066X.32.3.187

Substance Abuse and Mental Health Services Administration. (2008). *Screening, brief intervention, and referral to treatment*. Rockville, MD: Author. Retrieved from http://sbirt.samhsa.gov/about.htm

Substance Abuse and Mental Health Services Administration. (2011a). *SAMHSA's wellness initiative: Eight dimensions of wellness*. Rockville, MD: Author. Retrieved from http://samhsa.gov/wellness

Substance Abuse and Mental Health Services Administration. (2011b). *Screening, brief intervention and referral to treatment (SBIRT) in behavioral healthcare*. Rockville, MD: Author. Retrieved from http://www.samhsa.gov/prevention/SBIRT/SBIRTwhitepaper.pdf

Substance Abuse and Mental Health Services Administration. (2012a). *Mental health, United States, 2010* (HHS Publication No. [SMA] 12-4681). Rockville, MD: Author.

Substance Abuse and Mental Health Services Administration. (2012b). *Results from the 2011 National Survey on Drug Use and Health: Summary of National Findings* (NSDUH Series H-44, HHS Publication No. [SMA] 12-4713). Rockville, MD: Author.

Substance Abuse and Mental Health Services Administration, Center for Behavioral Health Statistics and Quality. (2012). *The NSDUH report: Physical health conditions among adults with mental illness*. Rockville, MD: Author.

Sue, D. W., & Sue, D. (2008). *Counseling the culturally diverse: Theory and practice* (5th ed.). New York, NY: Wiley.

Suls, J., & Rothman, A. (2004). Evolution of the biopsychosocial model: Prospects and challenges for health psychology. *Health Psychology, 23*, 119–125. doi:10.1037/0278-6133.23.2.119

Svendsen, D., Singer, P., Foti, M. E., & Mauer, B. (2006). *Morbidity and mortality in people with serious mental illness* (Technical Report No. 13). Alexandria, VA: National Association of State Mental Health Program Directors. Retrieved from http://www.nasmhpd.org/docs/publications/MDCdocs/Mortality%20and%20Morbidity%20Final%20Report%208.18.08.pdf

Swami, V. (Ed.). (2011). *Evolutionary psychology: A critical introduction*. Chichester, England: BPS Blackwell.

Szasz, T. S. (1971). The sane slave: An historical note on the use of medical diagnosis as justificatory rhetoric. *American Journal of Psychotherapy, 25*, 228–239.

Tarasoff v. Board of Regents of the University of California (1976). 17 Cal. 3d 425, 551 P.2d 334, 131 Cal Reptr. 14.

Task Force on Promotion and Dissemination of Psychological Procedures. (1995). Training in and dissemination of empirically validated treatments: Report and recommendations. *Clinical Psychologist, 48*, 3–23.

Taub, E., Uswatte, G., King, D. K., Morris, D., Crago, J. E., & Chatterjee, A. (2006). A placebo-controlled trial of constraint-induced movement therapy for upper extremity after stroke. *Stroke, 37*, 1045–1049. doi:10.1161/01.STR.0000206463.66461.97

Taylor, S., & McLean, P. (1993). Outcome profiles in the treatment of unipolar depression. *Behaviour Research and Therapy, 31*, 325–330. doi:10.1016/0005-7967(93)90032-P

Teasdale, J. D., Segal, Z. V., Williams, J. M. G., Ridgeway, V. A., Soulsby, J. M., & Lau, M. A. (2000). Prevention of relapse/recurrence in major depression by mindfulness-based cognitive therapy. *Journal of Consulting and Clinical Psychology, 68*, 615–623. doi:10.1037/0022-006X.68.4.615

Thase, M. E., & Jindal, R. D. (2004). Combining psychotherapy and psychopharmacology for treatment of mental disorders. In M. J. Lambert (Ed.), *Garfield and Bergin's handbook of psychotherapy and behavior change: An empirical analysis* (5th ed., pp. 743–766). New York, NY: Wiley.

Theobald, D. L. (2010). A formal test of the theory of universal common ancestry. *Nature, 465*, 219–222. doi:10.1038/nature09014

Tinbergen, N. (1963). On the aims and methods of ethology. *Zeitschrift für Tierpsychologie, 20*, 410–433. doi:10.1111/j.1439-0310.1963.tb01161.x

Tishkoff, S. A., & Kidd, K. K. (2004). Implications of biogeography of human populations for "race" and medicine. *Nature Genetics, 36*, S21–S27. doi:10.1038/ng1438

Tjaden, P., & Thoennes, N. (2000). *Full report of the prevalence, incidence, and consequences of violence against women: Findings for the National Violence Against Women Survey* (NCH 183781). Washington, DC: U.S. Department of Justice, Office of Justice Programs.

Tobler, N. S., & Stratton, H. H. (1997). Effectiveness of school-based drug prevention programs: A meta-analysis of the research. *The Journal of Primary Prevention, 18*, 71–128. doi:10.1023/A:1024630205999

Toro, P. A., Tompsett, C. J., Lombardo, S., Philippot, P., Nachtergael, H., Galand, B., . . . Harvey, K. (2007). Homelessness in Europe and the United States: A comparison of prevalence and public opinion. *Journal of Social Issues, 63,* 505–524. doi:10.1111/j.1540-4560.2007.00521.x

Trivedi, A. N., & Grebla, R. C. (2011). Quality and equity of care in the Veterans Affairs health-care system and in Medicare advantage health plans. *Medical Care, 49,* 560–568. doi: 10/1097/MLR.0b013e31820fb0f6

Trivers, R. (1971). The evolution of reciprocal altruism. *The Quarterly Review of Biology, 46,* 35–57. doi:10.1086/406755

Trull, T. J., Nietzel, M. T., & Main, A. (1988). The use of meta-analysis to assess the clinical significance of behavior therapy for agoraphobia. *Behavior Therapy, 19,* 527–538. doi:10.1016/S0005-7894(88)80021-2

Truscott, D. (2010). *Becoming an effective psychotherapist: Adopting a theory of psychotherapy that's right for you.* Washington, DC: American Psychological Association. doi:10.1037/12064-000

Turner, E. H., Matthews, A. M., Linardatos, E., Tell, R. A., & Rosenthal, R. (2008). Selective publication of antidepressant trials and its influence on apparent efficacy. *The New England Journal of Medicine, 358,* 252–260. doi:10.1056/NEJMsa065779

Turner, S. M., DeMers, S. T., Fox, H. R., & Reed, G. M. (2001). Guidelines for test user qualifications: An executive summary. *American Psychologist, 56,* 1099–1113. doi:10.1037/0003-066X.56.12.1099

Turnock, B. J. (2012). *Essentials of public health* (2nd ed.). Sudbury, MA: Jones and Bartlett Learning.

Tversky, A., & Kahneman, D. (1983). Extensional versus intuitive reasoning: The conjunction fallacy in probability judgment. *Psychological Review, 90,* 293–315. doi:10.1037/0033-295X.90.4.293

Tyson, N. D. (2008). *Time magazine interview with Neil DeGrasse Tyson.* Retrieved from http://lybio.net/neil-degrasse-tyson-the-most-astounding-fact/people/

Tyson, N. D., & Goldsmith, D. (2004). *Origins: Fourteen billion years of cosmic evolution.* New York, NY: Norton.

Ünal, B., Critchley, J. A., Fidan, D., & Capewell, S. (2005). Life-years gained from modern cardiological treatments and populations risk factors changes in England and Wales, 1981–2000. *American Journal of Public Health, 95,* 103–108. doi:10.2105/AJPH.2003.029579

United Nations. (1948). *Universal declaration of human rights of the United Nations.* New York, NY: Author.

U.S. Bureau of Justice Statistics. (2012a). *Correctional populations in the United States, 2011.* Washington, DC: Author. Retrieved from http://bjs.gov/index.cfm?ty=pbdetail&iid=4537

U.S. Bureau of Justice Statistics. (2012b). *Criminal victimization, 2011.* Washington, DC: Author. Retrieved from http://bjs.gov/index.cfm?ty=pbdetail&iid=4494

U.S. Bureau of Justice Statistics. (2012c). *State court caseload statistics*. Washington, DC: Author. Retrieved from http://bjs.gov/index.cfm?ty=tp&tid=30

U.S. Census Bureau. (2008). *An older and more diverse nation by midcentury*. Washington, DC: Author. Retrieved from http://www.census.gov/PressRelease/www/releases/archives/population/012496.html

U.S. Census Bureau. (2011). *Overview of race and Hispanic origin: 2010*. Washington, DC: Author. Retrieved from http://www.census.gov/prod/cen2010/briefs/c2010br-02.pdf

U.S. Census Bureau. (2012a). *Educational attainment in the United States: 2009*. Washington, DC: Author. Retrieved from http://www.census.gov/prod/2012pubs/p20-566.pdf

U.S. Census Bureau. (2012b). *Income, poverty, and health insurance coverage in the United States: 2011*. Washington, DC: Author. Retrieved from http://www.census.gov/prod/2012pubs/p60-243.pdf

U.S. Department of Health and Human Services. (2013a). *Framework: The vision, mission, and goals of Healthy People 2020*. Washington, DC: Author. Retrieved from http://healthypeople.gov/2020/Consortium/HP2020Framework.pdf

U.S. Department of Health and Human Services. (2013b). *General health status*. Washington, DC: Author. Retrieved from http://healthypeople.gov/2020/about/GenHealthAbout.aspx

U.S. Department of Health and Human Services. (2013c). *Health-related quality of life and well-being*. Washington, DC: Author. Retrieved from http://healthypeople.gov/2020/about/QoLWBabout.aspx

U.S. Department of Health and Human Services, Administration for Children and Families, Administration on Children, Youth and Families, Children's Bureau. (2012). *Child maltreatment 2011*. Retrieved from http://www.acf.hhs.gov/programs/cb/resource/child-maltreatment-2011

U.S. Preventive Services Task Force. (2013). *Recommendations*. Rockville, MD: Author. Retrieved from http://www.uspreventiveservicestaskforce.org/recommendations.htm

van Schaik, C. P. (2007). Culture in primates and other animals. In R. I. M. Dunbar & L. Barrett (Eds.), *Oxford handbook of evolutionary psychology* (pp. 103–114). New York, NY: Oxford University Press. doi:10.1093/oxfordhb/9780198568308.013.0009

Virani, A. S., Bezchlibnyk-Butler, K. Z., & Jeffries, J. J. (Eds.). (2009). *Clinical handbook of psychotropic drugs* (18th ed.). Ashland, OH: Hogrefe.

Von Foerster, H. (1972). Responsibilities of competence. *Journal of Cybernetics, 2*, 1–6.

Vonk, J., & Shackelford, T. K. (Eds.). (2012). *The Oxford handbook of comparative evolutionary psychology*. New York, NY: Oxford University Press.

Vyse, S. (2008). *Going broke: Why Americans can't hold on to their money*. New York, NY: Oxford University Press. doi:10.1093/acprof:oso/9780195306996.001.0001

Wachtel, P. L. (1977). *Psychoanalysis and behavior therapy: Toward an integration*. New York, NY: Basic Books.

Wachter, R. M. (2009). Entering the second decade of the patient safety movement: The field matures. *Archives of Internal Medicine, 169*, 1894–1896. doi:10.1001/archinternmed.2009.351

Waddington, C. H. (1957). *The strategy of the genes*. New York, NY: MacMillan.

Wade, N. (2006). *Before the dawn: Recovering the lost history of our ancestors*. New York, NY: Penguin.

Wahba, A., & Bridgewell, L. (1976). Maslow reconsidered: A review of research on the need hierarchy theory. *Organizational Behavior and Human Performance, 15*, 212–240. doi:10.1016/0030-5073(76)90038-6

Walfish, S., McAlister, B., O'Donnell, P., & Lambert, M. J. (2012). An investigation of self-assessment bias in mental health providers. *Psychological Reports, 110*, 639–644. doi:10.2466/02.07.17.PR0.110.2.639-644

Wallin, D. J. (2007). *Attachment in psychotherapy*. New York, NY: Guilford Press.

Wampold, B. E. (2001). *The great psychotherapy debate: Models, methods, and findings*. Mahwah, NJ: Erlbaum.

Wampold, B. E. (2007). Psychotherapy: The humanistic (and effective) treatment. *American Psychologist, 62*, 857–873. doi:10.1037/0003-066X.62.8.857

Wang, P. S., Demler, O., Olfson, M., Pincus, H. A., Wells, K. B., & Kessler, R. C. (2006). Changing profiles of service sectors used for mental health care in the United States. *The American Journal of Psychiatry, 163*, 1187–1198. doi:10.1176/appi.ajp.163.7.1187

Wang, P. S., Lane, M., Olfson, M., Pincus, H. A., Wells, K. B., & Kessler, R. C. (2005). Twelve-month use of mental health services in the United States: Results from the National Comorbidity Survey Replication. *Archives of General Psychiatry, 62*, 629–640. doi:10.1001/archpsyc.62.6.629

Ware, J. E., & Sherbourne, C. D. (1992). The MOS 36-item Short-Form Health Survey (SF-36). I. Conceptual framework and item selection. *Medical Care, 30*, 473–483. doi:10.1097/00005650-199206000-00002

Washington, H. A. (2007). *Medical apartheid: A dark history of medical experimentation on black Americans from colonial times to the present*. New York, NY: Doubleday.

Waskow, I. E., & Parloff, M. B. (1975). *Psychotherapy change measures*. Rockville, MD: National Institute of Mental Health.

Watson, J. B. (1925). *Behaviorism*. Chicago, IL: University of Chicago Press.

Weiss, B., Caron, A., Ball, S., Tapp, J., Johnson, M., & Weisz, J. R. (2005). Iatrogenic effects of group treatment for antisocial youth. *Journal of Consulting and Clinical Psychology, 73*, 1036–1044. doi:10.1037/0022-006X.73.6.1036

Whitaker, R. (2002). *Mad in America: Bad science, bad medicine, and the enduring mistreatment of the mentally ill*. New York, NY: Basic Books.

Whitaker, R. (2010). *Anatomy of an epidemic: Magic bullets, psychiatric drugs, and the astonishing rise of mental illness in America*. New York, NY: Broadway Paperbacks.

White, M., & Epston, D. (1990). *Narrative means to therapeutic ends*. New York, NY: Norton.

Wiggins, J. S. (2003). *Paradigms of personality assessment*. New York, NY: Guilford Press.

Williams, B. (1994). Patient satisfaction: A valid concept? *Social Sciences and Medicine, 38*, 509–516.

Williams, W. H., & Evans, J. J. (2003). *Biopsychosocial approaches in neurorehabilitation: Assessment and management of neuropsychiatric, mood and behavioural disorders*. Hove, England: Psychology Press.

Wilson, E. O. (1975). *Sociobiology*. Cambridge, MA: Belknap Press.

Wilson, E. O. (1978). *Human nature*. Cambridge, MA: Harvard University Press.

Wilson, E. O. (1998). *Consilience: The unity of knowledge*. New York, NY: Knopf.

Wolpe, J. (1958). *Psychotherapy by reciprocal inhibition*. Stanford, CA: Stanford University Press.

Wood, A., & Joseph, S. (2007). Grand theories of personality cannot be integrated. *American Psychologist, 62*, 57–58. doi:10.1037/003-066X62.1.57

Wood, C. C., Berger, T. W., Bialek, W., Boahen, K., Brown, E. N., Holmes, T. C., . . . Sweedler, J. V. (2006). *Steering Group Report: Brain science as a mutual opportunity for the physical and mathematical sciences, computer science, and engineering*. Arlington, VA: National Science Foundation.

World Health Organization. (1948). *Constitution of the World Health Organization*. Geneva, Switzerland: Author.

World Health Organization. (1978). *Primary health care report of the International Conference on Primary Health Care, Alma-Ata, USSR, 6–12 September, 1978*. Geneva, Switzerland: Author.

World Health Organization. (1992). *International classification of diseases and related health problems* (10th ed.). Geneva, Switzerland: Author.

World Health Organization. (2000). *The world health report 2000*. Geneva, Switzerland: Author.

World Health Organization. (2008a). *2008–2013 action plan for the global strategy for the prevention and control of noncommunicable diseases*. Geneva, Switzerland: Author. Retrieved from http://apps.who.int/iris/bitstream/10665/44009/1/9789241597418_eng.pdf

World Health Organization. (2008b). *The global burden of disease: 2004 update*. Geneva, Switzerland: Author.

World Health Organization. (2008c). *Primary health care: Now more than ever*. Geneva, Switzerland: Author.

World Health Organization Department of Health Statistics and Informatics. (2012). *World health statistics 2012*. Geneva, Switzerland: Author.

Yakubu, A., & Mabogunje, O. A. (1993). Skin cancer in African albinos. *Acta Oncologica, 32*, 621–622. doi:10.3109/02841869309092440

Zhang, T. Y., & Meaney, M. J. (2010). Epigenetics and the environmental regulation of the genome and its function. *Annual Review of Psychology, 61*, 439–466. doi:10.1146/annurev.psych.60.110707.163625

Zoellner, L. A., Feeny, N. C., Cochran, B., & Pruitt, L. (2003). Treatment choice for PTSD. *Behaviour Research and Therapy, 41*, 879–886. doi:10.1016/S0005-7967(02)00100-6

INDEX

Newton, Isaac, 36
Nielsen, S. L., 228
NNT (number needed to treat),
    220–221
Nonmaleficence
    in principlism approach, 84–86
    in treatment planning, 185
    and unintentional harm, 216
Nonpsychiatric mental health
    specialists, 278
Norcross, J. C., 33, 228
Number needed to treat (NNT),
    220–221
Nuremberg trials, 83
Nurture, nature vs., 46–52
Nurturing environments, 142

Oandasan, I., 282
Obesity, 126, 127
Obsessive-compulsive disorder (OCD),
    48–49
O'Donnell, P., 238–239
OECD (Organization of Economic
    Co-operation and Development),
    259
Ogles, B. M., 228
Okiishi, J., 228
Okiishi, J. C., 228
Ongoing care, in treatment plan, 199
On-site care model, 278–279
Oordt, M. S., 278
OQ-34, 242
Oregon, 130
Organization of Economic
    Co-operation and Development
    (OECD), 259
Origin of the Species (Darwin), 52
O'Sullivan, P. S., 173, 174, 178
Outcome Assessment Scale, 242
Outcomes (term), 241
Outcomes assessment, 235–253
    additional purposes of, 247
    in behavioral health care, 241–246
    best practices for, 249–250
    biopsychosocial framework for,
        236–240
    to ensure effectiveness of treatment,
        248–250
    generic vs. condition-specific,
        240–241

to improve treatment effectiveness,
    290
for mildly depressed patient (case
    example), 251–253
systematic monitoring for, 217, 245
Outcomes monitoring, 217, 237–238,
    245–246, 248
Outcome studies, of prevention
    interventions, 269–270

Paradigmatic era
    in behavioral health care, 289–290
    benefits of, 290–293
    tipping point to, 289
Pascual-Leone, A., 48
Paternalism, in principlism approach, 87
Patient (term), 7
Patient-centered medical home (PCMH)
    models, 279–280, 282, 284
Patient-Centered Medical Homes, 196,
    215
Patient-Centered Primary Care
    Collaborative, 279–280
Patient Health Questionnaire Anxiety
    Disorder Scale, 243
Patient Health Questionnaire
    Depression Scale, 243
Patient Protection and Affordable Care
    Act (2010), 88, 195–196, 215,
    276, 277, 280, 291
Patient Safety Indicators, 85
Patient safety movement, 85
    and communication/collaboration
        among health care
        professionals, 217
    and deaths from medical errors, 282
    and missed diagnoses, 154
Patient satisfaction, 247
PCMH models. *See* Patient-centered
    medical home models
Pearsall, P., 31
Penfield, Wilder, 47
PERMA model (positive emotion,
    engagement, positive relationships,
    meaning, and accomplishment),
    144
Permission, limited information,
    specific suggestions, and
    intensive treatment (PLISSIT)
    model, 195

Project Competence, 136
Prosocial behavior, evolution of, 69–72
Prosociality, 142
Protective factors
    defined, 139, 266
    in developmental perspective,
        139–142
    in public health, 266
Providers. *See* Therapists
Proximate explanations of behavior,
    39 40
Psychiatric disorders. *See also* Mental
        disorders
    most common, 213
    prevalence of, 104–105
Psychological abuse, 118
Psychological assessment guidelines,
    155–156. *See also* Assessment
    (initial)
Psychological dimension
    in biopsychosocial approach, 16–17
    most common disorders in, 213
Psychological factors, in human
    development, 135
Psychological flexibility, 142
Psychological functioning, 99–110
    assessing, 159
    mental disorders, 101–105
    need for broad perspective on,
        109–110
    possible interventions for, 202–204
    substance use and abuse, 107–108
    suicide, 105–107
    well-being and flourishing, 108–109
Psychology research and theory,
    advances in, 286–287
Psychopharmacological treatment,
    214–215, 222–224, 290–291
Psychotherapeutic drug use, 108
Psychotherapy. *See also* Therapists/
    providers
    clinically meaningful improvement
        from, 221
    evidence on safety of, 216–217
    factors in effectiveness of, 225–228
    failures of, 225, 229–230
    limits of, 249
    long-term benefits of, 221–222,
        290–291

medical treatments vs., 220–221
    psychotropic medication treatment
        vs., 222–224
    safety and effectiveness of, 218–230
    skills of therapists in, 228–229
    in treatment plan, 196–197
    in United States, 276–277
    variability in effectiveness of,
        224–225
Psychotropic medications
    concerns about, 86
    effectiveness of, 222–224
    prescribed by primary care
        professionals, 278
Public gatekeepers, assessment informa-
    tion from, 163, 164
Public health, 257–273
    and cost-effectiveness of prevention,
        271
    and costs of behavioral health condi-
        tions, 270–271
    effectiveness of interventions in,
        258–260
    effectiveness of preventive interven-
        tions in, 269–270
    and importance of prevention,
        272–273
    increases in, 291–292
    key features of, 261–262
    and limits of intervention, 271–272
    measuring, 262–265
    prevention approaches in, 267–269
    protective factors, 142, 266
    risk factors, 142, 264–266

Quality assurance, medical errors and
    failures of, 282
Quality of care, interprofessional col-
    laboration and, 282
Quality of life
    dimensions of, 240–241
    and lengthening of life span, 247
    measurements of, 128–129, 240
Quebec Suicide Brain Bank, 51

Race
    biological meaning of, 111
    and genetic variation, 43–44
    in United States, 112–113

Rape, prevalence of, 116
Rapport
    and emergence of new issues, 190
    and focus on strengths, 170
Rawls, J., 80–81
RDoC (Research Domain Criteria), 158
Rebirthing attachment therapy, 216,
    225
Recovered memories, 33, 85
Referrals
    assessment approach and, 161
    to more experienced professionals,
        188
    in multidisciplinary care, 279
Reflective equilibrium, 81
Relationship functioning, 115–116
Reliability
    of assessment information, 153–154,
        161–166, 244
    of safety measures, 236
    of self-reports, 244
    of treatment effectiveness measures,
        236
Religion, 119–120
Repressed memories, 216
Research
    history of, 30–32
    scientific tools for, 36–39
Research Domain Criteria (RDoC), 158
Resick, P. A., 222
Resilience, 139
    in converting problems to strengths,
        213–214
    as protective factor, 266
Risk factors
    for behavioral health problems, 266
    causal, 266
    defined, 139, 265
    in developmental perspective,
        139–142
    and preventive interventions, 266
    in public health, 265–266
Risks, imposed through omission, 216
Rogers, Carl, 143, 150
Rutter, M., 140, 266

Safety. See also Outcomes assessment
    as core need in health care, 216
    as ethical issue, 236–237

and improved interprofessional
        collaboration, 282
    and need for teamwork,
        communication, and
        collaborative care, 282
    of outcomes assessment data, 235
    patient safety movement, 85, 154,
        217, 282
    as priority, 216–217
    of psychotropic medication, 224
    reliability and validity of measures
        for, 236
    in science-based biopsychosocial
        approach, 185, 216–217
Safety needs, 170, 171
SAMHSA. See U.S. Substance Abuse
        and Mental Health Services
        Administration
Sandler, I. N., 142
SBIRT model. See Screen, Brief
        Intervention, Brief Treatment,
        and Referral to Treatment
        program
Schiff, G. D., 85
Schwartz, J. M., 48–49
Science, 29–59
    behavioral health care as
        paradigmatic clinical science,
        56–59
    in biopsychosocial approach, 24–25
    ethics vs., 62–63
    evolution of humans and human
        psychological characteristics,
        42–46
    as foundation of behavioral health
        care, 21
    history of psychology research and
        theory, 30–32
    lack of unified theory in, 52–54
    and metatheoretical biopsychosocial
        framework, 54–56
    nature vs. nurture in human
        development, 46–52
    necessity of both ethics and, 91–93
    and need for unified theory of human
        psychology, 52–54
    recent paradigm shift in, 14–15
    in science-based biopsychosocial
        framework, 39–42

Treatment planning, 183–209
  addressing severity/complexity of
      problems or needs,
      188–196
  from biopsychosocial perspective,
      185
  complicating factors in, 197–199
  education and experience required
      for, 190, 191
  general guidelines for, 189
  identifying alternative interventions
      in, 199–207
  initial decisions in, 186–188
  for mildly depressed patient (case
      example), 208–209
  ongoing care/follow-up in, 199
  psychotherapy and supportive
      counseling in, 196–197
  traditional, 184
Trivers, R., 70
Trustworthiness
  of therapist, patient's evaluation of,
      190
  as virtue of moral character, 90
Tuskegee syphilis study, 83–84
Tversky, Amos, 65
Tyson, Neil deGrasse, 295

Ultimate explanations, of behavior,
    39–40
Unemployment rate, educational
    attainment and, 115
Unified theory
  need for, 52–54
  traditional theoretical orientations
      vs., 13–14
United Kingdom, 194, 243, 246
United States
  cost-effectiveness of health care in,
      247
  deaths from medical errors in, 282
  health care delivery in, 283–284
  health care in, 239, 275–276
  integrated primary health care in,
      276–277, 279
  life expectancy in, 128
  life span in, 130, 143
  mental health care in, 276–277
  minorities in, 112–113

morbidity/mortality of individuals
    with severe mental illness in,
    283
multiculturalism in, 112
patient satisfaction with services in,
    247
potential impact of Affordable Care
    Act in, 280
poverty in, 115
primary care in, 278
"Universal Declaration of Ethical
    Principles for Psychologists"
    (International Union of
    Psychological Science), 74
Universal ethical principles, 74
Universal morality, 73–74
Universal prevention, 267, 268
U.S. Census Bureau, 112
U.S. Department of Health and Human
    Services, 117, 128
U.S. Food and Drug Administration
    (FDA), 223
U.S. Public Health Service, 83
U.S. Substance Abuse and Mental
    Health Services Administration
    (SAMHSA), 102–103, 107, 108,
    167, 194, 214
Utilitarianism, 77

Validity
  of assessment information, 153–154,
      161–166, 244
  of safety measures, 236
  of treatment effectiveness measures,
      236
Van Leeuwenhoek, Anton (Antonie),
    37
Vocational stability, 113–115
Von Foerster, H., 39

Walfish, S., 238–239
Wampold, B. E., 219–220, 227, 228
"Watchful waiting," 187
Watson, John, 32, 46
Well-being, 108–109
  in developmental perspective,
      142–144
  greater emphasis on, 292–293
  measurements of, 128–129

ABOUT THE AUTHOR

Timothy P. Melchert, PhD, graduated in 1992 from the University of Wisconsin–Madison with a doctorate in counseling psychology. He taught at Texas Tech University before moving to Marquette University in 1998. He served for many years at Marquette as training codirector, department chair, and assistant vice provost for graduate programs, and he also served on the State of Wisconsin Psychology Examining Board. He is a member of multiple journal editorial boards. His previous book, *Foundations of Professional Psychology: The End of Theoretical Orientations and the Emergence of the Biopsychosocial Approach*, was published in 2011.